The Ottoman World

The Ottoman World

A Cultural History Reader, 1450–1700

Edited by   HAKAN T. KARATEKE and HELGA ANETSHOFER

UNIVERSITY OF CALIFORNIA PRESS

University of California Press
Oakland, California

© 2021 by The Regents of the University of California

Library of Congress Cataloging-in-Publication Data

Names: Karateke, Hakan T., editor. | Anetshofer, Helga, editor.
Title: The Ottoman world : a cultural history reader, 1450–1700 / edited by Hakan T. Karateke and Helga Anetshofer.
Description: Oakland, California : University of California Press, [2021] | Includes index.
Identifiers: LCCN 2021004318 (print) | LCCN 2021004319 (ebook) | ISBN 9780520303430 (hardback) | ISBN 9780520303454 (paperback) | ISBN 9780520972711 (ebook)
Subjects: LCSH: Turkey—History—Ottoman Empire, 1288–1918—Sources. | Turkey—History—Ottoman Empire, 1288–1918—Early works to 1800.
Classification: LCC DR485 .O885 2021 (print) | LCC DR485 (ebook) | DDC 956/.015—dc23
LC record available at https://lccn.loc.gov/2021004318
LC ebook record available at https://lccn.loc.gov/2021004319

25 24 23 22 21
10 9 8 7 6 5 4 3 2 1

To Cemal Kafadar, who has inspirationally explored the uncharted territories of the Ottoman cultural world

CONTENTS

List of Illustrations   xiii

Acknowledgments   xv

Preface   xvii

1   **Letters of an Insecure Scholar, 1553**   1
    Zaifi, d. after 1557
    Translated by A. Tunç Şen

2   **Adversities at Sea: From Basra to Gujarat, 1554**   8
    Seydi Ali Reis, d. 1562
    Translated by Ármin Vámbéry

3   **Memoirs of an Ottoman Captive in Malta, 1597–98**   16
    Macuncuzade Mustafa, d. ca. Early Seventeenth Century
    Translated by Helga Anetshofer

4   **The Excommunication of a Greek Orthodox Priest, ca. 1642**   23
    Synadinos of Serres, d. after 1662
    Translated by Konrad Petrovszky

5   **Dream Letters of a Sufi Woman in Skopje, 1640s**   29
    Asiye Hatun, d. Second Half of Seventeenth Century
    Translated by Leslie Schick and Cemal Kafadar

6   **Diary of a Sufi Sheikh in Plague-Ridden Istanbul, 1661**   36
    Seyyid Hasan Nuri, d. 1688
    Translated by Mary Işın

7   Ramblings of an Eccentric Sufi Exiled on Limnos, ca. Early 1680s   44
        Niyazi-i Mısri, d. 1694
        Translated by Hakan T. Karateke and Ferenc Csirkés

8   Adventures of an Ottoman Officer in Captivity, 1690–99   53
        Osman Agha of Timişoara, Written ca. 1724
        Translated by Hakan T. Karateke

9   The Trial of a Heretic, 1527   60
        Told by Celalzade Mustafa, d. 1567
        Translated by Kaya Şahin and Cornell H. Fleischer

10   The Life and Works of Two Mediocre Poets   66
        Told by Âşık Çelebi, d. 1572
        Translated by Douglas Brookes

11   The Extraordinary Life Story of a Scholar   72
        Told by Mehmed Mecdi, d. 1591
        Translated by Helga Anetshofer

12   On Servants and Slaves   78
        Mustafa Âli, d. 1600
        Translated by Douglas Brookes

13   Children and Youth   86
        Court Records, Sixteenth and Seventeenth Centuries
        Selected by Yahya Araz; Translated by Hakan T. Karateke

14   Women at Courts of Law   95
        Court Records, Sixteenth and Seventeenth Centuries
        Translated by Hakan T. Karateke and N. İpek Hüner Cora

15   Prostitutes and Pimps   103
        Court Records and Imperial Council Registers, Sixteenth and Seventeenth Centuries
        Translated by Marinos Sariyannis

16   On Nocturnal Activities   111
        Court Records, Sixteenth and Seventeenth Centuries
        Translated by Hakan T. Karateke

17   Impostors, Frauds, and Spies   119
        Various Documents, Sixteenth Century
        Translated by Christopher Markiewicz

18   **The Madmen of Istanbul**   126
       Evliya Çelebi, d. after 1683
       Translated by Hakan T. Karateke

19   **Fetvas on Non-Muslims**   134
       Various Grand Muftis, Sixteenth to Early Eighteenth Century
       Translated by Cornell Fleischer and Amir A. Toft

20   **Conversion Among Ottoman Jews**   144
       Responsa by Various Rabbis, Sixteenth Century
       Translated by Matt Goldish

21   **Marriage and Divorce Among Ottoman Jews**   152
       Responsa by Various Rabbis, Seventeenth Century
       Translated by Leah Bornstein-Makovetsky

22   **News from Istanbul at the Turn of the Seventeenth Century**   162
       The Chronicle of Selaniki
       Translated by H. Erdem Çıpa

23   **Propagating the Faith in Constantinople**   173
       Catholic Missionary Reports, Seventeenth Century
       Translated by Paolo Girardelli

24   **An Armenian Chronicle of Crimea**   181
       Khachatur of Kaffa, d. 1658
       Translated by Naira Poghosyan

25   **On Revenants and Ghosts**   188
       Various Documents, Sixteenth Century
       Translated by Marinos Sariyannis

26   **Miracles of an Anatolian Sufi Saint**   195
       The Hagiography of Hacı Bektaş, ca. Late Fifteenth Century
       Translated by Helga Anetshofer

27   **A Dispute Concerning Sufi Tombs, 1619**   202
       Ömer Fuadi, d. 1636
       Translated by John Curry

28   **Preserving Public Health**   210
       Court Records and Imperial Council Registers, Late Fifteenth and Sixteenth Centuries
       Translated by Amir A. Toft

29	**Traditional Medicine for Everyday Ailments** 220	
	Anonymous, Late Fifteenth Century	
	Translated by Özgen Felek	
30	**Snake Medicine and Snake Charming in Cairo** 227	
	Evliya Çelebi, d. after 1683	
	Translated by Robert Dankoff and Sooyong Kim	
31	**On Smoking Tobacco** 236	
	Abdulmalik al-Isami, d. 1628; Katib Çelebi, d. 1657	
	Translated by Basil Salem and Geoffrey Lewis	
32	**Divining Past, Present, and Future in the Sand** 244	
	A Geomantic Miscellany, ca. Sixteenth Century	
	Translated by Matthew Melvin-Koushki	
33	**Reading Character by Appearance** 254	
	The Book of Physiognomy, Hamdullah Hamdi, d. 1503	
	Translated by Helga Anetshofer and Hakan T. Karateke	
34	**Religious Guidance for Hunters** 261	
	Ebu Bekr el-Kızılhisari, ca. Late Seventeenth Century	
	Translated by Christopher Markiewicz	
35	**Cultivating the Land** 269	
	The Splendor of the Garden, Sixteenth Century	
	Translated by Hakan T. Karateke	
36	**Wonders of Art and Nature** 277	
	Anonymous, Sixteenth Century	
	Translated by Ido Ben-Ami	
37	**On the Natural Advantages of Edirne** 284	
	Anonymous, Late Fifteenth to Early Sixteenth Century	
	Translated by Amy Singer	
38	**The Legend of the Construction of Constantinople** 289	
	Anonymous, Sixteenth Century	
	Translated by Dimitris J. Kastritsis	
39	**On the Construction of the Pyramids, ca. 1545** 297	
	Celalzade Salih, d. 1565	
	Translated by Giancarlo Casale	
40	**An Ode to Istanbul** 307	
	Eremia Keomurchean Çelebi, d. 1695	
	Translated by Henry Shapiro	

41   **Passion and Murder on the Bosphorus**   324

   Anonymous Tıflî Story, Probably in Circulation During the Later Seventeenth Century

   Translated by Helga Anetshofer

42   **Stories of Guilt and Repentance**   332

   Mehmed Nergisi, d. 1635

   Translated by Gisela Procházka-Eisl

43   **The Wiles of Women**   338

   Anonymous, Sixteenth to Seventeenth Centuries

   Translated by N. İpek Hüner Cora and Helga Anetshofer

44   **Social Criticism and Invective in Poetry**   348

   Various Poets, Fifteenth to Seventeenth Centuries

   Translated by Sooyong Kim

45   **Shrewd Witticisms by a Master Poet**   356

   Zati's Anecdotes, Sixteenth Century

   Translated by Helga Anetshofer

46   **Subversive Jokes Featuring a Folk Hero**   366

   Nasreddin Hoca Jokes, Sixteenth Century

   Translated by Kathleen Burrill

Index   375

ILLUSTRATIONS

1. The Ottoman territories in the early seventeenth century   xxii
2. Akçe, 1520   6
3. A four-master galleon, sixteenth century   11
4. Indian Ocean   13
5. Greek Orthodox priest, early eighteenth century   25
6. Hasan Efendi's family tree   37
7. Turkish funeral, 1553   39
8. Sorbet seller, 1581   70
9. Wine tavern, early eighteenth century   75
10. Slave market, Algiers, 1684   80
11. Woman and boy, ca. 1650s   89
12. Women at a court of law, early eighteenth century   99
13. Two pages from a court register, sixteenth century   105
14. Nighttime celebrations, Istanbul, 1720   117
15. An antinomian dervish   128
16. Men's bathhouse, nineteenth century   139
17. Shabbat in a Jewish home in İzmir, ca. 1648   148
18. Jewish woman, ca. 1650s   158
19. Kefe (Kaffa, Feodosia), early eighteenth century   182
20. The tomb of Sheikh Şaban-ı Veli, Kastamonu, Turkey, 2011   207
21. Market inspector, ca. 1650s   212
22. Circumcision of a male infant, ca. sixteenth century   215

23. Physician treating a patient, ca. 1466   224
24. Coffee house, early nineteenth century   239
25. Possible configuration of geomantic figures   246
26. Human limbs as they correspond to sixteen geomantic figures   252
27. Hunting scene, ca. 1580s   264
28. Images of humans and animals that help to cure illnesses   279
29. A stone that smells like mice   280
30. A dragon under a magic spell   282
31. Edirne, nineteenth century   288
32. Map of pre-Ottoman Constantinople, ca. 1420s   293
33. Pyramids of Giza, Egypt, seventeenth century   299
34. Map of Istanbul (view from north), seventeenth century   308
35. Map of Istanbul (view from east), sixteenth century   309
36. Land walls of Istanbul (view from southwest), nineteenth century   322
37. A barber, ca. 1650s   326
38. Women's bathhouse, eighteenth century   341
39. An Ottoman lady, eighteenth century   344
40. Governor general of European provinces (Rumeli)   352
41. A social gathering, sixteenth century   358
42. A rendering of Nasreddin Hoca, seventeenth century   367

ACKNOWLEDGMENTS

We extend our profound gratitude to the contributors of this volume for their hard work and their patience with our badgering emails asking them to rework translations. We hope they feel that their efforts were worth the trouble.

Ali Emre Özyıldırım, who possesses a penetrating understanding of Ottoman poetry and prose, was always prepared to brainstorm with us as we parsed obscure allusions in the texts, and we gladly acknowledge his insightful explanations. We also benefited from the linguistic expertise of Dzovinar Derderian for Armenian and Tahera Qutbuddin for Arabic. Amir Toft and İsmail Erünsal generously shared their expertise of the legal language used in court records with us. Mendy Chitrik provided us with his perspective on some of the texts in rabbinical Hebrew. We are grateful to them.

We have consulted many colleagues along the way and have sought their suggestions for possible texts to include in the reader—an extremely enriching experience for us. We included many recommended texts; others, owing to space and format, had to be left out. We appreciate the encouragement we received from Edith G. Ambros, Abdurrahman Atçıl, Hatice Aynur, Orit Bashkin, Yaron Ben-Naeh, Cornell Fleischer, Barbara Kellner-Heinkele, Vjeran Kursar, Ertuğrul Öktem, Claudia Römer, Zeynep Tezer, Dror Zeevi, and we appreciate their willingness to guide and help us. Our thanks also go to Ali Yaycıoğlu who kindly allowed us to use one of his wonderful paintings on the cover of this volume.

Some readers will note that almost all the court record entries in this volume have been translated from previously published volumes or theses. We did not venture into the archives in search of unpublished cases for our project, as this would have been far too time-consuming. However, we *did* view the originals of all documents translated here, and indeed sometimes preferred our own readings to published versions. The luxury of gaining access to the originals in such a short period of time would have been unimaginable a decade or so ago, before the digital revolution. We extend our sincere thanks to Melih Kayar, Muzaffer Doğan, Betül Kaya, Ahmet Arslantürk, Halil İbrahim Binici, and Tolga Cora for their assistance in gathering these documents from the archives and manuscript libraries. The Istanbul Court

Records project, initially spearheaded by the Center for Islamic Studies (İSAM) in Istanbul, was absolutely instrumental for us in bringing together court cases that presented a thematic coherence. (On the flip side, the availability of this documentation inevitably tilted the focus of cases in this volume to Istanbul.)

In the final phases of writing this book we received crucial feedback on the preface and the chapter introductions from our graduate students Katherine Costello and Theo Knights, as well as from Hakan Karateke's undergraduate students in the University of Chicago Study Abroad program in Morocco (2020): Alia Shahzad, Jessica Gitre, Ruth Dworin, Karolina Zachor, Katherine Howell, and Emma Mitnick. Their reactions were so insightful that we felt compelled to reorganize or rewrite certain sections in the chapter introductions. We have been lucky to have such brilliant students candidly share with us how this reader might be perceived by its targeted audience in the classroom. We heartily thank each one of them.

We knew when we first embarked on this project that we would at some point turn to Lydia Kiesling—author, literary critic, friend, and an old student of ours—to have a pair of professional eyes go over the translations. She did not turn us down, and as usual was generous with her time in copyediting many of the chapters to their final versions. Amir Toft was always prepared to edit the legal texts in the reader and search with us for the corresponding phrases in English of Ottoman legal terms. Sooyong Kim kindly read through the stories in the forty-fifth chapter and offered his elegant renderings. We are thankful to all these people.

The idea for a reader on Ottoman history originated with Eric Schmidt at the University of California Press. He approached our dear colleague Dimitri Kastritsis, with whom we sought ways to jointly administer the project. In the end, Dimitri lent us his full support and also contributed a translation to the volume, for which we are thankful. Our sincere thanks are due to Eric for his visit to us in 2017 at the University of Chicago, where he carefully listened to our pitch for a reader with a focus on cultural and social history and found it worthwhile to pursue. We are very grateful for his guidance through this long journey. We also sincerely thank Cindy Fulton and Gabriel Bartlett who very competently helped us during the production of the book and Fırat Ciftci for preparing the index.

Finally, we are thankful for the support we received from our home institution, the University of Chicago's Division of the Humanities, the Micro-Metcalf Program in the College and the Joyce Z. and Jacob Greenberg Center for Jewish Studies.

PREFACE

The Ottoman World is planned as a sourcebook with the objective of finding a variety of voices from across Ottoman society and bringing them into twenty-first century classrooms. It includes texts from the 1450s to 1700 and aims to supply instructors with narratives conveying the lived experiences of individuals—with attention to both the inner life and the material world—through texts that highlight human variety and accelerate a trend away from the "state-centric" approach to Ottoman history. Where possible, the texts emphasize the life experiences of real human beings—their hopes and fears, their disputes and ambitions, their prejudices and senses of humor, their social interactions and trajectories. By focusing on the lives that people, both common and uncommon, lived, we hope students will absorb events of the past on an emotional as well as an intellectual level. This approach brings a sense of relevance to historical study, connecting our modern existence with humans from a different place and time, and it provides fertile ground for class discussion. We suspect that students will be eager to shift their attention from the overly emphasized military character attributed to the Ottoman polity to more relatable topics.

Ottoman history has all too often been told as the history of the Ottoman dynasty and state. The existence of rich state archives and historical accounts produced by men invested in the Ottoman imperial project, while a blessing to historians, has made it too easy to represent Ottoman history as one limited to battles, imperial campaigns, conquests, complex institutions, careers of notables, luxurious palaces, and the like. New research trends have formed in the field of Ottoman studies in the last decades. On the one hand, more recent scholarship has focused on representations of power, ideology, and other "soft" aspects governing the relationship between state and society; on the other hand, an attention to new topics and perspectives relating to social and cultural history and material culture has emerged. Increasingly, studies are focused on unearthing viewpoints that do not necessarily reflect the imperial ideology of the Ottoman state.

The Ottoman World is designed in this spirit and it includes texts that we believe reflect alternative perspectives and understudied topics. In addition to the personal experiences of real human beings as outlined above, legends, biographical accounts, hagiographies, short stories, witty anecdotes, jokes, and lampoons provide us with exciting glimpses into popular mindsets in Ottoman society. Even when we included excerpts from widely circulated mainstream narratives produced for the imperial court, we tried to select pieces that covered topics beyond the rubric of "important affairs of the state." For the same reason, we abstained from including theoretical texts about government, ideals of kingship, or philosophical or doctrinal treatments of abstract concepts. A few prescriptive texts are included, since they address some of the contemporary interests and concerns of the wider Ottoman public. Some of the texts included are compilations based on works from pre-Ottoman times. We see these as features of the richness of Ottoman culture and find them valuable for exploring the foundations for Ottoman popular worldviews in the early modern era.

Also included in the reader are several chapters with examples of legal opinions issued by jurists, and records of court proceedings and imperial council meetings. These documents have long been hailed as rich sources for snapshots of the otherwise completely inaccessible lives of a wide variety of ordinary people who lived outside the hierarchy of power; they give us insight into the things they valued, the places where they spent time, their perceptions of others, and their interactions with the state apparatus. Despite their narrative shortcomings—among them, their formulaic legalistic language or the fact that they are written from the normative viewpoint of authorities—these documents offer information that historians of other early modern societies could only dream of accessing.

We looked mainly for interesting court cases, which may or may not have been representative of the routines of society. Thousands of registers and millions of court cases await interested students of Ottoman history who wish to pose new questions. These novel areas of inquiry will create opportunities to challenge persistent stereotypes about the individuals, practices, and traditions in this part of the world. We invite readers to look beyond the customary rhetoric that sometimes permeates prescriptive or legalistic texts, and to read these excerpts with fresh eyes.

The rhetoric of imperial ideology and state perspective, or of established religious dogma, is an unavoidable feature of much of the written documentation that has survived to date. Even though many narratives may not necessarily have been composed by propagandists of the Ottoman central polity, most written production was created at the hands of people educated in certain tracks—by bureaucrats, members of the scholarly establishment, or the clergy—and hence inevitably conveys particular perspectives. This hurdle is of course not exclusive to Ottoman studies. Nor do we wish to essentialize or in any sense demean those texts that historians categorize as state-centric. Certainly, that class of text can be read and mined in novel ways and with unconventional methodologies. That being said, the editors of this reader have set themselves the goal of deemphasizing this rhetorical register to the extent possible.

The Ottoman empire, which comprised the area extending from modern Hungary to the southern tip of the Arabian Peninsula, was home to a vast population with a rich variety of cultures and languages. Wide representation of differing customs, traditions, and languages is the only way to do justice to the vast geography we call the Ottoman World, and it obliges us to think about this early modern entity in novel ways. This reader offers a sample of the "alternative" riches of the Ottoman world; it is therefore a starting guide with which to begin exploring this realm. Admittedly, reflecting the incredible diversity within Ottoman society in a single reader is a daunting task, and we have achieved representation only to a certain degree. We have been perhaps even less successful in the purely geographical representation of Ottoman domains; the type of source material available and our respective expertise steered us to the central core lands of the empire—Anatolia and the Balkans. We hope that comparable collections will correct this imbalance in the future.

Translation is an intricate business. It was not easy to keep the balance between our desire to reflect the language register of the original texts and our wish to create a compelling translation in English. In order to provide students with a good understanding of the variations of language used in the sources and to allow them to explore narrative tropes and the disparate syntax employed in different genres, we strove to reflect the style of the original texts, from simple prose to embellished metaphorical styles and poetry. If the original text was ambiguous owing to missing words or an author's covert allusions, we filled in the blanks in brackets. If the text did not flow, we generally did not intervene to smooth out the narrative. Then again, keeping the many brackets, as we had in an earlier versions of the translations, proved cumbersome to early readers. Therefore, we kept the most essential ones, and omitted others that we thought were logically deducible from the flow of the original texts.

Most of the texts we selected were written originally in Ottoman Turkish; we chose them in part because of the linguistic background of the editors, but our choice is also a function of the significantly greater availability of material in Ottoman Turkish. We nonetheless included texts written in some of the many other languages used in the Ottoman realm—among them Arabic, Armenian, Greek, Hebrew, Italian, and Persian. For the majority of the chapters, we as editors selected the texts and asked our collaborators to translate them. We worked with these translators to arrive at a thorough understanding of the original texts and render them into English. Ultimately, we left final decisions about meaning and style to the translators. A few of the translations in this reader have been previously published. In some cases, we consulted the originals, reinterpreted the texts, and duly adjusted the translations. If we could not obtain the consent of the prior translators for our version because they are no longer living, we indicated this in the reference section of the relevant chapter.

These texts and their narrators and protagonists did not exist in a vacuum, and no centuries-old document is intelligible to modern readers without some sense of its context and references. Short introductions to each chapter are calibrated to provide the minimum contextual background for each text. We generally refrained from burdening the narratives with footnotes, with the exception of a few notes to some poems with double entendres. Our rationale was not to precondition the reader toward an interpretative direction but to let the documents speak for themselves and allow readers and instructors to collectively parse their meanings. Most of the subheadings in the chapters do not appear in the original texts, or not in the form we formulated them; we inserted these headers based on the topics of each section in order to make lengthy texts more approachable.

We first experimented with organizing the chapters under sections according to the topics they treat or the genre they represent. However, since several of the texts can be classified under multiple rubrics, we realized that classifying texts under one category would be more isolating than making them accessible. Currently, the chapters are arranged with a loose logic: At the beginning are autobiographical accounts (arranged chronologically among themselves); then come narratives about or biographies of certain individuals followed by texts dealing with groups of people. From here on special topics, city narratives, medical sources, and so on are mostly grouped together. At the end are fictional works, poetry, and jokes. We hope that a quick glance at the chapter titles and the subheadings within the chapters will allow the readers to get a first idea about the contents of the texts.

We hope that a balanced picture highlighting the diverse and cosmopolitan nature of Ottoman society emerges from this volume. Our sources portray some sense of what it meant to live in a multilingual, multiethnic, and multireligious premodern society. Contemporary life asks us to continually reevaluate what it means to coexist with people who are both like and unlike us, to question social stratification and division, and to reflect on our own vantage points. There are analogous moments in Ottoman history from which students may draw lessons, whether about Ottoman society, the contemporary Middle East, or the broader human family.

    Hakan T. Karateke and Helga Anetshofer
    Hyde Park, Chicago

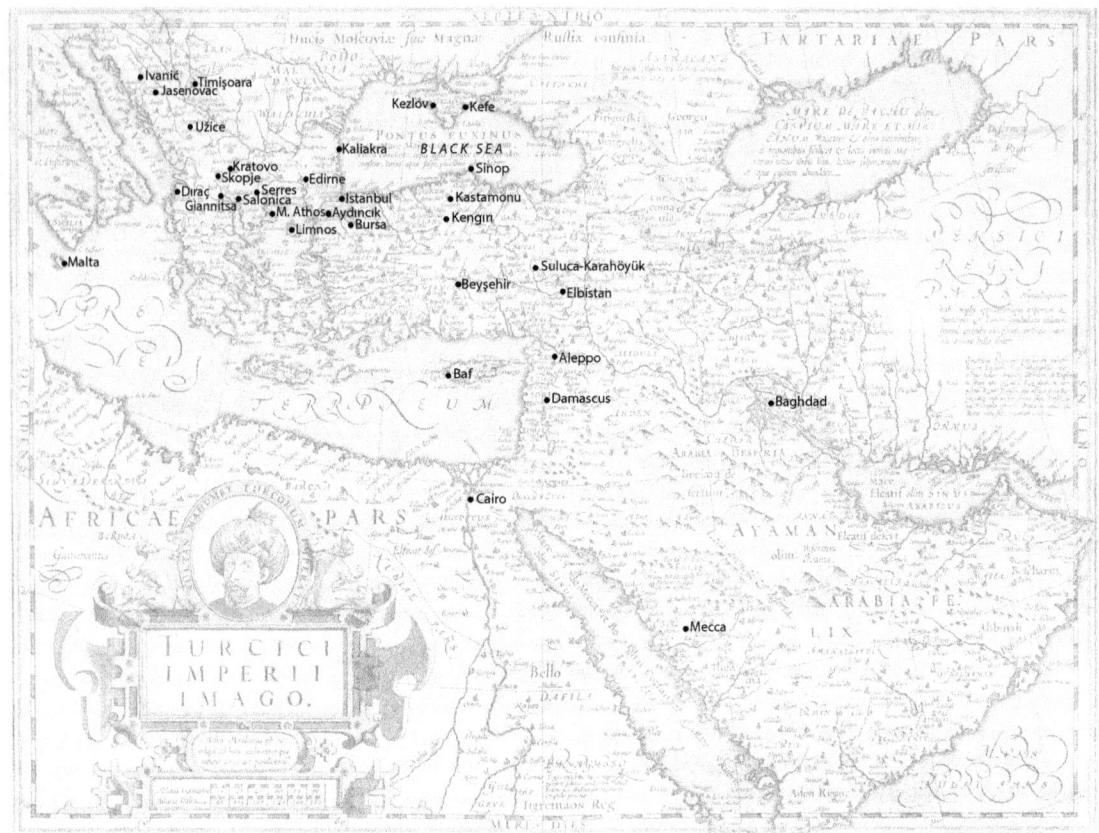

FIGURE 1. The Ottoman territories in the early seventeenth century. Note that the map is not exact to scale. The marked locations are approximate. Jodocus Hondius (cartographer). Gerardi Mercatoris, *Atlas sive Cosmographicae Meditationes de Fabrica Mundi et Fabricati Figura* (Amsterdam: Sumptibus & typis aeneis Judoci Hondij, 1613–16).

ONE

Letters of an Insecure Scholar, 1553

Zaifi, d. after 1557

TRANSLATED BY A. TUNÇ ŞEN

In the spring and fall of 1553, a scholar named Pir Muhammed bin Evrenos—better-known by his penname Zaifi ('The Frail One,' d. after 1557)—sent two petitions to grand vizier Rüstem Pasha (d. 1561). In these petitions, Zaifi asks for Rüstem Pasha's help securing an appointment to a higher paying teaching position, one commensurate with his career and age. The case of Zaifi, and of his candid descriptions of his professional grievances in particular, present us with an invaluable glimpse at the life and troubles of low- to midranking scholars in the strict hierarchy of the Ottoman scholarly establishment.

Zaifi was born ca. 1494, the son of a local learned man in Kratovo (in modern-day northern Macedonia). He traveled to Istanbul, likely in the early 1520s, after studying for several years in provincial towns. In his autobiographical account, which was completed in 1543, Zaifi relates his ill-fated career as a young aspirant to the scholarly life. In Istanbul, he enrolled in the *medrese* of the Eight Courtyards (Sahn-i Seman), which stood in Zaifi's time as the top institute of higher education. According to his account, Zaifi became the favorite student of the grand mufti, but the years of apprenticeship with a small stipend were too much of a financial strain. He became a private tutor to a wealthy bureaucrat's son, but the salary he received after a long delay was much less than he had expected. He began to doubt the financial prospects of private service and decided to return to his former career track in the scholarly establishment.

Strict regulations dictated the career paths of individuals within the scholarly hierarchy, from fresh graduates to the top offices of the grand mufti and the military judges. Medreses in the core lands of the empire were classified and ranked based on the daily wages of instructors. While a starting job in a low-tiered medrese would pay twenty akçe per day, the amount might gradually increase to as much as fifty akçe per day as the instructor climbed the ladder in the teaching track. (For reference, in the late 1520s, twenty akçe could buy around thirty-four kilograms of rice or eleven kilograms of mutton or five kilograms of olive oil. The daily salary of unskilled labor was around five akçe).

Zaifi's term of candidacy began in the mid-1520s, but the death in 1526 of his advisor added several years to Zaifi's waiting period before his initial appointment. Thanks to the support of a new patron, Zaifi obtained his first teaching job at a small medrese in Giannitsa (in modern-day Greece), receiving a salary of twenty-five akçe per day. His career did not advance straightforwardly over the next decade: Zaifi lingered at thirty-akçe paying medreses in less desirable locations and attended military campaigns with the hope of getting closer to men in charge of appointments in the scholarly establishment. Irked by the psychological and physical burdens of striving for a career in the hierarchy of learned men, he eventually decided to withdraw from the academic rat race and undertook a new venture merchandizing textiles. But after his house was robbed and he lost all his assets, he had to return, unwillingly, to professorial life.

In the second half of the 1540s, Zaifi's fortunes seem to have improved as he received his first jobs in a forty- and then a fifty-akçe medrese. Around the year 1549, however, he was dismissed from his fifty-akçe paying position for no apparent reason. In another work he openly accuses Rüstem Pasha for this dismissal. All his attempts in the next couple of years to obtain a position commensurate with his rank in the teaching track were to no avail. During this time, he stayed in Istanbul with his family under trying living conditions that he describes in the petitions below, as well as in his other compositions at the time. Zaifi never enjoyed an appointment to one of the Sahn colleges. Nevertheless, after Rüstem Pasha was reappointed to the office of grand vizier in September 1555, he granted Zaifi a handsome fifty-akçe pension, which must have provided relief in the final years of his life.

LANGUAGE: Turkish. Written in a mixture of elaborate formal and casual personal language—the latter arguably creating more of an emotional effect.

SOURCE: Manuscript: *Münşeat-ı Zaifi*. Topkapı Sarayı Müzesi Kütüphanesi, Istanbul, Revan 822. Letter 1: fols. 192a–193a. Letter 2: fols. 194a–b. Bibliothèque nationale de France, Paris, supplément turc 572. Letter 1: fols. 327b–328b. Letter 2: fols. 329a–b.

ZAİFİ'S FIRST LETTER TO RÜSTEM PASHA
ca. Spring of 1553

This is a copy of Zaifi's letter of supplication submitted to the illustrious grand vizier Rüstem Pasha around the time that the son-in-law of the king of the universe set out for the Persian Campaign. *[God] is the Merciful and the Sustainer.*

The petition of the insignificant, poor, and wretched shred of a man to the most honorable among the compassionate, the supporter of scholars, the source of beneficence, the mine of munificence, the protector of the poor, the benefactor of commanders, the crown on the heads of the viziers, is as follows:

The torments of poverty and trouble have overwhelmed and left me bereft of all my belongings. I have no assets to buy a house, nor do I have a mansion in which to live with my dependents in peace. My limbs and heart are in poor health; my children and dependents are abased like me. During summertime, they use rocks as pillows and the soil as a mattress. In wintertime, if they are lucky enough to find a blanket to cover themselves, they cannot find a mattress; when there is a mattress, there is no blanket. Their once splendid clothes have become sackcloth; their brocade coats have become coarse cloaks. Nor do I have a beast left to ride to visit your gate every day. Of my servants not even two remain so that I could leave one at home while taking the other with me when I visit your threshold. My feet are swollen from walking on foot. Whenever I see acquaintances mounted on Arabian horses while this humble servant walks on feet defiled by soil, I cannot help but suffer from spiritual pain. I had previously scrimped and purchased with my professorial income a modest robe [for each member of my family] to cover our disgrace. Lest people think we are impoverished, they put them on during religious festivals and similar special days, when they are exposed to other people's gaze. [The members of my household] are afraid that these robes will soon wear out if they don them all day long, as they know that I will not be able to replace them with new ones. What they wear every day at home are shabby robes and cloaks that are completely tattered. In accordance with the word of God, the Almighty, most worthy of praise—*The ignorant man supposes them to be rich because of their abstinence, but you will know them by their mark: they do not beg importunately from the people* (Qur'an 2:273)—we scrupulously avoid revealing our poverty and indigence to others out of dignity. We keep praying day and night to the Creator of the night and day, being fully resigned to Him in line with the [Qur'anic verse]: *Those who put their trust in God, He will suffice them* (Qur'an 65:3).

Nonetheless, as the saying goes, "a spear cannot be concealed in a sack," and some of the venerable and generous among the wealthy have become aware of and engaged with the conditions of these paupers. They have showed some attention, from time to time, by divine inspiration, and bestowed on us their benefaction, albeit at the level of meeting bare necessities. Praise be to God, Lord of the Universe, we have not yet been left hungry and dispossessed to date. In particular, the donation of your excellency, the mighty grand vizier pasha, in this month of Şaban, helped us replenish our stocks. However, that which is being spent will surely not last forever. If there is no [stable] income, the money in hand cannot meet expenses. Plants flourish by the blessings of clouds and the poor become gratified by the alms of the generous. People of rank fall from grace when they are dismissed [from office]; they have no bright day, only dark nights. For almost three years, the blade of dismissal has sickened my body and the cord of trouble and hardship has hobbled the feet of my mind. For that reason, I have become a desperate man with a thin, diseased body, despised by my fellows. I have not committed a sin so grave as to deserve this sort of reprimand; nor have I committed a crime so serious that I should earn such rebuke. Some that are only at the level of my students occupy high positions. Those who were previously under my guidance enjoy comfort and ease. This destitute one lives in a mansion as dark and narrow as the heart of a miser. When the weather is humid our courtyard becomes tar-like due to the clay. Our dependents can only walk around barefoot, as it is not possible to walk there with shoes. My current state is similar to that of a sick person, who ardently hopes for a remedy from the physician, but when he is close [to death] his friends and loved ones come and tell him, "while there is life, there is still hope."

It has become clear to me that you are the only one who can decisively solve this problem, but since you are soon embarking on a campaign toward distant countries there is no hope for my disease to be cured. There is nothing I can do but express my best wishes for your well-being. Judgment belongs to God. Would not it be more proper to implement a sort of action similar to that of the surgeon, who makes punctures with his scalpel and lets the body bleed [only] as much as he wants? He then puts salt on the wound and bandages it tightly. I could talk more about my current condition, but I shall not, lest people call me a grumbler. But in accordance with the saying, "Cautery is the end of medicine," you would deserve to be utterly admired by the public, should you treat my pained bosom with the mark of your favor and grace, and consider this slave—that is, me—as one of your marked and branded Indian (?) slaves. It is required to protect the honor and virtue of glorious sultans. When I was appointed to the Süleyman Pasha medrese in İznik, I did not take the appointment because it was not much distinguished in your view. Then, the professorship at the medrese of [Sultan] Orhan [in İznik], the grand ancestor of his excellency, our padishah—*may God glorify his helpers*—was assigned to me but I was dismissed before two years were up. Since then, for the last three years, I have not received an appointment. It is clearly an infringement of the virtue of the sultanate that [a dismissed scholar] remains so long desperate and deprived of means.

You submit [your recommendation] to the sultan that such and such scholar is a righteous person and learned in every science, which is then also written on our certificates of appointments. How strange it is that you reverse your opinion when that righteous and learned scholar reaches fifty or sixty years of age, after holding offices in many medreses! Yet, if you intend [to show your beneficence] again, it will doubtlessly happen. As for compassion, there has never been a vizier at the Ottoman court as benevolent as yourself. Your hand of support could lift a particle from the earth to the Pleiades, and the alchemy of your kindness could make soil like gold.

My felicitous lord! For God's sake, do not bother yourself with examining my dismissal or oppression by poverty and indigence. Since you are the lord of grace, show your utmost generosity, eminent grace, and benevolence for the destitute, and bestow on me, your servant, one of the medreses at the Eight [Courtyards]. Thereby I will be one of your special servants who will always wish the best for you. Since the day I was dismissed, I have not appealed to anyone else's gate. When Hudhud (the hoopoe) was missing [from the bird assembly], Prophet Solomon—*may God's blessings be upon him*—said, "*I shall punish it severely*" (Qur'an 27:21). The Qur'an commentators have interpreted this as Hudhud's peers being promoted to higher positions, and Hudhud being degraded. This humble one has been greatly suffering [like Hudhud]. Judgment belongs to God, yet we have not given up hope for reward. It is not uncommon that a master first reprimands his servant and then shows his benevolence to help him receive a reward. Your servant is not yet entirely without hope. If you decline my request, I will be a rejected servant; if you accept me, then I will be the one admired by people. The rest is upon God, Creator of all existing things and Provider for mankind and jinn.

[Signed:] The weakest of all servants, Zaifi, the humble one.

ZAİFİ'S SECOND LETTER TO RÜSTEM PASHA
ca. Fall of 1553

This is the petition of the feeble servant and weak slave of the most eminent of the honorable viziers, the most glorious of the respected commanders, the protection of poor scholars of the world, the confidant of the sultan of Arab and Persian lands, the cloud of generosity, beneficence, and grace, the rain pouring from the sky of prosperity onto the people, the exalted grand vizier, the mighty pasha:

As you embarked on the campaign toward an area as far as my farthest ambitions, this despicable one remained hopeless about a [teaching] position, like a diseased person despairing of remedy.

The spiritual efforts of the men of the unseen world, who are able even to uproot mountains, brought your far-flung imperial campaign closer and made certain that you return soon to your felicitous palace. This reanimated this sick one who had given up hope and made me realize that my request of attaining a position would, God the Compassionate willing, be soon fulfilled; *With [all] the hardship there is some ease* (Qur'an 94:6). It is hoped that with the abundance of your benefaction, these afflictions will come to an end and the requests this servant has made will be attained with ease. Amen! O God who responds to those who pray! Before you gloriously departed for the campaign, you had ordered those staying in the city to appoint me to a medrese. Although they had to observe the honor of my gracious and munificent lord and the dignity of the Ottoman sultans, they did not offer me a position appropriate to my rank, but one that would cause me to die from sorrow a thousand times over every day. While other scholars are [ordinarily] promoted from a medrese of forty akçe per day to one of fifty, or from a fifty-akçe medrese to a medrese at the Eight [Courtyards], or even higher positions, they offered this servant, who had previously enjoyed a fifty-akçe medrese, a shameful retreat to a medrese of forty akçe per day, saying, "We were only able to persuade the pasha of this level."

I said [to them], "The pasha is a generous person, famed for lifting his protégés from the ground to the sky." When I was offered the Davud Pasha medrese [in Istanbul], the professor whom I replaced there had previously held the judgeship of Egypt. The professor who was appointed there after me has [meanwhile] attained [a position in a medrese] in Üsküdar at the rank of [Eight] Courtyards. My distraught status, however, for the last three years has not been addressed with mercy and compassion at all.

Seeing that I was not being offered a teaching position according to my wish, I said, "I wish the pasha had not left for the campaign!" They said, "Hang on till he returns." I said,

FIGURE 2. Akçe, silver coin struck for Sultan Süleyman I, following his accession, 1520. Courtesy of Nuqud Gallery, Dubai.

"I hope I can!" The saying, "*The good thing that one was hoping for has actually happened*" is fitting here, and you have not been long and have returned sound and safe. The men of the unseen world, by divine command, have auspiciously brought you back to your place so that you now can carry out the [unfinished] affairs of many desperate people like me.

Oh my mighty and saintly lord, who shall remain seated for ages upon the throne of felicity! In order that God—*may He be glorified and exalted*—give you a long life, and that God may make you appear more gracefully and pleasingly in the fortunate sultan's blessed eyes, and that the Absolute Creator give my prosperous lord a beautiful noble son, light of everyone's eyes and joy of everyone's hearts, brilliant as the sun, sublime as the celestial sphere, with the character of an angel, a face similar to the moon, and a well-proportioned physique, with a long life—please do not leave this servant of yours bereft of an office of rank.

Scholars, commanders, and even commoners are taking pity on my current state. I have no possessions, no horse, no property or house to stay in. My dependents wear worn-out coats with no cotton filling left therein. I have suffered for years the burden of dismissal and have lived a debased life among my peers. Please bestow on me a medrese from the Eight [Courtyards] for the sake of the felicitous sultan's life. Don't let me go somewhere else with all my dependents; my children are innocent and sinless. We have in no way the strength and power to go half a day's journey. It is an easy thing for you to say, "I have appointed you to a medrese of the Eight [Courtyards]." For you it is not even as much as giving a silver coin to a pauper. [But] for us it is more valuable than receiving one thousand gold coins. A minimal commendation to the padishah (sultan) from you will cause him to fully approve of me. For the last three years, I have been striving every day to secure the livelihood of sixteen people or more [in my household]. It is not befitting to see, in the time of such a generous and benevolent vizier like my lord, that the garments of the dependents of a fifty-akçe professor are of lower quality than those of the children of artisans. *Just treatment is half of the religion!*

> Most of the artisans treated him justly
> So that he [too] became a just person

The Ottoman dynasty has never witnessed such a gracious, benevolent, generous, and bounteous vizier like my lord.

O my lord! Please show me your mercy and bestow on me your grace for the sake of God. The rest is up to God, Lord of the jinn and mankind, and Creator of day and night.

TWO

Adversities at Sea: From Basra to Gujarat, 1554

Seydi Ali Reis, d. 1562

TRANSLATED BY ÁRMIN VÁMBÉRY

Seydi Ali Reis was an Ottoman captain who was born in Istanbul in the beginning of the 1500s and died in 1562 in the same city. Having begun his career as an officer in the arsenal, he later participated in several naval campaigns, became an expert captain, and was eventually promoted to the rank of admiral. He was also an accomplished man of letters, with an interest in the mathematical and astronomical sciences. He is primarily remembered for the account of his adventures traveling from Basra to India by sea, and for his prolonged overland return trip to Istanbul—altogether spanning more than three years. The earlier part of his travel account is an outstanding document for gleaning the conditions on a ship in difficult waters. It also contains ample material for modern historians to study the dimensions of premodern cross-cultural encounters, as Seydi Ali travels through and spends time in the furthest reaches of the Islamic world, including the Mughal Empire, then in Central Asia and Iran—a sojourn relayed in the latter part of the book (not included in this chapter). It is thus a valuable document for exploring the cultural differences across Muslim-ruled domains that otherwise might too easily be presented as one monolithic civilization.

The sections translated below, however, are lively reflections of the political rivalry between the Ottomans and the Portuguese in the first half of the sixteenth century. The Ottomans attempted to expand their influence in the Indian Ocean during this period, which saw a continuous struggle between two powerful navies to control navigation on the Red Sea, the Persian Gulf, and the Arabian Sea. These struggles culminated in 1552, when another famed Ottoman admiral and a distinguished cartographer, Piri Reis ("Reis" denotes "captain"), led a fleet from Suez around the Arabian Peninsula, capturing the port of Muscat and briefly laying siege to the main Portuguese fortress in Hormuz. Fearing the arrival of Portuguese reinforcements from India, Piri Reis eventually withdrew from Hormuz and abandoned most of his fleet in the Ottoman port of Basra (an act for which he was executed shortly thereafter).

In 1554, Seydi Ali was charged with the task of bringing the Ottoman fleet, comprising fifteen galleys, from Basra to Suez. Seydi Ali arrived in Basra on February 3, 1554 and waited five months until the appropriate season for sailing, repairing the fleet over the winter. According to limited intelligence available to him as he set sail from Basra on July 2, 1554, there were only four small Portuguese vessels on patrol in the Persian Gulf (or "the Sea of Hormuz," as the Ottomans referred to it). But this intelligence proved to be false and Seydi Ali failed to reach the Red Sea owing to a combination of Portuguese attacks and violent storms. Several of his ships were lost at sea and others were taken by the Portuguese; those that survived were rerouted toward India, from where the captain and around fifty of his men would travel overland back to Ottoman territory.

The circumstances under which Seydi Ali composed his account have been debated by scholars. Since he failed in his mission to safely bring the fleet from Basra to Suez and it took him so long to come home, he would most likely have run into professional trouble after returning to Istanbul. For strategic reasons he might thus have inflated his importance at the Mughal and Central Asian courts during his overland return trip.

LANGUAGE: Turkish. Plain factual style with the standard number of periodic chain sentences. Interspersed with nautical words of Italian and Greek origin. Vámbéry's 1899 translation was partially revised and corrected by Hakan T. Karateke.

SOURCE: Seydi Ali Reis. *Mir'âtü'l-memalik*. Edited by Mehmet Kiremit. Ankara: Türk Dil Kurumu, 1999 (77–87). Translated by Ármin Vámbéry as *The Travels and Adventures of the Turkish Admiral Sidi Ali Reïs In India, Afghanistan, Central Asia, and Persia, during the Years 1553–1556*. London: Luzac 1899 (9–23). Partial translations are available in Kahane, Henry, Renée Kahane, and Andreas Tietze. *The Lingua Franca in the Levant: Turkish Nautical Terms of Italian and Greek Origin*. Urbana: University of Illinois Press, 1958.

On the first day of Şaban of 961 (July 2, 1554) we left the harbor of Basra, to be accompanied by the frigate of Şerif Pasha as far as [the end of] the Sea of Hormuz. [. . .] We arrived in Rey Shehr (Bushehr), a harbor on the coast of Shiraz province, and continued along the Persian coastline. We came across a spritsail and inquired about the whereabouts of the enemy, but the crew did not know. Thereupon we crossed over to the Arabian coast and arrived in the city of Katif situated near Hajar (Lahsa). There, too, we found a sailing vessel and asked about the enemy but received no information. Then we continued on to Bahrain, where I conversed with the commander of the place, Reis Murad. He confirmed that there is no fleet of infidels out at sea. [. . .] Next, we stopped at the Islands of Kays (Old Hormuz) and Barhat, and several other small islands in the Green Sea (Sea of Hormuz), and nowhere did we receive news of the enemy fleet. Thus, as we sailed out of the Sea of Hormuz, we dismissed Şerif, who had escorted us since Basra at [the governor of Basra] Mustafa Pasha's behest, with the message that Hormuz was safely passed.

CLASH WITH A PORTUGUESE FLEET

We proceeded along the coasts of Jalgar and Jadi, past the towns of Kumzar and Lima, and as we neared the town of Khorfakkan, forty days after our departure, which was the tenth day of holy Ramazan (August 9, 1554), in the late morning, we suddenly spotted the infidel Christian fleet coming toward us. The fleet consisted of four assault *bargia*s (galleys) as large as frigates, three large galleons, six Portuguese caravels, and twelve galliots—twenty-five vessels in all. We immediately struck the awnings, weighed the anchor, readied the guns, and, putting our trust in God Almighty and asking divine assistance from the prophets and friends of God, fastened the pennants to the masts. The flags were unfurled and, with full spirit and courage, yelling holy battle cries, we commenced fighting.

There are no words to describe the volleys from the guns and cannons. With God's help, we struck and utterly destroyed one of the enemy's galleons, which was carried away toward the island of Fakk al-asad and eventually sank. [. . .] An arduous battle continued until after sundown. Finally, when the admiral's lantern was lit (i.e., when night fell), the admiral of the infidel fleet got frightened and commanded that a signal shot for retreat be fired. The bargias tacked and headed toward the Sea of Hormuz and vanished from sight. Under the lucky star of the felicitous sultan and with the help of God, the enemies of Islam had been defeated. As darkness fell, suddenly a strong wind disturbed the calm waters. We put up the sails and pulled to a nearby shore. Using foliage as cover, we continued along the shore until morning. The bay waters became clear. It poured rain overnight.

CLASH WITH ANOTHER PORTUGUESE FLEET

The next day, we shoved off the coast, jibed, and continued our previous course. We arrived in Khorfakkan after a day's trip, where the soldiers took in water. Thereafter, we reached Amman (Sohar). We cruised another seventeen days and arrived in the vicinity of Muscat and Kalhat on the twenty-sixth of Ramazan—that is, the holy Night of Power. That morning, twelve large bargias and twenty-two *ghurab*s (pirate ships)—thirty-four vessels in all—under the command of the captain of Goa, the son of the governor (i.e., the Portuguese viceroy), advanced toward us from the harbor of Muscat. They carried a large number of troops. The bargias and the galleons obscured the horizon with their mizzensails and small sails all set. The caravels spread their round sails and embellished their ships with pennants.

With full confidence in God's protection, we prepared for battle on the coast side and awaited them. The bargias attacked our galleys. The battle that raged with cannon and guns, arrows and swords is beyond description. The balls of our basilisk cannons pierced the bargias like sharp knives and the *şayka* cannons tore large holes in their hulls. They, in return, turned our galleys into hedgehogs with javelins they threw down from the crow's nests of their ships, and showered stones on us like rain. [. . .] One of our galleys was set on fire by a bombshell, and yet by divine providence, the bargia that fired the shell also burned. Five of our galleys and as many of the enemy's boats were carried away toward the shore, where they

FIGURE 3. A four-master galleon, sixteenth century. Frans Huys (artist), ca. 1555.

sank and perished. One of their bargias ran aground with the thrust of its sails and was wrecked. In short, there were a great number of casualties on both sides. Our oarsmen grew exhausted from rowing against the current and from firing cannons. We were compelled to drop anchor, but moving the anchors to the stern, we continued to fight as best we could.

Finally, we let down the rowboats. Alemşah Reis, Kara Mustafa, and Kalafat Memi, captains of some of the foundered galleys, and Dürzi Mustafa Bey, the commander of the volunteers, with the remainder of the Egyptian soldiers and two hundred sailors, were taken on rowboats. As the rowers were Arabs, when they made it to the shore, they were hospitably treated by countless Arabs of Najd who came to help the Muslims and guided them onshore. The infidel ghurabs had likewise taken on board the crews of their sunken vessels, and as there were Arabs among them, too, they also had found shelter on the Arabian coast. God is our witness. Even in the war between Hayreddin Pasha and Andreas Doria no such naval action as this has ever taken place. When night fell, the bay of Hormuz once again churned and a strong wind arose. Their bargias each dropped two *ancorettas*—that is, large anchors—they made fast two sheet shots. They had the ghurabs rowed to the shore. Our galleys were carried toward the shore while dragging their anchors in the bottom of the sea. Though the crews were exhausted, we were compelled to move away from the shore, and had to set sail again.

OTTOMAN FLEET CARRIED AWAY TOWARD INDIAN OCEAN

That night we drifted away from the Arabian coast into the open sea, passed the province of Kerman, and finally reached the coasts of Jask. This is a coast with shallow waters and has no harbor. When we could see the shore, we let down the lines and roamed about for two days before we came to Kech-Makran, located in the province of Makran. As the evening was far advanced, we could not land immediately. We anchored close to the shore and spent another night at sea. A swell that lasted until morning tired out the crew. At last, after unheard-of troubles and difficulties, we approached the harbor of Chabahar early the next morning.

Here we came upon a pirate man-of-war along with a prize. As the watchman sighted us, their men disembarked and stormed our ship. We told them that we were Muslims, whereupon their captain came aboard our vessel. He led us to a source of water, for we had not a drop left; and thus our exhausted soldiers were invigorated. This was on the day of the Ramazan feast, and for us, as we now had water, a double feast day. Escorted by the pirate captain, we entered the harbor of Guador. The people there were Beluchistanis and their chief was Malik Jalaladdin, the son of Malik Dinar. The governor of Guador came aboard our ship and assured us of his unalterable devotion to our glorious padishah. He said that he shipped boats of supply and men when the Ottoman navy came to Hormuz, but the fleet had already left. He promised also that henceforth, if ever our fleet should come to Hormuz, he would undertake to send fifty or sixty boats to supply us with provisions, and to be of service to us in every possible way. We expressed our hope that they be ready for service when necessary, adding the saying, *"all affairs are contingent upon their exact time."* We then wrote a

FIGURE 4. Indian Ocean. Locations on Seydi Ali Reis's route. Note that the map is not exact to scale. The marked locations are approximate. Jan Jansson (cartographer). Detail from the 1658 map of the Indian Ocean, or Erythraean Sea printed in *Novus Atlas*.

letter to the native Malik Jalaladdin to request one navigator for the seas and a separate one for the shores, whereupon two skilled guides were sent to us—thereby demonstrating obedience to our felicitous sultan.

ANOTHER ATTEMPT TOWARD THE RED SEA

By God's mercy, with a favorable wind we left the port of Guador and sailed out to the Indian Ocean—that is, the Circumambient Ocean—and with the help of some wind again steered for Yemen. [. . .] We were out in the ocean for several days and presumably crossed beyond Ras al-Hadd, and arrived nearly opposite of Dhofar and Shihr, when suddenly from the west arose a great storm known as the "elephant's flood." We therefore turned back, but were unable to set the sails, not even the storm jibs. [. . .] The tempest raged with increasing fury. The foul weather in the western oceans is mere child's play compared to these tempests; and their towering billows are as drops of water compared to those of the Indian Ocean. Night and day became alike, and because of the frailty of our craft, all ballast had to be thrown overboard. In this frightful predicament, we had no option but to yield to our fate and trust in divine providence. We kept our unwavering hopes in God's aid and in divine assistance from the prophets and friends of God. [. . .]

FLEET ONCE MORE CAST TOWARD THE PERSIAN COAST

For about ten days the storm raged continuously, and the rain came down in torrents in the Indian Ocean. We never once saw calm waters. I did all I could to encourage and cheer my companions, and I advised them above all things to be brave and never to doubt but that all would end well. A welcome diversion occurred in the appearance of fish about the size of two galley lengths, or more perhaps. The navigators advised not to be afraid of these blessed animals. Strong tides occurred here. As the sea level rose very high, we approached the gulf of Kutch. We saw many unique creatures: Sea horses, large sea serpents, turtles in great quantities, and eels.

The color of the water suddenly changed to white. The navigators broke forth into loud lamentations; they declared we were approaching whirlpools and eddies. Whirlpools out in the Indian Ocean are a myth; they are, however found in two places: at Girdifon (Arkiko?) on the coasts of Abyssinia and in the bay of Kutch in the neighborhood of Sind, and hardly a ship has been known to escape their fury. So, at least, we are told in nautical books. We took frequent soundings and when we struck a depth of five arm lengths, we furled the mainsails, cleared the yard, let down the lines, [and] heeled over to the weather side as much as possible. As the ship stayed upright, we rowed all night and all day. At last, by God's mercy, the sea level fell low; the wind, too, made *drizza*—that is, it died down, and changed to athwart, perhaps even to a stern-prow, direction.

The following morning, we amained—that is, we hauled down and took the sail off. An able sailor from among the topmen was tied to the yardarm; the bare yard was hoisted to its highest point, then the *qazı* ("butt end of a lateen yard") was pressed down to the heel of the mast [so that] the *apli* ("upper end of a lateen yard") was raised to the height of an additional mast. Taking a survey of our surroundings, the sailor caught sight of an Idol-Temple on the coast of Djamher (Jamnagar?). The sails were drawn in a little more; we passed Porbandar and Mangrol, and directing our course toward Somnath, we passed by that place also. Finally, we came to Diu, but for fear of the unbelievers that control this place, we did not set any sails and continued on our course with all sails furled. Meanwhile, the wind had risen again, and as the men had no control over the rudder, large handles had to be affixed with long double ropes fastened to them. Each rope was held by four men, and with great exertion they managed to control the rudder. No one could keep on his feet on deck, so of course it was impossible to walk across to the forward part of the ship. Sailors' pipes could not be heard from the noise of the riggings. They communicated with the riggers on the front by transmitting the order from mouth to mouth. The captains and the sailing masters were unable to stand even a moment on the conning bridge, and finally, most of the hired sailors were packed into the hold. The storm took the rails from on board ship and carried them away. It was like doomsday.

SHIPS DAMAGED BY REEFS IN THE GULF OF KHAMBHAT

At last we reached the province of Gujarat in India; where exactly we were, however, we knew not. The navigators suddenly exclaimed, "On your guard! A rocky bank in front; watch out!"

Quickly the anchors were lowered, but the ship was dragged toward the bank with great force and nearly submerged. The rowers broke their fetters; the panic-stricken crew threw off their clothes. Some prepared barrels; others leather bags [to serve them as life preservers during the shipwreck], and they said their good-byes to each other. I also stripped entirely, gave my slaves their liberty, and vowed to give one hundred florins to the poor of Mecca [if I were to be saved]. Finally, one anchor broke off at the ring and the other at the bottom of the trunk [of the ship]. We quickly dropped two more anchors, secured them, and thus we cleared off the bank a little. The navigator declared that the bank was a shoal and is between Diu and Daman. If the ship went down here, no one would survive. We should immediately set the sails and strive for the coast. This humble one calculated the ebb and flow during the time we had been at sea; that is to say, I took its drift and, taking the bearing on the chart, I ascertained that the shore was near. I also searched for a sign in the Qur'an and found it wiser to not rush. We inspected the well rooms and found that the water filled up the frames and even covered the flooring in all the storerooms. The ships having taken in too much water, we started immediately to bail it out with pails. At various places we removed the skin of the ship and found leaks. The leakage was thus somewhat brought under control.

Toward afternoon the weather had cleared some, and we found ourselves about two miles off the port of Daman, in Gujarat in India. The other ships had already arrived, but being close to the shore, some of the galleys had suffered severe damage from constant clashing against the rocks. They had lowered their oars, boats, and barrels on the sea, all of which eventually were borne ashore by the rapidly rising tide.

THREE

Memoirs of an Ottoman Captive in Malta, 1597–98

Macuncuzade Mustafa, d. ca. Early Seventeenth Century

TRANSLATED BY HELGA ANETSHOFER

Little is known about Macuncuzade Mustafa, who was traveling from Istanbul to take up a new judgeship on Cyprus when his ship was intercepted by Maltese ships. *Kadı*s, or judges, were officials of the judiciary and the civil administration. As the representatives of the Holy Law and the Ottoman state, their responsibilities and job descriptions went beyond interpreting the law: They acted as judges, mayors, financial trustees, and mediators, among other things. Ordinarily, a judge would be appointed to a new post every two years. The term limit was in place to forestall the abuse of power that sometimes resulted from the relatively high authority judges possessed in rural areas. There was a strict hierarchy within the Ottoman class of *ilmiyye,* or scholars of Islamic jurisprudence. Kadıs were part of this ladder, and a judge's rank was indicated by the daily wage allocated to him. While a handful of prestigious judgeships were usually occupied by members of important scholarly families or those close to political authority, six hundred or more judgeships in smaller townships throughout the empire were filled with graduates of medreses in the early seventeenth century.

Macuncuzade remained in captivity for about two years and wrote down his experiences, which he recounted partly in prose and partly in poetry, contributing to a robust new tradition of Ottoman captivity narratives relaying the traumatic experiences of captives taken prisoner in battles or held captive by corsairs. The genre was extraordinarily popular: Not only did Ottomans write about their captivity in culturally alien and politically hostile lands but many European captives wrote in detail about their experiences in Ottoman lands. Such narratives served as vehicles through which readers learned about other cultures. Even though the genre is naturally prone to amplifications or embellishments by the authors, these accounts are extremely well-suited for the study of cross-cultural encounters. In addition to being engaging reading, they typically reflect the mindsets and worldviews of their authors and offer ample evidence of writers' cultural assumptions about foreigners at the time.

Taking captives and ransoming them back to their families was a well-organized and lucrative market in the Mediterranean in the early modern era. Capturing a high-ranking prisoner could fetch a handsome sum, and Macuncuzade, being a judge, was a potentially valuable prisoner of war. It was in the interest of captors to keep their captives alive—if only with the barest of necessities. Captives were urged to seek ransom money from their hometowns; if multiple members of the same family were taken captive, one of them would be allowed to return home to arrange for payment. All in all this was a robust, if deplored, business model in the Mediterranean. Five hundred gold coins (florins) were set as a ransom amount for Macuncuzade Mustafa, roughly equivalent to the price of a valuable residential property in late-sixteenth-century Istanbul.

LANGUAGE: Turkish. Rather unembellished but learned prose, interspersed with religious and literary citations in Arabic and Persian. Macuncuzade's own emotional verses make up about half of the text.

SOURCE: Ottoman print edition and partial facsimile: İz, Fahir, ed. "Macuncuzade Mustafa'nın Malta Anıları: Sergüzeşt-i Esiri-i Malta." *Türk Dili Araştırmaları Yıllığı Belleten* (1970): 69-122.

TRAVEL FROM ISTANBUL TO CYPRUS
April 1597

By divine decree and heavenly predestination, I was appointed from Constantinople, the Abode of the Sultanate and the city I was born in and hail from, to the judgeship of Baf (Paphos) on the island of Cyprus at the rank of 130 akçe [per day] on the thirtieth day of the venerable month of Receb in the year of 1005 (March 18, 1597) during the tenure of the chief military judge Damad Efendi. Thereupon, I bid farewell to my old friends and close intimates, and said the hemistich:

The following phrase gave the date of my appointment: "the kadı of Baf"
(i.e., the numerical value of the Arabic letters for this phrase adds up to AH 1005 / CE 1597)

I was getting ready to depart when I suffered an inflammation of the eyes. I had to rest until the last day of the month of Şaban (April 18, 1597). By then I had somewhat recovered, but the eye doctors did not allow me to travel by land under any circumstances. There was no other option but to travel by sea. Thus, I boarded the small galley of Mehmed Reis of Alanya, who lived in Galata [in Istanbul]. We set out in the late afternoon on Tuesday, the fifth day of the holy month of Ramazan (April 21, 1597).

MALTESE SHIPS INTERCEPT THE OTTOMAN GALLEY
May 1597

On the twenty-seventh of Ramazan (May 13, 1597), the day after the Night of Power, a Wednesday morning, we had long passed the spot called Cape Arnaoutis and were about seventy miles out of Baf when we encountered a gang of the wicked on four Maltese ships—

may God destroy them (Qur'an 9:30). They rammed us and a great battle took place until late morning. More than thirty of us Muslims were martyred—*may God have mercy on them*—and more than eighty of the cursed devils perished—*God's curse is on them,* and more than one hundred were wounded.

In short, two of our companions, Hüseyn and Osman, died—*may God have mercy on both of them.* This humble one was taken captive together with my slave Rıdvan. One of the judges, Bekir Efendi from Sivas, the judge of Pendaye [on Cyprus], and a substitute professor, his brother, and his steward were also martyred—*may God have mercy on them.* However, Abdurrahman Efendi of Antakya, the judge of Irbid and Ajlun (in modern-day Jordan), and Sinan Efendi, the judge of Gügercinlik were captured along with us.

We roamed the sea for twenty-six days, suffering all sorts of oppression, such that it is impossible to describe. It would be too much to count and enumerate all the pain and hardship that we suffered. All in all, they destroyed twelve sailing ships during this time.

PRISONERS TAKEN TO MALTA
June 1597

Toward the end of the month of Şevval (early June 1597), the cursed French captain by the name of Saint Aubin transported us, along with 283 prisoners, to Malta. They call the filthy residence that is the disgraceful abode of their overlords (i.e., the Knights Hospitaller) a "*palas*" or "palace." There they gathered us all together and displayed us to their overlords. Then they counted us and led us to the dungeon.

There was another judge, Haşim el-Haşimi, an old acquaintance of ours, in the dungeon. Just like me, he had been appointed the judge of Khirsofi (Khyrsokhou) in Cyprus, and while he was traveling by land out of fear of the enemy, he was captured at Ak liman when he passed Silifke. He had been a prisoner there for seven years (!), since mid-Şaban of the year 999 (early June, 1591). He greeted me [in Arabic], "*How are you doing?*" I responded with the following verse [in Persian], "*This was my destiny, it should not surprise / Slavery and being in foreign lands is extraordinary calamity.*" His old pain was refreshed, and the two of us suffering from the same pain cried and moaned together.

CONDITIONS IN THE DUNGEON

Discomposed as such, we waited in the courtyard of the dungeon from before noon until the evening. At that point, the door of the dungeon opened and a bad-natured executioner with an ugly face—he was hideous and his voice even more so—called out, "Come in!" to the group of prisoners in his infidel language. On entering, they gave us three pieces of brown bread and a bowl of soup. The bowls resembled earthen bowls for dogs and their soup was *food that chokes and a painful punishment [in hell]* (Qur'an 73:13). I entered the dungeon and noticed the noxious air and murky water.

Across from the door were a toilet and two uncovered stone basins in the shape of a trough. The water was stagnant and filthy. It was actually rainwater, but before reaching the reservoir it had been polluted by washing away dogs' and pigs' feces from the markets and the rubbish and waste from the roofs. There was no flowing water on that island, and the place was so crowded with masses of prisoners that it resembled the deepest pits of hell, demonstrating the meaning of [the Qur'anic verse] *and leg is entangled with leg* (Qur'an 75:29). [. . .]

You couldn't even see your hands in front of your face in the dungeon. With a thousand difficulties I located the aforementioned Haşim Efendi's cell and spent four nights there. When, during our conversation, he said metaphorically, "We are like corpses in the hands of the dead washers," this sad heart of mine could not help but wholeheartedly ask God to take my soul. For one year I persevered in this prayer. Wishing to die is obviously against the Holy Law—however:

Death is much better than this violence and torment.

But since I was obviously not destined to die, it did not happen. I was not able to give an answer to those prisoners who asked me what would become of us; I was lost and confused in a sea of thoughts; had no strength left; remained silent and thunderstruck.

When there is no strength to explain in words,
Describing in writing is beyond possibility.

All eternity was written down—in detailed expression, every single word,
So that 'the pen ran dry,' (i.e., it's irrevocable).

ADJUSTING TO THE CIRCUMSTANCES

When I rationally concluded that the reason for my captivity was the incapacity of my agency [to shape my fate], I consoled my sad heart to some extent:

Since death is coming anyway, what benefit is in my return?
[The calamities] of my misadventure are irrevocable.

The next day, I met in the courtyard of the dungeon another prisoner by the name of Seyyid Mehmed Çelebi [. . .] and his brother-in-law İbrahim Çelebi [. . .], who brought me to their family cells. Mehmed Çelebi's revered mother, and, indeed, all of them—although they were prisoners themselves—took good care of me and treated me with utmost generosity—may their kindness be eternal *as they deserve*. Until the end of the month of Şevval (June 16, 1597), I enjoyed their favors during the day, and slept in Judge Haşim's cell at night. This humble one also needed to be present in the cell, for an infidel by the name Antoine known as the "Foul-mouthed Ragusan" would count the prisoners cell by cell to check if we were all there.

> Whenever we were counted when I was a prisoner in the hands of the infidels,
> Grief was never ever missing from my heart.

On the first of the month of Zilkade (June 15, 1597), I fell ill and I stayed in the hospital of San Giovanni for two months. With their abundant favors and great generosity, my aforementioned benefactors brought to life the meaning of *"Friends are useful [when] in the dungeon,"* and through God's grace they became the final cause for my recovery.

AUGUST 1597—MAY 1598

On the first day of the blessed month of Muharrem of the year 1006 (August 13, 1597) I left the hospital. During that month, I paced the dungeon courtyard unrestrainedly during the day and it calmed me. İbrahim Çelebi found my *divan* (collection of poems) with one of the prisoners. I took the opportunity to make a copy of it and made a rough draft in his family cell. Because the evil infidels had taken all my belongings on the ship, I was left naked, apart from borrowed clothes, and in tears. [. . .]

The days passed in this manner as we unwound at Mehmed Çelebi's family cell. Even the pesky enemies stopped barking and howling at us like hungry dogs. But then, some malicious intriguers and envious, abominable men kindled the fire of incitement—commensurate with their malicious nature—because they didn't want anyone to be comfortable. They incited the Big (Elder?) Ragusan, the one-eyed dungeon keeper Marian the Rat, with the words, "This judge meets with the others for '*qonsel*' ('conseil')—that is, to consult with each other at the cell of the *çelebi*s," whereupon I was put in iron shackles and was incarcerated on the first of the month of Safer (September 12, 1597). With God's help I came out of the dungeon on the twenty-first (October 2, 1597) and continued to live in my old way in the same place. [. . .] I spent the days at Mehmed Çelebi's family cell, and during the night, went back to the dungeon sweeper Hacı Hasan's cell, which was the first one on the northern side when you entered the dungeon. If one swore by God that it was a part of hell, it would be an appropriate attestation. [. . .]

On the seventeenth day of Receb (February 22, 1598)—through God's grace—Hacı Hasan was set free. [. . .] I wrote an ode with a request for salvation and sent it with Hacı Hasan to the dust at the feet of Her Majesty Safiye Sultan [the imperial mother]. I hope that with God's grace, out of her general sympathy and her comprehensive generosity for scholars, dervishes, and imprisoned people she will not refrain from delivering this poor distressed one from the misfortune of captivity. [. . .] Hacı Hasan left on the seventeenth of Receb (February 22, 1598). I sent the ode and a refrain poem along with him and acted according to the meaning of the [Qur'anic verse]: *Those who put their trust in God, He will suffice them* (Qur'an 65:3). I kept praying humbly and wishing for help from the throne of the divine grace. I implored God during the obligatory prayers, "With one of your two mercies (God is *rahman*, the Most Compassionate, and *rahim*, the Most Merciful), rescue this wretched prisoner from the hands of the infidels!" [. . .]

PRISONERS AT HARD LABOR

When the holy month of Ramazan arrived, I lead the supererogatory night prayers in the aforementioned prayer room. On a Monday, the morning of the Night of Power (May 4, 1598), the infidels led us to a ditch, gave us wooden pestles, and accompanied by all sorts of rebukes and insults, forced us to hollow out the places where the cannon balls were to be placed. [. . .] The Maltese boys cursed our religion in their language, called the Holy Messenger indecent names, and said offensive nonsense about him that was absolutely inappropriate to describe his personality and qualities. They spit in our faces and hurt us with their sharp tongues or stoned us with their hard cruelty.

On the day of the Ramazan festival (May 7, 1598), the keeper of the dungeon, whose filthy nature was far from gracious, showed his kinder side and left us alone. We wished each other a blessed festival at the family cell of the aforementioned gracious friends. [. . .] Then, unintentionally, I started to cry. I was confused and didn't know what do say or to do. Thereupon [Mehmed Çelebi's mother Sakine] took a sigh and started to relate: "A while back, my son-in-law Baki Çelebi graduated from the medrese and was appointed the judge of the pilgrimage caravan at the rank of forty akçe. While traveling, he was killed on the ship. I said the following verse spontaneously:

What is happening to me is my troubled lot
The infidel took [him], all of us turned to You: oh God!

This involuntary crying and confusion that is happening to you right now happened to us too. But I have found no other remedy than beautiful patience." Her words comforted this humble one and, with a sign from the lady, I turned her verse into a poem. [. . .]

On the second day of the holy Ramazan festival, we thought we would start our previous work in the ditch again. Instead, they ordered us to carry rocks and soil to the architects. [. . .] All of us suffered this pain and torment and irredeemable misfortune for many days. My companions fell sick and could not recover. After a couple of weeks of exhausting work, this humble one felt increasingly helpless and weak. I started feeling like the walking dead. "No one will mourn me in this foreign land, let me mourn myself at least," I thought to myself. Self-reproach and yearning for salvation required dressing in black. My white turban cloth had turned pitch black from my tears, wounds, and heavy sighs in any case [. . .]. Finally, I pretended to be sick and laid in a corner of the dungeon for a few days like a dead man.

THE RANSOM AMOUNT FOR PRISONERS IS SET

Some time later, the superiors among the cursed infidels—*may God curse them until the end of the days*—gathered me before them in a place called Kond to set my ransom amount. They asked, "How much ransom can you pay?" I showed myself as poor and said, "I can give three hundred gold coins." Yet, they demanded one thousand coins from me. I said I couldn't afford that. "Enough already," they declared, called Judge Abdurrahman, and asked him the same question. He answered, "I can give four hundred florins." They gave him the same answer and sent us back to the ditches! On top of having stood in front of them bareheaded and ashamed, we came back to the dungeon hopeless and in despair. They set a price of five hundred florin coins for Judge Haşim.

We continued on for a while with [the following] prayer on our tongues: *We seek refuge in God from the evils of the infidels*, when, early morning on the day of the Feast of the Sacrifice (July 13, 1598), they said that they were taking us to that notorious place. They lined us up in front of the dungeon door, like a slave trader does at the gates of the market hall. Then they took us to the Kond. After having waited until late morning, we were taken back to the dungeon, as none of the cursed ones had come. [. . .] We were taken to the Kond and came back a few more times in the described manner. There was no kind of remedy for this pain. [. . .] Finally, after thousands of agonies, on the fourth day of the month of Safer in 1007, a Saturday (September 5, 1598), the price for Judge Haşim, who had been a prisoner for eight years, was set at five hundred florins. The cursed ones also set my price at five hundred florin coins—*may God destroy their stock.* [. . .]

GLIMMERS OF HOPE

It was before I dispatched the letter in which I communicated my ransom amount to Istanbul. There was no news from Hacı Hasan, and I was feeling confused and broken-down. At that time İbrahim Çelebi received a letter from his father Abdulvahhab Çavuş, in which he wrote that Mehmed Bey, the felicitous governor of the Morea, who was the son of her ladyship [the Ottoman princess] Gevherhan Sultan—*may her life be long*—had pledged to freeing this humble one, too. [. . .]

On the last day of Cemaziyelevvel of 1007 (December 29, 1598), Marco, who was the infidel mediator for İbrahim Çelebi, the son of Abdurrahman Çavuş, turned up. He also bore letters for the captives. I received a letter from the aforementioned Hacı Hasan, written and sent from Istanbul in Şevval of 1006, [that is, some eight months ago]. Another letter was from good friends of mine: Hakkı and Avni Efendis, Muhsin Agha, Helvacızade Mehmed Çelebi and others. They [first] thought that I had been killed, and even had a complete Qur'an reading dedicated to my soul—*My God protect and forgive them.* The joyful message in the letter was that his excellency the sultan, the refuge of the world, had shown the greatest kindness and protection by ordering the imperial chancellor Musa Çelebi issue a decree that a Christian captive be freed in return for my freedom. May God make his blessed self prosperous and joyful in both worlds. This good news tremendously delighted my wretched heart. [. . .]

FOUR

The Excommunication of a Greek Orthodox Priest, ca. 1642

Synadinos of Serres, d. after 1662

TRANSLATED BY KONRAD PETROVSZKY

Synadinos was a Greek Orthodox priest from the town of Serres (now in the eastern Macedonian region of Greece), whose population was composed of approximately 70 percent Muslims and 25 percent Christians by the middle of seventeenth century. According to his autobiographical chronicle, Synadinos, the son of a priest in a nearby village, was born on September 21, 1600. He first learned the craft of weaving from a Jewish convert to Christianity named Christodoulos. Later, following in the footsteps of his father and brothers, he entered the ranks of the clergy at the age of nineteen. Despite the many hardships he faced in his family life—all of his children died at a young age—Synadinos gradually climbed the ladder in the local church hierarchy and even attained some prosperity through his operation of several weaving shops. In 1639, however, his rise came to a dramatic halt when he was excommunicated by Daniel, the metropolitan of Serres, and ostracized from the community. Synadinos's personal reflections on this episode are the only extensive account of his excommunication, which was ultimately temporary, and its consequences. Abundant with hyperbole, pleonasm, and other rhetorical excesses, Synadinos's memoirs manifestly draw on the literary genres of the lamentation and the martyr tale to convey his feelings of hopelessness that must have continued for several months.

The precise reasons for Synadinos's temporary expulsion are difficult to glean from the author's vague and scrappy descriptions. He had previously accused the metropolitan of Serres of certain fiscal abuses. Thanks to additional documentation from surviving church registers, we have reason to believe that Synadinos wanted to prevent the metropolitan from taking control of a nearby family endowment bequeathed by his father Sideres to his descendants. Synadinos went before the patriarchal seat in Istanbul but failed to successfully make his case. The metropolitan, further incited by one of Synadinos's rival priests, retaliated against him for the attempted subversion.

It is not clear from his narrative how exactly Synadinos managed to settle his quarrels and get reinstated in office roughly one year after his expulsion. From allusions in the text we can infer that, after being encouraged by his brother, a priest on Mount Athos, Synadinos bought himself back into his former position by paying a substantial sum to the metropolitan. This, of course, also implies that his expulsion from Serres—the disastrous effects on family and psyche notwithstanding—did not result in his complete ruin. As we can learn from documents issued later, Synadinos continued to play an important role in the local church hierarchy until his death in 1662.

The author did not give a title to his work, but it is sometimes referred to as *The Chronicle of Serres* in modern scholarship. The translated excerpt is from a section in which the author reflects on his days of ostracization and psychological distress. But in addition to serving as an account of Synadinos's travails, it is also a local history recounting events that occurred in Serres between 1597 and 1642 with a markedly personal imprint and some plentiful advice to fellow Christians. It also includes many accounts of happenings in the Ottoman imperial throne city, which lay some 530 kilometers to the east of Serres. This narrative is esteemed by historians both for its rich and vivid descriptions of everyday life in the provincial center of Serres, and for the personality of the author that vibrates through the text. There does not appear to be a comparable self-narration from within the Christian communities of the Ottoman Empire in the seventeenth century.

LANGUAGE: Greek. For the most part the vernacular Greek of the Serres region, interspersed with many Hellenized terms and expressions of Turkish origin (transliterated in the translation).

SOURCE: Greek text and French translation: Odorico, Paolo. *Conseil et mémoires de Synadinos, prêtre de Serrès en Macédonie (XVIIe siècle)*. Paris: Association Pierre Belon, 1996 (140–50).

A PRIEST IN DESPAIR

The same year (1639), in the month of February, the entire town and all its Christians, young and old, expelled me, Papasynadinos, from Serres, away from home—my wife and my children, my belongings and my homeland. [The priests] held a synod and judged me and said to me, "From today on, we do not want you any more in our city. You don't belong to us, because you have brought us harm and ruin. Just tell us, you worthless person, have you become a respected man who deserves to have his hands kissed? No, you deserve only to be battered and pilloried. You dare to ask what you have done to us? Come on, let's beat him up!" Another one spat on me. Another said, "Do you think we will let you live?" And yet another said, "Let us hand him over to our *naziris* (town superintendent), who will keep him in *khapsi* (jail) and wait for the verdict of our master." And another one said, "Let's hand him over to our *zapitis* (military officer), who will chuck him on the ground and beat him until he is caned to death." And another one said, "It would be fair to stone him." And another one said, "From today on, if we see him in the church or outside, in the city, and if he keeps company with Christians again, we kill him, no matter what." And others agreed, "It's either us

FIGURE 5. Greek Orthodox priest, early eighteenth century. Jean-Baptiste Vanmour (artist), Jacques de Franssières (engraver) in *Recueil de cent estampes representant différentes nations du Levant* . . . (Paris: Chez Le Hay et chez Duchange, 1714), plate 67.

or him!" While others said, "Rather than suffering and bothering with one man and having *kavgades* (quarrels) all the time, we better let him perish alone and spare us the trouble. Let us go to his house and destroy it from top to bottom and not leave stone on stone, so that his case becomes an *ipreti* (warning example) for everyone and the unruly will be brought to their senses." And others said to me: "We thought you were a wise man, but apparently you have gone completely out of your mind."

Who can recount all the defamations they threw in my face? It is certainly impossible to write down all the chatter, all the complaints to the Turks and the nonlocals, and all their fabricated accusations against me. They drove me out of their midst and ousted me from office and eventually wrote an *artzi* (petition) and sent it to Constantinople. They brought against me two definitive depositions, which they read out in the churches on Holy Saturday (April 13, 1639), the time of the Epitaphios of Christ, so that all could listen to them—because there were also people there from Melnik (today in Bulgaria), peasants, priests, and strangers—and everyone would know [about it].

Thus they deposed me definitively and all anathematized me—young and old, in the church, and everywhere—and called me by the base name, "The wicked Synadi, the cursed." They drove me out of the church and took my parish and said that whoever met me; or broke bread with me; or whoever helped me; or gave me aid with his deeds or words; whoever did *alisphirisi* (business) with me; whoever bought my wine or even drank it; whoever served me; whoever came to see me or sent peddlers to me to whom I could sell things; whoever treated me as a priest or kissed my hand; whoever took me for a Christian; and many other such things. . . . Finally, as soon as I realized the dead end I was in, I took refuge in a house and stayed hidden there for seven days. There came a man who said to me: "You should know that they have learned where you are hiding and that they want the *voivode* to step in, so that he will come to take you, shackle you, and keep you in khapsi (jail) and then they will wait for the order from above. So get out of here for as long as you can, go elsewhere, and hide yourself in an unknown place." So I went to another house and stayed there hidden for another nine days.

[The people of Serres] were filled with joy during the *dunanma* (festivity). They ate and drank—everyone was at the celebrations [for the reconquest of Baghdad in December 1639]—whereas I did not even want to eat bread and was feeling dead all day. Someone said to me, "Today they will kill you," while another said, "Tomorrow they will kill you." One day a [fellow] Christian came and said to me: "Brother, I would rather not have eaten bread and salt with your Holiness, than to have to bring you this news. We have received information from a trustworthy man that this evening or tomorrow morning a man from Constantinople will arrive to arrest you, shackle you, and take you to Constantinople. Everyone agrees it is either you or them. It seems to me, brother, that they won't give you any *khozuri* (peace), they won't let you live. It is certain that you no longer belong here, but if you still want to live in this world, pack up and go somewhere else, to a distant and unknown place, and give up everything." [The person who] came to me told me these things and many more.

A PRIEST ON THE RUN

While considering these things, I saw the impasse, and called a spiritual father and confessed to him at night. Then I went out in secret and told no one that I wanted to flee, neither my wife nor anyone else. Clandestinely, I went to an unknown place on Mount Athos. There, I wanted to mingle with the monks to go to Wallachia, and then finally to Russia, to become a monk and stay there for the rest of my life. I knew that I was no longer made for this place, for the rest of my life. So, my beloved [fellow Christian] brother, there in exile, in a foreign place, my little heart was filled with great sorrow and the tears did not stop running from my eyes all day, as I was crying from the bottom of my soul. Indeed, exile and persecution are utterly sad and sorrowful. It is the most poisonous of all poisons and the bitterest of all afflictions and the saddest of all sorrows.

With many tears I said, "Alas, this is me, the strange, the miserable, the wretched me who has become poor among the poor and deprived of all things. Alas, I have been taunted, insulted, persecuted, reviled, and abhorred like an assassin—deposed! Alas, that this evil should come upon me! Alas, my misery! Alas, my misfortune! Alas, I am miserable three times over!" I read in the scripture that speaks of Job and Saint Eustace (! martyred ca. 118) and how they bore many sufferings; but it seems to me, the unfortunate, that far more and sadder things have happened to me and have befallen me. For Job, even though he lost his children and everything he had, at least he was in his homeland and all his friends and relatives and strangers went to see him every day and comforted him and felt sorry for him, because consolation does a lot of good. He also had his wife, and with all this he came to a greater happiness. In the same way, Saint Eustace, having lost his wife, his children, and all that he had, had at least confidence, because Christ had [appeared to him and] told him that he was going to find his wife and his children, and his heart was filled with confidence, too. So he returned to his previous condition.

What consolation can I, the unfortunate and the miserable, have? Whatever could I say or voice wherein I might find comfort? My children, to begin with, three girls and three boys, died one after the other and now, on top of the pain for each one of them, I have no child left. Whether my past misfortunes or the recent ones that have befallen me, from head to toe—which one to mourn, what to lament first? My wife, whom I will not see again in my life, or my children, or the absence of my brothers, relatives, and friends, or my house, or my vineyards, or my barrels, or all my possessions from the smallest to the largest? Or my parish, or my homeland, of which I was deprived so quickly and suddenly, so unexpectedly and in an unforeseen manner? Or the shame I incurred; or all the damage I suffered by envious men; or my many misfortunes; or every day, hour, and every night, when the tears do not cease to run from my eyes; or the great distress I feel; or the many injustices; or my great needs; or the great dangers; or internal conflict; or the denunciations; or the betrayals; or the false testimony; or the gossip: or the blames; or the threats; or the excommunications; or the anathemas; or the false reports and *artzia* (petitions) [about me]; or the deferments, or the final degradations, or the calumnies, or the machinations, or the unjust *tseremedes* (fines); or the theft, or the retention of my income, or the damages, or the envy, or the hatred, or the rallies, or the church synods, or the judgments, or the loss of my offices, or the turmoil, or my pains, or the loss of my parents! For which of these things shall I weep first, and for which shall I mourn from the depths of my soul and my heart, and for which shall I cry with no comfort and respite?

For henceforth, my country, I shall see it no more, and in a single moment, I have been deprived of everything so that I am *seventy-seven times* (re: Matthew 18:22) poorer than the poor; and therefore, into what precipice will I precipitate myself, in what river will I drown myself? Alas, earth! Open one of your tombs and accept me as soon as possible, so that I am free of all this! Alas, death, death, where are you? How good you would be for me right now! Woe, ah, bless me, alas, woe unto me, the forsaken and the stranger! Who will give me comfort? No one! But if only you, mountains, woods, rocks, stones, rivers, plains, flowers of all kinds, seas, reptiles, quadrupeds, beasts, and all that is on the earth come for once this time and console me, the stranger among strangers! These things and others, my brother, I said with many tears. And yet, Lord, Lord, if you will pardon my saying so, because you know that I am tormented by great pains, but give me, oh Lord, perseverance to endure this danger with patience.

One day [while I was hiding on Mount Athos], I saw my brother come in and he said to me: "Come, come back, stay hidden, and maybe we will make peace." So, I went, and I had the heart of some thief who was given the pole to wear on his shoulder while they take him to the gallows. Thus felt my heart and such were my looks. In the town and in the villages and everywhere else, in those days everyone at home had nothing else to talk about but me.

Anyway, to be brief, I had spent a whole year in misery, and they had taken my parish and wanted to give my office to Papakonstantas. They did not forgive me until I entrusted all my property as *amaneti* (pledge) to Khatzi Retzepougli (Hacı Recepoğlu). I gathered four hundred grosia and put [the same amount in] thousands [of akçe] in front of the icon of Christ. I prostrated myself three times and said, "You, my God, who decides that he who leaves his wife or children, and so forth, and [you, my God, who says:] 'Sell all that you have and donate it.' Here I am myself and I give you *a very small gift* and You shall take it as *the widow's mite*" (Mark 12:41–44 and Luke 21:1–4). This disaster cost me in all a hundred and twenty thousand [akçe], and so we reconciled and made peace, the night of the feast of Christ (January 5, 1640).

FIVE

Dream Letters of a Sufi Woman in Skopje, 1640s

Asiye Hatun, d. Second Half of Seventeenth Century

TRANSLATED BY LESLIE SCHICK AND CEMAL KAFADAR

The disciples in a Sufi community usually maintained a special attachment to a sheikh, or spiritual master, and received from him custom-tailored spiritual guidance and a distinct combination of daily litanies (*evrad*). The disciple was expected to regularly inform the sheikh of her spiritual developments; based on these reports, the master might or might not alter the prescribed formula for prayers.

Although uncommon, it sometimes happened that for spiritual or mundane reasons a sheikh sent his disciple to another master. Even less commonly, a disciple who felt that she could not spiritually flourish under the guidance of a particular sheikh, with the approval of all parties, might start to follow another master. This is exactly what happened to Asiye Hatun ("Lady Asiye"), who joined the Halvetiyye order (see chapter 27) in the late 1630s and initially appropriated Veli Dede as her master in her hometown Skopje (today in northern Macedonia). From her first letter below, we understand that her attachment to Veli Dede gradually weakened. Around that time, she must have heard from other Sufis about the more reputable Sheikh Muslihuddin of Užice (today in Serbia), some four hundred kilometers northwest of her hometown. As Asiye developed an inclination toward him from afar, she took the courageous step of conferring with a confidant called Mehmed Dede about her hesitations about changing sheikhs. She eventually attached herself to Muslihuddin (d. 1648), who was also a sheikh in the Halvetiyye order. Although spiritual guidance by way of letters was not too uncommon, it should be noted that Asiye never actually saw her new sheikh Muslihuddin before she decided to submit to him. It is likely that she acquired literacy through studying with her father, who may have been a member of the learned class.

By the time Asiye decided to switch to Sheikh Muslihuddin, she had already quickly progressed in her two years in the order, and she was far along enough to obtain permission to recite the "seven names of God" (*esma-i seb'a*), a significant step for a disciple. These names corresponded to the seven stages of the ego and were said to purify the inner self as the disciple advanced along the mystical path. In the order of ascending importance, these are: "There is no god but Allah"; "Allah"; "*Hû*" (Arabic for "He," i.e., God); "the Truth"; "the Everliving"; "the Eternal"; and "the Ever-Dominating." After Asiye started following her new sheikh, however, she would have to start reciting the seven names from the beginning.

Following her initial consultation letter to Mehmed Dede and his response (below), the collection of letters contains first-person descriptions of some forty-five dreams, the lengths of which vary from a couple of sentences to a page. Dreams are viewed in Sufism as a legitimate realm in which abundant spiritual communication takes place. The dream world is considered a realm more conducive to spiritual transmission than the material world, where people are thought to be limited by their senses and prone to the deceptions of their carnal desires. Not only is it possible for the disciple to receive spiritual guidance from her master in a dream but it is also not unusual that the guidance came from deceased great masters, and even the Prophet Muhammad. Dreams are the most common vehicle through which a disciple gleans indications about her progress or lack thereof. The references in Sufi texts to the "heart's eye" and the "body's eye" essentially point to the two realms: the dream world and the physical world, respectively.

Asiye Hatun must have dispatched these as letters to her sheikh in Užice over the course of a few years, keeping copies for herself and engaging a copyist to compile them into a booklet approximately sixty years after they had been written, and after she herself had passed away. Her compiled dreams present a rare insight into a Sufi's spiritual development, described in her own words.

LANGUAGE: Turkish. Epistolary format in conversational style with short sentences, often switching between past and present tense (left as they are in the translation). Simple, clear descriptions of mystical practices and experiences.

SOURCE: Manuscript: Asiye Hatun. No title. Topkapı Sarayı Müzesi Kütüphanesi, Istanbul, Hazine 388, fols. 46b–55a. Transcription: Kafadar, Cemal. "Mütereddit bir Mutasavvıf: Üsküp'lü Asiye Hatun'un Rüya Defteri, 1641–43." *Topkapı Sarayı Müzesi Yıllık* 5 (1992): 168–222.

ASİYE HATUN'S LETTER TO MEHMED DEDE

After kissing the noble, blessed hands of your excellency—my venerable, glorious sultan—and submitting prayers along with all manner of respect: My sultan, it is known to your holy self that my joining the righteous path occurred a few years ago without cause and out of no independent volition of my own. I, for my part, strove as much as possible and had developed great devotion to the sheikh [Veli Dede]. In accordance with [the customs of] the order, I was entirely obedient to his directives. Whatever he ordered, I heartily accepted. I had strong love and trust in him. Because of my love and belief, in the short time of less than two years, I completed the seven names [of God]. With the help of God, each of them manifested itself in some form. In short, my heart's eye had begun to open to some degree.

While in this state, the wisdom of God made it such that my love to my sheikh disappeared. With no cause. While overtly or covertly there was nothing about him that would give me distress, my love waned through the fault of my own self. My other [spiritual] states also declined—as if I remained in darkness. Much as I tried to improve my character, I failed. As I was in this state of grief and sorrow, love appeared in my heart for his excellency Sheikh Muslihuddin Efendi of Užice, and day by day it grew. Recently, I enjoined my father to send a man to him on some pretext. Merely to get acquainted. Wisdom belongs to God, acquaintanceship was followed by stronger love, and now he is so dominant in my heart that not a moment or an hour passes when my heart is free of him. Love has settled on the throne of my heart. To such an extent that if it were possible, it would behoove my soul to sacrifice itself for the ground on which he treads. However, as love for him grew dominant, the previous love abated. As this new noose of love wrapped itself around my neck, it is as if, to some degree, I have returned to my previous state.

My sultan, this is our state, which we present to your glorious presence. Of further matters, ask the teacher woman bearing this letter and she will tell you in detail. Now, my master, by God on high and by his messenger, let this secret be entrusted to you in this world and the hereafter. For some time now, it was hidden in my heart. It was known to no one but God. Now by necessity it has been revealed to the teacher woman. For she is my close friend and in all matters my confidante. Now my sultan, you shall be my brother in this world and the hereafter. I consider you dearer than my own brother. My sultan, you are knowledgeable. By the strength of knowledge and mind, what do you consider appropriate and what do you recommend? Is it advisable to declare my state to the honorable master or is silence preferable? If it is appropriate to inform him discreetly through your intervention, then let us do so. But only if it can be done discreetly. My sheikh should not be disappointed with me, for I have benefited from his kindness very much. But what can I do in my helplessness? Should I secretly convey this [to Muslihuddin] in writing? My sultan, by God on high and by the strength of knowledge and mind, find a solution to my difficulty. There is much pain in my soul. I know not if this state is a sign of the good or a trick of the [carnal] soul. It is a state outside my own will that has come [over me]. My sultan, what do you command? State your behest to the teacher woman and let her convey it to us. We eagerly await your reply. Let it be known to your glorious self thusly.

My sultan, I have read in manuals of the Sufi path that if a person is drawn to someone other than her own sheikh, then her inner self will not open to the One God. I wonder, my sultan, is it just that it will not open through my own sheikh, or by no means [will it open]? What does your learning say on this? Please give us the favor of your explanation. For there is strong grief in my heart. As for the rest, may the blessings of learning and knowledge be increased.

MEHMED DEDE'S RESPONSE TO ASİYE HATUN

After offering formal greetings [the content of the letter is the following]: Honorable woman, you have chosen this wretched one for a brother in this world and the hereafter. We have accepted. May you also be our sister in this world and the hereafter. Let God—*may he be praised and exalted*—allow us and all of the community of Muhammad to pass from this world to the next with complete faith.

The entire situation that you have conveyed has become known to me. The love for the honorable master that has been dominant in your heart is a beautiful state. May God on high bless it! And what is understood from your state is this, that by the wish of God on high your love has left a mark on the holy heart of the master (i.e., he knows of your situation through the communication of hearts). Thanks be to God on high; it is a great favor and kindness from God to you. Look on it as a Godsend. And give many thanks to God on high that he may increase it. This stage does not befall everyone. Let God, may he be praised and exalted, render it permanent. And what is necessary to those who join the order is only love and conviction. May God on high increase your love and conviction. And there is a large difference between your sheikh and [Muslihuddin Efendi].

Compare this with your recent dream, in which you reached Medina the illuminated through an alternate path. His excellency has very many such assistants and followers. May God—*His glory be exalted*—allow and have fated us and you to see the holy faces of many more masters through the body's eye. Your sheikh has brought you to that stage. The rest will, God willing, manifest itself through the master [Muslihuddin Efendi]. For this reason, your love for [the sheikh] has declined somewhat. You have completed the seven names; their purpose and objective are the purification of the self and the cleansing of the heart. Thank God, the goal has been reached. By the will of God on high, your love for the noble lord is evidence of this. To convey your state and dreams is quite sensible. Immediately write a letter as you intended and seal it. This wretched one hopes to dispatch it through a reliable man. We shall instruct him that this paper is very secret and that no one other than he must know of it. When in return [Muslihuddin Efendi] conveys his reply [to you], dispatch it to this wretched one by a reliable person, and instruct him that no one else's hand must touch it save this wretched one's.

We ask for your prayers. Do not neglect to pray for this wretched one, since being brothers and sisters [on the Sufi path] means that none of us forget each other in our prayers. May God—*may He be praised and exalted*—allow and have fated all of the community of Muhammad and all of us, all the desirous ones, to reach their desired goals auspiciously through the intervention of the saints and holy men. Amen. In veneration of the lord of prophets and messengers. The end.

DREAMS

The Monday before the holy feast, after having performed the morning prayer and recited the prescribed formula [by the sheikh] of daily holy litanies four hundred times and having performed the daybreak prayer, I rested for a while. In my dream a man says to me: "It is necessary for you to break relations with Skopje and go to Užice and marry the master. He has no wife. Become his wife and serve him. After being married, there will be intimacy between you, and he will touch your body with his blessed hand and any bodily illnesses that you may have will be healed externally and internally. All your wishes will be realized. Your heart has been entrusted to him, your feelings too should be under his rule. Certainly, certainly it is necessary to marry him," says he insistently to me. However, I could not tell who it was that spoke to me. But I do know that it was not a woman but a man. His words made me ashamed. "What are you saying? My love is spiritual. It is accepted by God on high. For this reason, my heart submitted," I reply. Again the man said, "That master has no human nature. In truth he appears as a human among humans, but he is pure soul. There is no humanity to him. But I tell you that after you are married and there is intimacy, he will gently touch your body and will bring relief to your grief and healing to your ills. If you have your wits about you, do not miss this opportunity," he advises me. And this wretched one, acting on this advice, begins preparations for breaking my relations with Skopje and journeying to Užice. In this state I awoke.

Then I fell back asleep. Again in my dream I saw that I had reached Užice. The honorable master is sitting somewhere. Under the roof is a pole that holds it aloft. And this wretched one stands across from him with clasped hands. Leaning on the pole, somewhat embarrassed, I stand before him. As though standing in prayer. But very close to the master. At that moment, his sons arrived. I went to them, and kissed the blessed hands of both, then returned next to the pole. As I stood before it, I awoke.

Again one day in [such] a state of perplexity, as I wondered at my state, I was taken by sleep. Again I dreamed that the master speaks to me and says, "We love the one who loves [us]. We are in love with the one who is in love with us. We grant the wishes of the one with whom we are in love," says he. It was as though a state of pleasure came over me, and I awoke. [. . .]

Again one night: I dreamed of a few ugly women. Their eyes are blind. Another woman sits before that blind one and acts as if she is applying some medicine to her eyes. From that blind woman a feeling of repugnance comes to my heart, and as I wonder, "Who is she?" she says to me: "Behold, I am the world. Know this and beware!" When I learn this, I am overcome with wrath, and I pronounce a major invective against her, "You cheater, swindler, enchanter; you deceiver of holy men, you who pretends to offer sugar and feeds poison. Get lost, do not come close to me. My siblings paid you the dowry and soon divorced you. But I have never married you so that I should give you a divorce. Be gone and do not come near to me." As I [thus] strongly admonish her, that accursed woman says to me: "If you had no fondness for me, red satin would not appeal to you," says she to me. Much wrath overcomes me, and with this wrath I woke up. This dream has yet more detail.

Another time: As I was performing the evening prayers on Friday night, [the image of] his excellency took shape in my heart, and I witness him with my heart's eye. He addressed me and said, "After the prayers, start on the second name [of God]. The time is auspicious." And as this wretched one (I) completed her prayers, and as though rehearsing with him sitting across from me, repeated the first name three times, and recited, "*Our Lord, accept [from us and bestow on us]*" to the end, and recited the holy opening chapter of the Qur'an, and rubbed my hands over my face, he said, "Now say it. With the help of God and much-blessed miracles of the messenger of God and with our license, permission has been granted to you for the second name. May God bless!" said he. And from where he was, he rehearsed with me according to the way it is done, and after reciting it a few times, said some prayers. And then he said, "To me you are not like the others. Do you think that only you feel love [for me]? Know that we feel tenfold love [for you]. Forego all hesitancy," said he. For in this wretched one there was hesitancy.

Again once: On the last Friday night of the holy month of Ramazan, I saw in the spiritual realm the Beloved of God [Prophet Muhammad]—*may God command and salute him*—and at this very place, his excellency [Muslihuddin] appeared from across. His excellency [the Prophet] said, "Greetings, my love, my soul! Beloved by God, cherished by the prophets!" That is to say that his excellency [Muslihuddin] sat next to the Beloved of God. [He] placed his blessed hand on his excellency [Muslihuddin]'s shoulder and said, "*Behold the pole of the saints of the age.*" As if he was declaring it to other men there present. After this, I fell asleep.

In the realm of dreams, I see a garden. Its trees and weeds had dried up. Such mean grounds as could not be imagined. I notice, there are snakes in it. I feel some degree of repulsion by this garden. And I fear lest one of those snakes should accidentally bite me. At that moment, a man appeared before me. A young boy is by his side. I request of this man that he should instruct the boy to cut the dried trees and weeds in the garden and clear it.

With this pain I awoke. Much grief took my heart. Thinking that the thorns and weeds in that garden were my acts, and those snakes my carnal soul, dejected and sad I attended to the nightly prayer, but my heart was not in it. Then it occurred to me that [it didn't make sense that] I would see such [a good dream] first, and then see this one. I started to doubt that [what I had just seen] really represented my state.

I then completed my prayers and busied myself with the recitation of the holy name [of God]. With my heart's eye, I witnessed his excellency in the spiritual realm. He said, "That garden that you saw is the world. The snakes that were in it are worldly possessions. Material things are snakes. With the intervention of God on high and with our influence, they showed you the world in such a way that all love for it would leave your heart. As you feared those snakes, so too will you hate worldly possessions. [What you saw] is the world. Why do you allow hesitancy in your nature? Do you not believe in us?" said he. And this wretched one answered, "God forbid, my sultan. I do not disbelieve in you. But my deeds are few and my rebellion great. For this reason, I cannot attribute such a state to myself." He said, "The mercy of God on high is certainly much greater than your rebellion." I collected myself from those thoughts.

Again once: In the realm of dreams, I saw that his excellency held me tight and embraced me. He squeezed me so tightly that my entire body felt like dough. But I felt no pain. Someone says, "When the caliph Umar embraced Islam, his excellency the Messenger [Muhammad]—*may God command and salute him*—embraced and squeezed him tightly like that. Omar's unbelief and polytheism exited through his toenail." And this wretched one said, "Thank God, I have no unbelief." Again he says, "May hunger and satiety leave you." This appeared when Mehmed Efendi was in Užice.

SIX

Diary of a Sufi Sheikh in Plague-Ridden Istanbul, 1661

Seyyid Hasan Nuri, d. 1688

TRANSLATED BY MARY IŞIN

The following extracts are from a diary kept by a dervish, or a disciple in a mystical order, Seyyid Hasan Nuri (1620–88) between 1661 and 1665. *Seyyid* is an honorific indicating that its bearer descends from the Prophet Muhammad. At the time of the composition of these entries, Seyyid Hasan was a distinguished member of the Sünbüliyye branch of the Halvetiyye Sufi order in Istanbul (see chapter 27). In 1665 he would be appointed sheikh, or spiritual master, of a dervish lodge in Balat, a neighborhood on the shore of the Golden Horn in Istanbul.

Almost all of the diary entries relate happenings, mundane as well as tragic, in the lives of the author, his family, friends, and acquaintances. There are records of numerous deaths from the plague that raged during the first few months of the diary. Seyyid Hasan conveys these tragedies in his diary with little or no emotional response, for reasons about which we might speculate. Despite its lack of affect, the journal is a rich source for identifying socioreligious customs: For example, Seyyid Hasan recounts eating boiled wheat when his son's first tooth appears, as well as eating the sweetmeat *helva* after a funeral. Details of his elder sister's divorce, at her own instigation, and of social interactions between men and women, provide firsthand insight into the lives of women, who in less personal sources remain almost invisible. The diary focuses above all on Seyyid Hasan's social life: visits to his sisters and other relatives, coffee drinking or walking with friends, dinner parties given by members of his close circle, and weddings and circumcision celebrations. Minute details of day-to-day life abound in the diary, including lists of dishes served at dinner parties, accounts of buying a watermelon or fish, sleeping overnight with relatives and friends, and visiting shops, the barber, and the public bath. The triviality of so much in the diary allows us to imagine the lives of ordinary people in seventeenth-century Istanbul.

The primary spiritual goal of Sufis was in theory the purification of the *nefs,* or inner self. In order to achieve this, mystical leaders generally prescribed an abstemious way of life, at least to

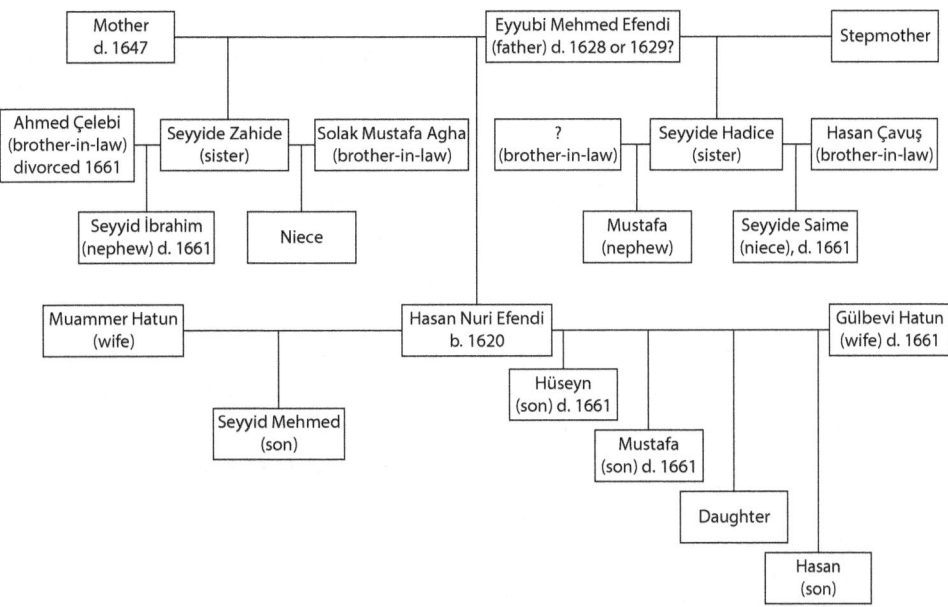

FIGURE 6. Hasan Efendi's family tree. Familial designations with respect to Hasan Nuri Efendi.

those who were committed disciples. As Seyyid Hasan's diary demonstrates, however, asceticism did not always translate to outright denunciation of worldly pleasures, such as feasting or socializing. Strict rules were not unknown in Islamic mysticism but were usually recommended only for certain individuals and for limited periods of time (for example, forty days of complete isolation with only bread and water). Differences in organization as well as approach to the religious way of life made the various mystical orders distinct from one other. A strict hierarchy within each order was a given.

The lives of the dervishes mentioned in this diary centered around the Sünbül Efendi lodge. Converted to a *tekke,* or a dervish lodge, from a church in 1486, this was the oldest convent of the Halvetiyye order in Istanbul and hence was considered the main lodge of the order (*âsitane*). Seyyid Hasan's father held the position of sheikh at this lodge until his passing in or around 1629 when Hasan was nine years old. At the time of the composition of this diary, the sheikh of the main lodge, who is regularly referred to in the text as the unnamed "noble sheikh," was Mehmed Alaeddin Efendi (d. ca. 1680s). Other personalities belonging to the highest echelons of the Sufi hierarchy, who are mentioned in the text below, include the *pişkadem*—that is, the deputy sheikh Hasan Çelebi (d. 1663), who was the son-in-law of the sheikh; the *zakirbaşı,* who led the rituals during which the dervishes gathered to recite litanies, God's names, and so on; and the *imam efendi*, who led the regular obligatory prayers at the lodge. Whether Şahbaz, whose passing is related in the text, was a daughter of Seyyid Hasan cannot be established, but she was evidently somebody dear to the family. She died in their house and Seyyid Hasan himself undertook her burial arrangements. Selim Kadın was a close neighbor who may have helped out with household errands. Several other names that appear in the text were fellow dervishes of the same order. The sunset marked the beginning of a day in the Ottoman calendar. Therefore, the "Saturday night" in the text below corresponds to the night of Friday in the widely used modern civil calendar system.

LANGUAGE: Turkish. First-person account in conversational language, generally with short sentences. Very limited use of elements of learned prose or metaphoric expressions.

SOURCE: Manuscript: Seyyid Hasan. *Sâlname* (*Sohbetname*). 2 vols. Topkapı Sarayı Müzesi Kütüphanesi, Istanbul, Emanet Hazine 1426, Emanet Hazine 1418. Sections translated here are from Emanet Hazine 1426, fols. 1b–2a, 18a–19a, 20a–21b, 29b–31b, 45b–46b, 50a–51a, 53b–54b, and 57b–58a. Family tree based on p. 49 in Durmaz, Tunahan. "Family, Companions, and Death: Seyyid Hasan Nûrî Efendi's Microcosm (1661–1665)." Master's thesis, Sabancı University, 2019.

THE BEGINNING OF THE DIARY

This notebook is for the year one thousand and seventy-two. The holy [month of] Muharrem began on a Saturday night (night of August 26, 1661).

Following the afternoon prayers on Sunday, Nim Barber shaved this humble one in my cell outside and adjoining the garden gate. Afterward, members of my family, my younger sister, and I ate dinner and passed the night at the house of my elder sister. On the following Monday, which was the third day of the said month, some of the aforementioned boarded the ox-drawn carriage that came from the village of Ali Bey to collect my younger sister. Only this humble one went on foot to the grave of my late [son] Hüseyn. This humble one arrived [at the graveyard] before the rest. While I was reciting prayers, the carriage also arrived and waited by the grave until the prayer. Those inside [the carriage] listened to some of my recitations and in the end we prayed together. Then we descended from the grave mound. I asked Mustafa Çelebi, the younger brother [by the same mother] of my younger brother-in-law Ahmed Agha, to get down from the black horse he was riding. I mounted it myself and set out in front of the carriage. [. . .]

SATURDAY NIGHT

Night of Friday, September 16, 1661

Following the nightfall prayers, I stayed along with some of the dervishes, particularly Nazmi Efendi and Amm Efendi and those who recite the litanies and Beşlizade in the hall. Musa Bey and the new neighbor were present and the latter's young son waited on them. Meanwhile, [my] deceased [niece] Seyyide Saime lay in the room that had been transformed from the hall. After the dervishes had departed, this humble one spent the night in the small room. When I awoke from sleep the sisters were reciting hymns (*ilahi*) nearby. I caught the words "You are God Omniscient" and the words "poor girl." I asked about it. It

FIGURE 7. Turkish funeral, 1553. Peeter Coecke, *Ces Moeurs et fachons de faire de Turcz*, woodcut (Antwerp, 1553).

appeared that Şahbaz had fallen ill of the plague and Selim Kadın had taken her home [to our house]. But the candle [of life] still burned.

In the morning of the next day of Saturday, prayers had been performed and [Seyyide Saime] had been buried within the courtyard [of the dervish lodge of Sünbül Efendi]. Emir Osman Çelebi had acted as muezzin for the funeral service and the function of imam and the final rites had been carried out by the noble [sheikh]. Then he had accompanied the family members to their villages. Likewise, I attended the funeral of the Imam Efendi's favorite concubine. As the company stood waiting at the side of the grave, this humble one visited our graves accompanied by my elder son. Then my son handed me the akçe coins left over from the expenses paid for Seyyide Saime's [funeral] and left to go to Silivri Gate via the main road. This humble one returned through the cemetery to the side of the Imam Efendi and stayed there a long time performing the final rites before going to the house of my elder sister and delivering the above-mentioned sum in her hall. Afterward I saw that they were kneading [dough for] *çörek* (i.e., a ring-shaped bun of leavened dough) for Mustafa's seventh day [of his passing] in our large room. [*Marginal addition*:] I saw Şahbaz lying on the bench in the kitchen; her head toward the door.

After the afternoon prayers I went to the house of Kavukçı Kadı Mehmed Efendi. [He] insisted that the deputy sheikh (pişkadem) Efendi and Amm Efendi and Şeyhzade and I, all stay. Nearing sunset, this humble one came to the mosque, performed the evening prayers. Taking the small stick behind the outer door of the cell to serve as a staff, and a lantern, I again went to the house of the aforementioned Kadı Efendi. Then we ate dinner there and I led the night prayers and we all stayed the night. —Except for Amm Efendi, who left. [. . .]

THE PASSING OF ŞAHBAZ

September 19, 1661

Poor little Şahbaz moaned and talked to herself all night long. Let it be known that she drank the cup of death in the presence of my elder sister, on the porch close to the railed platform on Monday the twenty-fourth day of Muharrem, following the night mentioned above, at the time of the noon prayer. Thus, this humble one arrived home to find her stretched out in the place to which she had been carried, right at the foot of the plank next to the railed platform.

Afterward, when I was leaving, having taken the measurement for her grave, someone called from Sunizade's shop asking what had happened. I replied that there was need for another grave. Then, after entering the courtyard [of the Sünbül Efendi tekke, or dervish lodge] through the bazaar gate, I encountered the tekke caretaker Şaban Dede next to the "Plated Cypress" (*zincirli serv*) near the fountain for ablutions and ordered a corpse washer and coffin from him. At that moment I spotted the deputy sheikh passing in front of Adli Efendi's tomb. Then I went to the cemetery, and unable to find a suitable plot near to our [brethren's] graves, I selected a place adjoining the grounds of the Bayrampaşa complex of charitable institutions close to the main road and next to our graves and went home. Thereafter, she was washed on the other side of the mulberry tree and placed in the coffin near to the wooden courtyard of my younger sister's garden and to the hawthorn tree. Her prayers were performed between the noon and afternoon prayers and were led by the Imam Efendi. It was prohibited to follow the funeral procession any further from the fountain for ablutions. Nazmi Efendi stood in front of Kullevi Emir Efendi's shop at İbrahim Pasha; a couple of times he wondered aloud if he should also go but he was excused. Afterward we buried her and returned. [. . .]

SATURDAY NIGHT

Night of Friday, October 8, 1661

All those present performed the sunset prayers and ate dinner. My son and I sang religious hymns (*esvat u ilahiyat*) and read from my younger sister's Turkish commentary on the hadith. We then performed the evening prayers—all in the main hall of the private quarters. Both this night and last night, my son slept and rested in the bay window and this humble one [rested] by the wall cupboard in the room with two openings (one to the guest section and the other to the private quarters). And that night there was a lunar eclipse.

SATURDAY

October 9, 1661

The next morning of Saturday, toward sunrise, together with my son and brother-in-law, we set out to visit the grave of [my nephew] Seyyid İbrahim. As we approached the threshing floor, we observed from afar my younger sister holding a staff and along with Handan in the cemetery and depart for the village. Then we arrived and paid a visit.

Today, later in the morning, we conversed much on spiritual matters in the aforementioned hall. After noon, my son and I, mounted on horseback, set out for Istanbul. This humble one dismounted on Şehidler Street and took [the horse] to a servant of the owner. But my son rode all the way home. Afterward, when I arrived at [the home of] Yıldızzade toward sunset, I found that my fur-lined robe of emerald green broadcloth had come from the furrier and was in his house. And Piri Çelebi was also there. Before sunset he ate the evening meal with us there in the hall. NOTE: But Yıldızzade was not present.

SUNDAY

October 10, 1661

On the following Sunday, the noble sheikh and his son, and Yorgani and Baki Dede and Kandilci Dede departed for the aforementioned Ali Bey village. And while this humble one was seated in the arbor [just outside] the deputy sheikh's cell, Piri Halifezade Süleyman Agha brought a copy of the *Münyetü'l-Musalli* (book on prayers by Sadiduddin al-Kashgari, d. 705/1305). He presented the book, explaining that the Turkish meaning was inscribed below the lines. When I saw it, I was delighted; I borrowed the book and took it home. When I went to my elder sister later, I even took [the book] with me.

MONDAY

October 11, 1661

At daybreak, while drinking coffee seated on the raised wooden platform of Zakirbaşı Halil Çelebi's cell with the deputy sheikh, Hacı Ali Dede came to the door of the cell and informed us that the aforementioned Süleyman Agha had caught the plague. I heard his voice, but I did not see him. At that point I attended the washing [of the corpse] of Şeyhzade's daughter. And I followed the funeral to the beginning of Nazmi Efendi's street. But Ayşe, the daughter of our younger brother-in-law Ahmed Agha by his concubine had died in Ali Bey village and her body was taken with recitations of the declaration of God's unity, and the noble sheikh spoke the final rites. [. . .]

NIGHT OF SATURDAY

Night of Friday, December 30, 1661

This is the tenth night of midwinter days (*erbain*) and the month of Cemaziyelevvel

In company with Mihribanzade Osman Agha
(1) Chicken; (2) hezarpare (i.e., fried pastry drops in honey and rosewater syrup?); (3) börek (layered pastry with a savory filling); (4) baklava; (5) pickles; (6) soup; (7) grapes. (In that order).

The next night of Sunday (i.e., Night of Saturday, December 31, 1661), I was the guest of my younger brother-in-law and younger sister near to the Butcher's Fountain. While in conversation with them, a fire broke out at midnight. My brother-in-law returned on horseback. It turned out to be a house and a bread shop very near the sea bath. The owner was a wealthy man who had formerly been an *odabaşı* (an officer in charge of a janissary barracks). [The house] had only just been built following the Great Fire (of 1660), and they had moved in. Owing to carelessness while melting fat, it had caught fire and they had been unable to save their property and possessions. Later, I slept and rested, and in the morning I drank coffee made by my younger sister and went to see the fire that had occurred in the night. And finding our İsmail Çelebi there, we watched together and returned to our neighborhood in his company. [. . .]

DIVORCE OF SEYYIDE ZAHIDE HATUN [AT HER OWN REQUEST]
January 13, 1662

In the late morning of Thursday, the twenty-second day of the midwinter days and [the month of] Cemaziyelevvel, in the guest quarters of the rented house near the Butcher's Fountain where they resided and in the presence of the noble sheikh, the deputy sheikh, Baki Çelebi, Küçük Hüseyn Dede, and acting judge our Kemal Efendi, and this humble one, my younger sister Zahide Hatun got a divorce from her husband Ahmed Çelebi—on the condition that she renounce the eighteen thousand akçe share of her dowry payable on divorce, the alimony, and her right to reside in the marital home. At that point, his elder brother Mehmed Çavuş, an old man in his father's service, and the aforementioned witnesses summoned to the court were present and apprehended the decision.

After the hearing, I attended a gathering for the first anniversary of the passing of Kambur İbrahim Efendi. There the noble sheikh gave a sermon and spoke words of counsel. The *Muhammediyye* reciter sang hymns (*taksim ve ilahi*). I saw the imam Mehmed Efendi of Nuri Dede [Mosque] and Peçeci Kenan Dede there. Let it be known that in coming and going to the aforementioned gathering I was also with the noble sheikh, the deputy sheikh, and my son. [. . .]

The following night, the night of Wednesday, after the evening prayers, I attended the noble sheikh's feast at the blessed cell. Let me note the brethren I saw there: The noble sheikh and his son, the deputy sheikh, Kemal Efendi and his son Hasan Çelebi, Sunullah Çelebi, Imam Efendi and his son, Piri Çelebi, Hasan Efendi, the judge of the illuminated city of Medina, Bezzazistani Mustafa Çelebi, Yorgani Ahmed Çelebi, Baki Dede, Fettah Dede, and this humble one, in addition to the others.

Let me list the delicious dishes: (1) goose; (2) salad; (3) meat stew; (3) stewed turnips in yoghurt; (4) dolma; stuffed cabbage leaves; (5) börek filled with bottle gourd; (6) triangular layered pastries; (7) spinach; (8) pilaf; (9) soft pudding with sweet-sour dried fruits.

[The noble sheikh] saw all of us off. Later, he returned inside and entered the bridal chamber by himself. Imam Efendi and his son accompanied this humble one up to the street where Ahmed Agha resided. Thereupon I entered Ahmed Agha's place and saw in his company the deputy sheikh, the litanies leader (*zakirbaşı*), Memiş Beşe, İsmail Çelebi, and

Osman Agha. The deputy sheikh related that today the [noble sheikh] Efendi went to Üsküdar to visit Hasan Efendi, judge of the illuminated city of Medina, and to see him off, and [crossing the Bosphorus] he got caught in a storm. [. . .]

MONDAY

February 6, 1662

While I was sitting outside drinking morning coffee at the deputy sheikh's [place], Kavukçı Kadı Efendi arrived. Afterward, since a strong southwest wind was blowing, the three of us watched the sea from both the pier and the mosque of Samatya. After eating our meal there, we walked to the house of Keresteci İsa Çelebi and on the uppermost floor we continued to contemplate the sea and ate a meal: (1) stewed calf's head and feet; (2) meat stew; (3) pilaf; (4) fish soup; (5) wheat soup; (6) black grape compote.

Let me list those at the table: The three of us, İsa Çelebi and his son-in-law Cerrah Yusuf Çelebi, Emir Osman Çelebi, and a person in a janissary colonel dress.

SEVEN

Ramblings of an Eccentric Sufi Exiled on Limnos, ca. early 1680s

Niyazi-i Mısri, d. 1694

TRANSLATED BY HAKAN T. KARATEKE AND FERENC CSIRKÉS

The extraordinarily eventful life of the Sufi master Niyazi-i Mısri (d. 1694) includes many anecdotes for modern readers to reflect on. Niyazi hailed from the eastern Anatolian town of Malatya. Although he was exposed to some measure of mystical Sufi learning in his youth, he eventually embarked on the career path of becoming a legal scholar in the provincial medreses, then traveled to Cairo for additional studies at the age of twenty-two and stayed there for three years.

The "exterior" (*zahiri*) sciences required to become a legal scholar—that is, the subjects one studied formally at a medrese (logic, exegesis, prophetic traditions, Arabic grammar, and many more)—and the "interior" (*batıni*) sciences that one acquired from a Sufi master to advance on a mystic path were very clearly differentiated. In reality, however, many scholars on the legal track also harbored Sufi tendencies and were simultaneously disciples on a Sufi path. Therefore, while a legal scholar made his living from a judgeship, he may also have practiced some form of mystical self-discipline. For many people in this situation, the two paths did not necessarily pose a conflict. If, however, one heard a calling and decided to become a full-time dedicated Sufi, then any mundane line of work would have been perceived by the aspirant as detrimental to the soul and as posing an obstacle to the spiritual journey.

Such decisive moments of renunciation of worldly things in the lives of famous Sufis were later told in legendary accounts. The tropes in these hagiographies include receiving life-changing advice in a dream from one of the great Sufi masters of old or throwing medrese textbooks into a river to signify the forsaking of exterior sciences. While Niyazi was in Cairo, he apparently saw in a dream Abdulqadir Gilani, the great master Sufi of the eleventh century, who instructed him to seek his own master if he wished to advance on the Sufi path. Soon after this, Niyazi quit his studies, left Cairo, and spent time in various Sufi lodges in western Anatolia before eventually advancing to become a sheikh or master.

A fiery preacher who apparently did not mince his words about statesmen or contentious topics, Niyazi soon became a controversial figure and was exiled by the authorities to Rhodes, where he was locked up in a cell for nine months (1674). On returning to Bursa he continued his denunciatory sermons. Alarmed by his growing group of followers, the authorities this time banished him to the island of Limnos, where he would be incarcerated for fifteen years.

Niyazi became increasingly preoccupied with the esoteric knowledge of *cifr,* which its practitioners used to make divinations based on the numerical symbolism of letters. Sometimes rendered as lettrism, this practice involved adding up the numerical values of the letters in certain phrases from the Qur'an, prophetic sayings, or other significant books to arrive at a date, and then interpreting the meanings of the phrases and discovering their connections to the date in order to make divinations. It appears that Niyazi also developed some form of mental agitation during his years in detention, if not earlier. Although his pervasive fear of persecution may have not been completely unfounded, his constant anxiety about being poisoned must have been taxing to his psyche. He believed he was the Mahdi—that is, the expected "messiah" of the Islamic lore—and also Jesus himself. Coupled with his involvement in lettrist divinations, he was convinced that he was receiving revelations. While he was regarded as a great Sufi by his followers at the time, others no doubt saw him as a deranged person.

Niyazi returned to Bursa once more in 1692, gathered a few hundred of his followers, declared that he would join the imperial campaign against Austria, and marched toward Edirne, the current seat of the throne. Only a quarter of a century earlier, Ottoman authorities had suppressed a civil disorder caused by a similar charismatic messiah at the same spot in Edirne, fomented by the Jewish "messiah" Sabbatai Zevi (d. 1676). Wary of what might become of this new dissidence, the authorities once more apprehended Niyazi and exiled him to Limnos, where he died in 1694.

The excerpts in this chapter are from his first incarceration on Limnos. Unlike hagiographies (see chapter 26), which relayed polished legendary accounts of great Sufis, these are Niyazi's haphazard personal reflections on the daily occurrences in his cell and as such they provide extraordinary insights into his confused mind.

LANGUAGE: Turkish. Discordant sentences written in a conversational register. The course of the narrative often changes abruptly. Clearly not premeditated entries but stream-of-consciousness jottings recorded as they occurred to the author.

SOURCE: Manuscript: Niyazi-i Mısri. *Mecmua-i Kelimat-ı Kudsiyye*. Yazma ve Eski Basma Eserler Kütüphanesi, Bursa, Orhan 690. Facsimile and transcription: Çeçen, Halil, ed. *Niyazi-i Mısri'nin Hatıraları* / Niyazi-i Mısri. Istanbul: Dergâh Yayınları, 2006 (33, 50, 52, 55, 97–101, 148–49).

NİYAZİ'S ILL-WISHERS: YUSUF AGHA

2606, Friday night: I swallowed so much poison that my lips got swollen. Afterward, as it was a little cold, I [went to] put on thin-soled boots, but one of them was taken. They had left a fresh stick leaning against the back of the door [in its place].

The evil Yusuf Agha sent food twice during his feast. He pulled off this mischief tonight. He has been trying to turn my brother against [me] since the second day of the holy feast. If [my brother] had come, and [Yusuf Agha] had carried out that plan of his, he would have soon reached his goal. Eventually, his aim is to kill my brother and me. He wants my brother to kill me, because then my brother would become a murderer. If [Yusuf Agha] had [my brother] killed as a punishment, he would be rid of both of us and become the vizier of the imam Karabaş (Alaeddin Ali, d. 1686). I was afraid of the food [he sent] because it did not look like the food of a feast. It was five or six pots of delicious food. There was surely something behind this. He would have sagaciously accomplished his goal as I described it.

O evil man, even if you give me something, not a day passes without one of your treacheries surfacing. O evil man, may a similarly pitiless fellow take my revenge on you. O evil man, do you think you screwed me by having that thin-soled boot stolen? Why don't you do your own dirty work, you pagan! Karabaş will not make you a vizier for [stealing the boot]. If you pulled my leg and made me fall from a ship, people would think the sailors did it. [If I had died because of the poison] how would Yusuf Agha be remembered for this feast? They would say, "He sent the sheikh food twice, both times enough for a whole feast. Yusuf Agha loves Mısri very much. Whoever did this, if Yusuf Agha catches them, he will shed their blood." People think so highly of you; why would evil assumptions come to mind now? Evil man, I leave you to Allah. However much evil you have in you, go on, don't stop. [. . .]

NİYAZİ'S ILL-WISHERS: SALİH AND HAKİM

You, tyrants, I don't expect you to leave me alive. You may scare me with snakes, snake charmers, and death, but I have been dead for a long time. Every hour of my life that my carnal soul is not chastised is harmful to me. It is better if I die. However, I have set your haystacks on fire such that they will burn the world from one end to the other. Consider it an accomplishment that I have given you a hard time (lit. "made your mother cry"). That mother works a lot.

My affairs have come to an end. Look at yourselves! You will see whether Mısri's death is just as much a waste as yours or as valuable. My being alive was not worth a bag of straw to you. See how much worth my dying is! You will see and understand how much trouble you have caused me this year. I have kept it hidden for a hundred and ninety-five days and not revealed your secret. You brought this doom onto yourselves; my fire won't be the cause of the doomsday, it will be you yourselves. The most terrible punishment will [be caused] by the [maledictions] that I will recite against you. You recite [some] on me [anyway?].

The Sheikh [Ibn ʿArabi]—may God be pleased with him—said in [his book] ʿAnqa [Mughrib] (The Book of the Fabulous Gryphon):

God protects us from the calamity of seditions (al-fitan),
and distracts the misfortunes (al-mihan) from us.

al-fitan [numerical value:] 561—tomorrow it will be so many [days] since Hakim arrived
al-mihan [numerical value:] 129—Salih, its numerical value [also]: 129

It is true that he said, "I am your spy." What more proof would there be? We seek refuge from someone whose name [Salih] [has the same numerical value as] "misfortunes" (al-mihan) and whose [number of] days spent in prison [is equal to the numerical value of] "seditions" (al-fitan).

"*God protects us from the calamity of sedition and distracts misfortunes from us.*" This should be my protection from now on. [The prayer has] the numerical value 2638. [...]

NİYAZİ'S ILL-WISHERS: THE SULTAN

2639, Wednesday, *Have you not considered your Lord—how He has spread the shade? Had He wished, He would have made it motionless—and then We made the sun a guide for it. Then We took it to us gently.* The Criterion (al-Furqan) chapter (Qur'an 25:45–46).

Nonrepeating merged geminates: B, D, L, M, M

Hundreds [unit]: 3200; ones [unit]: 37; verses: 3; altogether: 3240

Today at the noon prayer, this Qur'anic verse was revealed along with its meaning. Great legal scholars (müctehid) cannot comprehend what it means. Why? Because while they find a meaning by way of efforts in legal analysis—some by way of [following] transmission (nakl), others by [forming] reasoned opinions (re'y)—meaning appears to prophets (enbiya) by way of inspiration. That meaning is the following: God—*may he be praised and exalted*—says to Jesus—*peace be upon him,* "Have you not considered your Lord—how He has spread the shade?" Here, Lord means the padishah; shade means the mystery of his mother. Because [this mystery] was revealed, this time [the padishah] dispatched here a command by a ship and made [the venom of] a big snake pour into my throat. This is true, as the chronogram proves; since [the sum of the numerological values of] the merged geminates yielded the number thirty-seven. The news also came on that day.

On the eighth night, Tuesday, I became distressed. I had never been [ill] like that. Let me tell you what this means. This time [the padishah?] shall have [the poison] pour into God's throat! "Had He wished, He would not have extended [the shade]." Since [the padishah] did not want the prophet, he wished secretly to kill him. That's why he sent [the command]. The verse until this point is an allusion that it was undisclosed that the padishah [was behind the act]. When it implicitly says, "then We made the sun a guide for it," it refers to when it became apparent that it was the padishah who did it. "*Then We took it to us gently*" means that after completing his task, he secretly gathered [certain people] one by one around himself—some with the pretext that they fled, others with the pretext that they should be set free. Why would the stars have a shade? The shade belongs to the sun. When [the sun] hides, the shade becomes longer; when it appears, the shade retreats.

O padishah, so far it has been Mısri who has exposed you; from now on, it will be this verse that will make [your doings] public. You planned to murder Jesus—*peace be upon him*. Do what you have to do! Your affairs have also been taken care of! I will not regret my death from now on. Great legal scholars (müctehid) have remained powerless next to my knowledge, but next to the Divine Knowledge . . . (incomplete sentence). [. . .]

NİYAZİ'S ILL-WISHERS: KARABAŞ

2599. Let us leave that aside and return to what was happening to us. As the guard on duty did not let me sleep for two days, I slept a little during the day. Those swooping vultures grabbed the meat bowl and put a crippling poison in it. They instructed [the keepers of] the water taps and did not allow water to be brought. I would have purchased [water] myself, [but] they [also] instructed the water sellers, who [then] took other paths [than those close to me]. My insides were on fire. I ate four watermelons, but as much as I ate, so did my thirst grow. My belly became [swollen] like a drum, and still I thirsted. My belly was full; my chest became tight. In the morning, I had difficulty going downstairs. I could not walk upright.

I said to myself that I should talk to the congregation in the morning. The preacher before me started to cry when he was reciting the Yasin chapter [of the Qur'an]. "Have they poisoned him, too?" I wondered. Astonished at this, this time I began to laugh.

They have been stealing the cats [near me] for two days. Once I fed a cat this poisonous food; it fell ill and almost died. In order to conceal this, they removed the cats just like they added the poison [to my food]. If you ask who this was, it was Karabaş, Karabaş! Karabaş is a nobody. His preacher forgot to correct his mistake again in prostration and started [the sermon?]. O preacher, because of this advice of yours, how will I have to suffer at your hands? His Excellency the Sheikh [Ibn 'Arabi]—[*may His mystery be blessed*]—writes in his *'Anqa* when he informs of [the number] eight:

> *Seven of them of the earth are not incognizant,*
> *While the Eighth inseparably accompanies the stars* [. . .]

NİYAZİ STANDS HIS GROUND

2548, Wednesday: Yesterday, Tuesday, I said, "By God, I'll confront the challenge." Since it is appropriate here, as an introduction to that, I copy below a hymn that I had composed a while back in Uşak (ca. 1647–56). Calculate the chronogram of its first couplet and see if [its numerical value] is too much or too little [than what is required]:

He who finds a great gathering becomes pure
His body becomes an *H* and a *Q*

He does not claim to be a hero with his tongue
His grace is the *N* and *K* from his heart [. . .]

[The prophet] said—salutations and peace be upon him, "Whenever someone disheveled and [covered in] dust swears by Allah, [his wish] will be granted to him."

Yesterday He revealed these words. Today He verified them with the chronogram of the hymn and corroborated them with this hadith. Perfection is not in the words but in the skills; let us see how the skills are. And skills depend on your conduct. It is always like that. If it is not from you, nothing will come from this side.

The greater number of the first couplet is thus: Nouns in the thousands (?): 1729; what exceeds the hundreds: 747; letters: 45, dots: 22, [the letter] *elif*: 2, consonant doubling: 1; altogether: 1729+747+45+22+2+1 = 2546.

Its lesser number is from the day when [I] composed the hymn [that starts with the hemistich], "I have flown with one thousand and four hundred wings." Hundreds: 1100, letters: 45, [the letter] *elif*: 2, altogether: 1147.

Most or few of those who are sent away from the doors of [powerful] people attain such [a position] before God that if they say something will happen and [even] swear by it, God makes their promise worthy [of materializing]. While those who turn [them] away strive to falsify their words, God will make real what they said.

Now the hadith of the Messenger of God cannot be a lie. By God, I swear to God, and appeal to Him, you cannot fuck me over! If the padishah of the Ottoman dynasty descends on me and says to his aids: "Hold him and penetrate him. I will help you," and even if all the dead [padishahs] from the beginning of the Ottoman dynasty to date were alive, and they all came to help the padishah with a devoted heart, all of them would fail and would not reach their goal, and they would *lose both this world and the next* (Qur'an 22:11). This has given Mısri relief. *Praise be to God, and praise be to God!*

The chronogrammatic reading of the hadith [above] is also in accordance with this: Hundreds: 2500, letters (according to merging): 43, merged geminates: 4, [the letter] *elif*: 2; all together: 2549.

The number that exceeds the hundreds: 673, [the letter] *elif* 2, 673+2 = 675. The preacher attempted to have me leave the mosque (sentence crossed out). First, the language of the devil; the number is in it: 675. The nineteenth [day] after the coming of the Karabaş sheikh was a Monday (crossed out; written instead:) Tuesday, twentieth [day] was Monday [!] That's it for today! [. . .]

O tyrants, you are not looking for Mısri; you are looking for an ass. Those looking for Mısri cannot even find him in the spiritual kingdom, the highest heaven, or the divine [universe], yet you think you will find him in the earthly world—or perhaps in the stable!? You do not know the man and think he is an ass. Now you think an ass [could be] a man. If you do not know the difference between an ass and a man, how could you differentiate between one man and another man? You should just look at yourselves, for you have no idea how you have metamorphosed, and been effaced and annulled. When someone sees what is straight as crooked, it is their eyes that are crooked. Enough! O Mısri, enough of that! You [whose line is] cut off! The more you write the worse they get.

NİYAZİ'S TAKE ON THE OTTOMAN DYNASTY

2549, Thursday night: They made the snake [venom] pour [into me]. My face, eyes, and heart were swollen. Moaning, I was walking up and down in the mosque when I heard the words, "O [God], Worthy of Worship!" from outside. It turned out to be the [janissary] sergeant and the chief artilleryman. I said, "What do you want from me? I am not in the mood for visits. I am [filled with] snake [venom] inside, and my outsides are swollen. Look and see, so you know it! Sultan İbrahim (r. 1640–48), and Sultan Mehmed (IV, r. 1648–87), and this one sitting on the throne (Süleyman II, r. 1687–91) are all Jews. I will die at their hands. However, the throne belongs to the [Crimean] Tatar. Why should I be sad? Even if I die, I will have brought many over to Islam. Praise be to God! These will not be able to destroy the religion; the religion is going to destroy them!" [Hearing this,] they left.

O Muhammad's community! People of faith! People of Islam! Muslims! I will die soon anyway, but you should all know that it is [actually] Prince Mustafa who is sitting on the throne now. You should say, "We surely want to see our padishah; definitely!" If Sultan Mehmed (IV) shows himself to you, consider me false and punish me. If you find the prince on the throne, know that I am truly a prophet. When my prophethood is [realized as] true, know for certain that Sultan İbrahim and Sultan Mehmed (IV), and Prince Mustafa are Jews. In addition to being a Jew, your padishah will allow miscreants to fuck your wives and family members. If you consent to this, keep him on his throne. But the Tatar [ruler] is a Muslim and follows Islam. Go, bring him, and put him on the throne!

I have announced the truth to you. It's for you to decide. Since they (i.e., the Ottoman dynasty) descend from Jews, they zealously support the Jews; however, in terms of conviction, they belong to the Hamziyya [sect]. They permit everything that is religiously prohibited. There is justice in every people, but not among the Hamziyya. This is my last will to you. You will know whether to accept it or not. Since Sultan Mehmed fell off the horse and died—today being Thursday, the twentieth of Şaban—652 days have passed. This is a report of divine revelation. Check it! I [can be considered] wrong if he died just a day earlier or later than that. If you do not find it the way I say it is, I am not genuine and you should punish me. [But] if you find it [the way I say], take action, [or] you will repent afterward. *And the opportunity passes with the passage of the clouds, and God is the most knowing in terms of what is proper, and to Him is the reference and the return. God speaks the truth and guides to the [right] way.* (Qur'an 33:4). [. . .]

THE LEGACY OF PROPHETS AND SAINTS

See, tyrants! You are killing Jesus—*peace be upon him*—and who are you bringing to life? Tyrants, burn yourselves in the fierce fire for which you have gathered the firewood! You are like the deer that gave birth to a dragon. She [happily] suffered the trouble [of pregnancy] until she gave birth. She endured the ordeal for one day and [then] fled. Yes, those who are Jewish are glad. Those who are not concerned about their honor are pleased. This is a matchless fire that torments anyone who has religion and honor.

O tyrants, may you die! You worked hard until you murdered me. What you wanted to achieve was to blatantly make a Jew into padishah. At the beginning it was not known. He practiced his injustice with caution. From this day on, every mosque and medrese will be handed over to Jews. Jews will be esteemed, Muslims despised. [The day promised in the verse,] *On the day when the earth is changed to something else* (Qur'an 14:48) will arrive, and [the import of the verse] *When kings enter a settlement, they wreak havoc on it and humiliate its mighty* (Qur'an 27:34) will be apparent.

O Mısri, you say you are safe. Why are you? I did not say I won't die. I said I do not give a fuck about them. Even if I die, my religion will not. To say prophets are never defeated means they do not allow their religion to be plundered. Jesus—*peace be upon him*—was crucified, and St. George, Zechariah, John the Baptist—*peace be upon them*—and many others were martyred, but they did not die defeated; they gave up their bodies but revived their faith. While Nesimi (d. 1417) was being flayed alive, one of his dervishes went to his cell only to find him busy with his work. [The dervish] went back to the square and saw [Nesimi] getting flayed. He went back and forth a couple of times. In the end, Nesimi said to him, "O dervish, how many times have you come and gone!" The dervish replied, "My sultan, I am perplexed. How is it that your skin is being flayed in the square and you are sitting here free of care?" [Nesimi] said, "In order to get free from a bunch of dogs, I settled to give up my skin. Let them have it." [Thereupon] he said that he was leaving, put his skin on his back, and left, saying good-bye at all ten gates of Aleppo. Similarly, if I am a prophet, it is my miracles, and if I am a saint, it is my charismatic acts that will come forth after my death. Thank God, I do not receive favors from tyrants, and even if I do, I will not accept them. I will not be fooled. I am going to try and eventually become a martyr.

ON BEING AMBITIOUS

Karabaş, who is [supposed to be] the *baş* (head) of all, is an infidel. He could not have me fucked over by the people he brought, so he is attempting to kill me through thirst. He is trying to be Jesus and the Messiah and God. O tyrant, while you want them, they are running away from you. Have you not read the verse, *His eye did not swerve nor turn astray* (Qur'an 53:17), or have not you comprehended its meaning? It means that his eyes did not deviate from the right path, his heart did not stray from God, and his eyes and heart did not separate from each other. O tyrant, you should also unite your eyes and heart, and see if you can do such things. Would you pursue such improper suppositions?

A dervish once said to his sheikh: "My sultan, I had a dream last night. I saw you grow so big that your body filled the entire world. After that, you shrank so much that you became tiny like an ant." The sheikh wept and said, "My son, you too saw that?" "My sultan, what does it mean?" [the dervish inquired]. His sheikh said, "The [spiritual] pole (*kutb*) has passed on to the afterlife. I thought they were going to make me [the new] pole. I wanted it. Then I saw that they had brought a priest from the land of the Franks (i.e., Europe) and made him the pole. The only thing I wished for [then] was that they would not put his headgear (*şapka*) on my head; I no longer wanted to be the pole. I shrank so much that I became as tiny as a mote." [God does] not give it to the one who wants it, He gives it to whomever He wants. The created being should do its duties, and should not interfere with affairs reserved for God, in order not to be embarrassed in the end.

In order to display a miracle to one of his dervishes, a sheikh flew to a solitary place. He said to the dervish: "Would you also like to fly?" "My sultan, what else could I wish for?" replied the dervish. The sheikh said, "You cannot fly because you wanted it. If you had been content and had not wanted anything but to serve God [obediently], [then] you could have flown."

Jafar al-Sadiq (d. 765)—*may his soul be sanctified*—said to one of his dervishes, "Shall I show you God?" "That would be a great favor, my sultan," said the dervish. Next to Jafar was a huge lake. He said to his dervishes: "Take him and plunge him into the lake!" They did what he requested. "Keep him there a little!" They complied and waited a little. "Pull him out!" They pulled him out. He ordered it again, and they submerged him again. After waiting a little, he gave the order again, and they complied. [After waiting a little,] he gave the order again. [The dervish] said, "Mercy!," [but] they did not pay heed, and submerged him again. They did this a few times until [the dervish] did not ask [them] to stop any more. After that they held his head down. [When the dervish] came to his senses, the sheikh asked, "Did you see God and did you recognize Him?" The dervish said, "No." The sheikh said, "First you were begging the dervishes [to stop], but they had no mercy. Then you were begging me, but I showed no mercy, either. Afterward, the one you pinned your faith on was God. In other words, even though you lost hope in the best of people [being gracious], hope does not come to an end before the soul departs [from the body]. The one that you still have hope in at the end, that is God." [. . .]

Now, common people and even most of the greatest scholars and sheikhs are awaiting [the advent] of the Mahdi and Jesus, saying if only we could reach their time and see their faces. If they ask Mısri [about this], he will tell them, "If the two of them appeared in the east, I would flee to the west; if they appeared in the west, I would flee to the east; if they appeared on the earth, I would flee to the sky; if they appeared in the sky, I would flee below the ground seven stories deep, in order not to see their faces. By God Gracious, it is better and more comfortable to be imprisoned by infidels in the land of the Franks than to be the Mahdi or Jesus. If there is no other way out, it is better to abandon human form and enter that of the lowest of animals and hide in it than to be the Mahdi or Jesus, let alone to see their faces. I would rather see the face of [the Angel of death] Azrael than theirs."

EIGHT

Adventures of an Ottoman Officer in Captivity, 1690–99

Osman Agha of Timișoara, Written ca. 1724

TRANSLATED BY HAKAN T. KARATEKE

Osman Agha was born around 1671 in Timișoara (in modern-day Romania), the seat of a province and a strategic border town between the Austrian and Ottoman empires. Osman's father Ahmed was an officer in the Ottoman army and had moved to this town from Belgrade. Osman acquired some degree of literacy as a child, and some fluency in Serbo-Croatian, Hungarian, and Romanian, in addition to his native tongue Turkish. Later, he would learn German in captivity. He had a special interest in honing his military prowess. Osman would have been only fifteen or sixteen years old when he was appointed the lieutenant (*odabașı*) in the first cavalier division of Timișoara.

Conflicts between the Ottomans and the Austro-Habsburgs sporadically erupted in the latter part of the seventeenth century, culminating in the failed siege of Vienna by the Ottomans in 1683. Subsequently, in an alliance with the Holy League, the Austrians pushed into the Transylvania and western Balkans, capturing Belgrade in 1688.

In June of that year, Osman's regiment was charged with a mission to carry the salaries of the soldiers and officers of the Arad fortress to Lipova, located some sixty kilometers northeast of Timișoara, where the handover would transpire. While the party was in Lipova, the Austrian army attacked and laid siege to the fort. The fortress soon surrendered. The notables and officers were taken prisoner and distributed among the Austrian officers for ransom or servitude. Osman Agha became a captive to a certain auditor lieutenant Fischer. Soon after, Osman made an agreement with his new master for a ransom of sixty gold coins for his release. In order to obtain the sum, he arranged a guarantor from among the captives, made the trip back to Timișoara, and collected the money. Before he could bring it back to his master Fischer, however, he was robbed on the road by Hungarian irregulars. After this incident, he led the Austrians in pursuit of the bandits, reclaimed his money, and paid his ransom. Fischer, though, did not keep his side of the deal. He kept Osman, who was made to travel with him and even to endure tough conditions in a dungeon. Fischer attempted to sell Osman to a Venetian slave trader, but he escaped that bleak fate with the help of another officer. Each day of the five years he spent with Fischer was worse than the previous, we learn, until the Austrian died. Fischer's wife kept Osman for a year, then decided to send him to one of her relatives in Vienna.

Osman spent seven years as the bondslave of a count at a large mansion in Vienna. Here, Osman earned the trust of his new master and mistress for his diligence and integrity. He learned confectionery, waited tables, earned some money, and was, it seems, growing accustomed, although resigned, to the relative comforts of his new situation. In 1699, news spread quickly that the two empires had reached a truce at Karlowitz and that many prisoners of war were being exchanged. Suspecting that his masters would not free him because he had become integral to their household, he forged a travel permit with the help of the majordomo of the house and fled in the company of four other captives. Traveling partly by boat over the Danube, partly by land, he reached Belgrade (some 650 kilometers from Vienna), and finally made it home to Timişoara. He resumed his former position and put his knowledge of German to use as an interpreter on diplomatic missions. He would later get married.

The Austrians captured Belgrade in 1716 and Timişoara in 1717. We know that Osman Agha migrated to Istanbul in 1724 where, as an experienced and worldly wise man of fifty-three, he sat down to write his memoirs—mostly of his years in captivity. His attention to detail and memory for names is remarkable. In a candid vernacular, he masterfully builds tension and momentum in his narrative. The only copy of this book, in his own handwriting, is kept at the British Library.

LANGUAGE: Turkish. Simple narrative prose in conversational language, organized in long periodic chain sentences. Some specimens of German words in Viennese dialect pronunciation.

source: Manuscript: British Library, London, Ms. Or. 3213, fols. 35b–38b; 77a–79a, 79a–81b; 83a–84b, respectively. Ottoman print edition: Kreutel, Richard F., ed. *Die Autobiographie des Dolmetschers ʻOsmān Ağa aus Temeschwar: der Text des Londoner Autographen in normalisierter Rechtschreibung*. London: E. J. W. Gibb Memorial Trust, 1980. Translated into German by Richard Kreutel and Otto Spies. *Leben und Abenteuer des Dolmetschers Osman Ağa; eine türkische Autobiographie aus der Zeit der grossen Kriege gegen Österreich*. Bonn: Selbstverlag des Orientalischen Seminars der Universität, 1954.

THE TRIP FROM IVANIĆ TO JASENOVAC, 1690

After a few days, the man who was supposed to be my master [Fischer] wished to be released from the position of regimental auditor. We set out toward the Sava River and from there arrived at a fortification called Jasenovac. He settled his account with the regiment there and received his payment. Then he prepared to set out for Vienna and ordered me to ready the beasts. I saddled and prepared his blue roan gelding. For myself, I saddled up a short black horse whose two forelegs were lame. I fastened a large bag of clothes to the back of my saddle. Two Croatians on foot acted as guides. We proceeded with my master from the Ivanić fortress toward the Sava River for a day. However, it was winter, and it both poured and snowed. The roads were swampy and wet, and the conditions were difficult. After a few hours' march, my horse, with its extra load, could not move any further. The horse's forelegs were lame anyway. As I had only rawhide shoes, with no spurs and no whip in my hand, I was not able to urge the horse forward. The man who was supposed to be my master kept pushing me, saying, "Move, Turk!" His beast being sturdy, he approached from behind, prodded my animal and hit me two or three times as well. In short, by the time we reached the halting place that evening, I was almost dead.

Thank God, by God's wise plan, owing to the overflow of the Sava River it was not possible to ride with the beasts downward toward the Siska fortress. We had to take a boat on the Sava River. At the second halting place, in a Croatian village, my master left me with the horses and passed the night in a Croatian house. In this village, one of the sutlers of the aforementioned regiment was staying on for the winter. My master left me with him and traveled toward Jasenovac by boat.

I groomed the horses, and when I was done, I got acquainted with members of the household and the neighbors. [Curious that] a Turk or a Muslim had come to their village, men and women wished to chat with me. Some even took me along to festivities and feasts and wined and dined me. Each day, a new household provided me with food. The family whose turn it was would come and ask me what I'd prefer. I said not to cook anything with pork or lard. "I will eat whatever else you prepare," I said. Every single day, they brought me a *vukiyye* (ca. 1.2 kilograms) of wine and a meal.

I enjoyed myself for about fifteen to twenty days in that village—such that a young Croatian woman would take one of my hands and another girl would hold my other hand, and they would lead me to their private quarters. They showed me excessive kindness. We chatted for a few hours in private. They asked me to sing in the language of the Muslims (Turkish) and in Bosnian. This was of course in my youth; I was eighteen years old. If I was not particularly handsome, I was not ugly either; every creature looks pretty when young. It is a big accomplishment for someone to be able to preserve his chastity in youth when the opportunity presents itself. Out of his kindness and grace, God the most Holy imbued me with some chastity, so that I passed up such opportunities thousands of times. When I thought to myself, my carnal soul would say, "Look, you have the perfect opportunity. You are young and fresh. Those [women] by your side are game. What would happen if you had one of them? You are only a guest here for five or ten days. Nothing would come of it." Regret would overcome me. Then, as I weighed the situation on the scale of reason, and thought about it clearly, [I would say to myself:] "You are just a captive. If you commit such an offensive act and the news spread, whatever their customs or laws are, they would have to administer them to you. Who knows what kind of thing might arise? You would fall into a fraught situation for a little pleasure. What is more, if you left a seed of yours behind and begat children—you know what would happen!" With these kinds of thoughts and because of my aforementioned chastity, I was able to hold myself back and not seize many opportunities.

During this time, owing to all these invitations, I sometimes neglected to care for the horses properly. They lacked grooming and were underfed. One day, that sutler came to the place I was staying, inspected the horses, and figured out why their condition was such. It turns out that our master had instructed him to give me a good beating if I didn't look after the horses properly. The sutler called me to his house, saying he was going to tell me something. Without any foreknowledge, I arrived at his house, climbed the stairs, and stood on the balcony. I saw him take a rope and a thick club into the storeroom across the way. He had a ten-year-old slave named İmamzade Mahmud of Lipova. This slave came out of the storeroom with the son of the sutler. He had tears in his eyes. I asked why he was crying. "My brother," he replied, "My master will beat you. That's why I am crying." As soon as I heard this, I leaped down the stairs, and ran like a flash to the place I was staying, some four or five houses down the street. Without anybody noticing me, I hid inside the hayloft on the other side of the garden.

When the sutler came out of the storeroom and asked, "Where is the Turk?," those who were around replied, "He ran away." He immediately came to the place I was staying and inquired with the members of the household. Even if they had seen me, they wanted to protect me and did not give me away. When they replied, "We didn't see him; we don't know," the sutler searched for me all over. I learned later that when he could not find me, he panicked and said, "Oh my, I made a mistake. I let the Turk run away. If he escapes, his lord will demand [his worth] from me." In short, I stayed in that hayloft for two days and two nights. During the day, the daughters of the landlord brought me food and drink and comforted me. [. . .]

VIENNA, 1698

During my seven-year stay in Vienna, I acquired many skills. For four or five years, I served as a confectioner and waited on tables. I witnessed many good and bad things, and I also dealt with a lot of money, for I was responsible for keeping the pantry ledgers. Whatever was needed on a daily basis, I would purchase myself. At the end of each month a good amount of money would be left over. I was not paid a salary, but I would get tips, which amounted to more than a salary. Yet it was not possible to save anything. I would spend the money when I got together with my fellow countrymen to eat and drink. A few times a year there would be social gatherings at our mansion. I would prepare the necessary ice cream, fruit drinks, chocolate, and other things.

A lot of gold coins were collected from the money left on the card playing tables every night. That is, guests would play at twenty to thirty tables. Some would leave three, others four, and some two gold coins. It would amount to more than a hundred coins a night. Our mistress would pay out remuneration and tips to the [servant] girls. I also received a tip of ten to fifteen, sometimes twenty, gold coins.

I got along well with the members of the household. There were three female Muslims—two girls and one woman—at that mansion. The mistress, while she was [still] living in her own mansion, had the Muslim girls educated in a girls' monastery. When she later married and moved in with our lord, she brought those girls along with her. One of them was originally from Arad. The year that Buda was lost (AH 1097/1685–86), General Heissler marched on those regions with twelve thousand men and captured the Szolnok fortress, the Szarvas fort, and Arad, and he put them ablaze. This girl was the daughter of the late treasurer Ali Agha, who was taken captive there. She was seven when she was first captured, and fourteen when she arrived here with the mistress. She was an extremely pretty girl, well-behaved and of gentle birth. The majordomo of our household, Seyfried von Eyrsperg, was in love with this girl.

The other girl had been taken prisoner along with her mother when she was little, when Buda was seized through an offensive. She was separated from her mother and brought up in a monastery until the age of ten. When she was eleven, she came to our mansion. She, too, was a beautiful girl. However, she was a little licentious, and for that reason, was occasionally chastised by our mistress.

The third woman was the daughter of a *hacı* from Timişoara, and the wife of a Belgrade janissary officer of the rank of a *çorbacı* or *haseki*. When Belgrade was taken by assault (in 1688) by the German forces under the command of Bayerfürst (Max II Emanuel, elector of Bavaria) and the duke of Lorraine, a cavalier grabbed her and took her. When Count Mercy, the lieutenant colonel of that cavalryman, who today is the commander of the Belgrade fortress, saw this young, pretty, and nicely dressed lady in the hands of the soldier, he was attracted to her. He demanded the woman from the cavalryman, but despite his wheedling and his offer of payment, the soldier had no wish to hand over the woman, and he declined to do so. But according to the rules and customs in the regiments of the German army, all captives belong to the officers. If an officer wanted [a captive], he could have her; he did not have to pay an akçe. Accordingly, when the aforementioned Count Mercy wanted to seize the woman by force, the cavalryman drew two revolvers from his belt, and fired one gun at the woman's head. The ball wounded the side of her head. When the woman dropped to the ground, the soldier shot his other gun at her legs, puncturing her calves. He did this so that she would not belong to anyone.

Even though the woman was severely wounded, Count Mercy had her taken to his tent, assigned a surgeon, and treated with medication for a month or two until she recuperated. He later brought her to his mother in Metz, which was a large town located in his home district of Lothringen (Lorraine). She stayed there for a few years, but by some means escaped, and arrived in the city of Vienna. Cardinal Kollonitsch was seizing unclaimed captives there at the time, so he took her in too. Later, our mistress requested her from [Kollonitsch] and he agreed. That is how she come to our mansion. We stayed together in the same place for three or four years.

THE INCIDENT WITH THE MAJORDOMO, 1699

An issue arose between our majordomo Eyrsperg, whom I mentioned above, and myself. This became the main reason why I was eventually set free. Our majordomo was an extreme womanizer. He was originally from a town called Neustadt, which means the new city, some twelve miles outside Vienna. His father was the Bürgermeister—that is, the mayor—in that town. The renowned governor of Nógrád, Çonka Bey (after his conversion, Leopold Freiherr von Zungaberg) stayed in that town under their surveillance along with his family and children. Eyrsperg learned quite good Turkish from them and could speak the language.

One night, while our mistress and master were away in the countryside and no one else was around, [the majordomo] became somewhat intoxicated. Tipsy, he entered the maids' room. There was that young girl from Buda. She was just thirteen years old and not tall either—she looked like she was nine years old. As she lay in her bed, he approached her, fondled her body here and there, and by promising God knows what, deflowered her. When the act was finished, he used his own handkerchief to wipe away the spots of virginal blood in order to hide what had happened—but to no avail!

The next morning the girl came to me and complained: "My dear countryman! Something happened to me last night. If you ask me what it is: As I lay in my bed, our majordomo approached and seduced me like the Devil. Partly using nice words, partly through force, he assaulted me and took my virginity. My bed is all bloody. What will become of me? If our mistress learns about it, she will kill me. Most of all, I fear that I might have gotten pregnant; then there is no way to hide it." Thus she finished her words.

I wanted to laugh but I was also dumbfounded. I asked if she had talked to anyone about this matter. She said she had not. So I said, "Be careful not to tell anyone about this incident. Be very discreet about it. If it is disclosed and our mistress hears about it, she'll kill you—there's no doubt about it. You should do as I say." She took my advice and kept it to herself.

The next morning, I went to the majordomo's room, and was surprised to see that he had woken up early and was staring pensively out of the window at the square in front of the mansion. I greeted him. Then I asked, "Why is it that you look gloomy and unhappy? What is the reason for your concern?" His face flushed. He babbled a bit, and said, "What is there to be concerned about? Why would you ask?" I replied, "I don't know. It is just that the little girl came crying to me this morning and told me all that happened last night. She is terrified." When I added, "If our mistress hears about it, it won't be good," his face became even redder, and he replied, "What do you mean?" I said, "You know what. You took the girl's virginity. Now, she is frightened that she may be pregnant. This is no small business. You know what will happen if the word gets out. Besides, you are the manager of the whole household. You are supposed to prevent others from committing such acts, not perpetrate them yourself! How will you remedy the situation?" When I posed that question, he was perplexed and sank into complete silence.

"Don't worry," I said. "I can get this situation under control and cover it up. The girl will not report the incident to anyone else. I'll instruct her and warn her not to tell anyone. Word will not get out." The majordomo unwound a bit and started pleading. While his rank did not require him to ask me for any favors, the circumstances dictated otherwise this time. If our mistress and master became aware of this incident, they would not keep the majordomo an hour. A severe punishment would be inflicted on him. [. . .]

THE TREATY OF KARLOWITZ AND PREPARING TO ESCAPE, 1699

I thought about this for a few days and considered that there were other Muslim captives who had been apprehended by Cardinal Kollonitsch. Those captives would probably be sent down to the border and exchanged. If I went to the Cardinal [and requested that I be sent too], he would probably turn me down out of respect for our mistress and master. My intent would be obvious and I would draw detestation on me. There were also some captives and women who had converted to Christianity. All of them found some excuse—some with the pretext of going to Buda, others with different pretenses—to travel [near the border] and escape. Even a good many captives arrived from the province of Saxony, traveled by boat to the south, and probably found their freedom. Thank God, I had mastered quite good German and no one could recognize me [as a Muslim] from my looks, if he did not know me already. It would be best to leave in disguise, I thought, and I confided in our majordomo regarding my plan. He also found my idea plausible.

We deliberated about what to do next. We thought that it was necessary for me to obtain a valid travel permit, signed and sealed by my master. That would be easy, for it was mostly I who kept the keys to my master's room. When he was out of the house, I would lead the maids to his room and have them clean and make his bed. When the room was ready, I would lock up the room myself. The keys to the room stayed in the cupboard in the dining room. When our lord came, I would unlock the room. So I had access to the seal of my master. Another seal was with the majordomo. He would use this large seal for daily correspondence.

However, the signature needed to be written by the hand of [our lord] Christoph Dietmayr Graf von Schallenberg. We pondered what to do about that. We had many letters, and other papers and documents, signed by our lord. I practiced [imitating his signature]. When I put a blank paper on top of a signed one and pressed both against a glass, the signature could be seen clearly. Thus I traced the signature and forged it.

Now, since I was the only one the majordomo feared or felt shame from in the whole house, he reckoned that the best thing was to get rid of me so that he could do whatever he wished without having to worry about anyone. So he wrote a travel permit for me that said more or less that I was originally a Muslim but had converted to Christianity, [was thus freed] and was all by myself, and that I was allowed to travel to the Buda and Varadin regions and settle there. The letter counseled that no one hinder or bother me on the road to my destination or harass me in the places I passed through. We formulated his detailed travel permit, stamped it with the seal of my master, and signed it as described above. It turned out to be a handsome document. As my papers were ready, I waited for an opportunity [to flee].

NINE

The Trial of a Heretic, 1527

Told by Celalzade Mustafa, d. 1567

TRANSLATED BY KAYA ŞAHİN AND CORNELL H. FLEISCHER

Celalzade Mustafa (d. 1567) was a bureaucrat who served as chancellor at the central administration of the Ottoman state from 1534 until his retirement in 1557. During his long career, he wrote most of the sultan's official correspondence, helped administer imperial law, and established forms of chancery documents and practice. Mustafa was known as a gifted stylist. The excerpt below is taken from his major work, *Echelons of the Dominions and Hierarchies of the Professions* (*Tabakatü'l-Memalik ve Derecatü'l-Mesalik*), a history covering the period between 1520–55. Mustafa most likely wrote the section below after 1557, on the basis of recollections and contemporaneous notes. The excerpt features several passages that exemplify Mustafa's style: among these are criticisms he levels against two Ottoman officials; and descriptions of the virtues of the grand mufti in his narration of the trial of Molla Kabız. This highly metaphorical style of expression in Ottoman Turkish was very much inspired by Persian and Arabic literary works, and it relied on the adaptation of these languages' lexicons and stylistic elements into Mustafa's native Turkish.

While our knowledge of Celalzade Mustafa's career and activities is fairly extensive, we do not know much about Molla Kabız, whose trial is related in the excerpt below. Sources agree that Kabız received medrese training and joined the ranks of scholars of Islamic jurisprudence collectively known as the ulema. He lived in Istanbul for a number of years. He also appears to have made good use of the city's public spaces, most notably the taverns, to spread his ideas to his fellow city dwellers. Kabız believed that Jesus was the most prominent of God's prophets, and that he was thus superior to Muhammad. He constructed his argument from an Islamic perspective, using the fundamental texts of the Muslim tradition. This argument contravened Islam's fundamental claims that Muhammad was sent as the last prophet, and that Islam was the final and most perfect form of revealed religion. Even though scholars of Islamic jurisprudence were generally staunch champions of a literal interpretation of Islamic tenets, Kabız lived in a time in which Islam did not necessarily represent a unified dogma in the Ottoman realm or a universally agreed on historical narrative but was instead open to multiple interpretations. Kabız's arguments would not therefore have seemed too radical to some who were familiar with ongoing debates about the meaning of sainthood and prophethood.

The Kabız case raises a few questions about the interaction between Islam and Christianity in a society that was managed by a Sunni Muslim elite, some of whose members were themselves recent converts from Christianity. As an Abrahamic religion that expanded politically and culturally in a geography previously dominated by Christianity, Islam early on developed a fairly detailed narrative about the lives of Mary and Jesus, as well as refutations of Christian dogma. Islamic societies in the Middle East always contained large Christian communities until the modern period. In the Ottoman case, Islam was presented as the true inheritor of the Gospel of Jesus, while Muslim scholars were keen to isolate the Muslim faithful from exposure to Christian dogmas and rituals. The alarm of the Muslim scholarly establishment with regard to an unexpected intrusion of Christian dogma is apparent in the Kabız incident.

A religious trial had to follow certain procedures in order not to seem arbitrary and mismanaged. Kabız was denounced to the political authorities by fellow scholars, who were reportedly worried both by his arguments and by the popularity he had begun to enjoy in Istanbul. The sultan's insistence on passing judgment on the basis of the Holy Law rather than imperial customary law (*kanun*) also demonstrates the attention to procedure and precedent given in a legal procedure. At the end of the trial, Kabız was invited to renounce his beliefs and repent, since a Muslim could not be summarily put to death for a transgression of religious law according to the Holy Law. He was executed on November 4, 1527.

LANGUAGE: Turkish. Long sentences, written in a formal chancery style that was being developed in this period; ornate imagery, especially in the descriptions of the mufti and the kadı.

SOURCE: Manuscript: Celalzade Mustafa. *Tabakatü'l-Memalik ve Derecatü'l-Mesalik*. Staatsbibliothek Preussischer Kulturbesitz, Berlin, Ms. or. quart. 1961. Facsimile: Kappert, Petra, ed. *Geschichte Sultan Süleyman Kanunis von 1520 bis 1557, oder, Tabakat ül-Memalik ve Derecat ül-Mesalik von Celalzade Mustafa genannt Koca Nişancı*. Wiesbaden: Steiner, 1981 (fols. 172b–175b).

KABIZ'S TRIAL BY THE MILITARY JUDGES

This section concerns the case of Kabız, who, in the city of Istanbul, entered the unacceptable path of free thought (*zendeka*) and heresy (*ilhad*) and who, therefore, died by the drawn sword of the Holy Law.

Once again, o pen of oceanic perfection!
Your tongue contains every form of speech

Tell a story to the learned
Relate a few anecdotes

The intention here is to tell an exemplary story
Indeed, every story has various delights

Words become a lamp that sheds light
The spoken word has effects, it leaves its marks

Truthfulness and verification are the ornaments of speech
Such speech is accompanied by divine guidance

Truthful speech is like the breath of Jesus
Without truthfulness it is the noise of the [church] bell

The felicitous reign of his majesty the emperor, who is accompanied by God's approval—*may God strengthen the foundations of his rule*—happened in the most distinguished time. All classes of people lived in perfect comfort under his imperial shade. The universe was in perfect order, and the world was in complete calm. All at once, the elevated character of a scholar named Kabız entered the path of free thought and heresy. His faith was corrupted; he strayed from the true path; he grasped the coin of perdition and rebellion; he lost himself in the taverns. He became known for his banter in drinking houses. A number of zealous scholars were unable to endure his transgression of the limits of the Holy Law and etiquette. They brought him to be judged by the Imperial Council, saying that he proclaimed the superiority of Jesus over Muhammad—*may God's peace and blessings be upon him*—and thus displayed the signs of heresy. It was the year 934, the eighth day of the month of Safer (November 3, 1527).

At that time Fenarizade Muhyiddin Çelebi (d. 1548) was the military judge of Rumeli, and Kadiri Çelebi (d. 1548) was the military judge of Anatolia. The viziers referred this matter to their exalted offices and ordered the military judges to adjudicate the case. They had the aforementioned heretic brought in front of them. When he affirmed his claims based on his corrupt belief, both military judges were overcome with anger and rage. In unison, they ordered his summary execution. The heretic insisted on his claims. He cited and interpreted Qur'anic verses and prophetic traditions to support and explicate his claims. He remained firm in his assertions by citing scriptural evidence. The military judges were unable to refute his claims in accordance with the Holy Law. They did not have a grasp of the legal issues [under dispute]. They were filled with pride of status and rank, and they were covered by the blanket of the armies of negligence. One of them, of unstable character, had come to the position of military judge by virtue of his lineage. The other one was not without ability but had come to prominence by virtue of his connections. In fact, he was not adorned with the gem of piety, and not decorated and distinguished with the jewel of religiosity. He was completely [devoted to] acquiring gold and cash; his virtues were limited to adorning and embellishing [himself] with servants and attendants. In the case of the aforementioned heretic, they were unable to refute his assertions according to the Holy Law. In a state of anger, they passed a judgment on the basis of executive law (*örfi*). The grand vizier İbrahim Pasha (d. 1536) repeatedly excoriated the military judges, telling them, "If this person's assertion is contrary to the Holy Law and is erroneous, then show where the error is. You must discover and reveal the belief and suspicions that are firmly settled in his mind. Answer according to the Holy Law. It is improper, for men of learning and reason, to judge with anger and rage, and to display rudeness and bad manners." Finding an opportunity, the heretic was fortunate enough to prevail over the other side. On the face of things, the heretic appeared triumphant. Out of necessity, the viziers concluded the session and released the heretic from the Council.

His majesty the emperor, of perceptive heart and armed with justice, had built an exalted throne, an elevated gallery fit for a king, above the outer Council chamber where the viziers held court. There, he had established a hidden vantage point from which he could observe the Council chamber below. In this fashion, he was able to observe in person the dealings of the Council, and to be informed of the truth of the matters under discussion. That day, by happenstance, he watched from there and heard the proceedings with his imperial ears. As the viziers later entered the throne chamber and were graced by the world-adorning presence [of Sultan Süleyman I, r. 1520–66], the sultan presented the pearls of his felicitous, jewel-laden speech: "A heretic comes to our Council and he asserts the superiority of Blessed Jesus over our Prophet, the pride of the two worlds—*God's blessings and salutations be upon Him*. To prove his claims, he resorts to fallacious statements. The suspicions [he sowed] have not been dissipated, and his refutation has not been provided. Why has he not been condemned?" He thus expressed his imperial chastisement. İbrahim Pasha replied: "Our military judges were unable to refute him according to the Holy Law; they responded simply out of anger and rage. What could we do? We disbanded the session." His majesty, the refuge of the caliphate—*may God exalt his supporters*—ordered, "The military judges are not the sole learned people. Invite the mufti of the Muslims who issues fetvas, and the chief magistrate (kadı) of Istanbul, to the Council. Adjudicate tomorrow according to the Holy Law." After the viziers exited, they dispatched pursuivants and had the aforementioned heretic held. They also went to the mufti and the kadı of Istanbul and invited them to the Imperial Council.

KABIZ'S TRIAL BY THE GRAND MUFTI AND THE KADI OF ISTANBUL

At that time, the late Mevlana Kemalpaşaoğlu Şemseddin Ahmed (d. 1534) was the mufti—*may God envelop him in His mercy*. It is true that he was unique in his time thanks to his virtue and perfection, and he was first and foremost in the abundance of his knowledge and wisdom. His exalted person was adorned with nobility and grace; his subtle essence was famed for its wealth of virtue and perfection. In accordance with the verse *Are those who know and those who do not know equal?* (Qur'an 39:9), it is impossible to express and describe accurately and in a fitting manner the arts and sciences concentrated in his exalted person, and the perfections adorned with virtue that were afforded to his felicitous nature. His pure mind was full of light and shining with the ornament of perfections; his resplendent nature and perception, like the shining sun that disperses bright light, sparkled and gleamed. Of the sciences of the ancients and the moderns, there was not a single one whose intricacies and problems were beyond the scope of his perfumed, roving mind. Was there any field of virtue and perfection that his enlightening mind did not contain and command? He was like a phoenix who flew, almost without equal, in the highest spheres of scholarly virtues. In the dominions of perfections and sciences he was like no other. He was a world conqueror of virtue who solved all riddles. He was a prince and emperor in the dominions of the divine sciences. His fragrance-expressing fingers were adept and superior in displaying the precious jewels and bright stars of virtuous writing. The writing composition of his honey-like, delight-inspiring tongue, in the explication of knowledge and wisdom, was like that of a singing nightingale or a parrot. One can find out about the learned of the past and the skillful critics of the latter days from his books, which are products of his learning; the outcome of the considerations of his sunlike mind is to be found in his writings. His elite standing among the learned is clear; this is even more apparent and obvious than the light of the sun to the men of learning. In particular, his world-adorning knowledge of prose composition, and his treatises that reveal extraordinary beauties, are wondrous examples of orthography. This is conform to the truth-displaying meaning of the expression, *That is God's bounty, which He gives to those whom He wishes* (Qur'an 62:4). Those luscious jewel-scattering pearls are most fitting to the stature of his interlocutors. The Exalted God—*may He be glorified*—bestowed on him so much in this regard. Until the end of the world, and the conclusion of the life of the mind, it is unlikely that one tenth of one tenth of his extraordinary capacities and special abilities, one thousandth of the signs of nobility and virtue concentrated in his person, indeed his stature and capacity, and his skills and fortitude, would be granted to another intelligent person.

> His high estate and pure essence
> Manifested in his person the bright star of felicity
>
> He was a rose garden for the flowers of learning
> He was a shining sun in the firmament of virtue
>
> Even though he resided on Earth
> The heavenly spheres were the coursing ground of the noble steed of his character
>
> Kemal reached perfection in his time
> His words were like the sweetness of flowing, fresh water
>
> His blessed face was a shining sun
> The light of faith shone on his cheeks
>
> He pardoned mistakes, he paid compliments
> He was spirit-like, and angel-fashioned
>
> His speech was as welcome as well-ordered pearls
> One's spirit would joyfully submit to his words
>
> If all knowledge were a physical body, then he would be its soul
> He was the emperor of the realm of the sciences

From head to toe he embodied spirituality

His like shall not emerge from the dominion of nonexistence.

The kadı of Istanbul, Mevlana Sadeddin (a.k.a. Sadi, d. 1539), was likewise well respected among the learned of the time. He was happily endowed with virtue; he was adorned with knowledge and perfection, and he was known for his integrity. On the path of knowledge, he was sought out; in the gatherings of scholars he had participated in many discussions on learned matters. He was a highly regarded individual who knew both the intricacies of the material and the protocols of discussion. He was a noble man of learning, a person of virtue. In every respect, his fulfillment of religious duties, his good deeds, his excellent character were well known.

These two wise and learned men were invited to the exalted Council of the felicitous emperor. The following day, the two presented themselves together, at the Sublime Porte, to the Council. The chief military judge of Rumeli, resentful of the promotion of the mufti over him, got up and left the Council. In fact, the reason for his departure was his concern about the learned discussion: if his turn to speak came, his capacity [or lack thereof] would be revealed, and he wanted to avoid that. Those who were unaware [of the truth of the matter] attributed [his departure] to his dedication to the path of learning. In fact, he was an ignoramus whose sole relationship to learning was his name [Fenarizade].

At the supreme Council, the exalted mufti sat on the left of the grand vizier: the kadı was seated before him. The aforementioned heretic was brought in. The mufti of all Muslims, with perfect restraint and courtesy, inquired about his assertions. [The mufti] listened to his speech carefully, with the ear of verification. He had him recite the proofs and evidence that he had derived from Holy Scripture and prophetic tradition. When he had disclosed the entirety of his belief, the mufti, in accordance with the rules of scholarly discussion, demonstrated [the heretic's] misunderstanding, and completely refuted his suspicions. He explained the meaning of the Qur'anic verses and the point of the prophetic traditions with complete confidence. Thus was the truth revealed. Kabız was dumbstruck, and he was powerless to utter anything else. He was defeated, unable to respond. One more time, the mufti addressed him graciously: There you go, the truth has been revealed. Do you have anything more to say? Do you foreswear your incorrect belief and accept the truth?" The defeated heretic insisted in his incorrect belief and refused to accept the truth. Since, by virtue of his false belief, he remained firm in his resistance, the mufti referred the matter to the kadı, and thus completed his task as issuer of legal opinions. He told the kadı to pass judgment as the Holy Law requires. The kadı of the Holy Law asked the heretic, "Have you now returned to the path of the Pure Belief, the way of the people of tradition and consensus (Sunnism)?" Thus was an opportunity presented, but [Kabız] would not affirm the truth and, as before, he remained steadfast in his false belief. Therefore, his execution was ordered in accordance with the Holy Law. The Council meeting ended. Then, as required by the Holy Law, the aforementioned heretic was annihilated by the sword of the victorious Holy Law.

TEN

The Life and Works of Two Mediocre Poets

Told by Âşık Çelebi, d. 1572

TRANSLATED BY DOUGLAS BROOKES

Âşık Çelebi (the pen name of Pir Mehmed) was born in 1520. He came from a line of poets and scholars, evincing a lineage that opened doors for his excellent education on a wide variety of subjects, particularly literary culture. Trained in law, he entered the legal profession and became a judge. However, poetry, not the law, was his true calling. His style in verse reflected his nature; he was a keen observer, genial, and devoted to friends. His writings were imbued with a rich palette of emotion and human interest, in contrast to the rather stiff style of the typical Ottoman poet of the day. His poems could be suggestive, even raunchy, but he always arranged his colorful words with an amazing command of literary embellishments: alliteration, internal rhyme, puns, simile, satire, and plentiful proverbs and anecdotes. His style in verse indicated that he was a keen observer and devoted to friends. His verse also reflects his affinity for young men, like his pen name of Âşık, or "Lover." Relationships between men and much younger men or older boys were common among the Ottoman elite, and allusions to these relationships were frequent themes for the Ottoman literati. Âşık Çelebi was prolific enough to eventually compile a compendium of his poems, and he also translated notable Arabic works into Turkish. His literary fame won him appointment to a judgeship in the Ottoman town of Üsküp (today's Skopje, northern Macedonia), but, struggling with ill health, he died there in 1572 at the age of fifty-two.

The two entries in this chapter are from Âşık Çelebi's most celebrated work, *The Assemblies of Poets* (*Meşairü'ş-şuara*), a compendium of biographies of Ottoman poets in the mid-1500s. The work fits into the Middle Eastern literary genre of *tezkire* (literally, "memory aid") a literary trend that descended from centuries-old Arabic and Persian predecessors and flourished in sixteenth-century Ottoman literature. Âşık Çelebi began compiling the work in the 1540s, inspired by the first Ottoman tezkire that was then making the rounds. When he finished it in 1568, it contained entries for close to four hundred Ottoman poets (or more, depending on different manuscripts), embellished with insights on the many poets and artists he knew personally, along with biographies of the Ottoman sultans.

Meşairü'ş-şuara swiftly became, and has remained, one of the most famous works in Turkish literature. What made the work extraordinary was Âşık Çelebi's groundbreaking inclusion of his own playful, even shocking, commentary in the text. This is no dry list. Thanks to his colorful writing, it is a rich description of social life that touches on a vast number of topics including Istanbul literary circles, the villas of great men, parties, gardens, public baths, dervish convents, and booksellers. As the genre dictates, it is written in a mixture of prose and poetry. The poetry is relatively straightforward. But the prose, terse and succinct, showcases the master's clever and entertaining style, marrying rich vocabulary with wide-ranging allusions and literary embellishments, all of which make it a challenge for later generations to follow, even while impressing us deeply with the author's brilliance.

LANGUAGE: Turkish. Prose written in rather short sentences with straightforward grammar, but with lots of poetic imagery.

SOURCE: Facsimile: Meredith-Owens, G. M., ed. *Meşa'ir üş-şu'ara, or Tezkere of 'Aşık Çelebi* / edited in facsimile from the manuscript Or. 6434 in the British Museum with introduction and variants from the Istanbul and Upsala manuscripts. London: Luzac, 1971; *Hasbi,* fols. 86a-87a; *Hüseyni,* fols. 88a-88b. Transcription: Kılıç, Filiz, ed. *Meşa'irü'ş-şu'ara: İnceleme, Metin* / Âşık Çelebi. Istanbul: İstanbul Araştırmaları Enstitüsü, 2010.

HASBİ: THE CONVICT POET

Younger brother of the late Keşfî is he, the town of Gedüs (Gediz) in Germiyan province his place. At the beginning of the late İbrahim Pasha's viziership (in office from 1523 onward) and his administration, [Hasbi] was tried in a council concerning a murder, and the Pasha ordered him tortured [to extract a confession]. The police superintendent brought him to his quarters and strung him up by his arms, whereupon [Hasbi] uttered this impromptu couplet:

The pain of the wound of love [is such that] not even Kaf Mountain can bear;
This frail heart of mine endures it well—have mercy on it.

It so happened that [at that time] the police superintendent's daughter quite suddenly died. This the superintendent attributed to Hasbi's being innocent, and he intended to let him go. He took him to the Pasha and said, "I tortured him much but he did not confess." [Additionally], on the way a tree branch scratched Hasbi's eye and injured it. Fearing for his life, he became half dead from the pain of that wound. When, on the following day, he came into his presence, the Pasha saw that his eye was wounded. "Molla Hasbi, what happened to your eye?" he asked. Hasbi said, "Sir, it didn't like where it was, it wanted to get out." To which the Pasha replied, "Your eye has something yet to see" and ordered him locked up again. Hasbi modified his pen name into *Habsî*, "the prisoner," under which name he has quite a few odes and lyric poems.

The prominent poets Basiri, Zati, Keşfi, and Kandi teamed up and greeted the Pasha on the way to the Imperial Council meeting. Each one submitted a praise poem and a piece of ornate writing to intercede for [Hasbi's] release. The Pasha was inclined to soften his stance and act with gentleness, but some hypocrites denounced Hasbi by saying "Does the poets' satire really frighten our master?" They made the Pasha's impetuous disposition on the field of anger flare up again. The Pasha submitted the matter to the Padishah and had the unfortunate Hasbi bound in chains. He made of him an eternal prisoner in the castle known as Ketayun Palace (Kızkulesi, Maiden's Tower), opposite Üsküdar. Ten years he lay there as an eternal prisoner. Just like that fortress, he was plunged into the sea of the tears of remorse. At that time he coined the following quatrain; full of misery it is:

Let me utter an "ah" again, so that the era weeps in misery
May my laments rise to the firmament; may the revolving sphere of heaven weep;
When it sees my tears, may the ocean weep;
May infidels pity my state, may Muslims weep.

Since parting from you, with yearning, O moon,
The separation fills my eyes with tears whenever I call it to mind
Ah! Separation. Alas! Separation. Difficult it is, O friends.
May infidels pity my state, may Muslims weep.

When the cupbearer of the age proffered me the chalice of separation
The evening of separation has obscured the world to my eye
Alas! The days of separation have slain me, the one sick at heart.
May infidels pity my state, may Muslims weep.

Tell him that my exalted sultan cast a glance upon me
I am his slave; may my khan show favor and grace
If my friends show not compassion for me in my exile.
May infidels pity my state, may Muslims weep.

On the day of İbrahim Pasha's execution, some of his followers had their eyes gouged out, others their head cleaved. Hasbi was freed from prison.

He had a propensity to madness in his nature. Uneducated and simpleminded, a drunk, he talked a lot, but mostly words devoid of meaning. He uttered all kinds of so-called poems, but they were nonsense.

When [his brother] Keşfî died he left behind much property, which went to his son Atâ, the prettiest of the boy-beloveds. He in turn earned just as much again, by putting to use his silver ingots (i.e., his buttocks) and the sweat of his forehead, he [bent over and] put his face on the ground for some people and bowed his neck to others [to perform oral sex on them]. Later he joined the janissary cavalry and collected from infidels incalculable *harac* tax and [tax mixed up with] pig's blood, which was detestable twice over. When he died the money went to Hasbi. [The saying] *"Bear tidings to the miser's gold of accidents or heirs"* fits the mark exactly, for Hasbi, too, died without having spent a single akçe. It was apportioned among various churls and filthy wretches from Gedüs. Harlots earned it, pimps spent it. Those who heard about it said:

> *My God, my God, who squandered what had been gathered together?*

This chronogram about the killing of Prince Mustafa is his:

> Judgment is to God, the Overpowering One,
> Praise to him who created fate

> Prayers for the pure soul of Muhammed
> All who have come to the world will depart it

> Many a measure mankind takes
> God is the one who commands

> The Lord has added the soul of Prince Mustafa
> To the ranks of martyrs for the faith

> The believer resigns himself to fate
> When he has reached the destined end of his life

> Recite the Fatiha for his soul, Hasbi
> Its date is nine hundred sixty (1553)

> Two divine inspirations, two chronograms;
> May they be the pretext for one prayer

Poem:

> With desire for your lips the tulip charred its breast
> Out of jealousy, the cup foundered in blood.

> Whenever the goblet receives a kiss from your lips
> Blood of [my] liver becomes an appetizer for me.

He buried his brother Keşfî and [Keşfî's] son Atâ on an [elevated] platform outside the Edirne Gate, on the road to Ebu Eyyub (Eyüp), where he had also prepared a burial place for himself. He had these couplets inscribed:

> Whichever persons pass by this grave
> What is fitting is that they offer a prayer for the buried ones

> May God grant mercy to those who see this chronogram:
> "May they offer prayers for Keşfî and Atâ."

FIGURE 8. Sorbet seller, 1581. Melchior Lorck (artist), woodcut (Antwerp[?], 1581).

This occurred in the year nine hundred fifty-five (1548–49).

HÜSEYNİ: THE CONFECTIONER POET

Emir Hüseyn-i Helvayî ("the helva maker") is he, Edirne his native town and place. In his day he possessed such a degree of beauty that if [the Umayyad caliph] Yazid (d. 683) had known that such a lovely beauty would spring from among the descendants of [the Prophet's grandson] Husain, he would not have made His Excellency Husain the martyr of Kerbela.

The henbane (*beng*) and opium addicts used to stand at respectful attention on the road down which he passed, saying:

> If I die an addict of henbane, let them wash me with fruit drink
> Let them place me on the paths where the helva maker beauty passes by

They used to teem like ants around his shop, as though

> *They are flies 'round a sweet*

Those [lovers] whose appetites were aroused (lit. were smeared with honey on their mouths) with the hope of a union with him were more innumerable than flies. But compared to the giddy ones who fell for the honey of his promises, they were fewer in number than the wings of a fly. His red cheeks underneath the green turban wrapped around his head looked like the rainbow in his face that shone like the sun. For this reason, the unjustly treated [lovers] would shed showers of tears like the clouds of spring.

He considered it better to bear a tray of Chinese porcelain [on his head, to carry helva] than a royal crown. Because his [face] resembled a round helva cake surrounded by a large tray, [it was as if] he was carrying the moon on his head surrounded by a halo. He would take [the tray] from alley to alley and nook to nook. Those who ate his *sabuni* helva would wash their hands of other helvas—even if [their] syrup was the water of life. Those who ate his *zülabiyye* thought it more precious than a cup of ruby red [wine]. Yearning for his lips and eyes, libertines became addicted to [his] helva with almonds. People, lifeless and alive, would flock to his shop as though they were already dead, and declare, "Let his helva be the helva prepared to commemorate our death." Those who ate his *peşmine* helva would allow themselves to be led by the nose by him. Those who tasted his *kadayıf* would lose control over their affairs. If his helva were sold for the price of a life, those who hear about it would offer their lives as a tip. Seeing this marketplace of sweetmeats, the sugar crystals would become the prisoner of the flask of envy like a demon and from amazement they would coalesce into candy on a stick (lit. bite the willow stick) as though it were a finger bitten in astonishment. Even though all poets and refined persons of wit were admirers of his, saying the helva maker beauty is sweeter [than his sweetmeats], their unmatched chief was Baba İshak. Every day on the way to the madrasa he would pass by his shop and at times cast a glance out of the corner of his eye and sometimes emit an unexpected "Ah!"

With the idea that "Lying is acceptable in poetry," the above-mentioned gentleman [Hüseyni] had adopted the practice of lying not only in poetry but also in prose. Claiming that "All that lovers possess belongs to me," he would recite the poems of all poets as if they were his. Indeed, Emri Çelebi converted the meaning of this into verse:

The prince of poets, Helvayi,
Tells tales to every gazelle[-eyed boy]

Saying "The very best of poets are liars"
He lies in whatever he speaks

Verses by [Emir Hüseyn-i Helvayi]:

I waded into the ocean of your love, thinking it was shallow
Suddenly a wave of misfortune washed over my head, ah!

Mount Bisutun is grieving for Ferhad
O Husrev, the [cloudy] sky around its top; do not think it mist

As you are capable of a cloud of smoke of a sigh, O heart!
Your burden, as big as a mountain, you too pile up on top

ELEVEN

The Extraordinary Life Story of a Scholar

Told by Mehmed Mecdi, d. 1591

TRANSLATED BY HELGA ANETSHOFER

The following biography is from the Turkish translation of Taşköprülüzade Ahmed's (d. 1561) *Crimson Peonies Among the Scholars of the Ottoman State* (*Shaqa'iq al-numaniya fi ulama al-dawlat al-Uthmaniya*). This biographical encyclopedia of more than five hundred scholars and Sufi sheikhs who lived after the rise of the Ottomans was the first one of its kind in Ottoman literature. Taşköprülüzade held the position of the judge of Istanbul until 1554, when he resigned owing to failing eyesight. Although his native language was Turkish, he dictated this work in Arabic between 1554 and 1558. It was not unusual among sixteenth-century Ottoman scholars to compose their scholarly works in this language. The compilation quickly became immensely popular; there were several attempts to translate it into Turkish and make it widely accessible. The entry below is from the author and poet Mehmed Mecdi's translation, *Gardens of Peonies* (*Hada'ikü'ş-Şaka'ik*), which was carried out in 1587. Mecdi strove to turn the unassuming plain language of the original work into an embellished courtly style. The excessive use of various terms related to alcohol consumption in the entry below was an interpolation on the part of the translator Mecdi, for such a style both pertained to the topic and was considered integral to the art of eloquent writing. Mecdi's work represents an attempt to produce new work from the original source material.

The ulema, or the scholars of Islamic jurisprudence, make up one of the segments of Ottoman society about which today's historians know most. The reason for this is obvious: they were the most educated societal class. Accordingly, they wrote more and left more evidence for modern historians. Many composed works about their subject of study; others occasionally recorded their reflections on society or drafted autobiographical accounts. Biographical dictionaries, like Taşköprülüzade Ahmed's, detailing their subjects' lives and achievements also facilitated their reception as a distinctive class within Ottoman society. Yet, owing to the theme of study—namely, Islamic sciences—members of the ulema are often characterized in modern scholarship as a monolithic bloc of people without personal histories. Attention has primarily been given to their intellectual achievements. Their scholarship notwithstanding, there is much to be learned from their various life trajectories.

The biographical entry below details the rather unusual story of the poet and scholar Melihi (d. early sixteenth century). The honorific title "Mevlana" in front of his name (also written as Molla or Monla in the Ottoman context) is customarily used for scholars of Islamic jurisprudence. Students in this track usually attended a medrese—an institution offering secondary through higher education—for over ten years, studying Arabic, Qur'anic exegesis, and Islamic law, among other things, in order become jurists or medrese professors if they were lucky enough to find a position (see chapter 1). It was fairly common for ambitious students to travel to other cities to study with a renowned scholar. Melihi travelled to Herat (in modern-day northwestern Afghanistan), the seat of the Timurid court at the time, and became classmates with Abdurrahman Jami (d. 1492), who would become one of the most prominent poets and theologians of the Persianate world.

Melihi's life story took an extraordinary turn when he returned to Istanbul following his studies and gradually fell into alcoholism. It was illegal to sell alcohol to Muslims, although surely many Muslims drank it. His constant intoxication became a growing problem. The text indicates that Melihi could easily get hold of wine—that is, until the sultan specifically ordered the tavern-keepers not to sell it to him. Apparently, he had a pleasant personality and was often called to the palace to serve as a boon companion to the sultan. Mustafa Âli, the author of another biographical encyclopedia, reports that the sultan felt that a feast without Melihi was like "food without salt" (a pun on the Arabic root of his name, which means both "salt" and "wit"). Melihi is not known to have held any office, so apart from the stipend mentioned in the text, it is not clear how he made his living.

LANGUAGE: Turkish. Literary prose, with a high degree of elaborate and metaphorical language. Interspersed with Arabic quotations and Persian poems.

SOURCE: Ottoman print edition: Translated by Mehmed Mecdi. *Tercüme-i Şakaik-i Numaniyye* (a.k.a. *Hadaik al-Şakaik*). Istanbul: Daru't-Tıbaati'l-Amire, 1269/1852 (232–34).

Mevlana Melihi—*may God have mercy on him*. He hailed from the province of Anatolia. When he studied the advanced sciences with the virtuous scholars of his time he supplicated to God: *My Lord! Increase me in knowledge!* (Qur'an 20:114). Consequently, he was endowed with an abundance of divine grace, excelling his peers.

Since advancing to higher ranks and progressing to higher standards is an innate part of human nature, Mevlana Melihi went to the land of the Ajam in order to rise high on the ladder of virtues. During his studies with the scholars of that land, he became companions with Maulana Jami, who was intoxicated with the cup of pure and true [spiritual] wine. After

Melihi imbibed from the cup of virtues through the grace of Jami's companionship, he returned to his noble and bountiful home and settled in the protected city of Constantinople in the early days after the conquest (1453). He had indeed drunk an excessive amount from the cup of knowledge: if those who are used to sipping from the bowl of divine virtues take even a sip of what he drank, they would become drunk, unconscious, and bewildered. Just one drop of the wine that he swallowed would make all the people of the world intoxicated.

> If one of the droplets we drank fell on the world, vines would appear
> From just one berry of our grapes all things would get drunk.

As he was so intoxicated with the tipsiness of the carefree cup, he became a wine lover and drinker until the end of his life: just like the wine jar he was never empty of wine. In all his life nothing made his heart and eyes blossom like a rose so much as a fragrant and pomegranate-colored wine. If he was not dead drunk, he was not himself. The tulip of his pinecone-shaped heart would only open up with the help of rose and tulip-colored wine. The withering rosebud of his mind would only become succulent with wine, and the dew-crying rose of his heart would only be calmed by the same. [. . .] He was not able to function properly unless the warming intoxication of the wine that bestows life and increases the spirits—which, in elegant speech, they call "the second spirit"—entered his body like a flowing spirit or flowed into his veins like the blood of life. Without drinking a few cups of wine he would not eat even one bite. [. . .]

The author of the *Shaqa'iq* (i.e., Taşköprülüzade Ahmed) has narrated from his father that the Arabic dictionary of *Sihah* by Jawhari (d. 1009) was preserved on the thread of the memory of this omniscient augur like pearls on a string. If one had difficulty with an Arabic word and explored it, Melihi would accurately recite from memory all the phrases and expressions related to this word from that dictionary.

One of the trusted pious friends told the following story: "When I was going to travel from Ajam to Rum (i.e., Greater Persia to the Ottoman lands), I visited his excellency Abdurrahman Jami and asked, 'I am going to Rum. Is there anything I can do for you there?' He answered, 'I have a companion there by the name Melihi. I am hearing that he now resides in the protected city of Constantinople. This treatise is my gift to this most virtuous man. Please, bring it to him.' When I arrived in the protected city of Constantinople a while later, I started asking around for Mevlana Melihi among the members of the group of the pious ulema, thinking he was one of them because he was friends with Molla Jami. One of them told me, 'Melihi is not a member of the ulema, who are steady in rectitude and prosperity. Instead, he dwells in the house of drunkenness—that is, the tavern—like a misfortune-bringing cup of wine. Go there, that's where you will find him.' Thereupon I searched for him, and indeed found him in a tavern. I conveyed to him the greetings of Maulana Jami and handed over his virtuous treatise. On [hearing] my message and words, he started weeping bitterly and said, 'The divine decree and the predetermined plan of fate have led me to

FIGURE 9. Wine tavern, early eighteenth century. Artist unknown. In *Hamse-i Atai*, Walters Ms. W.666, fol. 44a. The Walters Art Museum, Baltimore.

sin and iniquity, while they have led Maulana Jami to rectitude and prosperity. *The commandment of God is certain destiny* (Qur'an 33:38).' [. . .] After that, learned man (Melihi) spoke of scholars who defended fatalism, and blamed predestination and fate for his own plight, he said, 'Men of bad plight like me are not worthy of seeing such an unequaled treatise,' and he returned it to me. He remained at the spot where he was and continued with his unlawful ways. [Later,] he regretted his past deficient actions, and thought that there will be no good end for him because, despite [his ability for] jugdment, he had acted contrary to the things forbidden by divine law. So he filled the cups of his eyes with tears of remorse and let his teardrops flow and flow from his cheeks." [. . .]

They say that once Sultan Mehmed Khan Ghazi heard that Mevlana Melihi drank wine in the covered bazaar and sprayed his unclean sips on Muslims. As a result of this spraying incident, the sultan became concerned and ordered the wine-sellers not to give any wine to Mevlana Melihi. He threatened them with capital punishment and promised again and again a swift penalty. With this measure Mevlana Melihi had to refrain from the wine glass. As he no longer set foot in a tavern, he was designated a daily stipend of twenty-five akçe for his necessary expenses and lived for a few days abstemiously and virtuously. *Perhaps God is granting me virtue.* About this issue Mevlana Melihi made the following joke: "How on earth did the noble sultan believe them when they said about me, 'He spit wine on people'—me, who holds every glass of pure wine in high esteem, and who would not give away one drop of that precious jewel for all of his treasury!"

One day, some hateful and malevolent men saw the aforementioned virtuous Melihi drunk and complained to the sultan about him: "Mevlana Melihi is again secretly abusing the crystal cup that used to be the eye he saw through and the hand that held him; he is secretly longing for the sound of wine gurgling out from a narrow-necked vessel and the clamor of the beak-spouted jug. While he had previously promised in the presence of the comely sultan, he now broke his promise because of the goblet, and made the keeper of the tavern his spiritual guide and the 'staff of the old men' (i.e., wine) his helping hand."

Mevlana Melihi was a strange person,
The keeper of the tavern was his spiritual guide.
When he was not able to walk any more,
The goblet became his helping hand.

The noble sultan sent for him immediately and had his breath checked. Yet there was no smell of alcohol. He asked how this was possible, and urged and reproofed him, "What is the reason for your tipsiness? Speak the truth!"

If you desire in the world someone with a face like the sun,
Tell the truth like the true dawn.

Mevlana Melihi told him the circumstances and said, "The cup of my promised agreements is still intact. I have not crushed it with the rock of violation. Only I, who am ill from deprivation, gave myself an enema with this vital force and water of life as a remedy for my disease. That is what made me tipsy." Sultan Mehmed Khan Ghazi took pleasure from these words. He laughed heartily like the gurgling sound of liquor poured out from a pitcher, and he pardoned him for his sin.

Honesty is what brings God's satisfaction,
I have not seen anyone who was lost from the right way.

Sultan Mehmed Khan Ghazi's—*may God's grace and approval be upon him*—cup of living filled up and eventually the goblet of his life broke. Afterward Mevlana Melihi drank even more. From then on, he was preoccupied with drinking alcohol until his death. Like a bubble he always lusted for wine. Whenever he saw a cup of wine he would simply flop. He would spread out an old mat and take the place of honor wherever he spotted a goblet of wine.

. . . . Abstain from the elixir of life (i.e., wine),
For drinking one drop of it brings a thousand calamities.

We ask from God, *whose grace is wide and majesty is high*, that He—after Melihi has entirely drunk the wine of death from the hand of the cupbearer of the hour of death—may quench his thirst with the water of paradise [from the river of Kauthar]. May God let Melihi, who was ill with sinful thirst, obtain fresh life and immeasurable freshness through the stream of His forgiveness of which He has spoken in the verse: *A spring whence those brought near to God drink [in the gardens of paradise]* (Qur'an 83:28). Amen.

May God's grace be his friend and companion,
May Your forgiveness be the guide on his path.

NOTE: Melihi was a skillful poet who could write beautiful poetry. There was elegance in his witty poems, and sweetness in his pleasant works.

TWELVE

On Servants and Slaves

Mustafa Âli, d. 1600

TRANSLATED BY DOUGLAS BROOKES

A vast market in which tens of thousands of enslaved people changed hands year after year operated in the Ottoman lands. Most slaves were captured in wars or in raids on Christian villages to the north and northeast of the Black Sea or seized by slave traders on the Mediterranean Sea or in sub-Saharan Africa. Ownership of enslaved people constituted one of the markers of high social standing for all religious groups in Ottoman realms. Wealthy men and women seem to have owned the majority of slaves, who formed an important part of the workforce in upper-class households. Enslaved women, in addition to performing domestic duties in the households where they were held, were also often kept for sexual purposes. Enslaved girls had fewer rights than wives, which made them more convenient targets for slave owners' abuses—an arrangement that was likely also preferable for the wives. However, a child born to an enslaved woman was free and had a claim to the estate of her owner equal to that of a child by his legal wife.

  The sections below were composed by Mustafa Âli (1541–1600), a highly class-conscious bureaucrat born to a family of educated merchants. In 1560, he completed his studies at the leading Ottoman medreses of the day in Istanbul, showing great talent for writing both prose and poetry early in his life. To make a living, Âli took up positions in government and advanced to increasingly important posts. But life in the Ottoman bureaucracy was tough, with brutal competition and corruption, and long periods of unemployment punctuating his career. Âli used these periods to produce a staggering number of written works, mostly history texts and social commentaries. Sharp-tongued, imaginative, and quick-witted (any of which traits might have sabotaged his career), in 1581 he turned to penning the kind of works that would come to define his oeuvre: mordant, gimlet-eyed social commentary—lashing, humorous, brilliant, and never dull.

Âli's last major work before his death, *Tables of Delicacies Concerning the Rules of Social Gatherings* (*Meva'idü'n-Nefa'is fi Kava'idi'l-Mecalis*), is written in this vein. The wide-ranging social commentary—touching on wine taverns, narcotics, music, and sex, to name but four topics—was written with the purported goal of ridding society of corruption, and in the process revealed its perspicacious author's opinions on the customs of his day. In this excerpt he concentrates on household servitors (both enslaved people and hired servants). This was a favored theme of Âli's since it allowed him to vent on one of his pet peeves, incompetence among servants. He also expanded this theme into an allegory for the contamination, in his view, of the highest levels of the Ottoman bureaucracy by undeserving "rabble" (as he called them) among the few praiseworthy office holders. One suspects that for Âli this explained his failure to achieve the heights he deserved in government service. Perhaps unexpected is Âli's presentation of sexual intimacy between adult men and prepubescent boys ("beardless youths," to use his term) as the accepted norm in his world; what earns his reprobation is not this; it is the complaining ingrates and crude and incompetent bumpkins among his servants.

LANGUAGE: Turkish. Elaborate prose, embellished with internal rhymes, alliterations, double entendres, and puns, but overall in a chatty style, as if talking to an old friend, although a very well-educated one.

SOURCE: Facsimile: Baysun, M. Cavid, ed. *Mevaidü'n-Nefais fi Kavaidi'l-Mecalis* / Gelibolulu Mustafa Âli. Istanbul: Osman Yalçın, 1956. Transcription: Şeker, Mehmet, ed. *Mevâ'ıdü'n-nefais fî-kavâ'ıdi'l-mecâlis* / Gelibolulu Mustafa Âli. Ankara: Türk Tarih Kurumu Basımevi, 1997 (308–342). Translated by Douglas S. Brookes as *The Ottoman Gentleman of the Sixteenth Century: Mustafa Âli's Mevā'idü'n-Nefāis fī Kavā'idi'l-Mecālis (Tables of Delicacies Concerning the Rules of Social Gatherings)*. Cambridge, MA: Department of Near Eastern Languages and Civilizations, Harvard University, 2003 (60–104). The translation below slightly differs from the 2003 edition.

THE MANIFESTATION OF INCOMPETENCE IN SERVANTS

Servants (*hizmetkar*) used in buying and selling, or shameless and idle ones employed in matters connected with the bazaar sometimes display incompetence and laziness. When one says, "Go get such-and-such at the market," they say, "They don't have it," or they answer, "The shops are closed today." In short, they give some answer accompanied by a false claim without budging from their spot, without even going to the market in search of the requested object—that is, they invent pretexts and excuses and procrastinate. This demonstrates that they deserve chastisement and corporal punishment without delay, and merit immediate insult and humiliation. For, according to intelligent people, servants [must be] far away from indolence and apathy.

In fact, anyone who is too lazy to go to the market or who thinks of giving answers rooted in laziness and indolence should never in his life become a servant (hizmetkar). In the event

FIGURE 10. Slave market, Algiers, 1684. Jan Luyken (artist), in Pierre Dan, *Historie van Barbaryen, en des zelfs zee-roovers* . . . (Amsterdam: J. Ten Hoorn, 1684), 384–85.

that they do choose that line of work, intelligent people must not employ types like them. To open the mouth and give an answer right off without inquiring diligently into the matter to say, "They ran out" and "They don't have it," are most inappropriate situations quite extraneous to proper behavior. It is neither suitable nor acceptable for a servant (hizmetkar) who wants to be [called] a reliable person.. If this should occur, he will be simply a torment for his master (seyyid), and a signature with the words *Sahh 'indi* ("Correct in my estimation") to the document of his own indolence and neglect.

THE CONDITIONS OF SERVANTS AND OTHERS IN THE HOUSEHOLDS OF GRANDEES

If a servant (hizmetkar) detects a change in attitude in his benefactor (velinimet), and if he is clever at reading and writing or is a capable person skillful at comprehending and intuiting, he must first review his own actions along the lines of "My lord's (efendi) mirror has certainly clouded over. This was caused either by my own words or deeds, or else by the malicious chatter and duplicity of one of my enemies." Then he should diligently inquire into what manner of fault or transgression he may have committed.

Should the deficiency become apparent; should the cause for his having offended his master become clear, is it possible to clear the matter up by writing an entreaty as a petition and submitting it or else by finding an opportunity when they are alone together to confess his offense and ask forgiveness? He should not prolong matters but rather find a solution to the issue. He should realize that if he delays to do this, his illustrious master will grow more displeased and disgusted with him by the day, so that the outcome of the matter will not be good.

SERVANTS WHO ARE UNSUITABLE AND OF BAD STOCK

Slave girls (*kenizek*) of bad stock cannot become a lady of the house (*kadın*) simply because well born people show them interest and attention. Nor can low-bred female slaves (*karavaş*) take the place of women from a good family by virtue of their bedchamber service. For the thorny acacia cannot become a fruit-laden date palm just because it grows along the road to the Kaaba; nor does anyone hope for delicious, sweet fruit from a prickly shrub.

A lady of the house (*hatun*), who entrusts kitchen and pantry to her female slaves (*cariye*), and thinks that entrusting all her possessions to her slave girls (kenizek) is what being a "kadın" means—the meals prepared by this sort of respectable woman (*afife*) will possess no flavor; her conservatorship of the pantry will not be blessed. Because when the lady of the house does not enter the kitchen, she will never find the right flavor to suit the householder's palate. In truth, the worthiest among the female class are those who love to keep house. The ones who are prudent are those who personally watch over their favorite treasury and their chest of precious jewels.

Slave girls (kenizek) who are concerned about their livelihood, in particular the slave girls (cariye) of the bedchamber, guard themselves as far as possible from behavior and actions that disgust the heart. If they have the strength to do so, for their entire lives they do not let their lord notice when they go to the privy. This kind of cleanliness, self-supervision, and endeavoring to shun behavior that elicits disgust, are incumbent on not only slave girls but also houri-faced ladies. For their refinement and elegance of manner must surely be superior to that of the slave girls (karavaş).

This sort of behavior, which has as its goal modesty and good manners—specifically, avoiding the vulgarity of obviously going to the privy—is incumbent on the servant boys (*içoğlan*) and on the menservants (*harem hizmetkarı*) in great houses. They need to act like virgin maidens (*duşize*). As much as possible, they too must avoid situations that disgust the heart.

The beardless boy servants (*sade-ru hizmetkar*) most deserving of being put to death are those who malign their lords, who instead of constantly praising them in one way or another, heap vituperation on them. Next are those who ask permission to seek service in another house on account of some particular matter at which they took offense but should overlook. According to wise persons, it is then improper to retain in service the kind of servant (hizmetkar) who even dares to ask for permission. He should ask for what he lacks and make his needs known by saying, "I have no more undergarments or shirts or robes or shoes"—on condition that that he only does it when necessary and not all the time.

For the peerless moon-faced ones, the beautiful slave girls (cariye) and boys in household service (*gılman-ı harem*) who are usually mentioned as a pair like the houris (*hûr*) and the handsome young men (*gılman*) of paradise, the observance of good manners lies in not looking into the face of anyone other than their master and in imitating one another in wondrous modesty and reticence. Unacceptable behavior includes frequently entering and exiting a room, darting about with quick motions and not staying still in one place, and bending the knees when offering pure water or sherbet or coffee, by which I mean bending over and sticking out the behind when serving, so as to make those present at the gathering hope for different joys and pleasures.

Furthermore, the servant boys in household service (harem hizmetkarı) and bedchamber and mattress slave girls (*hizmet-i firaş ü bister cariyesi*) always reveal their utter absurdity when they repeatedly gather to a place and complain about their master; when, with eyes wide open, they follow the path of base ingratitude even while drowning in the sea of comfort and happiness provided by their master; when their warped notions cause them to turn up their noses at the gifts and favors offered them; when they view with complete nonchalance the boundless protection and courtesy extended them; when, after living thus for some time under their master's care, they say, "Well, what have I been able to get out of him?" and when they complain that, "So-and-so's servants (hizmetkar) have it easy; compared to them we've got nothing but trouble!" Even if this reflects the actual state of affairs, their blameworthiness and treachery stand revealed. For disdaining the manifold favors and generosity bestowed by the honorable personage who is their transitory worldly lord is the same as the error of rejecting the bounty of the Creator of the Universe, who is their real Lord.

Even those who are present when these complaints are aired but who say nothing are guilty of ingratitude. Those who do not hush this talk but rather listen with pleasure, even though they be purchased slaves (müştera kul), and those who do not report to their master those servants who habitually spout this kind of disparagement, are coconspirators and coequals in treachery with that vile person.

Verses by the author:

> Do those who constantly criticize their master
> Never improve, in this world?

> Even though all that they eat and wear are his,
> They deny this and thus fall from his favor.

> They are as one with the dogs
> Who howl day and night at their masters.

> Blasphemy is one thing, ingratitude is a second;
> They must not hope to see paradise.

> Almighty God is the Great Avenger;
> Do not hope that he will improve them and let them reach [paradise]. [. . .]

To sum up the lot of these despicable servants (hizmetkar), these ill-famed, contemptible, disgraceful servitors (gulam), whether they be a few treacherous boys in the inner service, or whether they be the no-account vermin who figure as ingrates in the outer service: they consume the delicious food of their lord and then afterward criticize him when they should be thanking him; and they wear clothes which protect them from the ravages of heat and cold both day and night, and which cover their outer immodesties both winter and summer and adhere to the proper way of dressing, and use their brocades and silks as undergarments and overgarments. But then after communicating their plentiful devotion and sincere praises to, first, the Creator of the Universe, and then to their master, instead of endeavoring to offer up a prayer for their good fortune to continue, they insult him in accordance with their perverted thinking by whining, "We are absolutely nude!" And they deprecate him by saying, "He practically makes us walk around stark naked!" even as they are drowning in all kinds of clothes. According to the conjecture of the educated class and the reasoning of the virtuous sheikhs and the confidants of intelligent persons, clearly the two selected angels who are the "Illustrious Scribes" immediately copy down the insults of these unfortunate persons in their book of evil deeds. They will first be astounded at their ingratitude and curse them all; then inform the illustrious angel who is entrusted with these matters by Almighty God. [. . .]

In sum, the legitimate members of this class—that is, the straight-grown cypresses worthy of the religion and the state—whether they be purchased slaves (*kul cinsi*) or hired servants (*huddam*), must consider both appointments and dismissals by their master with equanimity. Indifferent to poverty or wealth, they must not permit the perpetration of any situation that harms [the master]. This is because God, may his name be praised, who is the true benefactor of those who do not err while in the service of ephemeral masters, is the guarantor of arranging their affairs. Happiness in this world and the next belongs to those servants who on all occasions put their trust in God.

The purchased slaves (*gılman-ı müştera kul*) and hired servants (*yanaşma cinsi*) who will obtain their share of happiness are those wise servitors (*huddam*) who ask the Creator of Worlds for what they desire. While in household service they absolutely never allow the desire for an income to penetrate their thoughts. They are not so bold as to ask of their lord: "What will be my lot today or tomorrow?" They conduct themselves according to the meaning of *Say: All things are from God* (Qur'an 4:78). They put their trust in God, abandoning those vain hopes that are censured by both Almighty God and the people of this earth. [. . .]

If they should find [their lord's] house empty, they must not go and sit down on his mattress; if one of them does exhibit such impertinence and sits down in this fashion, they must not approve of it. Whatever is given them, regardless of whether it is a valuable gift or not—and let us suppose it has absolutely no value at all—nonetheless they must exhibit the purest joy. They must accept it and keep it with a thousand thanks as "our benefactor's gift," and act as true servants (*abd*). They must not give it to someone else in turn for as long as they live. They must believe that it carries special blessing and so never let it out of their possession. [. . .]

A dog is better than a slave (kul) who does not understand the obligations of gratitude—although the one is human and the other canine. An ungrateful slave looks like a human but is a lowly pig. He is a wild pig in the swamp of deviates. Whosoever always talks about his own work in service but does not remember the bounty of his lord, whosoever in his misguided thinking says, "I've given service for years," who utters, "I've received nothing from my owner (*mâlik*) except unfairness and punishment," will not improve his lot in this world, nor know the comfort afforded by good fortune and happiness. Neither will he establish a household and know the company of kith and kin, nor will he share in the joys of life and taste the fruits of the garden of sons and daughters. He is never able to improve his lot; he is doomed to misfortune until the end of his days; he becomes an ill-starred mendicant. If he is a slave (kul), he will not escape being sold from door to door. If he is a paid servant (yanaşma), he will not be able to make ends meet. He will become a marked man deserving to be put to death.

For beardless boys in household service (saderu harem hizmetkarı) to brand their arms constitutes utterly improper behavior, rebelliousness, and contrariness. Furthermore, inflicting slash wounds on themselves and tattooing their arms, but then to show them bandaged on some pretext (?) out of fear that the lord might see, is a form of rebellion necessitating that the culprit be tied up. These types must have their wings trimmed or broken without stopping to question or investigate. If a strong intercessor should appear on their behalf, he should be surreptitiously thrown into the sea.

This is because, if, despite his youth, he commits such impudence as to say, "I've fallen in love with one of the servants (huddam)," then he has committed treachery against his benefactor. If he says, "I am aflame with one who loves me secretly," then it is plain that he is inclined to forfeit his life. In both these situations, it is necessary to remove him. If tolerance be shown, then one decimates the modesty and proper breeding of the servants in that household (haremdeki hizmetkar).

But if they become addicted to hemp gum and opium and eat whatever they find out of desire for an opium paste and henbane dust, they must be thoroughly thrashed with a stick. Whipping and beating them with a rod is imperative and inescapable, to serve as a warning to others and that it becames obvious that they need to carefully resist each such addiction. However, it is only considered acceptable for them to drink coffee. Permission is granted for them to occasionally drink it provided that it is without hemp gum or opium. [. . .]

THE MANNERS OF SERVANTS: A SUPPLEMENT

To expect good manners and dignity from anyone of Albanian stock, to entertain the hope of fidelity from the impure Kurds, is the same as telling a hen who is cackling while laying eggs to stop cackling. Or it is the same as imploring a burglar or robber, "Don't kill me!" And it is utterly impossible for a slave girl (cariye) of Russian origin not to be a whore, or for a beardless page (sade-ru gılman) of Russian origin not to be a catamite. Similarly, it is baseless fancy to think that wine will not be the disgrace of the Cossacks, who are of that blood, or that degenerates among the black-faced Africans (*siyeh-ru Arab*) will not become infamous with the disgraceful acts they commit due to their addiction to wine and [the fermented] *boza* drink.

Pure-hearted, well-proportioned, polite, modest, and honest-behaving Bosnians and Croats are numerous. In the same way, intelligent, wise, and refined European Christians, elegant of dress, pleasing of gait and walk, nimble and agile, are abundant. That most of the abominable Georgians are soiled of clothing, filthy and dirty from top to bottom, whether they are wearing silk or linen, is manifest. Looking at their eyes and eyebrows, one might think them Circassians, perhaps opine that they are not without good breeding, but one would make a mistake in that reasoning and be deceived. On the other hand, the cleanliness of the Hungarians, and their nimbleness and quickness in service, are evident. Still, the treachery of some of them, and their offences against their lord owing to stubbornness and pertinacity, are legion.

Now, the beauty and courage of Circassians and Abkhazians, and the delicacy in their eyes and eyebrows and eyelashes, are indisputably apparent. However, owing to lack of intelligence some occasionally behave contumaciously and perversely toward their benefactors. But the infidels of Wallachia, Transylvania, and Moldavia resemble one another in character. Their beauty is somewhat pleasing, but their wickedness is ugly. That is, compared to the Hungarian and Croat infidels, their morals and temperaments are vile and offensive. Meanwhile, the lewdly dissolute Voynuks are a group of infidels devoid of beauty and comeliness.

Masters talk of the domesticity and friendliness of the stock called Amhara, Marya, and Damot from the Abyssinian people, of how with their gentle nature they are much grieved and offended at just a mild reprimand, of their effeminate behavior in making up and spreading out bedding, and of their familiarity with gentleness, like virgins. Compounded in many ways are the wicked characters, warped temperaments, and various foul and repellent qualities of other black-faced Africans, apart from the Nubians and the Takruris. However, it is impossible for any people not to have some good members among them. Yet, as they say for something low in number or few in quantity, "As rare as naught."

THIRTEEN

Children and Youth

Court Records, Sixteenth and Seventeenth Centuries

SELECTED BY YAHYA ARAZ; TRANSLATED BY HAKAN T. KARATEKE

It is generally very difficult to find comprehensive sources in the premodern world dedicated to "insignificant" groups of people. Children, who were thought to contribute to society only in the most marginal sense, are certainly one such group. Historians thus mine a variety of alternative sources for information about children—how they lived and how they experienced the world. Ottoman historians are lucky to have court records documenting the activities of underage people. That said, apart from the records that functioned as notary documentation, most cases handled by the court were criminal cases. Therefore, the cases in this chapter do not necessarily focus on the joyful moments in Ottoman children's lives and they should be viewed through their particular legal and/or punitive lens.

Most of the concepts we use today to delineate the ages that constitute childhood and adulthood derive from modern law. A "minor" or "underage" person in modern Western law is usually a person under eighteen years of age. The Ottoman law, following Islamic legal notions, accepted that adulthood began sometime between the ages of nine and fifteen. A person's biological growth and maturity, and not strictly his or her age, were taken into account when defining adulthood for legal purposes. Similarly, terms like "teenager," "youth," or "adolescence" are culturally determined and may not have exact counterparts in premodern societies.

The terms most commonly used to describe children in Ottoman legal documents are *sagire* (female) and *sagir* (male), which we understand generally as a person who has not reached puberty. A plethora of other designations are encountered in documents, and these only approximately correspond to certain periods in a child's or young adult's life. *Sabiye* or *sabî*, *oğlancık*, and *uşak* were usually used for children in their infant and toddler years. Among the common terms that were used for postpubescent youth are *mürahık*, *oğlan* (male or female), *emred* (a beardless young man), and *şabbe* (young woman). Normally, a girl was legally considered an adult (*baliğa*) after the age of nine, provided that she had reached biological sexual maturity and had started menstruating. The age for reaching adulthood for boys (*baliğ*) was twelve. The upper age limit for both sexes was fifteen; even if they had not biologically matured by that point, people were regarded as adults after that age. Legal adulthood meant, among other things, that individuals could make decisions about marriage, enjoy the legal right to inheritance, and assume criminal responsibility.

As with all premodern societies, children in Ottoman lands joined the workforce quite early in life. Many children helped their parents with chores or were employed in commerce or business in towns or cities. Outside urban areas, agriculture required an enormous labor force, and every soul was indispensable in farming communities. Many young girls were put in service as maids to wealthier families in larger towns. Such arrangements were often made for extended periods of time—sometimes until the child reached puberty. If full legal adoption was not possible in Ottoman law, legal agreements indicate that almost all rights and responsibilities of the child in service were transferred to the family that assumed the childrearing (*besleme*). These could be orphans or children who were surrendered by their biological parents because of economic hardship. The Ottoman courts functioned as notaries in these instances. On paper, the court determined a daily amount for the maintenance (*nafaka*) of the child for the biological family to pay to the caretaker family. In practice this was sometimes a guarantee for the latter to preserve their rights and deter the biological family from demanding the child back. But we should be careful about interpreting the position of a child taken into a household solely through the prism of the employer-employee relationship. The responsibilities of the caretaker family included the rearing and perhaps education of the child, as well as arranging their marriage when the time came.

Children in the neighborhoods of larger towns stood a chance of attending elementary schools (*sıbyan mektebi*), which were mostly for boys, but some were for girls as well. Middle or higher education was only possible for Muslim male individuals in medreses, following which employment opportunities were restricted to the judicial professions. Christian and Jewish children obtained literacy in neighborhood temples and "Sunday schools."

LANGUAGE: Turkish. Uncomplicated, formulaic legal language interspersed with technical terms.

SOURCE: Document 1: Üsküdar Court Records 17, fols. 3b. Doc. 2: Tophane Court Records 2, fols. 3b. Doc. 3: Beşiktaş Court Records 2, fol. 68a. Doc. 4: Istanbul Court Records 3, fol. 4a. Doc. 5: Istanbul Court Records 3, fol. 40b. Doc. 6: Manisa Court Records 64, p. 12. Doc. 7: Istanbul Court Records 12, fol. 38b. Doc. 8: Hasköy Court Records 23, p. 173. Doc. 9: Manisa Court Records 124, p. 53. Doc. 10: Hasköy Court Records 10, p. 57.

---

1. YORGİ IS ACCUSED OF BEATING AND VIOLATING A CHILD, 1548

The occasion for drafting the court record is the following: Mihal bin Yanni from the village of Çengel brought forth a claim in the court of law and said, "This Yorgi bin Nikola beat and violated (*vat'*) my young son (*sagir oğlum*) Aleksi."

[Yorgi] was questioned in the presence [of the plaintiff]. He denied. After his denial, Mihal was asked to produce proof in support of his testimony's truthfulness. He could not. Thereupon, Yorgi was asked to swear—in accordance with their false rites—on the Bible. He swore as per Mihal's demand.

Yorgi was acquitted from the charge. [The procedure] was recorded on request.

Date of the recording: Middle of Zilkade, year 955 (December 11–21, 1548).

Witnesses to the procedure: Kara Yusuf bin Abdullah | Ramazan bin Hüseyn | Hasan bin Abdullah | Gavra bin Yanni | Petroz bin Nikola | İstirati bin Dimo | Manos bin Kosta, carpenter | Nikola bin Poli | İstefan bin Dimitri | Kosta bin Marko | Yorgi bin Dimitri and others.

2. İSHAK BEATS A YOUTH AND VIOLATES HIM, 1558

[The occasion for drafting the court record] is the following: The youth (emred) named Beyti bin Nuh brought charges against İshak bin Yakub in the court of law and stated, "İshak happened across me when I was at the quay of the superintendent [of the customs] along with a boy [servant] of an agha. He made me come along and took me to a bachelor flat. As they drank wine there, he also forced me to drink some. Later, he came on to me and wanted to violate me, and when I refused, İshak beat (?) and violated me."

İshak was examined. He denied [the accusation] and said, "A janissary [introduced?] me to Beyti. I am acquainted with his uncle. The youth and I did sleep in a bachelor flat. I did not let him go that night." Recorded on request.

Date: Tuesday, fourth of the month Safer, year 966 (November 16, 1558).

Witnesses to the procedure: Mevlana Ahmed Çelebi, inheritance officer | Ali bin Mahmud | Durmuş bin Ahmed | Ahmed bin Dede | Muslihiddin bin Abdullah.

3. EMİR GIVES AWAY HIS DAUGHTER TO FOSTER CARE (FOR HOUSEHOLD HELP), 1561

The occasion for drafting the court record is the following: The individual named Emir bin Kemal stated, "I have given my biological young daughter (*sulbiyye kızı sagire*) Sitti Mümine, without maintenance, to the care of the holder of this document, Ali bin Selim, a porter, until she reaches puberty. I handed over [to Ali bin Selim] her lawful share of 121 akçe passed down from her deceased mother Şahi. Ali, the porter, may request one akçe per day in living allowance from me for however long he takes care of my daughter." [Ali bin Selim] accepted and confirmed the statement of the aforementioned applicant as explained above. On request, it was recorded in the register as it transpired.

FIGURE 11. Woman and boy, ca. 1650s. Artist unknown. Cod.Rål. 8:o no. 10 (*Rålambska dräktboken*), fol. 127. Kungliga Biblioteket, Stockholm.

Written on the twenty-second day of the month of Receb, in the year 968 (April 8, 1561).

Witnesses: Mahmud Bey, cavalry soldier | Ali bin Abdullah | Hasan bin Abdullah, butcher | Sadi bin Yusuf, chief of police | İlyas bin Abdullah, foot soldier | Ferruh bin Abdullah | Mehmed bin Mustafa, court officer and others from the present party.

4. BLOOD MONEY FOR A CHILD WHO WAS KILLED, 1617

Dimitri bin Mihal, a Christian from the inhabitants of the Kreseva village in the jurisdiction of the Dag county from among the counties of the district of Yenişehir in Rumeli gave a statement and expressed his thoughts in the presence of the *zimmi* Todoro bin Papa, the possessor of this document, at the exalted court of law: "My biological son (*sulbi oğlum*) Panayot, who was approaching the age of puberty (mürahık), was the apprentice of the aforementioned Todoro. Forty days before the composition [of this document], my son was found killed through injuries inflicted in [Todoro's] shop, located in Avratpazarı [quarter] of the protected [city of] Istanbul. As I am his rightful heir, we had a few lawsuits concerning the blood money for his killing. At present, owing to the mediation of some reconcilers, I dismissed said claims, we settled for ten thousand akçe, and I accepted the mentioned settlement. I obtained the mentioned amount of settlement money in full from the mentioned [Todoro's] hand.

I release him from all my claims, demands, oaths, and disputes related to the mentioned matter, and give up all my rights [pertaining thereto]. From this day on, if any claim is brought by me or my representative against the contents of this document, it should not be heard or accepted by the honorable judges."

After approval [of the parties] in person, it was recorded as it transpired.

Written on the twenty-fourth day of the auspicious [month of] Safer, in the year 1026.

Witnesses to the procedure: Haydar Agha, fief holder | Hüseyn bin Hasan | İnal bin Abdullah | Mehmed bin Hızır | Mehmed Çelebi bin Ahmed | Mustafa bin Mustafa and others.

5. AYŞE HATUN'S SON ABDUCTED AND A RANSOM IS DEMANDED, 1618

Ayşe Hatun binti Ömer, inhabitant of the Magnisa[lı] Çelebi neighborhood in the protected city of Istanbul, brought a claim in the exalted court of law in the presence of the individual named Mehmed bin Hasan from the "Arab" lands (*evlad-ı Arab*), "My biological son (*sadri oğlum*) Hüseyn bin İsa disappeared two months before the composition [of this document]. It was uncertain if he was dead or alive. Mehmed came to my house in the aforesaid neighborhood one day before the composition [of this document] and said: 'Your son is with me. If you give me [a payment or a present for] good news, I will deliver him to you.' He still employs pretexts to avoid handing my son over to me. I ask that he be interrogated and that he surrender my son to me."

[Mehmed] was questioned. He denied [the accusation]. The muezzin Musa bin Eyyub and Hüseyn bin Mustafa were present in the court of law in order to provide information. On being asked, they stated, "Mehmed indeed came a day before the composition [of this document] to Ayşe Hatun's house and declared in our presence: 'Your son is with me. If you give me [a payment or a present for] good news I will deliver him to you.'"

Recorded on request as it transpired. Written on the twenty-seventh day of the [month of] Cemaziyelevvel, in the year of 1027 (May 22, 1618).

Witnesses: Mehmed bin Ömer | Hüseyn bin Ahmed | Hüseyn bin Ali | Musa bin Yusuf | Ahmed bin Abdullah and others.

6. MEHMED SODOMIZES ABDULLAH (THREE YEARS OLD), 1630

[The occasion for the court record] is the following: Ali Efendi ibn Mustafa—*pillar of esteemed professors and eminent among the illustrious scholarly authorities*—currently a professor with the rank of fifty akçe per day at Sinan Bey medrese in the protected city of Magnisa (Manisa, in modern-day Turkey), requested the youth (*şab*) Mehmed bin Osman, a [law] offender, to the exalted court of law and filed a complaint against him in his presence, "Three days before the date of the writing [of this document], before sunset, Mehmed seized my three-year-old son Abdullah off the street and brought him in the house, in which he lived, in our neighborhood. As he was—*by God, atrociously*—committing an indecent assault, the child howled and cried. Hearing his screams, the Muslims came [to his help] and saw that the aforesaid criminal ran into the inside of his house while he tied the waistband of his trousers. They rescued the child. I demand that [Mehmed] be questioned and the law be executed."

On examination and denial, the aforementioned Efendi was asked to produce proof in support of his allegation. Mehmed bin Hüseyn, Arslan bin İbrahim, and Mehmed bin Ebubekir, competent Muslim witnesses, appeared in court in order to testify. After they were asked to testify in the presence of the aforesaid denier, they said, "In fact, at the said time, we heard the screams of the child [from] within the house. As we entered the house, Mehmed raised himself from atop of [him] and, tying the waistband of his trousers, fled into the inner part of the house. We saw Mehmed in this situation. We are witnesses to this matter and do testify." After they performed their legal testimonies, they were appraised and were accepted.

Thereupon, the Muslim residents of the aforementioned protected city who had knowledge of Mehmed's reputation were asked to submit information. El-Hacc Zati Beşe ibn Ahmed, Seyyid Mahmud Çelebi ibn Seyyid Mustafa, Durmuş Beşe ibn Abdullah, Yusuf bin Mustafa, and others appeared at the honorable court. They stated, "In truth, Mehmed is a criminal and an evildoer. He is never free from such despicable and abominable acts. From among his many despicable acts was to sit at the intersection of three streets in the mentioned protected city and expose his private parts. As we saw him take his penis in his hand in public and perform the cursed act, we drove him away. He is a pervert who commits all sorts of depravity and wickedness. It is necessary that his evil be repelled from Muslims." As they reported thus, [the court] acted as if to say "*The galleys are dearer to him*" (in reference to Qur'an 12:33) and handed [Mehmed] over to Abdullah Agha—*treasure among his peers*—the governor (voivode) of the said protected city, in order to be delivered to an official ship of the state.

> Recorded on request as it transpired. Written on the twenty-second day of the victorious [month of] Safer, in the year of 1040 (September 30, 1630).

> Witnesses to the procedure: Mehmed Çelebi bin el-Hac Cafer | Hüseyn Efendi ibn Abdullah | Sinan Efendi, professor | Mehmed Efendi ibn el-Hac Rıdvan | Hamza Efendi ibn Halil | Abdurrahman Efendi ibn Süleyman | Mustafa Çelebi bin el-Hac Ali | Mustafa Efendi ibn el-Hac İbrahim | Hatib Mahmud Çelebi ibn Abdülkerim | Ali Efendi bin el-Hac Mehmed and others from the present party.

7. HÜSEYN ADOPTS A YOUNG ORPHAN, 1663

Hüseyn bin Ali, gatekeeper at the imperial palace, one of the inhabitants of the Molla Gürani neighborhood in the protected city of Istanbul, stated in the exalted and respectable court of law and said, "The parents of this child (sagire) Rabia, who is under my care for upbringing, had died previously. It appears that she does not have anyone from her relatives or next of kin. It is my request that the child be left in my care and that a fair maintenance sum be assessed upon a rightful petitioner [of custody]."

The esteemed judge who has signed this document—*bliss be his and a fair resort [in the Hereafter]* (in reference to Qur'an 13:29)—ruled that the aforesaid child, Rabia, be left with Hüseyn Bey for adoption and upbringing, and he assessed and determined a maintenance sum of four akçe per day according to a rightful petitioner. It was permitted that, if necessary, a loan be taken out to be spent on the child and then, once a rightful petitioner is found, recovery be sought.

Recorded on request as it transpired. Written on the fifth day of the noble Zilhicce, in the year of 1073 (July 11, 1663).

Witnesses to the procedure: Davud Çavuş ibn Şaban | Mustafa Çelebi ibn Ali | Hızır Çelebi ibn Abdünnebi | Abdi Çelebi ibn Hüseyn | Şükrullah Çelebi ibn Mustafa | Receb Çelebi ibn el-Hac Murad | Mehmed bin Ramazan.

8. HALİL BEŞE ADOPTS A BEDRIDDEN CHILD, 1638

Halil Beşe bin ——, one of the inhabitants of the Kağıthane village, which is under the jurisdiction of the district of Havass-ı Aliyye (Eyüp), appeared at the district court and gave [the following] statement: "I found the child, called Yusuf, who is approximately ten years old and present in this court, close to the mentioned village and brought him to your presence. He suffers from an illness, is bedridden, and is not able to work. Since he does not have a guardian, I request that he be given to me for legal adoption and upbringing, and that a certain amount of akçe as a loan be assessed as maintenance for a rightful petitioner [of custody]."

Public proclamations were made. None of the child's relatives, who would be required by law to provide for him, was found.

The esteemed judge who has signed this document—*bliss be his and a fair resort [in the Hereafter]* (in reference to Qur'an 13:29)—as per the reason of public guardianship, gave the child to Halil [for adoption], and [Halil] accepted him for adoption and upbringing. Thereupon, a daily allowance of five akçe was assessed for [the boy's] subsistence, clothing, and other necessities. Permission was granted for a loan to be taken out, to be spent on the child, and thereafter recovery to be sought from a rightful petitioner for [custody of] the child.

Recorded as it transpired on request. Written in the beginnings of the sacred [month of] Muharrem, in the year 1048 (May 15–25, 1638).

Witnesses to the procedure: Yusuf Efendi ibn Bayram, preacher | Mehmed Çelebi ibn Ömer Usta | Ahmed Çelebi ibn Ali | Mehmed bin İsmail and others.

9. HALİL EFENDİ ACCUSED OF DEFILING THE CHILD HAVVA, 1665

Kurt bin Kayalı, an inhabitant of the Alaybegi neighborhood in the city of Magnisa, brought a claim in the court of law in the presence of the one responsible for composing this document, Halil Efendi ibn Nasuh, who is the imam of a blessed mosque located in the Deveciler neighborhood, and said, "Fifteen days before the composition [of this document], I left Havva, my biological deflowered young daughter (*sulbiye-i sagire seyyib kızım*), who is present in this court, with the aforesaid Halil Efendi, in order for him and his family to accommodate her, bring her up, as it is allowed by the law, put to work at tasks she can handle, and Halil Efendi to take care and supply her clothes. He took her into his home. Later, ten days before the composition [of this document], during the holy festival, at night, he approached Havva's bed in her sleeping quarters, put his hand in her bosom, and had sexual intercourse (*tasarruf*) with her. I request that he be questioned, his statement recorded, and his reputation investigated with the inhabitants of his neighborhood."

After questioning, Halil Efendi accepted the mentioned points but denied the adultery. The aforementioned plaintiff, Kurt, was asked to produce evidence in support of his allegation. He could not.

The aforementioned Halil Efendi's reputation was investigated with the inhabitants of the mentioned neighborhood. El-Hacc Mehmed bin Osman, Ömer bin Mustafa, El-Hacc Mehmed bin Mehmed, Mehmed bin El-Hacc Hızır, Veli bin El-Hacc Hamza, El-Hacc Ali bin El-Hacc Veli, Musa Çelebi ibn Mehmed, professor, İsmail bin Hasan, Şaban bin —— Mustafa bin El-Hacc Ali, and others appeared in the court of law in order to provide information. After legal inquiry, each one reported his good reputation by way of testimony, "In fact, Halil Efendi is a quiet, righteous, and pious person. To this day, we have not witnessed any wrongdoing of him. He has been the chosen elder [of our neighborhood] until now."

The aforementioned Kurt was prohibited from appealing [the case] with no cause.

Recorded on request as it transpired. Written on the eighth day of the honorable [month of] Şevval, in the year of 1075 (April 24, 1665).

Witnesses to the procedure: Ahmed Efendi ibn el-Hac Mahmud—*pride of the professors* | Muharrem Resmi Çelebi ibn Mustafa—*treasure among the professors* | Nabizade Abdullah Çelebi—*exemplar of the professors* | Bayram bin Hüseyn | Ebubekir bin Osman | Mehmed bin Ali Balı | El-Hac Ahmed bin Osman | Kadri, officer of the court | Hüseyn bin Halil and others.

10. MEHMED, A MUSLIM CONVERT, IS ORDERED TO PAY CHILD SUPPORT TO HIS FORMER WIFE, 1678

—— binti ——, a Christian woman, one of the inhabitants of the Piri Paşa neighborhood of the town of Hasköy, which is in the jurisdiction of the Havass-ı Aliyye (Eyüp) district, gave a statement and expressed her thoughts at the exalted court of law, "Mehmed bin Abdullah, who was formerly my husband and became honored with the glory of Islam gave me a definitive divorce. It is my request that a maintenance and clothing support be assessed from Mehmed's property for the sustenance, clothing, and other necessities of my minor biological son (*sadri sagir oğlum*), Ahmed and my biological daughter (*sadriye kızım*), Hadice, who are dependents of their father, Mehmed."

Five akçe per day for maintenance and clothing support was assessed from the property of their father, Mehmed, for each of the two minors (*sagiran*). [The woman] is permitted to take out the money as a loan in case of need and recovery should be sought from [Mehmed].

Put down and recorded as it transpired on request and handed over to the requester.

Written on the eighth of the month of Rebiülahir, in the year 1089 (May 30, 1678).

Witnesses to the procedure: Halil Efendi bin Ömer | Bali bin Mustafa | Ali Çelebi bin Abdurrahman | Dilaver Bey bin Abdullah | Abdullah Beşe bin Mehmed and others from the present party.

FOURTEEN

Women at Courts of Law

Court Records, Sixteenth and Seventeenth Centuries

TRANSLATED BY HAKAN T. KARATEKE AND N. İPEK HÜNER CORA

Historical sources were almost exclusively written by men about powerful men. Women featured very modestly in premodern historical accounts and usually only to the degree that they "meddled" in state affairs, had interactions with great men, or were members of the highest court society. Women from modest backgrounds were almost completely absent from historical narratives. If women did feature in fictional works, they were usually represented by stock characters with sexualized or devious overtones (see chapter 43). As feminist approaches in historiography emerged in the latter part of the twentieth century, historians attempted either to reread historical narratives in search of female perspectives or to look for new sources from which to glean details about women's lives. As has been pointed out in the chapter about "Children and Youth" above (see chapter 13), Ottoman court registers are one source offering a wealth of information about "insignificant" people who would not have been noted elsewhere.

Historians have been turning to these court records as one method of determining the socioeconomic involvement of women in Ottoman society, and in order to better understand their rights and how they were able to exercise them in the legal arena. Since people ordinarily went to courts only to resolve contentious issues or to have a transaction notarized, noncontentious elements of middle-class women's lives can only be ferreted out between the lines of legal documents. One historical approach to the particular lens of legal documents has been to systematically examine similar cases involving women (for example their economic activities) within a time period and to look for patterns in women's societal status. Some historians have been imaginative in reconstructing the stories of individual women if a court case is detailed enough or if the same woman appears several times in the register, thereby allowing us to learn more about her.

Examining these documents for clues about the lives of women in premodern Ottoman society has been enlightening; we now know much more about their social, economic, religious, and spiritual activities. The documentation of real women going about their lives sheds light on their varied socioeconomic class, linguistic and religious backgrounds, vocations, and ambitions, and it allows modern observers to be attentive to the diversities inherent in individuals. The historical record left by these documents cautions us to be careful about making sweeping generalizations about categories like "Middle Eastern women" or "Ottoman women."

One persistent perception of women in the Middle East has been that they held a servile position in the socioeconomic order. Modern historians have been challenging this essentialist view—mostly held by Western observers—as an increasing number of sources show examples of some women's independence in the social and economic spheres of the premodern Ottoman world. While we still lack sweeping comparative studies on women's activities, a much more diverse and less monolithic picture of women's lives emerges from the documents. This picture defies the long-standing prejudicial perceptions of Middle Eastern women, and it forces us to be especially cautious about accepting women's status as prescribed by religiolegal normative works as a pure reflection of reality.

The court records of a region, like the ones from Istanbul in this chapter, should not be taken as absolutely representative of the lives of all Ottoman women. They are valuable snapshots from a section of Ottoman society at a given time in a given area.

LANGUAGE: Doc. 7 in Arabic, the rest in Turkish. Uncomplicated, formulaic legal language interspersed with technical terms.

SOURCE: Document 1: Üsküdar Court Records 1, fols. 41a–41b. Doc. 2: Üsküdar Court Records 26, fol. 64a. Doc. 3: Galata Court Records 5, p. 128. Doc. 4: Üsküdar Court Records 56, fol. 40b. Doc. 5: Topkapı Sarayı Müzesi Arşivi 692, fol. 36a. Transcription: Doğan, Muzaffer. "Balıkesir Şeriyye Sicilleri: TSMA 692 No'lu Defter vr. 1b–45b." Master's thesis, Marmara University, Istanbul, 1989 (109). Doc. 6: Topkapı Sarayı Müzesi Arşivi 692, fol. 39a. Transcription: Doğan, Muzaffer. Ibidem, p. 119. Doc. 7: Galata Court Records 20, fol. 34a. Doc. 8: Ahi Çelebi Court Records 1, fol. 4b. Doc. 9: Galata Court Records 90, fol. 4a. Doc. 10: Eyüp Court Records 90, fol. 79a.

1. HÜSEYN TAKES AN OATH NOT TO TAKE A SECOND WIFE, 1515

The reason for drafting the document is that Hüseyn bin Mustafa gave the following statement in the court of law: "If I marry [a second wife] without the permission of my wife Gülbahar, the woman shall be divorced from me with a threefold [final and irrevocable] divorce the moment I marry her." This being the case, it was recorded in the register at the aforementioned Gülbahar's request.

Written in the middle days of [the month of] Rebiülevvel, year 921 (end of April 1515).

Witnesses to the content [of the proceeding]: Han Agha bin Ali | Mehmed bin Pir Ahmed | Ramazan bin Ahmed | Yusuf bin Abdullah | Şirmerd bin Abdullah.

2. HÜSNA HATUN BUYS A HOUSE, 1564

The occasion for drafting the record is that İlyas bin Hasan, a resident of Üsküdar proper, appeared at the noble court of law and voluntarily gave the following statement in the presence of Hüsna Hatun, who had built a mosque in the Sultan neighborhood and acts as a trustee in her own endowment: "I sold the house in my ownership in the Davud Pasha neighborhood, enclosed and separated by the boundaries on one side by Hacı Ahmed's property, one side by the house of Köse Şeyh, one side by Şaban's property, and one side by a public road. [I sold the house] with its fixtures and appurtenances by way of *istiglal* (whereby the old owner continues to use the property and pays rent) to the possessor of this document Hüsna Hatun for the current value of 1500 akçe."

After both parties completed the transaction, [İlyas] stated, "I accept the renting of the mentioned house for 150 akçe for a full [year] from the drafting of [this] document." As Hüsna Hatun also confirmed and verified [the transaction] in person and verbally, the legality of the rental and the sale was decided. It was recorded on request.

Happened thus and was recorded during the final ten days of Cemaziyelahir, year 971 (beginning of January 1564).

Witnesses to the proceeding: Ali bin Hacı Behram | Ali bin Abdullah | Ali bin Süleyman | Mustafa bin Mehmed | Mustafa bin Mehmed.

3. AYŞE GRANTED DIVORCE FROM MEHMED BECAUSE OF HIS APOSTASY, 1576

Mustafa Çelebi bin Bali Bey—*pride of his peers and notables*—a steward (*müteferrika*) of the imperial court and the women whose names are Fatıma binti Abdullah and Cansever binti Abdullah, testified in the presence of Mehmed Bey bin Abdullah, a former commander in the *segban* regiment (*segban beyi*) of the exalted [Imperial] Council, "When Mehmed Bey saw his wife Ayşe Hatun binti Bali Bey—*pride of virtuous women*—read the glorious Qur'an, he said: 'I crap on your head. I crap on the Book you read. Go read your Qur'an in the brothel (*zübhane*).' We were present and heard [what he said]."

Abdi bin Mehmed and Mustafa bin Hüseyn testified in the presence of Mehmed Bey: "When they informed [us] that Mehmed Bey [saw] his wife Ayşe Hatun read the Qur'an and said, 'I crap on your head. I crap on the Book you read. Go read your Qur'an in the brothel,' [and we confronted him about it], he replied: 'I said it. So what!'" After legal confirmation, their testimonies were deemed acceptable.

It was ruled that Ayşe Hatun be separated from Mehmed Bey because of his apostasy. What transpired was recorded on request.

Written on thirteenth of Zilkade, year 983 (February 13, 1576).

Witnesses to the proceeding: Hacı Mahmud bin Sinan Çavuş | Üveys Çelebi, bookkeeper | Murad Çelebi bin Mustafa Çelebi, bookkeeper | Mehmed Çelebi, bookkeeper | Mehmed bin Şeyh Mah——

4. AYŞE CONFRONTS HER HUSBAND FOR FOOLING AROUND, 1583

[The occasion for drafting the record] is the following: Ayşe binti Abdullah, a resident of the Mamure neighborhood, rendered the following deposition in the court of law in the presence of her husband, Mehmed the lampmaker: "Mehmed is constantly together with a woman named Cihan, who had been his wife before, whom he [later] divorced. When I confronted him [by saying], 'You go to Istanbul and many other places together [with Cihan]. You drink wine and, in addition to much mischief, you carry on with her [even though] she is legally marriageable to you,' Mehmed said in response, 'So, I carry on [with her], what of it? Even if I divorced her, she is my previous wife.' I demand the necessary action."

On questioning, Mehmed denied [having said those words] and stated, "Indeed, I divorced Cihan, and have not yet married her [again]. My wish is to marry her, [which is why] I carry on with her."

On the summoning of witnesses, Himmet bin Mehmed and Derviş bin Abdullah testified, "When [Ayşe] accused Mehmed in the quoted fashion, he uttered in our presence, 'So, I [carry on with her]; she was my wife.'" Their testimonies were recorded at the request of Ahmed, the chief of police.

[Date: ca. end of June 1583].

Witnesses to the proceeding: Mirza bin İbrahim, market supervisor | Mehmed bin Abdullah | Mehmed bin Şaban | Ahmed bin Mahmud | Murad bin Abdullah.

5. RAHİME MARRIES A NEW HUSBAND, 1593

[The reason for drafting the record] is the following: Muslihuddin bin Ali, the legal representative of the person named Süleyman bin Ramazan, appeared at the noble court of law. He set forth a claim in the presence of Mehmed ibn Ramazan, the husband of Rahime binti Abdullah, who is the bearer of this document, and said, "When my client Süleyman had gone to Istanbul, Rahime was in marital bond with him. Without [Süleyman] divorcing

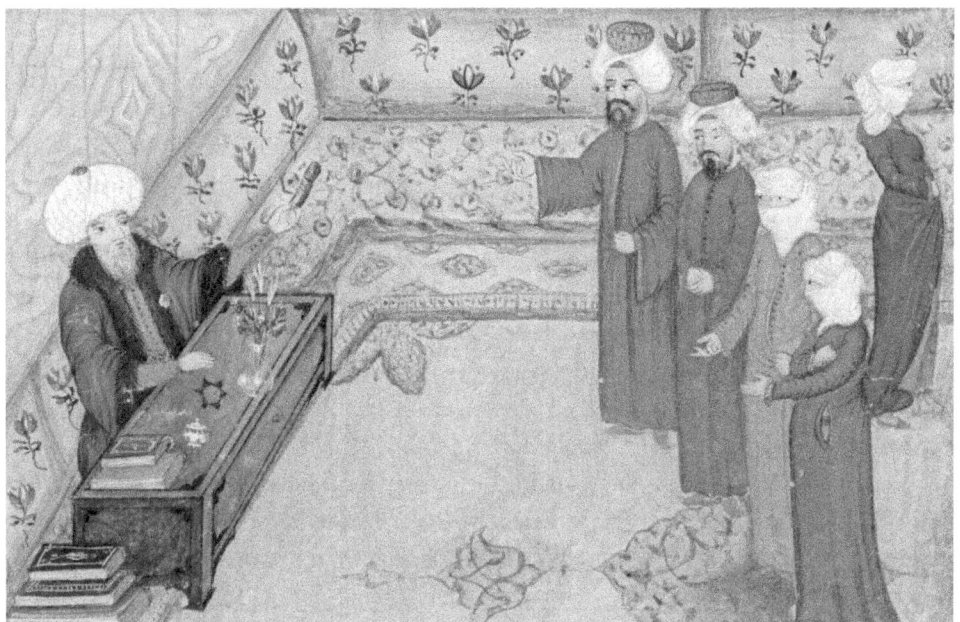

FIGURE 12. Women at a court of law, early eighteenth century. Artist unknown. In *Hamse-i Atai*, Walters Ms. W.666, fol. 51b. The Walters Art Museum, Baltimore.

her she married another [person]; [in other words,] after Süleyman's departure, Mehmed wed her. At present, I request the aforesaid woman['s return] on behalf of my client Süleyman."

Mehmed stated in response: "Previously, Süleyman had stolen the mule of Hacı Bekir. When he had been suspected and [later] apprehended, he had stated: 'If I do not bring the mule within a month and hand it over to Hacı Bekir, my wife Rahime shall be divorced with a threefold [final and irrevocable] divorce,' thus pronouncing a conditional divorce. [Süleyman] did not deliver the mule to Hacı Bekir within the stated time period. When he left for Istanbul, the condition was fulfilled [for the annulment of the marriage]. After his departure, [Rahime] married me."

Muslihuddin denied this. When [Mehmed bin Ramazan] was asked for proof, el-Hac Turgud bin Mahmud and İbrahim ibn Abdi were present at the court as witnesses and confirmed his statement as elucidated. Their testimony was deemed within the realm of acceptable, and thus [Rahime] was [confirmed] as belonging to Mehmed.

[Recorded] on the aforementioned date [as in the previous cases] (ca. mid-August 1593).

Witnesses to the proceeding: —— | Mehmed ibn Kasım and others.

6. AYŞE DEMANDS HER DOWRY FROM THE HEIRS OF HER LATE HUSBAND, 1593

[The reason for drafting the record] is the following: Ayşe binti Ali, the wife of the deceased Ahmed bin Ali, who was from the village Yakub, a dependency of the town of Balıkesri, summoned Şaban bin el-Hac Memi, who is the legal guardian of the late Ahmed's young daughter, and Meryem binti Maden, who is Ahmed's other wife, to the court of law. [Ayşe], who initiated [the drafting of] this document, rendered the following deposition in their presence: "Previously, my deceased [husband] had in his possession my deferred dowry, worth a thousand akçe, and also the upfront payment of my dowry consisting of a quilt, two mattresses and two pillows. I demand these. [Şaban and Meryem] should be questioned."

They were questioned and, on [their] denial [of any knowledge of the dowry agreement], two people named Ahmed bin Gökmen and Memi bin Süleyman, who were present at the noble court of law as witnesses from among the disinterested and fair-minded Muslims, testified, "Indeed, the late Ahmed had married Ayşe in our presence by providing her with two mattresses, a quilt and two pillows as the upfront payment of the dowry and a thousand akçe as deferred dowry. We were witnesses to this matter and do testify." Their testimonies were found in the realm of acceptance.

Ayşe was asked to take an oath to the effect that she had not forgiven the aforementioned amount of thousand akçe to the deceased. She swore by God, and [the proceeding] was recorded as it transpired on request.

[Date: Beginning of Muharrem 1002 (early October 1593)].

Witnesses to the proceeding: Mehmed bin Sevim | Mustafa bin Şaban and others.

7. KAMİLE SEEKS HER FREEDOM FROM SLAVERY ON HER OWNER'S DEATH, 1597

Mevlana Mehmed bin Hüseyn, the imam of the Kassab Halil mosque located in the guarded city of the Constantinople; el-Hac Hüdaverdi bin Hasan from the Sirkeci neighborhood, which belongs to the neighborhoods of the town of Kasımpaşa; and el-Hac Yusuf bin Mehmed from the same town appeared at the noble court of law. On being called to testify to the legally cognizable claim brought at the request of the holder of this document, Kamile binti Abdullah—who is blond, hazel-eyed, and of Russian origin—they testified in the presence of el-Hac Mustafa bin Mehmed, who had been appointed as the legal guardian of Fatıma, the young daughter of el-Hac Süleyman, who had previously passed away on his way to pilgrimage to Mecca. They attested that the plaintiff [Kamile], who was in the possession of the deceased [el-Hac Süleyman] at the time of his death, had attained the status of a "mother of a child" (*ümmü'l-veled*) because she had given birth to Fatıma, and [thus] became free after the death of her owner. As their testimonies conformed to the conditions of admissibility and were legally acceptable and valid, [Kamile's] freedom has accordingly been granted.

Occurred thus and was recorded in the beginnings of [the month of] Cumadelula, year 1006 (mid-December 1597).

Witnesses: Hüsrev bin Abdullah | Mehmed Yusuf | Musli, court officer, and others.

8. FATIMA AND HER OPPONENTS AGREE ON THE OWNERSHIP OF A DIVIDER WALL, 1653

Fatıma Hatun binti Halil Çelebi, a resident of the Üskübi neighborhood of the protected [city of] Istanbul, is currently the occupant—through the upfront payment and recurrent rental—of a shop belonging to the Rüstem Pasha endowment located outside the Zindan Gate, which is one of the gates of the fortress of the protected [city of] Istanbul, and a storeroom belonging to the Mehmed Agha endowment.

Mehmed Bey bin Ahmed—whose power of attorney in the matter below was legally established, in the presence of [Fatıma's] legal opponents, through the testimonies of Mehmed Beşe bin Hüseyn and Muharrem Beşe bin Mustafa—who are recognized by law as knowing the person of [Fatıma].

El-Hac Mustafa bin el-Hac Bali and Mehmed Çelebi bin Ahmed el-Yesari are tenants in common—through the upfront payment and recurrent rental—of a shop and a storeroom belonging to the endowment of late Ahi Çelebi, which are again located in the mentioned site.

[These two parties] were present at the court of law. Each one of them gave the [following] statement and deposition in the presence of the other: "A wooden divider on five pillars was put up between the shops and the storerooms that are at our disposal, as mentioned above, by the permission of the [endowment] trustee. Half of it having been constructed by the client Fatıma Hatun and the other half by el-Hac Mustafa and Mehmed Çelebi, the divider does not belong solely to any of us but is a shared [property]. We [therefore] request that it be recorded in a legal document."

After each of the deponents confirmed the statement of the other, [the proceeding] was recorded as it occurred on request.

Written on twenty-third of [Cumadelahire], year 1063 (May 21, 1653).

Witnesses to the proceeding: el-Hac Mustafa bin Şaban | Himmet Beşe bin Ahmed | el-Hac Mustafa bin Ahmed | Mahmud Beşe bin Şaban and others.

9. İSMİHAN SEEKS DIVORCE AFTER REACHING PUBERTY, 1663

İsmihan binti Sarı Ali, a virgin adult resident in the Bedreddin Bey neighborhood from among the neighborhoods of the town of Kasımpaşa, which is a dependency of the protected [district of] Galata, gave the following statement and deposition in the presence of the holder of this document, Bayram bin Mustafa, at the court of law:

"Rabia binti Perviz, who is my mother and present in this court, had me marry and conclude a marriage contract with Bayram for a deferred dowry of 1,500 akçe while I was a minor. I am currently not consummated in marriage, and as I reached adulthood, I demanded separation by my own volition in the presence of a legal arbiter. Following the legally required oaths, the contract between us was annulled by the judge. I renounced my right to the mentioned dowry at the amount of 1,500 akçe and released Bayram from all my claims and gave up all my rights [pertaining thereto]. From now on, I have no claims from or disputes with him related to the mentioned matter by any manner or means."

After legal ratifications, [the proceeding] was written on request as it occurred.

On twenty-fourth day of the peerless [month of] Receb, year 1073 (March 4, 1663).

Witnesses [to the proceeding]: Abdullah Çavuş bin Abdullah, usher [of the court] | Mustafa Çelebi bin Mehmed, foot soldier | Mehmed bin Şaban | Mehmed Çelebi bin Abdullah | Mustafa bin Ahmed | Mehmed bin Hızır | Musa bin Receb | Zülfikar bin İbrahim | el-Hac Cafer bin Yakub.

10. SALİHA REACHES SETTLEMENT IN HER LAWSUIT, 1680

A Gypsy woman named Saliha binti Derviş, resident of the Avcıbey neighborhood adjacent to Egri Gate, which is one of the gates of the fortress of the protected [city of] Istanbul, [appeared] at the exalted court of law.

She voluntarily gave the following complete statement and deposition in the presence of the Gypsy man named Mehmed bin İsmail, who bears this document: "Previously, when I had brought suit against Mehmed, saying, 'You deprived me of my virginity,' he had denied my claim, after which lots of quarrel and strong hostility occurred between us. At present, reconcilers acted as mediators and established a settlement based on denial (*an inkar*) between us concerning my lawsuit for the amount of twenty [Dutch] lion *guruş*. I too accepted the mentioned settlement and took full physical possession of the twenty lion guruş of settlement money from Mehmed's hand. I release Mehmed from all my claims related to the mentioned matter and give up all my rights [pertaining thereto] with no possibility of [further] dispute."

After legal approval, [the proceeding] was recorded on request as it transpired in the [abovementioned] manner.

On eighteenth day of the peerless [month of] Receb, year 1091 (August 14, 1680)

Witnesses to the proceeding: Hüseyn Agha bin Kaya | Hüseyn bin Mehmed | Hüseyn bin Oruc, chief of Gypsies | Mustafa bin Mehmed | Mustafa bin İsmail | Sefer bin Hasan | Hasan bin Derviş | Bayram bin Mustafa | Sefer bin Mehmed.

FIFTEEN

Prostitutes and Pimps

Court Records and Imperial Council Registers, Sixteenth
and Seventeenth Centuries

TRANSLATED BY MARINOS SARIYANNIS

Although prostitution was a widespread phenomenon in Ottoman society, it is hardly visible in most historical sources. The laws have little to say on the matter; if caught, a sex worker would normally be accused of *zina* or extramarital sexual intercourse, meaning that she was liable for a fine, but there is nothing specific to the punishment that differs from that of an adulteress. The Ottoman code of law prescribed monetary fines for adultery; fines were collected from persons who committed fornication according to their wealth and their marital status. The seventeenth-century version of the Ottoman code of law stipulates that "if the fornicator is married and rich, possessing one thousand akçe or more, a fine of three hundred akçe shall be collected from him," whereas an unmarried fornicator of the same means was to pay one hundred akçe (the fines for females were comparable). Regulations were stricter against procuring or trafficking, and they were more analytical when the procuring or trafficking interfered with the functioning of the slave market. Procuring usually incurred corporal punishment or imprisonment or both in addition to monetary fines. Judges determined the precise sentence in accordance with the severity of the crime.

There are relatively few cases of prostitution recorded in the judicial registers. This is owing in part to the strict statutes of Islamic law, which required the eyewitness testimonies of four adult males to prove illicit sex, but it is also because none of the involved parties would be eager to go to court. Still, there are a few cases in which the chief of police, the *sübaşı*, would bring a girl to court with the accusation, not of adultery, but of associating with strangers (*na-mahrem*). More frequently, "decent" residents of a neighborhood would ask for a "morally deviant" woman or sex worker to be expelled. It is always difficult to understand whether a given judicial case concerned professional prostitution, adultery plain and simple, or even flirtation that disturbed the rectitude of the neighborhood. It has been argued that

Ottoman legal practice was deliberately euphemistic in labeling infringements around adultery in order to flexibly adjudicate and move away from strict punishments. Decrees and prohibitions are sometimes more informative, since they are not constrained by the limitations of Islamic law and are explicitly concerned with public morality and order.

The examples below represent the main patterns of urban prostitution in Ottoman cities. It was typical that a sex worker received customers in her own house; frequently, more than one girl would be associated with the business. Sometimes the house would belong to a procurer or a procuress (who may be a sex worker herself). Poorer girls, hanging out in taverns or streets, are also seen in the documents. We can also discern from some legal documents and imperial decrees another, more formal pattern of trafficking, whereby slave traders rented out concubines using legal loopholes. Romani populations or other nomadic groups were often accused of organized prostitution.

In general, it seems that by the sixteenth century jurists had reached a consensus that prostitution in and of itself was tolerable, whereas procuring, by contrast, was a crime according to both Islamic law and the Ottoman legal codes. Sex workers were mostly prosecuted at the behest of neighborhood inhabitants, and the defendant usually faced nothing but expulsion to another neighborhood, or in more serious cases, to another city. As in other criminal cases, there was no permanent branding of sex workers by the authorities; it was public opinion that constituted the main threat to their activities.

LANGUAGE: Turkish. Court records in uncomplicated but formulaic language interspersed with technical legal terms. Records of the Imperial Council (*mühimme*) in an uncomplicated and formulaic language, with their specific pompous phrasing.

SOURCE: Document 1: Mühimme Registers 5, p. 121, case 281. Doc. 2: Mühimme Registers 7, p. 226, case 623. Doc. 3: Üsküdar Court Records 51, 55a. Doc. 4: Mühimme Registers 52, p. 7, case 22. Doc. 5: Üsküdar Court Records 56, 69b. Doc. 6: Üsküdar Court Records 84, 39b. Doc. 7: Mühimme Registers 91, p. 73, case 233. Doc. 8: Galata Court Records 90, 28b. Doc. 9: Eyüb Court Records 90, 117a. Transcription: Documents 1–2, 4: Ahmet Refik [Altınay], *On Altıncı Asırda İstanbul Hayatı (1553–1591)*. Istanbul: Enderun Kitabevi, 1988 (38–39, 42). Transcription and facsimile: Document 7: 91 *numaralı Mühimme Defteri (H. 1056 / M. 1646–47): Özet, Çeviri Yazı, Tıpkıbasım*. Istanbul: T.C. Başbakanlık Devlet Arşivleri Genel Müdürlüğü, 2015 (p. 150, case 233).

---

1. ARAB FATI AND HER COMPANIONS ENGAGED IN PROSTITUTION, 1565

Order to the judge of Galata: Since you have sent a copy of the judicial register to my Abode of Felicity, and reported:

People from the neighborhood of the mosque of the deceased prince [Cihan]gir— *may he rest in peace*—outside Galata came to the court of law and declared the

FIGURE 13. Two pages from a court register, sixteenth century. Galata court register, no. 20 (1596–99), fol. 33b–34a, İstanbul Müftülüğü Şeriyye Sicilleri Arşivi. Reproduced in *İstanbul Kadı Sicilleri: Galata Mahkemesi, 20 Numaralı Sicill (H. 1005–1007 / M. 1596–1599)* (Istanbul: İSAM Yayınları, 2012).

following, "In our neighbourhood the women named Arab Fatı, Narin, and Kamer, and Balatlı Ayni, who are also known as Nefise of Crete and Atlu Ases, are notorious for their promiscuity (*yaramazlık*)."

An officer was sent to summon Arab Fatı but she went missing. The other [women] came [to the court], and the community of the Muslim [inhabitants of the neighborhood] testified in their presence that they were promiscuous. Professor Mevlana Muhyiddin, the scribe Mehmed, İlyas, Sinan Halife, and other Muslims from among the people of the neighborhood [further] gave testimony that especially Balatlı Ayni is notorious for her promiscuity. When previously, the imam, the muezzin, and our congregation came in front of [Balatlı Ayni's] house in order to inspect her ways, she scolded: "Damn your imam and your judge and your shari'a!" Previously, she had been caught in the Kalafatçı neighborhood with a stranger. Besides, she had been also caught with a stranger in Arab Fatı's house. [Her house] is a place of depravity and baseness. We request that her house be sold and she be expelled from our neighborhood.

I order that, as soon as my noble decree arrives, you shall force the aforementioned women to sell their house and expel them from the city. As for the wife of the janissary who blasphemed, after making her take a renewal of faith, you shall imprison her until her husband returns.

So written.

[Deliberated] at the [Imperial] Council on 2 Rebiülahir, year 973 (October 27, 1565).

The military judge presented [the case], the order was recorded and drafted accordingly.

Handed over to the chief sergeant-at-arms.

2. MEN MARRYING ARRESTED PROSTITUTES TO FREE THEM, 1568

Order to the judge of Istanbul: It has been heard that some individuals wish to marry the prostitutes (*fahişe*) who were caught during the [recent] inspection and imprisoned. I order that, as soon as [this decree] arrives, you admonish those marrying prostitutes, such as these, that after marrying them they shall not stay in Istanbul but shall take [their wives] and move to other places. After having warned them, if such men stay in Istanbul with the prostitutes they have married, let [the women] be once again imprisoned.

So written.

Handed over to Sergeant Hacı Hızır on 5 Receb 975 (January 5, 1568).

3. ALİ BALİ CONFESSES TO KEEPING A PROSTITUTE AT HIS PLACE, 1580

The occasion for drafting the record is the following: The people of the neighborhood filed a complaint saying that Ali Bali bin Karagöz, a falconer and an inhabitant of the Hamza Fakih neighborhood, in the protected [district] of Üsküdar, would constantly keep prostitutes (*fahişe avrat*) at his bachelor apartment and engage in acts of depravity. When Ali Bali was summoned to the noble court, he voluntarily confessed, "I have a whore (*kahbe*) in my bachelor flat; she watches over it." On request [the proceeding] was recorded.

In late Safer, year 988 (April 6–15, 1580).

Witnesses to the proceeding: el-Hac Mustafa bin Muharrem | Nasuh bin Hamza | Cafer bin Abdullah and others.

4. PROCURERS TRAFFICKING CONCUBINES FOR PROSTITUTION, 1583

Order to the judge of Istanbul: You have sent a petition and submitted that a large group from among the people of the covered bazaar of the guarded [city of] Istanbul, the slave sellers, the brokers, and other experts had come to the court of law declaring the following:

> Contrary and contradictory to the old custom, a group from among the urban dwellers, going by the name of "women [slave traders]" or "young [girl] slave traders," [had the idea to] bring the concubines of some Muslim men and women to the market in order to sell them. They pretended to make a transaction with some ne'er-do-wells who passed for customers. The [dealers] take a few akçe for the sale. [The buyers] go to their rooms to see [the concubines], then take them and leave. After having possessed these concubines for some days, they give them back to their dealers—and the concubines have formed the habit of not running away.
>
> There are other dealers who bring their own wives as customers to the bazaar. While the concubines of some Muslims are being auctioned, they make a [selling] gesture with their foot (?) with a pretext, saying that the alien woman [purchaser] has a bid, and take the [concubine] to their wives at a lower price than she is worth.
>
> There are other brokers with no guarantors (i.e., without a license) who bring some concubines from women slave traders as an unclaimed slave to the rooms of ne'er-do-wells, producing much corruption. Those who cause such offenses and detestable acts are prostitutes and brokers with no guarantors, who pass themselves as slave traders, [but] buy and sell [temporary] contracts.
>
> From now on, women should be prohibited from slave trade. Dishonest brokers with no guarantors should also be removed. Thus will not only the damage to the society be eliminated but also the affairs of the slave traders be organized.

You said that they petitioned you about their circumstances with such mischief makers. I order that, as soon as [this decree] arrives, you do as you must concerning this matter: From now on, do not allow those kinds of women in the slave trade and prohibit them. Also, remove the brokers with no guarantors and warn [people] and arrange [the circumstances] such that there is no possibility of misconduct and mischief as described above. If, after warning, there are [still] some who do not take heed and who continue with their mischievous conduct, you shall deal with them according to the unswerving law. You shall report on the measures you proceed with.

By the hand of Muhyi Efendi.

[In the month of Şaban 991 (August–September, 1583)].

5. CARAVANSERAI RAIDED, FATIMA APPREHENDED DRUNK, 1583

[The occasion for drafting the record] is the following: The janissary Bekir bin Abdullah, from among the patrolmen of the Mamure neighborhood, appeared at the court of law and stated, "I was informed that some toughs bring prostitutes to the caravanserai of Arpacı Hüseyn. I went there together with the undersigned Muslims, [but] the fellows fled. One left his raincoat, his jacket, his vest, his belt, two old felt caps, an old shirt, and his muslin; two *şahi* [coins] were also found in his clothes. After much tumult [and searching] we found this Fatıma binti Mehmed with them and brought her here. She is still drunk, her mouth smells of wine."

When the aforementioned woman was asked, she was unable to deny. On request, it was recorded that she was drunk and that her mouth smelled of wine. It has been recorded that [the woman] was given over to the chief of police Ahmed.

Written in the latter portion of the honorable [month of] Şevval, year 991 (October 18–27, 1583).

Witnesses to the proceeding: Mehmed bin Abdullah | Şaban bin Abdullah | Ferruh bin Abdullah | Hüseyn bin Hasan.

6. MUSTAFA'S HOUSE RAIDED, TWO WOMEN AND ONE MAN CAUGHT IN ONE BED, 1592

[The occasion for drafting the record] is the following: The chief of police in Üsküdar, Müstedam Bey bin Abdülmennan—*pride of his peers*—stated in the court of law that "There are prostitutes in Mustafa's house in the Toygar Hamza neighborhood, and it is likely that they will engage in the shameless act during the blessed days [of Ramazan, which is to begin tomorrow]. I request that [a representative of the court] go and investigate."

From the part of the court, Mevlana Mehmed bin İbrahim, a righteous man, went and inspected the aforementioned apartment. Satılmış bin Hızır [and] the women by the names of Fatıma binti İbrahim and Huri binti Hüner Çelebi were apprehended while all three were on one mattress. When they were asked, they confessed, "We succumbed to Satan's temptation." It is hereby recorded that they are subject to flogging.

Wednesday, the twenty-ninth [day] of the exalted [month of] Şaban, year 1000 (June 10, 1592).

Witnesses to the proceeding: Same as before.

7. GYPSIES RUNNING A PROSTITUTION RING, 1646

Order to the judges in the subprovince of Kengırı: The judge of Kengırı sent a letter, informing us the following:

A nomadic tribe of Gypsies has arrived, setting up tents in the surroundings of the town and the villages. Vile and abominable people go there. Every one of these [Gypsies] takes money according to the beauty of his wife or daughter and gives permission to her to commit adultery while he himself waits at the door of the tent. In this manner, every day there is adultery happening in a hundred places. The local deputies of the governor take some money and allow it, and thus depravity is at hand. The inhabitants of the region have repeatedly asked for my illustrious decree in the matter of prohibiting this.

In order to prevent such acts and not to have the authorities allow them from now on, I hereby order: As soon as [this decree] reaches you, you shall act according to my command, driving away and henceforth disallowing such depravities in the aforementioned subprovince. If [these acts] are not prevented, you shall write [a report] detailing them and submit [it to me].

So ordered.

Early Cemaziyelevvel, year 1056 (June 15–24, 1646).

8. AYŞE, SAİME, AND CANAN ARE ACCUSED OF PROSTITUTION, 1663

In compliance with the noble decree, which has arrived addressed to this humble one, [ordering me] to inspect the women engaging in mischief in the neighborhood of Firuz Agha, at the Tophane neighborhood in the guarded [district of] Galata, the individual named İsmail Bey, who is the steward of Siyavuş Agha, the voivode of the mentioned district, summoned to the court of law the women by the names Ayşe known as Tüfekçi Kızı ("the daughter of the musket maker"), Saime, and her daughter-in-law Canan, who live in the said neighborhood. He brought a suit against them in their presence, stating, "The aforementioned are promiscuous women (*yaramaz avratlar*), prostitutes (*fahişeler*) who do not abstain from [associating with] strangers. I request that the inhabitants of the neighborhood be asked about their reputation and that their testimonies be recorded."

The imam Mustafa Efendi bin Ahmed, the muezzin Mahmud Halife bin Mehmed, Mahmud Efendi bin Hasan, Kasım Bey bin Mehmed, [and forty other] inhabitants of the aforementioned neighborhood, all present in this court, were asked about the reputation of Ayşe, Saime, and Canan. In response they testified and informed [the court thus]: "The aforementioned are not good women, and they do not refrain from [associating with] strangers. They are constantly carousing with music and merrymaking in their house. In short, the aforementioned are well-known for [engaging in] prostitution. We all demand that Ayşe, Saime, and Canan be expelled from our neighborhood." Recorded on request as it transpired.

Written on the fourteenth day of the holy Şevval of the year 1073 (May 22, 1663).

Witnesses to the proceeding: Mustafa bin Receb | Ebubekir Beşe bin Musli | el-Hac Kenan bin Abdullah | Musa bin Receb | el-Hac Mehmed bin Abdullah | Muharrem bin Receb.

9. PROSTITUTION RING IN EYÜP, 1680

You, the dignified and virtuous judge of Haslar (Eyüp), shall inspect this:

> May my most excellent and felicitous Sultan be hearty and hale! The petition of your humble servants from the neighborhood of Nişancı in [the district of] his excellency Eyyub-i Ensari is the following:
>
> The six rooms known as the Rooms of the Mufti's Daughter are full of prostitutes, constantly engaged in acts of depravity. [The tenants] roam armed with swords all through the night until morning, and no matter how many times we warn them, they cannot be stopped. For the sake of the God Most High, His Prophet, and your noble self, we request an illustrious decree to the effect that these rooms be emptied with legal warrant, the prostitutes expelled, and the rooms sealed. The final decree belongs to my Sultan.
>
> [Signed:] The humble slaves, the inhabitants of the neighborhood.

A decree [was issued] ordering that the chief of police and the captain of the guard summon the imam, the congregation [of the neighborhood], the superintendent [responsible for these] rooms, and the prostitutes before me.

[Decree] to the effect: Dignified and virtuous judge of Haslar (Eyüp)! From this day forward expel the prostitutes from those rooms, and do not let such prostitutes settle in the rooms. Rather have them rented to decent people who are approved by the inhabitants of the neighborhood.

On 3 Ramazan, year 1091 (September 27, 1680).

SIXTEEN

On Nocturnal Activities

Court Records, Sixteenth and Seventeenth Centuries

TRANSLATED BY HAKAN T. KARATEKE

Nights were pitch-black in the premodern world, not only in the countryside but in cities as well. The course of a day was delineated by the onset of dark, and life was regulated around natural light. At night, simple oil lamps or wax candles were used inside homes for necessary chores, and torches or lanterns for travel outside the house. Perhaps some Muslims walked to the neighborhood mosque for night prayers, which are performed roughly ninety minutes after sunset. Unless there was a full moon and clear skies, walking about in the open at night was not only difficult but also dangerous. It was common for people to retire to their homes at dusk and stay inside until morning. In fact, more often than not, those without some legitimate business that required them to be out were not permitted by law enforcement officers to wander around at night.

Houses of worship, dervish lodges, taverns, and some coffee shops (after their proliferation) had modest lighting inside, but not more than that. The oil lamps used in households were the main cause of fires, which were a major threat to neighborhoods with densely packed wooden houses. Although fire departments were well-organized, the technology was not always efficient enough to stop the spread of fires. Large cities were decorated and illuminated with oil lamps and torches for special occasions, such as religious festivals, celebrations of military achievements, or the births of princes or princesses.

While small explosive firecracker devices were known in the Chinese world in the late medieval period, complex forms of fireworks became a significant element of celebrations in Europe and in Ottoman lands after the advent of gunpowder technologies in the fourteenth century. The intensity of nighttime dark in the preelectric era would have made fireworks an even more dazzling spectacle than they are today. Most fireworks craftsmen were initially members of the army's armorers division, but as fireworks became increasingly elaborate, a group of highly skilled artisans assembled to work on complex public displays. As the pyrotechnic technologies, aligned with other forms of technological advancement, progressed from the sixteenth to the eighteenth century, fireworks performances became more sophisticated by applying narrative techniques and staging dramatic shows involving large puppets and light-emitting substances.

Public street lighting with lanterns gradually spread in some European cities toward the end of the seventeenth century. The development of these technologies should be seen in correspondence with the expansion of nightlife in the early modern period. The expansion of the social uses of nighttime is an overlooked but a critical marker of modernity. Common people (or more accurately, common men) of the early modern era gradually grew accustomed to socializing in the evening and nighttime hours in a variety of prescribed legitimate secular public spaces, such as coffee houses. Some scholars call this development "nocturnalization" or the "conquest of the night." Gas lamp lighting, which burned gas distilled from coal or wood and conveyed through pipes, became widespread in European cities like London and Paris from the beginning of the nineteenth century. In Istanbul, first the imperial Dolmabahçe Palace, and quickly thereafter some large thoroughfares, would be illuminated with the same technology after the mid-nineteenth century.

This chapter includes translations of court documents that deal with a variety of offenses that occurred at night in the sixteenth and seventeenth centuries, as well as others that give us a good idea about how watchmen oversaw nighttime in the city.

LANGUAGE: Turkish. Uncomplicated, formulaic legal language interspersed with technical terms. Patronymics starting with *veled-i* (reserved exclusively for non-Muslims) have been translated as "son of . . ." For example, Dimitri veled-i Nikola, which means Dimitri son of Nikola.

SOURCE: Document 1. Üsküdar Court Records, 14, fol. 35a. Doc. 2. Tophane Court Records, 2, fol. 37b. Doc. 3. Hasköy Court Records, 5, p. 317. Doc. 4. Istanbul Court Records, 22, fol. 169a. Doc. 5. Üsküdar Court Records, 9, fol. 83a. Doc. 6. Üsküdar Court Records, 14, fol. 60a. Doc. 7. Üsküdar Court Records, 17, fol. 39a. Doc. 8. Üsküdar Court Records, 56, fol. 54b. Doc. 9. Cyprus Court Records, 1, pp. 40–41. Doc. 10. Hasköy Court Records, 5, p. 90. Doc. 11. Istanbul Court Records, 12, fol. 148b.

---

1. FARMING OUT THE DUTY OF A NIGHT WATCHMAN, 1547

The occasion for drafting the record is that Nikola bin Yorgi and Dimitri bin Buber, who are collectors of revenues in the village of Çengel, said in the presence of Nikola bin Dimitri from the aforementioned village at the court of law: "He will patrol the village at night and arrest whomever he finds [out on the streets], refer to the judge, [and collect] whatever small [amount of fines that might] accrue. We farm out [this duty] for sixty akçe for a full year from the first of [the month of] Muharrem."

Nikola [bin Dimitri] confirmed it in person orally. Recorded on request.

Date of the drafting [of the record]: Beginnings of the sacred month of Muharrem, year 954 (late February 1547).

Witnesses to the proceeding: Papa Yanni bin Nikola | Duka bin Tiranoz | Mihal bin Nikola.

2. VIOLATORS OF THE NIGHT CURFEW, 1559

Ali Bey bin Abdullah, the brother and the legal representative of Behram the voivode, the current fief holder and the police superintendent of Galata, has rendered the [following] deposition: "I have found [and apprehended] these two [fellows], İsmail bin Abdullah and Hacı Hüseyn Kulu, along with the individuals named Dimitri son of Nikola and Hasan on a two-oared boat cruising out on the sea at night against the imperial order. They should be questioned."

After questioning, their confessions were recorded at Ali Bey's request.

[Date: ca. 15 Şevval 966 (July 21, 1559)]

Witnesses to the proceeding: Mustafa bin Hamza | Ferhad bin Abdullah.

3. APPOINTMENT OF A WATCHMAN AND GATE GUARD, 1612

Jews by the names Solomon son of Eliya, Kalevi son of Eliya, Afda son of Solomon, Udeh son of Eliya, David son of Avraham, Sa'd and his brother Moshe, who are residents of the village of Has, a dependency of the district [named after] his excellency Ebu Eyyub el-Ensari—*may the Creator's mercy be upon him*—all appeared at the noble court of law and explained themselves and gave the following statement in the presence of Yahuda son of Nesim: "There are three gates in the neighborhood of Has village. We have appointed Yahuda son of Nesim, a Jew, as guard to close the doors tight at night in said neighborhood." Since he also accepted the [position of] guard and undertook the required duties, it has been recorded as it transpired.

Written in the beginnings of the noble [month of] Zilhicce, year 1020 (early February 1612).

Witnesses to the proceeding: İbrahim Bey, expert horseman | Kasım Hoca | Hüseyn bin Mehmed | İbrahim, court officer.

4. NIGHT WATCHMEN NOT PERFORMING THEIR DUTIES, 1696

To the honorable and virtuous Efendi, the judge of Istanbul:

It has become evident, [and in fact the shopkeepers] themselves verbally informed us that the neighborhood watchmen in Istanbul do not patrol at night [but rather] sleep until the morning in front of the shops without lanterns. Now, you shall summon all the neighborhood imams, warn them, and warn them forcefully that from now on [the issue] will be scrutinized, and that if a neighborhood watchman is caught lying or sitting around with[out] a lantern until the morning, he will be given corporal punishment and the imam of his neighborhood will be dismissed. You should pay attention accordingly.

So ordered.

[Written] in the guarded [city of] Constantinople, 7 Şaban [1]107 (March 12, 1696).

5. GRAPES STOLEN FROM THE VINEYARD, 1535

The reason for drafting the record is that Ahmed bin Hasan, the steward of the heaths in the village of Bulgurlu, appeared at the noble court, brought a claim against Memi bin Hüseyn, whom he had summoned [to court], and testified, "I caught him picking grapes from my vineyard at night."

Memi was questioned. He denied [the accusation]. After his denial, [the court] asked for proof [from the plaintiff] for his accusation. [The case] was established by the testimonies of Hasan Baba and Erli Ali bin Timur, who were competent Muslim witnesses, and was recorded.

Written on the first day of Muharrem of the year [9]42 (summer of 1535) (*approximate date*).

Witnesses to the proceeding: Durahan bin Hasan | Hamza bin Veli | Hacı Süleyman bin Abdi | Hızır bin Ahmed and others.

6. FISHING NETS STOLEN, 1547

The reason for drafting the record is the following: Yanni bin Nikola from the village of Çengel brought a suit against Captain Kosta bin Yorgi from the [village of] Yenice in the district of Eyyub in his presence and stated, "On Monday, the fourteenth day [of the month] of Zilkade [year 954], I left (cast?) eleven pieces of fishing nets in the sea near the poplar tree close to our village. You came in the middle of the night, took them, and left."

Kosta was questioned. On his denial, [the court] asked for proof [from the plaintiff]. Zimmis named Mihal bin Yanni, Yorgi bin Manol, Dimitri bin Todora, and Azfurapulo bin Azfurapulo testified: "We are witnesses and do testify, 'On Monday night, [Yanni] had left eleven pieces of fishing nets in the sea near the poplar tree. You came, took them, and left.' After appraisal [their testimonies] were [found] in the realm of acceptance. [The proceeding] was recorded on request."

Written in the middle days of [the month of] Zilkade, year 954 (end of December 1547).

Witnesses to the proceeding: Hasan bin Abdullah, court officer | Ramazan bin Hüseyn | Karaca bin Yusuf | Hamza bin Ali | Duka bin Tiranos | Yorgi bin Yanni | Papa Yanni bin Nikola.

7. TAIL OF A HORSE SEVERED, 1550

The reason for drafting the record is that Ali bin Abdullah and Mehmed bin İlyas of the village of Kadı appeared at the court of law. Ali brought a claim and said, "One of my horses walked loose at night and entered your vineyard, and you cut off its tail as punishment."

Mehmed was questioned. He denied [the allegation]. When proof was demanded of Ali, he was incapable of producing any. Mehmed was asked to swear by God three times, from which he abstained. It was recorded in the register on request.

Written in the beginnings of [the month of] Cumadelula, year 957 (late May 1550).

Witnesses to the proceeding: Hasan bin Hızır Dede | Ahmed bin Nebi | Ali bin Mehmed | İskender bin Abdullah | Ali bin Hacı Fakih and others.

8. ATTEMPTED ROBBER APPREHENDED, 1583

Himmet bin Piri, resident in the Mamure neighborhood set forth a claim in the court of law in the presence of zimmi named Mosko: "The mentioned zimmi is a carpenter. After having fixed some parts of my house [during the day], he came and had the intention to enter my house through the window after the night prayer that night. I woke up at his movements, [but] hearing that I approached the window, he fled. I shouted, 'Catch the thief.' Hasan bin Mustafa and Ahmed bin Mahmud were sleeping [just] outside my house. They woke up at my cry for help, got up, and ran to the street. The zimmi ran before them along with an accomplice of his and entered a boza seller shop that belonged to a certain Mustafa."

On questioning, the zimmi responded by denying [the accusation].

Hasan and Ahmed were asked [to relate] the incident; they said, "Indeed, as Himmet stated, as we got up and came on the street, the zimmi fled before us with an accomplice. We followed them and ran to [Mustafa's] boza seller's shop. There was a moon at night, so we exactly identified him as he had worked [at the house] for a day. Thus is the true course of the incident." Recorded on request.

[Date: Middle of Şaban 991 (mid-September 1583)]

Witnesses to the proceeding: Hüseyn bin Haydar | Kerim bin Mehmed | Hüseyn bin Abdullah | Mehmed bin Abdullah, the tailor.

9. AN ORPHAN FOUND DEAD IN THE MORNING, 1594

A meeting was held with Hüseyn Bey—*may his dignity be raised*—who was appointed the commissioner for the following case by *the pride of the illustrious and honorable,* Mustafa the steward—*may his dignity be raised*—the deputy governor of his excellency the felicitous governor Ramazan Pasha—*may God help him attain whatever he wishes for*—and İdris Çavuş bin Emrullah—*may his dignity be raised*—on the part of the current superintendent of the public and imperial treasury Perviz Bey.

The holder of this document, Hüseyn bin Resul, appeared at the noble court of law in the presence of inhabitants of the village of Konya—Bostan bin Ali, the foot soldier, Ali bin Abdullah, Musa bin Şuayb, Receb bin Abdullah, Bilal bin Abdullah, Ali bin Bekr, another Ali bin Abdullah, Mehmed bin Abdullah, Cafer bin Pir Aziz, Veli bin Nebi, and other residents of the village—and made the [following] statement:

"The minor orphan Acemoğlu İlyas bin Alaeddin took care of and grazed the donkeys in the aforementioned village. He was alive at night [but] was dead in the morning. What is the cause? Did he die by beating, or did he die by God's command (i.e., naturally)? The residents of the village should be questioned."

After questioning, the residents of the village said in response: "İlyas was sick and frail. [That] night there was a feast. The residents of the village got together for the feast and gave İlyas food. Being weak, he did not even eat the food; he went to bed sick, and by morning he died by God's command. We buried him with the Muslims."

After this statement, Hüseyn was asked to bring forth proof for his statement that [İlyas] died by beating at the hands of the village residents or by some other means. He was incapable of producing any. Each of the villagers was asked to swear, and they swore by God. [They were all] absolved of [the accusation]. It was recorded in the register as it transpired.

Written in the glorious month of Şaban, 1002 (middle of May 1594)

Witnesses to the proceeding: The chief of police Hızır bin Abdullah, the foot soldier | Mehmed bin Memi, a.k.a. Rıdvan Agha | Nasuh bin Ali, the foot soldier | Mirza bin Receb, soldier at the fortress | Yusuf bin Abdullah, soldier at the fortress and others from the present party. [Further] witnesses to the proceeding: Mehmed Bey | Mehmed bin —— | Hasan bin —— | Receb bin ——.

10. COMPLAINT ABOUT A TAVERN MAKING NOISE, 1637

[The reason for drafting the record] is the following: The Jew named Kemal son of Marol, a resident of the village of Has, has summoned zimmis named Kostantin son of Yorgi and İstemad son of Yanni to the noble court of law and made [the following] statement in their presence: "Kostantin and Yorgi rented in partnership the tavern just next to my [house] and [they] sell wine there. Yet, apart from operating the tavern during the daytime, they fail to shut it with the onset of night, [continue to] sell wine into the wee hours, fill [the place] with

FIGURE 14. Nighttime celebrations with fireworks and other pyrotechnical devices, Istanbul, 1720. Abdülcelil Levni (artist), in Vehbi's *Surnâme*, Ahmed III 3593, fol. 100b. Topkapı Sarayı Müzesi Kütüphanesi, Istanbul.

vile people at ungodly hours, play music, and make loud noises. The fire in their tavern continues to burn all night long. It is possible that their conduct may cause all sorts of depravity in the neighborhood. It is my wish that they be questioned and prevented from such conduct."

Following the interrogation and the [accused party's] denial of [the allegation], Kemal was asked to present proof in support of his claim. Jews named Avraham son of Navin and Yahya son of Eliya were present at the noble court of law in order to give testimony. They gave their legal testimonies as follows: "Indeed, Kostantin and Yorgi run the tavern, which they rented in partnership, at night, and they sell wine until the wee hours. They fill [the place] with vile people at inappropriate hours, play music, and make loud noises. The fire in their tavern continues to burn until the morning. We are witnesses to this situation and do testify." Their testimonies were appraised as being conforming to the conditions of [legality and credibility] and were accepted.

Kostantin and Yorgi were warned not to commit such depravities. Recorded as it transpired.

Written on the twenty-fifth of [month of] Cumadelahire, year 1047 (November 14, 1637).

Witnesses to the proceeding: David son of Mordehay | İsak son of Yakov | Konpor (?) son of Revon and others from the present party.

11. ISTANBUL TO BE ILLUMINATED IN CELEBRATION OF THE CONQUEST OF UYVAR, 1633

To the honorable Efendi, [the judge] of Istanbul:

Thanks be to God, the Sovereign Lord. As the conquest and subjugation of the Uyvar fortress (Nové Zámky, in modern-day Slovakia) was facilitated [by God], a noble order and a felicitous imperial decree was issued to hold illuminations in the city for seven days and seven nights. It is necessary that the doors of the shops and houses in markets and bazaars in the city of Constantinople be illuminated for seven days and seven nights; and, in accordance with the imperial decree and the noble order, [people] should occupy themselves with praying for the continuation of the life and fortune of the padishah.

So ordered.

On 16 Cemaziyelevvel, 1074 (December 16, 1633)

SEVENTEEN

Impostors, Frauds, and Spies

Various Documents, Sixteenth Century

TRANSLATED BY CHRISTOPHER MARKIEWICZ

In the sixteenth century, the Ottoman Empire established an extensive bureaucracy capable of administering vast territories. In this regard, the empire, like most of its early modern counterparts, embraced a bureaucratic culture of documentation that has left us with one of the richest archival collections from the early modern period.

The core of this bureaucracy was developed in the period after the conquest of Constantinople in 1453. The central administration grew substantially after the expansion of the empire into eastern Anatolia, Syria, Egypt, and the Hijaz in the 1510s. To administer this vast empire, the state relied on the production and maintenance of accurate records, especially those that pertained to the principal sources of revenue for the state. Fundamental to the development of this central bureaucracy were the land surveys that were carried out in each province roughly once every generation. These determined the extent of taxable agrarian production and the beneficiaries of this production—most significantly, provincial cavalrymen (*timarlı sipahi*) who were entitled to collect tax revenue in exchange for military service. The central bureaucracy employed a growing number of secretaries who kept detailed registers of these land surveys, recorded revenue and expenditures, and registered important developments in the provinces that pertained to matters of justice and administration. In the course of these duties, Ottoman officials were regularly dispatched to the provinces to investigate contentious matters and report back. Some issues took weeks, if not months, to be resolved.

Written documents were therefore central to the state and to wider Ottoman society. Through them, information was obtained from across the empire and beyond its borders. Equally, written documents lent authority to individuals when they interacted with officials as they sought to press certain claims or assert particular privileges. The four documents presented here all address issues of individual identity and the problems fraud could pose to the political, religious, and social order. In the eyes of Ottoman officials, the people at the center of these documents might be viewed as impostors, fraudsters, or double agents. In all cases, the authorities sought or produced written documents to evaluate the claims of the individuals involved or to decide on a course of action.

This bureaucratic culture of documentation also presented opportunities for individual exploitation through forgery. Indeed, documents 2 and 4 both detail cases of individuals who presented Ottoman officials with dubious documents when their claims to certain rights and privileges were scrutinized. For Hüsam, his deed of a pious endowment, if authentic, entitled him to revenue produced from property that had been allotted to provincial cavalrymen. For Ali from the Maghreb, his papers in Magrebi script substantiated his status as a descendant of the Prophet Muhammad, a status that entailed widespread respect within Ottoman society, certain sartorial privileges, exemption from taxes, and immunity from certain punishments.

The extensive reach of the central authority and the culture of documentation suggest firm state control over all peoples and territories of the empire, yet such control was often illusory. Provincial rebellions were common, and for this reason, Ottoman authorities were particularly concerned with the Turkmen nomad who claimed to be the Safavid Shah Ismail II (r. 1576–77) and who roamed the mountainous regions of Anatolia gathering supporters. Even when the state compiled reports, the information they contained was not always reliable, as is suggested by the activities of the double agent referred to in the first document.

LANGUAGE: Turkish. Uncomplicated language that adheres to the appropriate and occasionally pompous bureaucratic formulae, including the use of technical legal terms. Doc. 1, being a memorandum, includes a more personal touch.

SOURCE: Document 1. Topkapı Sarayı Müzesi Arşivi, Istanbul, 754/22. Facsimile and transcription: Gurulkan, Kemal, Ersin Kırca, Numan Yekeler, Mehmet Selim Temel, İskender Türe, Yılmaz Karaca, and Vahdettin Atik, eds. *Arşiv Belgelerine Göre Osmanlı'da İstihbarat*. Istanbul: T.C. Başbakanlık Devlet Arşivleri Genel Müdürlüğü, 2017 (40–41). Doc. 2. Mühimme Registers 6. Facsimile and transcription: *6 Numaralı Mühimme Defteri (972/1564-1565)*. Ankara, 1995, case 166; p. 113. Doc. 3. Mühimme Registers 32, pp. 206–7, case 392. Transcription: İzgi, Şuayib. "986 (1578) Tarihli 32 Numaralı Mühimme Defteri." Master's thesis, Marmara University, Istanbul, 2006 (6–7). Doc. 4. Topkapı Palace Museum Archives, 692, fol. 45a. Transcription: Doğan, Muzaffer. "Balıkesir Şeriyye Sicilleri: TSMA 692 No'lu Defter vr. 1b-45b." Master's thesis, Marmara University, Istanbul, 1989 (134).

---

1. NİKOLA THE MYSTERIOUS SPY, CA. 1481–1512

His glorious and fortunate Majesty!

After dedicating and presenting innumerable good prayers and boundless pure salutations, which are clear and obvious from the source of purity and the wellspring of sincerity, the petition to the luminous heart of the sun-faced [Majesty] is this:

The unbeliever named Nikola of Filibe (Plovdiv, in modern-day Bulgaria), for seven to eight years, as has been known to your Majesty, set out to sea many times in service and brought information back. The truthfulness of the information that he brought was never known. His main business is deception and cheating. I, your sincere servant, have been saying, "He is a liar; there is no truth to his information." His lies were completely exposed. Because the seafront is somewhat of an unusual case (?), his lies were not noted; you had ordered that he should continue to come and go for the time being. Previously, the letters that he brought addressed to your well-wisher (i.e., to me) from the sea were also sent here from Istanbul.

When that one (i.e., Nikola) came now with the intention of meeting me, I said [to him], "For some time, you have been going out for service at sea, yet you have not brought any sound information. All along, your main business has been deception and cheating. Your desire has been to go about spying on us for them and them for us. Just you wait, I will bring a great calamity on you." After saying these enraged words, I gave him to the custody of a gatekeeper, saying, "Lock him up."

[As] the gatekeeper brought him [to his confinement], because of his delusions, [Nikola] removed his hat and said to the owner of the house where he would be locked up: "If you do not burn what's inside it, tomorrow I'll make you pay for it!" The gatekeeper heard what he said and grabbed his hat. Papers with the writings of unbelievers (i.e., in Greek or Roman script) came out [of the hat]. As [the gatekeeper] brought these to me, we had them read, and saw that on these papers it was written, "I, who am Nikola, shall appear like the heavens and I shall trample like one tramples on earth! May the Great Sultan Bayezid Han, the chief treasurer, Mustafa Bey, the chief sergeant-at-arms Kasım Bey, and Şirmerd Bey be like [silent] owls; may they be like chickens whose chicks have just hatched and whose feathers have been plucked. I am Nikola, servant of God. I have cast a spell on their tongues many times over. May their [evil] tongues and eyes not be on me." There was more writing but because [the paper] was damaged, it could not be deciphered. I enclose the papers that were found in his [hat].

After the papers were viewed, he was asked to explain them: "Why did you do this?" He said, "The Dragoman Süleyman, who died in prison, did this to me." These papers that are enclosed should be shown to a Christian, who knows about these things, because they are magic; according to what he says they should be burnt or pulverized in water. It should be done as he says.

So, it is requested that a great punishment be ordered against this accursed fellow so that his example may serve as counsel and a lesson to cheats like him so that they not do as he has done. This is not a little matter. May it be known to His Majesty. Finally, may the sapling of your Majesty's eternal life be extended in perpetuity through the dignity of Muhammad and his honored family.

The weakest of servants, Mustafa, the poor one.

2. HÜSAM THE ENTERPRISING FRAUDSTER, 1564

Imperial order to Bayezid Bey who is the commander of Beyşehir and is on a special investigation in [the province of] Karaman:

In the province of Karaman, someone known as Hüsam Abdullah created a dervish lodge and wrote for himself a deed of a pious endowment. He established its property boundaries and, under the cover of night, he loaded stones and charcoal in a wagon and placed the stones wherever he liked and poured charcoal underneath and recorded these markers in the deed. Since the above-mentioned places are prebends belonging to [provincial] cavalrymen and fortress guards, they requested [an inquiry]; [Hüsam] submitted the deed of the pious endowment and the forged court documents that he wrote under the names of previous judges. He harassed the opposing party and made them drop the case.

While Ebu'l-Fazl Mehmed was previously undertaking a land survey of the province, the prebend holders complained [to him] of the above-mentioned [Hüsam Abdullah]. So, [Ebu'l-Fazl] sent a letter to the judge of the province saying, "Go to the places that [Hüsam Abdullah] said belonged to the pious endowment of his dervish lodge. Inquire of trustworthy people whether in actual fact there has been a dervish lodge since olden times in the above-mentioned places and ask how much revenue is produced by these places that are supposed to belong to this pious endowment." When the judge, in turn, went to [those] places and inquired of trustworthy Muslims [on this matter], they replied, saying [it produces] approximately ten thousand bushels [of grain] according to the Konya bushel. They bore witness that there had been no lodge there in the past and that he had created it himself.

Because the judge announced [this assessment] to the above-mentioned [Ebu'l-Fazl], and [the latter] was on his way to my Imperial Palace, Hüsam also came to the palace without the knowledge of his legal opponents. He submitted [the case to the imperial council] and obtained an imperial order stipulating that the judge had investigated the endowment of his lodge without an imperial order.

[Thereafter, Hüsam Abdullah] mobilized an itinerant judge and two investigating judges and arrived [back in Karaman]. As for the investigating [judges], he took two deputy judges suitable to his aim and, without informing the itinerant judge, he had them write petitions suitable to his aim after suborning each one of them completely. He himself wrote the petition in the place of the itinerant judge. He carved a seal [in place of the judge's seal] and imprinted it [on the document]. He conveyed it to [Ebu'l-Fazl]. [Thus,] by fraud and deceit, he had it recorded in the old and new [cadastral] registers. The poor [prebend holders] were not able to press their claims.

[Subsequently, Hüsam] apparently confessed to the itinerant judge that he had written the forged petition in that manner. He supposedly humbled himself, saying, "I wrote such a petition in your place. Forgive me." That [itinerant] judge is currently the judge of Seydişehri. In case there is doubt, [the judge of Seydişehri] may be interrogated.

Because he [Ebu'l-Fazl?] notified my Threshold of Felicity of this [matter], I order the following:

Inquire of this matter from the judge of Seydişehri, Mevlana Dervish. Go yourself with some trustworthy people and investigate these places. Was there in actual fact a longstanding lodge in that place? In the case that these places were endowed and recorded in the new imperial register, what are the borders of those places? What were its old boundaries? Did it previously have boundaries? If not, were these subsequently fabricated? You should get to the bottom of the matter. You should write an explanation and make known what occurred.

So written.

Handed over to the chief sergeant-at-arms on 6 Rebiülahir year 972 (November 11, 1564).

3. A CHARISMATIC IMPOSTOR OF THE SAFAVID SHAH, 1578

Imperial order to the commander of the Turkmen subprovince, Şah Murad—*may his glory be perpetuated*—is as follows:

The judge of Elbistan (in modern-day southeastern Turkey), Mahmud sent a letter informing [us] that the notables of Elbistan came to the court of law [and stated], "Someone from the Şam Bayad Turkmen clan arrived from Arab lands to this province claiming: 'I am Shah Ismail (II).' They constructed about thirty houses in arduous terrain in the vicinity of Sultan Korusu. A contingent of two hundred mounted riders gathered at night engaging in brigandage and robbing people around [Sultan Korusu]—but they are not to be seen during the day. In order to gather many more troublemakers, they went to the Seven Sleepers [cave and mosque complex] and made sacrificial offerings. Apparently, there is a *halife* (i.e., a Kızılbaş delegate-propagandist) in Bozok; they came to his [location] and made sacrificial offerings. From there, they went to [the mausoleum of] Hacı Bektaş and also offered a sacrifice. They left there and set out to continue acts of sedition and disorder."

Ahmed, the governor-general of Dulkadir [province]—*may his fortune be perpetuated*—also sent a letter and stated, "As some people were travelling to Elbistan, a Turkmen clan came on them, robbing whatever people had and stripping them bare. Some of these were apprehended and executed; however, the people of Elbistan fear these brigands completely. They are already starting to cause disorder again. There is a likelihood that they would cause great disorder once the troops head out [for campaign] and leave your [Şah Murad's] province empty." [Ahmed] petitioned that it be considered appropriate for you [Şah Murad] to remain [in the country] to safeguard it.

You are ordered to refrain from joining the campaign in order to protect and defend those areas and carry out the important business of collecting the imperial revenue. Imperial orders were also sent to Çerkes, the commander of Bozok; Keyvan the commander of Ayntab; and Memi Şah, the commander of Kırşehir—*may their glory be perpetuated*—from among the commanders who are appointed for safeguarding [the domains] in order that they apprehend that troublemaker who calls himself Shah Ismail and the rebels beside him along with the brigands claiming to be halifes and execute them.

[In light of the above-mentioned,] I order that on receipt of this rescript, in accordance with my order, refrain from joining the campaign. In the service of safeguarding [the domains] and collecting imperial revenue, protect, guard, and save as required those places that have been frightened and threatened. You should act with heightened caution to prevent any loss or damage to anyone's life or property. You should give no quarter to the unlucky sort who came out in the name of Shah Ismail. You should endeavor to move against him with the Turkmen clans and the irregulars of the region, apprehend the rebels alongside him, and execute them.

If you are unable to apprehend them independently, you should consult with the commanders mentioned above, embark immediately on the best plan for the apprehension of [this] rebel along with his followers. With [the help of] the provincial cavalrymen appointed to the protection [of that territory] and the irregulars of that region, you should also apprehend the brigands who, like the Shah Ismail pretender, claim to be halifes. You should have them executed in whatever manner so that it becomes a lesson and a counsel to other brigands. Yet you should take extra precautions to not use this as a pretext to meddle and show hostility to those who were not involved.

Handed over to Nalbandzade Mehmed, sergeant-at-arms.

On 8 Cumadelahire, year 986 (August 12, 1578).

4. ALİ THE MAGHREBI DESCENDENT OF THE PROPHET, 1593

Someone named Ali, originally from the Maghreb and now resident in Balıkesri, claimed to be a descendant of the Prophet Muhammad and donned the green turban reserved for descendants of the Prophet. He has been incessantly drinking wine and committing immoral acts and vice in that town. When a vagabond named Süleyman passed by the town, spent the night at an inn, and departed, the rogue [Ali] allied with some brigands, went after Süleyman, killed him, and stole his belongings.

[Ali] repeatedly confessed voluntarily in the presence of Muslim [witnesses at the court] to allying himself with the above-mentioned [brigands], saying, "They killed Süleyman. They took the cash that he had on him and gave me the murdered man's mule and merchandise." The same belongings that they appropriated were found in his possession and recorded in the court register.

When it was investigated whether it was true that this individual was a descendant of the Prophet and whether he had a title deed of his status [issued by] the members of the noble lineage and the great scholars who have been chief officers of the descendants of the Prophet in Ottoman lands, he had no signed and sealed family tree with the signature and seal of the chief officer, but only a couple sheets written in Maghrebi script. When these were looked at, and his name and the names of his forebears were asked of him, and his responses were compared, the truth of his lineage was not established. His contradictions became apparent.

In fact, because the papers he had on him were not sound evidence, Ali was prevented from donning a green turban. It was recorded on request as it occurred.

> Written in the middle portion of the first of the two Rebi [months], year 1002 (early December 1593).
>
> Witnesses to the Proceeding: Mehmed bin Kasım | Mustafa bin Ali | Ali bin Mustafa | and others.

EIGHTEEN

The Madmen of Istanbul

Evliya Çelebi, d. after 1683

TRANSLATED BY HAKAN T. KARATEKE

It was apparently common to see people with mental illness in public in Ottoman cities. People with mental illness were primarily the responsibility of their families and the neighborhoods in which they lived. Mental asylums were rare and therefore mentally ill people, at least those who were not dangerously aggressive, were accepted as a part of everyday life. Modern asylums were opened in the later nineteenth century in the Ottoman lands and were regulated with bylaws in 1876. One of the requirements of modernity was that the state assumed the role of caretaker for its mentally ill citizens. More importantly, "madness" was now regarded as a topic of modern medical study.

In the premodern world, mentally ill people were commonly regarded on a continuum that approached sainthood. There were mystical orders whose members contravened social norms and displayed antinomian tendencies. Most committed Sufis strove to achieve some degree of detachment from the mundane ambitions of everyday life, which inevitably created a disconnect between their behavior and normative mainstream comportment. In particular, people of mystical *Melami* persuasion deliberately sought public reproach by disregarding social and religious mores; this was their strategy for focusing on God and freeing themselves from aspirations to worldly recognition. As a result, for many people there was likely a thin line between perceptions of madness and holiness.

The Arabic term *uqala al-majanin* was one of the designations for individuals whose actions went against social norms. The term is sometimes translated as "wise fools." *Mecnun* (Arabic *majnun*), in fact, denotes that the person is possessed by evil jinns (see chapter 25). In Islamic theology, jinns are regarded as created beings, just like humans, and subject to the ordinances of the Qur'an. Therefore, there are good jinns, who abide by the Holy Book, and bad jinns, who do not. They were created from smokeless fire (as opposed to humans, who were created from clay) and could potentially pester or possess humans. Other designations for people with mental illness include *meczub* (Arabic *majzub*). The word implies holiness, as it literally means "attracted" (by divine grace or obsessed with divine love). It is interesting to note that modern Turkish speakers sometimes make an interplay of the two similar sounding words *deli* (Turkish for "madman") and *veli* (Arabic for "friend of God, saint"). We understand that these "fools" were unconcerned with their appearance or conduct. Some walked around naked or half-clad; others displayed one or more obsessions that came to be their hallmark. Contemporary sources do not necessarily distinguish between the different varieties of illness. The conditions of these men likely included a wide range of behavioral disorders and illnesses.

Evliya Çelebi (d. after 1683, see chapter 30) attributed a certain degree of wisdom to what he called madmen in his log of eccentric people in Istanbul. He does not dismiss them as outcasts, but shows appreciation for their sagacity—in fact, the excerpts below are taken from a broader section listing the holy men of the city. These eccentric people were believed to have access to hidden knowledge, the invisible world, and the future. The anecdotes demonstrate that people occasionally solicited these men, no doubt partly for amusement, for divinations. Some are also mentioned as having performed miracles. Although so-called madmen were not necessarily always held in high regard by society, and undoubtedly were figures of derision to some of their contemporaries, the perception of mentally ill people as having mystical powers must have made it easier for society to incorporate the people who did not follow its norms.

LANGUAGE: Turkish. Evliya Çelebi uses many uncommon words, and has a peculiar grammar of his own, employing a lively narrative technique. In fact, there is a separate dictionary for the unusual words that Evliya uses.

SOURCE: Manuscript: *Seyahatname.* Books 1 and 2: Topkapı Sarayı Müzesi Kütüphanesi, Istanbul, Bağdat 304. Excerpts from fols. 106b–115b. Transcription: Dağlı, Yücel, Seyit Ali Kahraman, and Robert Dankoff, eds. *Evliya Çelebi Seyahatnamesi.* Book 1. Istanbul: Yapı Kredi Yayınları, 1996.

MEHMED ÇELEBİ, THE HAWKNOSED (A.K.A. "MORNING" LOONY)

His father had been superintendent of the janissary guards of the —— corps since the capture of Eger (in 1596) by Mehmed Khan, the conqueror of that city. When the janissary aghas went out on patrol as is customary, the madman Çelebi's father would make the rounds with them, apprehend any of his son's criminal friends, and incarcerate them. One day, the madman Çelebi became dismayed with his father and told him that he would die the next morning. By God's wisdom, his father passed away at dawn. Ever since, whenever someone says "morning, morning" to this madman Çelebi, he bangs his head on the rocks and, as God is omniscient, his head makes a dull "thud" sound like a gourd from Adana.

He also possesses such an aquiline nose that he is Minkarizade himself, as it were (the "Son of the Hook-nosed," a contemporary scholar). Whenever he gets angry at someone, he

FIGURE 15. An antinomian dervish (left). Some people perceived these dervishes as "holy fools" in the sixteenth century. Nicolas de Nicolay (original drawing), Louis Danet (engraver), in *Les navigations peregrinations et voyages, faicts en la Turquie* (Antwerp: Par Guillaume Silvius, 1576), 192.

discharges, with a puff, an oystery mucus from his nose so that the poor elegant person's clothes become all soiled with mucilage.

SCENE ONE: Once we chanced on this lunatic on the procession route when a few friends and I were going to watch the Imperial Council procession. He wore a tattered, tall hat of the palace guards and carried the stock of a musket on his shoulder. He was mounted on a stick as a horse; holding the bridle, he rode his stick horse toward us, doing all kinds of improper things and shouting ribald remarks to the shopkeepers on both sides as he went. As he passed us, he said, "Beware, my horse kicks," and hit the leg of our friend with the lower side of the stick so hard that he started limping. "You crazy asshole!" yelled our friend and slapped the madman in the face. In return, he squeezed his nose with his hand and shot a snot rocket from his giant nose into the face of our companion. Our friend started screaming, "Oh my God! My eye came out of its socket." I thought the madman must have had a stone in his hand, which he threw and thus poked out our friend's eye. But then I looked closely and realized that the vicious madman had ejected a booger from his nose that had grown rock-solid over the course of a month. Thinking the snot was the white of his eye, our companion was freaked out. "Come on, open your eye, brother," I said. "Your eye is just fine. It was his booger, not a rock." He then opened his eye and heaved a sigh of relief: "Thank God, it was just the booger of the madman."

In truth, his nose was half the size of a money changer's board. But the size of his nose was not a reflection of snootiness. He was a cheerful madman living in his own world. Just as salt is the spice of life and is found in everything we eat, this hawk-nosed madman, too, is present at every gathering, at all places and festivities, on land or sea—he does not sleep day or night, but roams about Islambol (Istanbul).

SCENE TWO: The mother of this madman was once imprisoned for smoking tobacco. He went to the Imperial Council presided over by Kara Mustafa Pasha to plea for her release. The chief sergeant-at-arms Boynueğri said to him, "Wait a bit. The pasha is busy." When, in reply, the madman said, "Don't give me that shit! The pasha is expecting me," the members of the Council snickered. At that moment, Mustafa Pasha heard the yelling and the quip, approached, and asked, "What is it, Çelebi?" In order to calm the situation, the chief sergeant-at-arms quickly responded, "My lord, the Çelebi's mother was incarcerated for owing some debt. He came to ask for her release." The madman snapped at the chief sergeant-at-arms: "He is lying—giving you crap! My mother does not owe any debt. They arrested her for smoking tobacco and put her in jail." He implored, "Let them take her out of the women's prison and put her in the men's prison—for I do not have a father." All the members of the Council were dumbfounded at this request and disputation, and they were beside themselves with laughter. Finding him delightful, Kara Mustafa Pasha bestowed on the madman a handful of money, ordered his mother's release, and counseled his assistant that the mother be married to someone. The late pasha was a protector of lunatics.

SCENE THREE: He used to be present at all occasions and at all times. Often, he would walk in front of the funeral processions side by side with the Qur'an reciters and presumptuously sing nonsensical words. He would also jump ahead of the procession, take a seat in the boat, and paddle the oars [if the corpse was being carried by sea]. *A peculiar story:* One day, this madman came across the funeral of a Jew named Nesim in the company of a crowd of three hundred Jews. He swiftly mingled with the Jews, placed his own palace guard hat on a Jew's head, and put the Jewish cap on his own head. As he walked, chanting like a muezzin in front of the corpse, the Jews exclaimed, "Çelebi, man! This is a Jew, not a Muslim." Thereupon, he discharged phlegm onto some and snot onto others—and punched a few people too. As he attempted to run under the coffin, the Jews panicked and dropped the casket right there on the street. Apparently, according to the false beliefs of the Jews, when a Muslim passes underneath a Jew's corpse, or leaps over it, the corpse becomes bewitched and goes to hell. The carcass (*laşe*) of the Jew remained unattended on the street. Finally, some Muslims gave a few coins to this madman to pacify him. But after he was pacified, he—pardon my language—indecently exposed his penis and pissed on the carcass of the Jew, spraying it everywhere, and then ran away with the [Jew's] hat on his head. He was such a loon.

If I reported every one of these incidents, it would fill a whole book. The tales of his ribald humor are well-known, just like the Nasreddin [Hoca] jokes among comedians and impersonators. They tell them at gentlemen's gatherings. He is a crazy man, but not without depth.

SCENE FOUR: Once he yelled, "Fire on the Red Islands (Princes' Islands)!" for three days and three nights. Thinking that it was just a madman's blabber, no one paid heed. By God's wisdom, on the fourth [day], in (date missing), a massive fire broke out. It progressed from Odunkapu to Yedikule and its other flank traveled all the way to Molla Gürani [district]. The fire continued for three days and three nights.

In short, he was not a madman without wisdom. I do not know where he is buried.

SEFER DEDE OF UNKAPANI

At Unkapanı, [this madman] entered the scorching hot bakery of Ali Çelebi and took a restful nap. Then he came out, bid farewell to everyone, jumped into the sea, and disappeared. The people of the neighborhood know this incident well. Seven years later, when the captains Kara Hoca and Ali Peçenoğlu returned to the Port of the State (Istanbul) from Algeria with their galleys, the madman Sefer Dede was with them on their galleys. He took up residence in Unkapanı again. But he had become mute. He did not eat anything but the ragged shoes that he found in dumps.

The crews of Kara Hoca and Ali Peçenoğlu related thus: "Seven years ago, we chanced on this Sefer Dede of Kapan mounted on a fish floating on the Surrounding Sea (Atlantic Ocean) outside of the Strait of Gibraltar and took him aboard. As we journeyed with agreeable winds toward Algeria, the big fish that Sefer Dede had mounted continued to follow us. As we reached Algeria, the fish, too, entered into the harbor, but it went aground on the shore and died. At Sefer Dede's request, we buried it." All these [sailors] testified to it.

That's the kind of intrepid, ecstatic, and distinguished madman the late Sefer Dede of Kapan was. That year, he passed away in the granary of Unkapanı and was buried outside of the district, next to Horosi Dede—*may his grave be hallowed.*

SIMPLETON DEDE

He used to be at Sarrachanebaşı district. Always wandering around silently like a *deaf, dumb* (Qur'an 2:18), he would pick up the useless rocks that rolled around on the main roads. It was his duty to clean the streets, as it were. I do not know where he is buried—*may God have mercy on him.*

CRAZY SMOKER DEDE

This was one of the mute lunatics who had a nose like a boulder. He was addicted to sniffing nose-weed (snuff). Some kids would put dirt in his hands telling him that it was nose-weed. He would probably sniff up a hundred *dirhem* (ca. 320 grams) or more in a day. Some miracles of his are reported.

THE NIGHTINGALE MADMAN OF EYÜP

He carried around a nightingale in a cage during winter and summer. While nightingales ordinarily sing during spring, his sang a thousand tunes in the winter. This was a strange mystery that astonished all friends.

THE PRIEST MADMAN OF GALATA

This was an infidel (Christian) worth seeing. Whoever saw him enjoyed and was astonished by his gestures and mode of conduct—the way he walked and talked. All distinguished gentlemen knew him.

DURMUŞ DEDE OF RUMELİHİSARI

All the boatmen, who sailed out of the city and arrived [at their destinations safely], made offerings to him. He used to say to some of the captains: "Don't go that direction, go to such and such place." Those who went to the places he suggested would travel safely, have favorable outcomes, and collect spoils. Those who went to the places he advised against would experience harm and come by little or no profit. Durmuş Dede was a stable, stationary, and calm [person], who possessed hidden knowledge.

THE HORNED AHMED DEDE OF KASIMPAŞA

He used to dwell in the home of a janissary by the name of Kocamışoğlu. He would seat himself on the bridge by the Kasımpaşa slaughterhouse all day long and snipe at passersby: "God willing you will go to the Kaaba, Ahmed Çebü (garbled form of the title "Çelebi")"; "God willing you will go to the Kaaba, Mehmed Çebü." The odd thing was that he would call people whom he had never met in his life by their names and honorifics—[that is,] "so and so Çebü." When he spotted a guy whom he had not seen for twenty years, he would get up, jump, and say, "Good to see you, so and so Çebü, son of Mrs. so and so."

He carried the horns of sheep, oxen, goats, lambs, deer, elk, and gazelles on his bosom and under his arms. ODDITY THREE: Some wags would come to him, curious about divination, and ask, "Ahmed, where is my horn?" By God's wisdom, if the guy was married, he would reply according to the guy's wife's [moral] conduct: "Here is your horn," brandishing a small horn to some and a large horn to others. ODDITY FOUR: If the guy who asked, "Where is my horn?" was single, [Ahmed Dede] would say, "Your horn has not grown yet." This was a curious scene.

ODDITY FIVE: Some Christians and Jews disguised themselves [as Muslims] and took me with them to see this madman Ahmed. When he saw us, he identified us as "so and so Çebü," and chatted with us, but did not talk to any of the non-Muslims. When this humble one and my friends asked him, "Ahmed Dede, why don't you converse with these [guys]?" he identified them as, "Infidel Beşe," "Jew Agha," became furious, and displayed his private parts.

ODDITY SIX: When somebody said, "Ahmed Dede, I'll give you a horn if you dance for me," he would straightaway stand up and snap the fingers of his right hand, making a sound similar to that of a stork. He would dance so hard that you would think he was Zühre, the dancer. People would then present a horn to him. ODDITY SEVEN: If, after a month, you inquired, "Where is my horn?" by God, he would take out of his bosom the horn you had given him and say, "There is your horn." This, also, is a strange puzzle.

ENIGMA EIGHT: If he said three times in a row, "God willing you shall go to the Kaaba" to someone, that person certainly would travel to Mecca.

In short, he was a cheerful, pretty faced, friendly madman. Since he journeyed off into the regions of Ethiopia, Sudan, and Aswan, I have not heard any news of him.

THE SIEVE EATING MADMAN

This was a mute madman. By God's ordinance, he did not eat anything but [the silk mesh of] sieves. The sieve seller women used to walk alongside him, for the madman would point at someone, and then that person would purchase a sieve. The madman would promptly break the sieve apart, throw away the frame, and devour its silk mesh, his mouth watering, enjoying it as if it were a sweetmeat. The oddity is that when the executioners torture a thief in prison, they first force the robber to swallow silk mesh. As they pull it back out by a string, it rips out the thief's gall bladder and stomach, which come out of his mouth. Silk mesh is a bad thing [to eat], but the sieve eater madman eats it like it was rock candy from Hama. Strange spectacle! At the same time, no one has ever seen this madman urinate or defecate. That's that!

Most of the time, he would wander around naked, just like he was born from his mother's womb. While he never ever uttered a worldly word, one day before he took his last breath, he went to a person named ——, greeted him, and said, "God willing, ritually wash and wind me in a shroud, [paid for by] your honestly earned money, and bury me outside the gate of the ——! Those who have a condition of arrhythmia shall make a pilgrimage [to my tomb], take some earth, mix it with water, and drink it up. By God's ordinance, they shall be cured." This was his testament. He then went to the alluded place and breathed his last. Later, that person [he spoke with] came and buried him according to his last will. His tomb outside [the gate of ——] by the bridge is still a pilgrimage place for all sorts of people. Those who suffer from palpitation find cures by the decree of God.

NINETEEN

Fetvas on Non-Muslims

Various Grand Muftis, Sixteenth to Early Eighteenth Century

TRANSLATED BY CORNELL FLEISCHER AND AMIR A. TOFT

For many of us today, law has a kind of totalizing quality. Many people take for granted, at least in theory (although there is often a discrepancy in practice), that a given territory's system of laws ought to address itself equally to all members of the polity. There is a stated presumption that all people are to be afforded equal protection of the laws unless some truly compelling interest demands otherwise. This legal regime—equality under a unitary law—has obvious benefits. It satisfies a basic demand for fairness, and it aspires to protect the interests of smaller and more vulnerable groups against the tyranny of the majority. Many people are content now to live under legal systems that do not apply a different set of rules for different ethnic or religious communities.

Readers of this chapter, however, are invited to consider the historical incongruity of this modern legal regime. Law today tends to erase forms of legal identity other than membership within the nation. But what if certain social groups, living in a single polity, desire not to be subject to a uniform set of laws but rather to be allowed, for a variety of issues, to apply their own community's customs and legal usages? Such a communitarian vision of the law was more at home in a world before nation-states. In the Ottoman context, that vision of law, as well as the complications arising from it, is illustrated well by the numerous Ottoman legal opinions (fetvas) on the ehl-i zimmet, a collective term for all non-Muslim communities living under Ottoman rule and protection. The selections below cover questions of religious conversion, social intercourse with non-Muslims, intercommunal space, and taxation. These opinions may be read as an attempt to facilitate intercommunal relations while maintaining the sociolegal integrity of each community. Sometimes that endeavor led to outcomes that appear rigid or offensive to today's sensibilities. Yet this sampling of opinions urges us to consider a society, now largely gone, in which people defined their communal identity in terms radically different from our own.

What practical role did the fetvas play in the constitution of Ottoman law and in the practice of Ottoman courts? Islamic jurisprudence (fıkh) functioned interactively with dynastic law (kanun) to create a uniquely Ottoman legal system. However, Islamic jurisprudence, being a learned science, covered a limited range of doctrinal issues. One way that Muslim jurists, both Ottoman and non-Ottoman, addressed the gaps as they arose was through the fetva (Arabic fatwa). Sometimes called a legal responsum, the fetva was simply an answer to an individual's legal query. Hence the question-and-answer format that fetvas often take. The opinions of prominent or prolific jurisconsults were often compiled in book form after their deaths. The fetvas you read here are selected from such compilations.

The fetva was fundamentally a single jurist's opinion. This means that, unlike a judicial decision, it did not have any intrinsically binding power. Ottoman fetva petitioners were given a piece of paper, signed and sealed, containing a summary of the question and the jurisconsult's answer. They could then use that document to strengthen their case before a judge, but their doing so was entirely voluntary. One may therefore question whether these opinions can tell us anything about actual Ottoman legal practice; however, for two reasons, they can. First, fetvas could, and in many instances did, form the basis of a court ruling. Second, it is wrong to regard the legal opinion as pure theory. As answers to real questions, these opinions expressed an authoritative legal statement on various issues, whether or not those issues saw the inside of a courtroom. The practice of law is not reducible to the practice of courts. The fetvas, therefore, suggest to us how people did conduct—or would have conducted—their affairs in the shadow of the law.

LANGUAGE: Turkish. Interspersed liberally with legal terms. Despite the jargon, most of the questions are straightforwardly formulated. Some excerpts from authorities of the Hanafi school are quoted in Arabic as a postscript to the fetva, probably added as a note in the course of compilation.

SOURCE: If no name appears after the fetva below, the issuer is not specified in the source. Manuscripts, Ottoman prints, or transcriptions: 1. Şeyhülislam Esad. *Fetava-yı Esadiyye* (*Esad* hereafter). Istanbul Müftülüğü (no. 157/2, 27b). 2. Şeyhülislam Menteşizade Abdurrahim. *Fetava-yı Abdurrahim* (*Abdurrahim* hereafter). Istanbul: Darü't-tıba'ati'l-ma'mureti's-sultaniyye, 1243/1827. Vol. 1 (p. 73). 3. *Abdurrahim*. Vol. 1 (p. 62). 4. İbrahim bin eş-Şeyh İsmail el-Kastamoni, *Fetava-yı Halli* (?) (el-Kastamoni hereafter). Istanbul Müftülüğü (no: 1193, fol. 97a). 5. el-Kastamoni (fol. 85a). 6. *Abdurrahim*. Vol. 1 (p. 19). 7. *Abdurrahim*. Vol. 1 (p. 125). 8. Şeyhülislam Erzurumlu Feyzullah, *Fetava-yı Feyziyye ma'a n-nukul* (*Feyziyye* hereafter). Istanbul: Darü't-tıba'ati'l-amire, 1266/1850 (p. 46). 9. *Abdurrahim*. Vol. 1 (p. 160). 10. Düzenli, Pehlül, ed. *Gayrimüslimlere Dair Fetvalar.* Istanbul: Klasik, 2015 (no. 573). 11. Veli bin Yusuf (compiler, d. 1590), *Mecmuatü'l-fetava* (*Mecmua* hereafter), Istanbul Müftülüğü (no: 178, fol. 38a). 12. *Esad* (no. 157/1, fols. 61b–62a). 13. *Abdurrahim*. Vol. 1 (pp. 125–26). 14. *Esad* (no. 157/2, fol. 81a). 15. *Esad* (no. 157/2, fol. 27b). 16. *Esad* (no. 157/2, fol. 27a). 17. el-Kastamoni (fol. 6a). 18. Şeyhülislam Yenişehirli Abdullah. *Behcetü'l-fetava* (*Behcet* hereafter). Istanbul: Darü't-tıba'ati'l-amire, 1289/1872 (p. 167). 19. *Behcet* (p. 168). 20. Salih bin Ahmed el-Kefevi, ed. *Fetava-yı Ali* (*Fetava-yı Ali* hereafter), Istanbul: Sahafiye-i Osmaniye Şirketi, 1311/1839 (p. 174). 21. *Abdurrahim*. Vol. 1 (p. 14). 22. *Fetava-yı Ali* (p. 171). 23. *Mecmua* (fol. 77b). 24. *Feyziyye* (p. 154). 25. *Feyziyye* (p. 155). 26. *Feyziyye* (p. 155). 27. *Mecmua* (fol. 78b). 28. Ataullah Mehmed, *Fetava-yı Ataullah*. Istanbul Müftülüğü (no. 144, fol. 27a). 29. *Esad* (no. 157/1, fols. 75b–76a). 30. Osman bin Mehmed Tosyevi. *Fetava-yi Tosyevi*. Istanbul Müftülüğü (no: 310, fol. 64b). 31. *Mecmua* (fol. 79a). 32. el-Kastamoni (fol. 96a). 33. el-Kastamoni (fol. 97b). 34. *Abdurrahim*. Vol. 1 (p. 77). 35. *Abdurrahim*. Vol. 1 (p. 76). 36. *Feyziyye* (p. 152). 37. *Feyziyye* (p. 153). 38. *Abdurrahim*. Vol. 1 (p. 76). 39. *Mecmua* (fol. 76b). 40. *Esad* (no. 157/2, fol. 39b). Transcription: Düzenli, Pehlül, ed. *Gayrimüslimlere Dair Fetvalar*. Istanbul: Klasik, 2015.

CONVERSION AND ITS IMPLICATIONS

1. Andrea, a zimmi, sells to Atanasi, a zimmi, a dwelling place in his possession. Atanasi in turn [promises to] lodge Andrea in his shop. The aforementioned parties accept the condition that "whichever one of us breaks his word must leave his religion and become Muslim." Afterward, if Andrea honors the condition, while Atanasi goes back on his word and does not honor the condition, should Atanasi legally be forced to convert to Islam?
ANSWER: Yes (Grand Mufti Hocazade Esad, d. 1625).

2. Zeyd, a zimmi, a resident of a village, gets offended at the people of his village over some matter, and says, "From this day forward, if I ever reside in this village, may I be a Muslim." Thereafter he moves away from that village to [another] township and lives there for some time. If he subsequently returns to the mentioned village and resumes residence there, is Zeyd considered to be a Muslim?
ANSWER: No (Grand Mufti Menteşizade Abdurrahim, d. 1716).

3. Zeyd, a zimmi, a resident of Muslim territory, breaks his covenant [as a zimmi] and betakes himself to hostile territory, where he is accepted by the ruler. As he has no heirs in Muslim territory, Bekr, the superintendent of the public treasury, seizes his possessions, and by a special decision of the authorities, sells them to Bişr, a Muslim, for their appraised prices and turns them over. After some time, Zeyd leaves the hostile territory and comes back to Muslim territory, where he is graced with the honor of Islam. Can he then reclaim those possessions from Bişr, citing that they had formerly belonged to him?
ANSWER: He cannot (Grand Mufti Menteşizade Abdurrahim, d. 1716).

4. If a few people compel Zeyd, a zimmi, to convert by bidding him come to Islam, and Zeyd under duress enters Islam, is his conversion valid?

ANSWER: It is. But if he retracts, he is not to be killed, but imprisoned until he becomes a Muslim.

5. After Hind, a Christian, is graced with the honor of Islam, if she renounces her Islam, saying, "I was drunk when I converted," what should be done with her?

ANSWER: She should be imprisoned and not released until she returns to Islam.

6. Zeyd, a zimmi, has been graced with the honor of Islam, and thereby his minor daughters, Hind and Zeyneb, have also become Muslim. If Hind, after reaching legal majority, refuses to accept Islam and reverts, should she be buried in a Muslim cemetery or an infidel cemetery?

ANSWER: She is not to be buried in either. She is to be cast into a ditch and buried as a dog would be (Grand Mufti Menteşizade Abdurrahim, d. 1716).

7. After being graced with the honor of Islam, Zeyd, a zimmi, dies and is buried in a Muslim cemetery. If Amr and Bekr, two priests, disinter Zeyd from his grave and then take him to an infidel graveyard and bury him there, what should be done with them?

ANSWER: Severe beating (Grand Mufti Menteşizade Abdurrahim, d. 1716).

8. Is Zeyd, whose father alone is Muslim, an equal in marriage for Hind, whose father and grandfather are Muslims?

ANSWER: No (Grand Mufti Erzurumlu Feyzullah, d. 1703).

MARRIAGE

9. While Zeyd, a zimmi, is abroad, his wife Hind, a Christian, is graced with the honor of Islam. Thereafter, without conversion to Islam being offered to Zeyd, and while he is still abroad, Hind marries herself to Amr, a Muslim. This being so, Zeyd returns and is graced with the honor of Islam. Does he have the capacity to separate Hind from Amr?

ANSWER: Yes (Grand Mufti Menteşizade Abdurrahim, d. 1716).

10. If Zeyd, who is in charge of a township, forcibly marries Hind, a Muslim, to Amr, a zimmi, and gives Hind to Amr, what should be done with Zeyd?

ANSWER: Severe corporal punishment and incarceration.

11. If Zeyd, a Muslim, after marrying a zimmi woman and consummating [their marriage], dies or divorces her, is it permissible for her to marry an infidel after the legal waiting period has passed?

ANSWER: It is (Grand Mufti Ebussuud, d. 1574).

12. Hind, a Muslim woman, states, "Nikola, an unmarried zimmi, [forcibly] committed fornication with me." What by Holy Law should be done with Nikola?

ANSWER: If any supporting evidence comes to light, then severe beating and incarceration shall be necessary (Grand Mufti Hocazade Esad, d. 1625).

13. Hind, a female Christian, has married herself to Bekr, a zimmi, with judicial permission. Thereafter, if Amr, a priest, along with Bekr declares, "The judge doesn't know our marriage conventions," and then proceeds to marry Hind once again to Bekr according to their false rites, is Amr punishable by fine?

ANSWER: He is punishable not by fine but by corporal punishment (Grand Mufti Menteşizade Abdurrahim, d. 1716).

SOCIETAL REGULATIONS

14. If the predominant dress of the zimmis of a particular region is green, and the zimmi women too wear a green garment called *füstan*, is the legal authority permitted to forbid the aforementioned from wearing green clothes?

ANSWER: No. But they must be distinguishable from Muslims (Grand Mufti Hocazade Esad, d. 1625).

15. Most of the population of a particular region is Jewish. Muslims and Jews are not distinguishable in the bathhouse. When [an individual] claims precedence over Muslims and takes a [prominent] seat at the marble wash basin, and it is not known whether he is a Jew or a Muslim, is it then permissible in that province to impose on the Jews the wearing of an insignia that will suffice to distinguish Jews from Muslims?

ANSWER: Yes (Grand Mufti Hocazade Esad, d. 1625).

16. The Jews living in the township of Ana, near Baghdad, which belongs to Muslim territory, cover their heads with a "Persian headcloth" such that it is not possible to distinguish between Muslims and Jews. If, for this reason, insult and harm befall the Muslim population, is the authority of the specified township, in order to prevent said harm, able, according to the Holy Law, to require the wearing of the broadcloth skullcap that Jews wear [in the rest] of the Muslim territory?

ANSWER: It is necessary to distinguish [Jews from Muslims] on condition that it not constitute oppression (Grand Mufti Hocazade Esad, d. 1625).

17. Zeyd, a Muslim, and Amr, a zimmi, live in the same dwelling. When that dwelling burns down, Zeyd and Amr also burn to death, such that it is not possible to distinguish the Muslim from the zimmi in any way. How, then, should the matters of ritual washing, funeral prayer, and burial of the corpses be handled?

FIGURE 16. Men's bathhouse, nineteenth century. M. J. Starling (engraver), in Thomas Allom, *Constantinople and the Scenery of the Seven Churches of Asia Minor* (London: Fisher, Son & Co., 1838), 34–35.

ANSWER: Each of them should be ritually washed and then buried separately in an empty lot of the cemetery; however, their graves should not have burial mounds but rather be leveled. Prayer is allowed on condition of intention to pray and supplicate for the Muslim.

18. Zeyd, one of the Armenian priests, enters the dwellings of some Armenians without their consent and converses with women who are not unlawful to him in marriage (*nâ-mahrem*). The male householders forbid Zeyd, saying, "We do not consent to your entering our houses." If Zeyd refuses to except the prohibition, citing that it is permitted in their religion, can the authority, at the request of the Armenians, forbid Zeyd from entering their dwellings?

ANSWER: It can (Grand Mufti Yenişehirli Abdullah, d. 1743).

[NOTE:] If they bring the matter before a Muslim judge, or become Muslim themselves, it is necessary to apply the Islamic ruling, as in the case of marriage among unlawful relatives. See "Marriage of the Protected Classes" in *al-Mabsut* (by al-Sarakhsi, d. 1090). In *al-Multaqa* (*Multaqa 'l-abhur* by Ibrahim al-Halabi, d. 1549), citing *Ashbah* (*al-Ashbah wa-l-Nazair* by Ibn Nujaym, d. 1563) on laws pertaining to the zimmi, it is written, "Everything prohibited to the Muslim is prohibited to the zimmi, except for wine and swine."

INTERCOMMUNAL SPACE AND PLACES OF WORSHIP

19. In a township in Muslim territory, zimmis purchase homes in a neighborhood where Muslims reside and take up residence. If the mosque of that neighborhood loses its congregation and falls into disuse, can Zeyd, who is the township's legal authority, remove those zimmis from the neighborhood and relocate them to another neighborhood where there are no Muslims?

ANSWER: Yes (Grand Mufti Yenişehirli Abdullah, d. 1743).

20. Endowed apartments attached to the walls of a mosque precinct are rented by Zeyd, the trustee, to infidels. While this does not diminish the congregation, some of the congregation's members say, "We don't consent to renting to infidels." Can they force Zeyd to remove the infidels?

ANSWER: They cannot (Çatalcalı Ali, d. ca. 1620).

21. In an infidel village, an ancient church falls into decay and an empty lot remains. Furthermore, the population of that village, over the years, has all become Muslim, and no infidels remain. That lot becomes unused and has no known owner. Is it permissible for Zeyd, a benefactor, to buy the lot from the communal treasury and build a mosque in its place?

ANSWER: It is (Grand Mufti Menteşizade Abdurrahim, d. 1716).

22. The [original] residents of a village were zimmis, and in that village is an ancient church. The population having become dispersed, if some Muslims then take up residence in that village, can they have the church demolished?

ANSWER: They cannot (Çatalcalı Ali, d. ca. 1620).

[NOTE:] In *Fath al-Qadir* (by Ibn al-Humam, d. 1457) [it says], "Know that, according to all received opinions, old synagogues and churches in the countryside may not be demolished." See *al-Bahr al-raiq* (a commentary by Ibn Nujaym on *Kanz al-daqaiq* by al-Nasafi, d. 1310) at the beginning of the discussion on the poll tax.

23. If, in a city taken by force, there is a church in the middle of a Muslim district, are the Muslims allowed to tear down the church and erect a mosque in its place?

ANSWER: When it is legally established that [the city] had been taken by force, they have imperial permission (Grand Mufti Ebussuud, d. 1574).

24. A few Muslims, concerning a church located in a township in Muslim territory and in the possession of zimmis, have claimed that, the township having been taken by force, it was not permissible to allow the church to remain. The zimmis who use the church have argued that the township had been taken by treaty and that the aforesaid church had been confirmed for use by the protected people. Owing to the passage of time there is no longer anyone alive who witnessed the conquest and therefore legal testimony is not possible. There is

no reliable document in the hands of the ulema to establish whether the conquest was by force or by treaty. Because the zimmis hold the presumption in their favor, can the township, by means of their sworn oath, be confirmed as conquered by treaty and the church be confirmed to remain in the zimmis' possession?

ANSWER: Yes, it can (Grand Mufti Erzurumlu Feyzullah, d. 1703).

[NOTE:] From a commentary on *al-Siyar al-kabir* (by al-Sarakhsi): "If they have a church in one of the Muslim metropolises and the Muslims seek to bar them from worshipping therein, and the parties dispute, the infidels claiming, 'We belong to the protected people who concluded a treaty for our lands,' and the Muslims claiming, 'Rather, it is we who took your lands by force, after which you were entered into protection;' and if, moreover, so much time has elapsed that what transpired is not known, then the ruler (imam) is to see whether he can find some evidence, with the jurists or the keepers of records, concerning how the occupants came to hold the land. If he finds some reported evidence, he is to act on it. But if he finds no such evidence with the jurists, or finds the evidence to be conflicting, the ruler is to make it a treaty land and resolve the matter in favor of its inhabitants because they are in current possession of it. For it is they who hold the presumption, while it is the Muslims who seek to interfere either by barring them from using the church or by demolishing the church itself. The matter is to be resolved in favor of those who hold the presumption in spite of their beliefs."

25. After the aforementioned township had thus been lawfully taken by treaty, certain Muslim individuals claimed that, because the church was established after the township was conquered and had become one of the Muslim metropolises, it should be proscribed. The zimmis, for their part, cited that it was ancient and, at the time of treaty, confirmed to remain in their possession. Whose claim is superior?

ANSWER: The claim of the zimmis. Evidence must be presented for its establishment after the conquest. It can be proscribed if such evidence is presented. If it is not possible to produce evidence, it is to be confirmed to remain in the possession of the zimmis (Grand Mufti Erzurumlu Feyzullah, d. 1703).

26. When an ancient church of the Christians located in Edirne in Muslim territory burns down as a result of a natural disaster, should those Christians be prohibited from repairing the church to restore it to its prior condition?

ANSWER: They should not (Grand Mufti Erzurumlu Feyzullah, d. 1703).

27. There is an ancient church on a mountaintop. Infidels ascend to a raised platform on top and ring the bells, and other infidels gather around it. Their priests, in accordance with their false rites, deliver sermons, and the congregation weeps and laments. Are the Muslims legally able to destroy the church?

ANSWER: If there is no [Muslim] population around it at all, they should not be accosted. If there is, they should be restrained and prohibited from displaying such emblems of unbelief (Grand Mufti Ebussuud, d. 1574).

28. Half of a large village belongs to Muslims, the other half to infidels. The Muslims have a congregational mosque and a congregation sufficiently large that it cannot fit completely into the mosque, thus giving the village the legal status of a metropolis. If the infidels in the village ring the bells of their ancient churches at certain times, do the Muslims have the legal authority to prohibit them from ringing their bells in this manner?
ANSWER: They do (Ataullah Mehmed, d. 1715).

29. Infidels have seven or eight churches in a town, while the Muslims have no mosque at all. Because their need is pressing, the judge of the province presented the Muslims' request to have one of the churches made into a mosque. The order was issued by the sovereign that one of the churches be made into a mosque, pursuant to which one church has been converted into a mosque. After it has been used for some time for the performance of prayers, can the infidels then return the mosque to its original state as a church on the grounds that, because the city had been taken by treaty, it was their property and they did not agree for it to be made into a mosque?
ANSWER: They cannot (Grand Mufti Hocazade Esad, d. 1625).

30. The original Greek Orthodox (*Rum*) inhabitants of a township possess an ancient church. If the Armenian infidels living in that township should take over the church by force, can they take back their church from those Armenians?
ANSWER: They can.

31. Next to a neighborhood formerly inhabited by Muslims, there are houses of infidels and taverns, because of which the Muslims, being disturbed by immorality and debauchery, have sold many of their homes to infidels and moved to another neighborhood. Can the Muslims remaining in the neighborhood, citing that their mosque no longer has a congregation, force the sale of the infidel houses located close to the mosque?
ANSWER: It is both lawful and necessary that their sale be compelled at their fair value (Grand Mufti Ebussuud, d. 1574).

32. There is a town, possessing both a congregational mosque and a neighborhood mosque, that is inhabited by Muslims and infidels. When the priests of the ancient church proceed to another church together with the infidels, they light candles, and they bring out, display, and parade the cross while raising their voices and in this fashion demonstrate and perform their vain rituals, thereby vexing the Muslims. When the Muslims make the case known to the authority, is the authority able to prohibit them from performing these abominable acts?
ANSWER: He is, and he absolutely must.

TAX REGULATIONS

33. Zeyd, who is charged with collecting the poll tax, requests the tax from Amr, a zimmi. If Amr says, "I am a Muslim! Since when is the poll tax collected from Muslims?" is he to be considered Muslim because of these words?

ANSWER: Yes.

34. Zeyd, a zimmi, is a poll tax payer in a particular village. He has paid the annual poll tax due from him to the village's poll tax collector. Afterward, when he travels from that village to a town nearby to buy some things, can Bekr, who is the poll tax collector for that town, collect for a second time the poll tax due for the same year?

ANSWER: He cannot (Grand Mufti Menteşizade Abdurrahim, d. 1716).

35. Zeyd and Amr are monks who live in a monastery and have no contact with other people. Can the poll tax be sought from them?

ANSWER: It cannot (Grand Mufti Menteşizade Abdurrahim, d. 1716).

36. Can the poll tax be required of Zeyd, a zimmi, who suffers from permanent insanity?

ANSWER: It cannot (Grand Mufti Erzurumlu Feyzullah, d. 1703).

37. Can the poll tax be taken from Zeyd, a zimmi, who is poor, disabled in both hands, and therefore incapable of earning a living.

ANSWER: It cannot (Grand Mufti Erzurumlu Feyzullah, d. 1703).

38. Can the poll tax be collected from Hind, a Christian woman?

ANSWER: It cannot (Grand Mufti Menteşizade Abdurrahim, d. 1716).

39. Are monks exempted from the poll tax and *ispenc* [poll] tax, or are they to be collected from them?

ANSWER: Absolutely not, as long as they are not in contact with people and earning money (Grand Mufti Ebussuud, d. 1574).

40. By Holy Law, are the legal poll taxes that are required of the *reaya* (here: non-Muslim subjects) to be collected at the beginning of the [fiscal] year or at the end?

ANSWER: They are to be collected at the end of the year (Grand Mufti Hocazade Esad, d. 1625).

TWENTY

Conversion Among Ottoman Jews

Responsa by Various Rabbis, Sixteenth Century

TRANSLATED BY MATT GOLDISH

The Jewish law encompasses all aspects of life and is quite complex, like any well-developed legal system. In Jewish tradition the number of biblical commandments is calculated at 613, and there is an authoritative oral tradition explaining how these commandments are to be carried out. When Jews were faced with new situations or issues touching on these laws, they would ask their rabbis what to do. Over a long period, it became common for some rabbis to keep notebooks of the more interesting or complicated cases with which they dealt, along with the answers they gave to these questions. They would edit the material in various ways, often eliding individual names, which would be replaced with the anonymous Reuben, Simeon, Levi, Rachel or Leah. These collections were studied by students and other rabbis as a form of case-law or precedent for deciding other cases. Such questions with their answers are called *responsa*, or, in Hebrew, *she'elot u-teshuvot* (questions and answers). Below is a selection of responsa given by Sephardic rabbis in the Ottoman Empire.

During much of antiquity the Israelites, or Jews, lived in the region which was then called Judea, later called Palestine by the Romans and Muslims, and, which is today in the region of Israel. Roman armies captured this region from the Jews in a war lasting from 67 to 70 CE. Some Jewish inhabitants were able to remain in their land while many others were exiled or sold as slaves all over the Middle East, the Mediterranean, and Europe. Over time large communities aggregated in various parts of the Byzantine and Roman Empires. Sizeable communities existed in Syria, Iraq, Iran, Egypt, Yemen, Italy, Spain, Germany and France, among other places.

In 1492, the large and ancient Jewish community of Spain was given an ultimatum by the Catholic Monarchs, Ferdinand and Isabella. These Jews, called Sephardim, could convert to Catholicism and stay, but if they remained in their Judaism they would have to leave. Some stayed and converted. Many of those who fled went to the then-expanding Ottoman Empire. In addition to the Jews who came to Ottoman lands in 1492, a constant trickle of former Jews who had converted to Catholicism—as well as descendants of such Jews—escaped illegally from Spain and Portugal and came to the Ottoman Empire. These people were called conversos, Marranos, or New Christians. Their status in Jewish law could be highly problematic.

These Iberian Jews found a diverse, longstanding community of Byzantine Jews (Greek speaking Romaniotes), North African Berber Jews (Amazigh speaking), and Arab Jews (Arabic speaking Musta'ribim) already present in these regions. Sometimes the newcomers mixed easily with the older groups and sometimes there was conflict. Most Sephardim continued to use their dialect of Castilian, later called Judeo-Spanish, Judesmo, Ladino, or Haketia. The majority of Jews lived in urban centers, such as Salonica, İzmir, Aleppo, or Cairo—where the community was organized as congregations (kahal) usually attached to a synagogue. Istanbul was home to one of largest Jewish communities. The material in this group of responsa reflects the lives and struggles of Jews, including former conversos, living in the Ottoman Empire during the sixteenth century.

LANGUAGE: Rabbinical Hebrew. Includes many biblical and Talmudic wordings or quotations as well as acronyms, mostly written for a target audience of rabbinic scholars familiar with the allusions.

SOURCE: Case 1: Eliyahu ha-Levi. *Zekan Aharon.* Constantinople: [s.n.], 1734; #25. Case 2: Berab, Jacob. *She'elot u-Teshuvot.* Jerusalem: [s.n.], 1958. First published 1663 by [s.n] (Venice); #39. Case 3: Berab, Jacob. *She'elot u-Teshuvot.* Jerusalem: [s.n.], 1958. First published 1663 by [s.n] (Venice); #44. Case 4: Tam ibn Yahya. *She'elot u-Teshuvot Ohale Tam.* Edited by J. Tzemah. Jerusalem: [s.n.], 1998. First published 1620 as part of *Tumat Yesharim* by [s.n] (Venice); #91. Case 5: Ibn Abi Zimra, David. *She'elot u-Teshuvot Rabbi David ibn Abi Zimra.* Part IV. Jerusalem: [s.n.], 1972; #1086. Case 6: Capusi, Hayim. *She'elot u-Teshuvot Rabenu Hayim Capusi.* Jerusalem: Makhon Yerushalayim, 2010-11; #66. Some cases have been translated and published before. See, for example, the following titles: Goldish, Matt. *Jewish Questions: Responsa On Sephardic Life in the Early Modern Period.* Princeton, NJ: Princeton University Press, 2008. Goldish, Matt. "Jews and Muslims in Egypt at the Turn of the Seventeenth Century: Two Responsa of Hakham Hayim Capusi." In *From Catalonia to the Caribbean: The Sephardic Orbit from Medieval to Modern Times,* edited by Federica Francesconi, Stanley Mirvis, and Brian M. Smollett, 330-38. Leiden: Brill, 2018.

---

1. THE JEW ACCUSED OF HERESY
Early Sixteenth Century

You asked about Reuben, who said to Simeon before many people: "It is forbidden to pray with you, because you are a sectarian heretic. When other people pray, they say, "God of Abraham and God of Isaac;" but when you pray you say, "God of Aristotle!" Reuben said this and similar things in front of many people, forcefully pouring out his wrath in public. He screamed like a child in the crowd, opening his mouth and cursing. He showed no concern about [the dicta]: "Do not cause your friend's face to blanche" (Babylonian Talmud, Tractate Berakhot 43v) and "Nor take up a reproach against his neighbor" (Psalms 15:3).

RESPONSE: (He begins with a strong attack against embarrassing or speaking badly of people, especially scholars). I must add that this mocker who came to Simeon did not denounce him alone, but holy people of the land as well. For he slandered the heads of the ancient Babylonian academies (*ge'onim*) and learned medieval scholars (*rishonim*), who studied the sciences, such as Rabbi Sa'adiah Ga'on and Rabbi Hai Ga'on, as well as other sages like Ibn Gabirol, Rabbi Judah ha-Levi, Rabbi Abraham ben Ezra, Rambam (Rabbi Moshe ben Maimon, i.e., Maimonides), and sages of every generation. They established a great fortress with ramparts to fend off those who speak falsely against our holy Torah. Rambam composed introductions to prove the truth of God's existence that were copied, commented on, and used for betterment by the scholars of other nations. He brought proofs concerning the secrets of the Torah and its meanings, thereby banishing many doubts from the hearts of people who were confused by them in both earlier and later generations—all through learning the Torah and establishing "what to answer the heretic" (Avot 2:14). [. . .]

There is no doubt that anyone who ridicules wisdom in general also derides those who study it—that is, the great wise men of ages past. Although the words of the philosophers contain falsehoods in the matter of divine providence, some of which impinge on the foundations of Torah, those who study their works must not be disgraced. For their issues depend not on faith, but on physical proofs and demonstration—demonstrations visible to the eye. These are easily dismissed by anyone who has filled himself first with the bread of Torah, for he has consumed the nourishment of the mighty. Furthermore, many of [the philosophers] argue about these matters as well. Thus, anyone whom God has granted eyes to see and supplied with understanding will see with his eyes and understand with his heart that man's grasp is too limited to comprehend what is above him; it cannot be proved by demonstration. The true tradition is decisive in nullifying false conclusions that arise in the words of the philosophers. It is about such things that it is said, "Let not our pure Torah be like the idle chatter of others" (Babylonian Talmud, Bava Batra 116r). Everyone who fears the word of God will choose their [the rabbis'] words, which are efficacious and conform to our faith, in the manner of, "He ate the fruit and discarded the shell" (Babylonian Talmud, Hagigah 15v) like Rabbi Me'ir. He will make of them "perfumers and cooks" (I Samuel 8:13). [. . .] (By Eliyahu ha-Levi; fl. early sixteenth century)

2. A CONVERSO AND HIS FLEMISH CONCUBINE

Early Sixteenth Century

QUESTION: Reuben was in Portugal at the time of the persecution and was forcibly converted among the other conversos. At that time, he went to Flanders and took a certain woman from among the Christians of that land as a concubine. She bore him a son. After that he left the non-Jewish woman, who retained her status as a Christian gentile of that place, for she had no wish to convert, only to remain among her nation in her birthplace.

After a time, Reuben fled from under that government and settled in Turkey (Togarmah). He brought the son who had been born to her [the concubine] in order to convert him.

Reuben now married a proper Jewish woman according to the rules for Jewish men, with a canopy and a wedding ceremony. She bore him sons and daughters.

After a time, the son of that gentile concubine died, leaving behind daughters born of a Jewish woman to whom he had been married with a canopy and wedding ceremony. Then Reuben died.

Now, the daughters of the son of that gentile concubine have come, wanting to take part together with the children of [Reuben's] Jewish wife in the inheritance of their [grand]father. The Jewish children say that they [the concubine's granddaughters] have no part in their inheritance, for their father had been born of a different woman, one who came from a completely gentile family, who had been taken with the understanding that she was not at all Jewish. Thus [they said] it is obvious that the son born of that gentile woman is not [Reuben's] son and has no [legal] family relationship with him or with his children. He is like a complete gentile born of a gentile man and woman.

Instruct us now, righteous teacher, whom the law favors, and may your reward be multiplied by heaven.

RESPONSE: (Hakham Berab (d. 1546) agrees that only the family of the Jewish mother inherits).

3. A CONVERT REPUDIATES HER MARRIAGE

Early Sixteenth Century

QUESTION: To our rabbi and teacher; teach us, our rabbi: A certain gentile woman came to find protection under the wings of the divine presence and became a convert. She also brought with her and converted a baby girl whom she had found abandoned in front of their houses of idolatry (a church) and raised in her home. When this girl reached the age of about eight and a half years, a certain converted man accepted money from another converted man earmarked for [the latter's] engagement to this converted girl. She herself received nothing. She was immediately brought to the wedding canopy with that convert who had sent the engagement money to the other convert—[now] the husband of this converted girl.

After the marriage, she had not lived with her husband more than about eight days, when he left. They immediately took the girl to the court of Rabbi Zakhariah, of blessed memory, and before him she formally repudiated the marriage. The rabbi investigated and examined and concluded that this girl was a minor. The rabbi gave her a certificate of marriage repudiation.

Two and a half years later, her husband returned. They hid the converted girl and told him that she was not in town. Seeing this, her husband said explicitly that he would go and inform on them to the gentiles that there were people who had originally been gentiles and

FIGURE 17. Shabbat in a Jewish home in İzmir, ca. 1648. Former Permanent Exhibition of Beit Hatfutsot. The Oster Visual Documentation Center, ANU Museum of the Jewish People, Tel Aviv.

had been converted by the Jews. Out of fear and terror, they brought out the converted girl, and she was alone with her husband with no wedding ceremony or anything else. Afterward, he stayed with her about fifteen days. During that time, he took money and coins from people because he was a silversmith; then he vanished.

Immediately they sent the girl and her nurse out of the region so that, should her husband return, he would not find her there. They say that all this time [the husband] was running about among the gentiles and eating forbidden foods with them. Meanwhile, the converted girl had reached the age of eleven years and eight months.

Now, for everything that is written here, the only testimony is that concerning the marriage repudiation, given by Rabbi David, the son of the rabbi mentioned (R. Zekhariah), before whose father the matter was carried out; and that of the converted girl and her nurse, on whose testimony everything is based.

RESPONSE: This woman is permitted to marry. It is a clear matter and there is no need to expand on it because it is so simple. (By Jacob Berab, d. 1546)

4. BEQUESTS OF CONVERSOS AND THEIR STATUS AS JEWS
Early Sixteenth Century

QUESTION: There are Jewish conversos in the kingdom of Portugal, some of whom come to this kingdom in order to shelter under the wings of the Divine presence (i.e., revert to Judaism), but they leave behind their relatives. When they pass away and leave property behind, what is to be done with it? Should the rabbinic court appoint a custodian for it? Or, if they have some relative here, should it be given to that person until the heirs arrive from Portugal? Inform us, our teacher, what the law dictates, for we do not know whether they should be considered captives or fugitives. Your vision will enlighten us.

RESPONSE: (The response is not from the collection's author, but from a contemporary, Hakham Joseph Shalom. He opens with a fourteenth-century precedent about the treatment of such cases, then moves on to the present case.) This is how it is with these conversos: They derive from the hope of Israel, despite the fact that they have been immersed among the idolaters. Their hope and righteousness endure forever—[the hope] that they will come to a city that is a haven for them in the lands of the Turk's righteous rule, may God raise him up. Furthermore, when they come to be included among the Jews, they are simply circumcised; they are not immersed [in the ritual bath] like converts who were never part of the Jewish people. They do not have the status of converts, whose goods are given to the first in line (i.e., their gentile relatives have no prior claim). So, [the inheritance of dead conversos] is to be held by the rabbinic court until an heir arrives. Or those who are living in the lands of idolatry in Portugal should be informed about it. If they either give up on [the inheritance] or choose to donate it to some charity, the individual or charity they designate should get it.

Out of my love of brevity I have kept it short. So speaks the one who completed it, a worm and not a man, Joseph Shalom. (By Tam ibn Yahya, d. ca. 1542)

5. LENDING MONEY TO APOSTATES AND THEIR DESCENDANTS
Sixteenth Century

QUESTION: I was asked concerning the descendants of apostates—that is, people whose ancestors became Turks (i.e., Muslims). They come to Alexandria with merchandise. Is it permissible to lend them money at interest or not?

RESPONSE: There is a long-standing disagreement concerning apostates. Rashi (Solomon ben Isaac), of blessed memory, wrote in a responsum that it is forbidden to lend them money at interest because, though they have transgressed, they remain Jews. There is also the matter of "Thou shalt not place a stumbling block before a blind man" (Leviticus 19:14). Others have also subscribed to his view. The R"I (Isaac ben Samuel ha-Zaqen) states that one may lend them money at interest, for the passage "that your brother may live with you" (Leviticus 25:36) does not apply to them, for you are not commanded to help them make a living.

It appears to me that this [latter ruling] is correct with reference to the Karaites who have rejected the oral law. This argument would also mean he [who lends them money at interest] does not transgress [the verse] "Thou shalt not place a stumbling block before a blind man." To borrow money from them [at interest], however, is forbidden according to all authorities, for it would constitute "placing a stumbling block." In the *Book of Commandments*

[Maimonides] writes that it is forbidden to lend at interest to the kind of apostate who eats forbidden foods to satisfy his appetites; but it is permitted to lend to the kind of apostate who did it to antagonize, because regarding taking interest, it states "your brother. [. . .]"

Now, even though the ancestors of these who come to Alexandria were forced converts, at this stage they are considered apostates intending to antagonize, because if they wished, they could return to Judaism as others have done. This is even more true for those who go to secure lands where they are their own masters. We might wonder whether there is a distinction between the actual apostates and their descendants. [In] the *Haggahot Maimuniyyot* [Me'ir ha-Kohen] writes that [with reference to] the arguments about descendants of apostates, it should be understood that there is no distinction between them [and the apostates themselves.] This is indeed the law, for, since he can return [to Judaism] and does not return, he is himself an apostate.

All this applies when we know that the mother is also an apostate, for if the mother is a foreigner (*nokhrit*), the offspring follow her status, since we maintain the principle that when a Jew has relations with a non-Jewish woman, the [religious] status follows the woman. In situations where there is a doubt we generally follow the principle that doubtful situations pertaining to Torah law follow the stricter ruling. Here, however, since there is both a difference of opinion and a doubt, we are lenient and [allow the] loan of money at interest. This is all the more so in the case of people who are several generations removed [from the actual apostate] and have already assimilated among the Turks. Furthermore, had they wished, they could have returned to the Jewish religion as we wrote above.

Although I am unworthy of deciding [a dispute] among the earlier authorities, it appears to me that it would be permissible to lend money at interest even to the apostates themselves, in accordance with the R"I and the SeMa"G (*Sefer Mitzvoth Gedoloth*), of blessed memory. For, because they rejected the God of Israel and embraced idolatry, they are to be considered complete idolaters in this matter. Even though their betrothals are effective, we are strict about this, for it cannot be otherwise. [. . .]

This is how it appears in my humble opinion. (By David ibn Abi Zimra, d. 1573)

6. A CONVERSA JEWESS TESTIFIES ABOUT A MURDER
Spring 1598

At the assembly of the three [judges] sitting together there appeared the young man Jacob ibn Shevet Yedei Hendi, may his Creator protect him. He said that one day, about a month previous, he purchased some silver scraps from a certain gentile. He brought the man to his home in order to pay him what he owed, and he placed a meal before him. Jacob then asked him, "From where have you come?" for the man appeared as if he had just arrived from a journey. The gentile replied, "I have come from Rashid (Rosetta), and on the way I stopped at a village about a day's distance from Rashid. There I saw a certain gentile who said to two Jews: "Would you like to buy silver?" They told him, "Yes." He brought out a broken silver necklace weighing almost a hundred drachma (ca. 310 grams). They bought it from him, and the gentile said, "Give me payment." They gave him the money, and after they had paid the money another gentile came up from behind them, struck them, and knocked them to the ground. He then slaughtered them, dragged them to the brick furnace, and threw them in."

On the same day, at the assembly of the three [judges] sitting together, there appeared Gutzna the wife of Mr. Samuel al-Zouari. She said that during their return from Rashid, on her arrival at the neighborhood of Abu Ali, she went to purchase bread for her journey at the marketplace of the abovementioned town. There she ran into a certain gentile woman, who said to Gutzna: "*Shema Yisrael!*" Gutzna was amazed by this and said to the gentile woman, "Who taught you this phrase?" She responded that she had been a Jewish woman, but she was coerced [to convert]. Now she is married to a gentile and has consumed all her assets. She cried about her conversion, sighing and saying that when she smells the odor of a Jew, her soul goes out of her.

Immediately, during her sighs, she said to Gutzna: "Did you know those poor Jews who were murdered here—Imanu and his friend?" She replied, "No." The gentile woman said to her: "In our multitude of sins, those Jews came with [the Muslim silver sellers] to sleep here [in the inn] with them. Out of my love for the Jews I said to them in Spanish: "Take care that you do not sleep [under the same roof as] these men, for they are murderers who kill every Jew who crosses their path." Imanu responded to me, "I am not afraid of them! I am a Maghrebi (from North Africa) and I will strike them a death blow!" That very night they murdered them and threw their dead bodies into the pit. In my jealousy on behalf of the children of my nation I wanted to shout, but my husband yelled at me and prevented me from crying out. My husband said, "I am by myself, and I fear that if you cry out, they will say that I am married to a Jewish woman. They will come, gang up on me and beat me. Therefore, remain silent and do not cry out." That same night I saw that they lifted [the bodies] out from the pit and brought them to the lime furnace, where they burned them together with the lime. Since that night I am ill with a head sickness." She further said to Gutzna: "If you know of some cure, inform me of it."

This [testimony] was given on Tuesday, the twenty-ninth day of the month of Nisan in the year 5358 since the creation here in Cairo.

Hayim Capusi Solomon son of the honored Rabbi Me'ir Somekh ha-Kohen David son of the honored Rabbi Sa'adya 'Adani, of blessed memory.

[RESPONSE: This testimony is fully acceptable, and the wives may remarry. (By Hayim Capusi, d. 1631)]

TWENTY-ONE

Marriage and Divorce Among Ottoman Jews

Responsa by Various Rabbis, Seventeenth Century

TRANSLATED BY LEAH BORNSTEIN-MAKOVETSKY

The Ottoman legal system allowed the family and inheritance laws of different religions to exist side by side. Adjudication in an ordinary Ottoman court of law was carried out by a kadı, or a judge, according to Ottoman secular law and the Islamic Holy Law (sharia). Yet, zimmis—that is, protected denominational groups such as Christians and Jews—were free to use their own customary family and inheritance laws. Therefore, the judicial codex commonly used by a kadı was not forced on non-Muslim denominations of the Ottoman population unless the dispute fell in the realm of penal law or if one of the litigators in a lawsuit was a Muslim.

The option to bring a case either before a denominational court or before a kadı was not regulated and was thus at the discretion of the litigants. Documentation suggests that most Jews used the rabbinical courts, but there were quite a few who made use of the kadı's court. A litigant's preference for a kadı's court over a rabbinical court might be ascribed to lower fees, speedier adjudication, one or the other judge's reputation for lenient rulings, or an attempt to make use of the "loopholes" between legal traditions—but also to the kadı's power to have his rulings enforced. Displeased by this, some rabbis issued warnings to their flocks against ratifying their marital contracts or resolving their disputes anywhere other than in the rabbinical courts; even so, neither the rabbi nor the community possessed real coercive power.

The rabbinical court was founded on Jewish law and jurisprudence (halakha) based on the Talmud. The responsa—that is, legal opinions, issued by various prominent rabbis—were later compiled into books, and served as legal compendia for legal scholars to study (see chapter 20). The narratives of some of these cases suggest that they may have been partially theoretical legal exercises; nonetheless, a wealth of information about seventeenth-century Jewish life can be gleaned from these documents. While these documents were primarily composed with rhetorical sensitivity to correspond with rabbinic legislation, social and cultural historians look for the details of the real lives that emerge from between the lines.

The documents suggest that modesty and a strict observance of the religious commandments—especially around kashrut, or dietary laws, and family purity—generally held a central place in the societal expectations for Jewish women. Women were married at approximately age twelve to a husband usually chosen by their family. Polygamy was also possible among Ottoman Jews; the rabbinical court frequently permitted a husband to take a second wife, particularly in cases where the couple remained childless after ten years of marriage. While Jewish law gives the right to dissolve the marital bond only to the husband—a prerogative that created difficulties for women who could not get out of complex situations—a woman could seek divorce by paying her husband to persuade him to give her a *get*, or a divorce document. In rare cases, the wife could also initiate a divorce on the basis of detesting the husband (case 2 below). Importantly, women in unhappy marriages did not want to lose their right to the monetary support conferred by the ketubah, or marriage contract.

The cases below provide snapshots from domestic entanglements of Jewish women in a variety of Ottoman regions such as Egypt, Palestine, and greater Syria in the seventeenth century. The complexity of the actual situations could only be addressed by proper references to the intricate halakhic body of knowledge.

LANGUAGE: Complex rabbinical Hebrew with abundant legal references and prayers. The translations below were carried out with a degree of simplification and truncation to make the cases accessible to modern audiences.

SOURCE: Case 1: Rabbi Yom Tov Tzahalon. *Maharitatz New Responsa.* Jerusalem: Makhon Yerushalayim, 1980, section 38. Case 2: Ibid., section 172. Case 3: Rabbi Daniel Estrosa. *Responsa Magen Gibborim.* Salonika: [s.n.], 1754, section 9. Case 4: Ibid., section 75. Case 5: Rabbi Mordekhai ha-Levi. *Responsa Darkhei Noam.* Venice: [s.n.], 1697, Even ha-Ezer, section 53. Case 6: Rabbi Avraham ha-Levi. *Responsa Ginat Veradim.* Istanbul: Bi-defus Yonah ben Ya'akov mi-Zlozits, 1716, Even ha-Ezer, section 4:21.

---

1. AN ABANDONED WIFE SEEKS LEGAL DIVORCE
Early Seventeenth Century

QUESTION: Concerning a certain Jewish male who married a woman here in Damascus, lived with her for some time, and then traveled out of the country. He left his wife here in eternal widowhood and converted from our faith. Just as he did not have any contact with his wife while he was still a Jew, he continued on without contact after his [spiritual] death. Things continued until a few gentlemen of his new residence approached him and, speaking gently, asked, "Is it good of you to oppress and abandon this fine woman, leaving her moaning, wrapped in poverty and eternal widowhood?" They offered monetary incentives until the man was willing to release her with a legal divorce document (get). They brought him to a court in the city of Bursa. He wrote the document and appointed an agent from his town to deliver it to her.

When the get was brought before us with a document, in which the messenger of the get was appointed, we saw that the documents were garbled and written in incoherent words—such that they wrote in the get about someone called Levi, whereas the man['s name] is not Levi. The mistake in the document stemmed from the fact that the man was orphaned when he was a small child and grew up with his relatives who were Levites. He grew up ignorant and never went to the synagogue where his name was declared; he never put on *tefillin*—as his end proves his beginning.

Now his wife, this poor woman, is sitting weeping for her youth, because she was hoping to get a divorce and now it is not happening. She asks the court to legalize the divorce. It is possible that the husband acted wickedly and intended to thwart the divorce. I (Rabbi Yisrael Najara) asked several women who were his relatives and they said that they used to call him Levi because of his relatives. According to the testimony of the get's emissary, the court gave permission to the scribe of the court and the judges (*dayanim*) to write a get in order to allow the woman to marry another man.

(The answer was signed by Rabbi Yisrael ben Moshe Najara (d. 1625). It was [then] sent for the approval of Rabbi Yom Tov Tzahalon (d. 1638) in Safed. He agrees to approve the get.)

2. A MARRIAGE GONE SOUR

Early Seventeenth Century

QUESTION: Rachel, daughter of Simon, rebelled against her husband, saying that she did not want to be with him owing to their strife and contention. Both of them came to the court to bring their claims. This is what the woman said three times before me in the court in Ladino: "I don't want him." The court asked her, "Why? Have you not loved each other since childhood?" She responded that from the first night of their marriage he has searched for libelous claims to give her a bad name, as is known [in the community], in order to divorce her without paying the monetary obligation of the marriage contract (ketubah), or at least to lower the payment. From then on, her heart has not been with him, and therefore she said that she does not want him nor his marriage contract. It is now nine months that they are married. There have been many quarrels and harsh disagreements between them. He was living at his father-in-law's house according to [the latter's] promise to support the couple for two years, but he left until peace was brokered between them so that he would return. The husband complained continuously that she didn't love him. She, in turn, responded that he did not show her the face of love and peace. This time he left in anger; he has argued with his wife and even with his in-laws. She spoke brazenly and said, "I won't see your face again; you are disgusting!" Will the court please judge in righteousness to determine if this woman is considered rebellious (*moredet*).

The Rabbi (Yom Tov Tzahalon) is asked to look into this case and write a judgment if the law of the rebellious wife applies to that woman. The rabbi is also asked to determine whether she is entitled to keep the clothes that her husband gave her as a bride price (*mohar*) and a gift, and to establish that the husband does not have permission to sell them, despite the fact that she is a "rebellious woman." Will the clothes she took remain with her, because she now lives in her father's house? Some believe that if she lives there, she is not allowed to keep the clothes given by her husband and has to return them within twelve months of the day she declared herself a "rebellious woman," and can keep only the clothes she received from her father.

ANOTHER QUESTION: If, after twelve months of marriage, the wife continues to be rebellious and the husband does not want to divorce her, thus effectively making her an *agunah* (an abandoned wife), can the assets that she kept be grounds to force the husband to divorce her? Is it possible to say that if forcing a divorce through the use of flogging or a Muslim court is considered, it will be a divorce out of coercion, and the get will thus not be valid?

DISCUSSION: Does the husband have the right to marry another woman? The question is if he has halakhic permission to marry another woman within twelve months, and if it is possible to find a halakhic permit to break the oath that he swore to his wife not to take a second wife. To this end the husband will bring forth the rationale that he has a [natural] instinct that demands him [to remarry] and that he must also fulfill the commandment of procreation. Perhaps during the course of twelve months he and his wife will again become committed to their marriage.

ANOTHER DISCUSSION: Is it possible for the court to impose a boycott on the woman in order to demand her to tell the truth? She declared that from the first night she hated him. However, the husband claims that her father and mother instructed her to say so.

RESPONSE: This woman is subject to the law of a woman who hates her husband and is therefore considered a rebellious woman. In my humble opinion, it is likely that the dayanim would threaten to censure her if she did not tell the truth. It seems that she sincerely hated him, and that her father and mother did not coach her to utter this claim. Until the husband divorces her, he will not be able to marry another woman. If he does so, he is an offender who breaks the oath of God.
(Signed by Rabbi Yom Tov Tzahalon, d. 1638).

3. A WIFE REFUSES TO MOVE WITH HER HUSBAND TO A DIFFERENT CITY
Early to Mid-Seventeenth Century

He had sworn to his wife an oath not to marry a second woman. It so happened that he was forced to flee to another city owing to his debts. He found refuge and sent for his wife to come and live with him, but she did not want to go. He remained eight years without a wife. The court released him from his oath not to remarry. Now he asks if the permit is valid. Rabbi Moshe Hayim [of Salonika] ruled that he was exempt from the oath. The halakhic response was sent to Rabbi Daniel Estrosa [of Salonika] who wrote, "I have seen the words of the Rabbi, my good friend Rabbi Moshe Hayim, that if [the judges] cancelled the oath, the husband is released from the oath."

This man asked his wife to come to Salonika or Istanbul or to any other city [with him]. He cannot go back to his old town, where she lives, because of his debts there. The rabbis wrote to the city's Jewish leaders to ask her to follow him, but she did not answer and did not obey the words of the rabbis. So, the permit he received to marry another woman was valid.

(Signed by Rabbi Daniel Estrosa, d. 1654).

4. A WIDOW TAKES POSSESSION OF THE WHOLE INHERITANCE

Early to Mid-Seventeenth Century

QUESTION: Reuben died and left behind two sons from two wives who had died in his lifetime, and a widow with two sons, and an engaged daughter. He left behind a bequest of money and goods he had bought on credit, with bills and documents relating to these goods from Jewish and European merchants, and real estate as well. There was a dispute about how to divide the inheritance between the sons, and also between the sons and the widow.

The widow took possession of everything that her husband owned: silver, gold, copper, household items, bills, notes, and accounts, as well as her husband's notebook in which he recorded all his negotiations with people from his town and from Frankia (Italy). She claims that she is taking the gold for her livelihood. In regard to the courtyard and the houses she owns in which she dwells, she claims that she took them to cover her marriage contract, saying that she wants to be secure, although she does not intend to collect [the amount indicated in] her marriage contract during her lifetime.

The heirs claim that it is not proper to withhold so much property when it is many times the value of her marriage contract, and that it is causing them harm because the bills and the accounts and the notebook of the deceased are lying in a box and the money is lost. She is required to provide them with the bills, the accounts, and with the notebook so they can manage and use them. In addition, the heirs claim that if she wishes to collect the amount noted in her marriage contract, that this amount is invested in land that the deceased left for the express purpose of repaying her marriage contract; if that is sufficient for her, they agree to fulfill her demand. They claim that she lives in one of the houses and would rent the other houses and make a living from the income. If the money she receives is not enough for a living, [the heirs] promise to supply the remainder of the sum, or even give her a document of assurance, as required by the Jewish court. Who is right in this quarrel, the heirs or the widow?

RESPONSE: The seizure of assets by the widow is illegal. A trustee should be appointed to manage the estate and ensure that the value of the estate is increased, so that the widow and the heirs will divide the profits.

(Signed by Rabbi Daniel Estrosa, d. 1654).

5. A WOMAN BUYS HER DIVORCE FROM A GOOD-FOR-NOTHING HUSBAND

1680

Moshe Guta was in prison on account of his debts to gentiles. At various times he sent messages to his wife requesting that she save him and pay off his debts. He appeared before our court and made a claim against his wife. She responded that nothing remained of his estate at all, or of his jewelry, because everything had been sold in order to support the family. [She added] that he had not worked a day since their marriage and had not dealt with the settlement or worked to put food on the table.

He had no response. He returned to prison where he remained for a long while. Ultimately, his wife agreed to sell off a part of her dowry for the sum of seven thousand *maydis* silver coins if he legally divorced her. She would take care of the children and forgo all monetary claims that she may have against him. She gave him the sum required to pay the debts to secure his release from prison. She would give him the additional sum [of seven thousand maydis] when he divorced her. When [the defendant] reached the Jewish court, the dayanim tried to mediate between them, but they did not succeed. He just wanted to write her the divorce document.

The protocol of the divorce is as follows: "Before our court, Moshe Guta ben Yom Tov came to us and asked us to write him a kosher (legal) divorce document to divorce his dear and modest wife, Mrs. Irmuza, the daughter of the late Hayim Reuben. He had already agreed with her on the amount [determined by] her marriage contract to be paid, and for every claim and demand that she requested. We asked him the reason for the divorce—whether it was because of a quarrel between them, in which case we would try to mediate and reconcile them in the manner most appropriate to them. Moshe replied that he had no desire to reconcile with his wife, and that it was gratifying for him to divorce her, because he was unable to provide her and her children with bread and water. We came back a second time and told him that despite all these details, we would try to reconcile them, and asked that he try to live with her for a month or even some years—maybe God would pity him and grant him a livelihood. We told this to him three times, but he objected and said he had no desire to live with her. We suggested that perhaps because of the debts he owes, he wants to take money from his wife to pay the creditors, and that this is why he wants to divorce her. If this were the real problem, we would make an effort to find him the money to pay off his debts, and he would continue to live with his wife as is customary among Jewish men. The woman would agree to take thirty silver maydis from him every week and provide him and his sons with food. He replied that he had no desire to live with her.

As we witnessed his efforts to divorce her, we demanded to know, with the force of the Torah and all the biblical signs written in the Torah, whether he divorced her out of coercion and not out of free will—perhaps his wife or someone representing her was forcing him to divorce her. He stated with all the power of the aforementioned decrees that he was not coerced. We, the rabbinical court, saw that the situation was real and that he was divorcing her with absolute will. Therefore, we wrote a divorce document for her according to the

FIGURE 18. Jewish woman, ca. 1650s. Artist unknown. Cod.Rål. 8:o no. 10 (*Rålambska dräktboken*), fol. 72. Kungliga Biblioteket, Stockholm.

Jewish law. And he divorced his wife on the twenty-eighth of the month of Iyar 5440 (May 27, 1680) here in Cairo."

After divorcing her, it took him about a week to appeal the validity of the divorce on the grounds that he had not divorced her of his own free will. He brought a notification of duress (*moda'ah*) without the signatures of the witnesses, which he himself forged and signed in place, because they could not write or read what was written in the bill.

The following is the language of the witnesses' statement: "Because we, Avraham son of Samuel Makazich and Isaac ben Nissim Atroti, have entered prison, we met there Moshe Guta ben Yom Tov Guta. He told us that he had been in prison for seven months because of a debt. He said to us: "You two will testify in court how I divorced my wife against my will." We asked him: "What is the reason?" He answered that his wife, Irmuza bat Hayim Reuben, took everything he had, silver and gold and jewelry and the house's chattels and copper and carpets. More importantly, she took his sons, and he had not seen them for a year. She also took six thousand silver coins from his mother. He asked her for one object that belonged to him so that he could get out of prison. She told him that she would not give him anything, [upon which] he told her that he does not want her. She sent to him an official (*kapıcı*) of the superintendent of the janissary guards (*baş çavuş*), who told him that he was authorized by her to represent her in this case. He found no way to save himself from prison.

We testify that she sent [the official] to tell him that she would give him six thousand maydis and, [in return] he would give her a divorce document. But he refused the offer. When his debtors heard about this, they told him to accept this offer. They organized seven thousand maydis so that he could give her a divorce document. He came to us and told us that we were witnesses that he did not want to divorce his wife, and that he gave her the divorce document against his free will. He stated that the forgiveness he will give her is not a forgiveness and that the oath he will swear is not an oath, and that everything his father left him was in her home. He divorces her because he does not want to remain in jail. We, the witnesses, realized that he was acting out of coercion. He told us that the notification of duress (moda'ah) is valid and cannot ever be annulled. Even if he annuls it before the court, the annulment is against his free will. He gave us this testimony to be handed over to the court and to the Holy One, blessed be He. He swore a solemn oath not to annul the notification of duress and told us that it will be in effect for as long as he has it. And all this happened before us on Tuesday, 22 Iyar 5440 [May 22, 1680] here in Cairo."

Then the court saw this unsigned document and we, the court members, ordered the two witnesses to the court. They came from the prison and we received their testimony orally; each of them testified separately. They testified in slurred language because they are ignorant. One of them testified that Guta had vowed not to divorce, and the other testified that Guta had sworn not to cancel the notification of duress.

A SECOND RESPONSE: My heart trembles at the Jewish criminals who follow the whims of their hearts and distress the daughters of Israel, who are like captives in the hands of hard masters. These criminals conspire to rob them of their wealth and cause them to deviate from the straight path. These women are like slaves who have been taken captive in a war. We must help the women while husbands lie and say that the divorce bill that they gave is not kosher and was obtained through coercion.

I (Rabbi Mordekhai ha-Levi) did not attend [the court proceeding] when this divorce was arranged and my soul is saddened to see this evil act. When I left the court, the dayanim who stayed told me that the husband had returned with a criminal named Avraham Kajiji who entered the court with brazenness and testified about the notification of duress. It seems that he is helping the husband appeal the divorce. I decided to investigate this case and am writing a ruling.

In the case in question, he was put in prison not because of his wife and relatives but because of his debtors. The woman did not act to save him with her own money and the assets of her dowry unless he divorced her. The woman had already denied several times that she had taken assets away from him. He had no assets left because he had sold them off, and she did not have to give him her own assets to pay off his debts. He had lost even the jewelry that he had brought her when he married her, and she blamed him for losing it. Even if all the jewelry were still there, they are, according to Jewish law, "assets of iron" that belong to the woman. The husband is forbidden from selling or pawning these assets without the consent of his wife. This law is valid even if the husband cannot earn a livelihood.

The husband wrote in the notification of duress that the woman has sent an official (kapıcı) of the superintendent of the janissary guards (baş çavuş). It is possible to deduce that the husband sent her a message every day asking to collect money from her to pay his debts. That is why she sent the kapıcı as her representative, so he would save her from her husband's demands. That is what the woman said when she was asked about this case.

When the husband and the offender (Kajiji) who supported him saw that we canceled what he had done, they came together to the court where we sat with one of the witnesses of that notification of duress. The criminal Avraham Kajiji came before the court and asked why we, the court, are cancelling the notification. He said that we knew after all that the kapıcı came to talk to the husband in prison and told him that he had no way out of jail unless he divorced his wife and gave her a divorce bill. And that therefore, he was forced to divorce her. Then, when the husband and the criminal who supported him saw that we, the dayanim, had canceled what he had done, they came together to our court. Two men (Kajiji and another man) appeared with the husband to speak against the court, and they dared to face the court. We, the judges, asked them if they were telling the truth, and why they did not write all this down in the notification of duress. We told them: "You cannot be disrespectful to us. You just have to give the court evidence." We asked them: "What do you care if a solution is found for the woman? You are criminals who wanted to act against her." The rabbinical court judges left the court angrily. My heart burned like fire. I was afraid people would say there was a problem here and that the woman would be an agunah. Thus, I sat down to write the ruling.

A THIRD RESPONSE: The husband had to interrogate the kapıcı about whether or not the wife talked to him about the divorce. The woman denies this. She undertook to pay his debts and get him out of jail on the condition that he would divorce her. This does not annul the validity of the divorce contract.

(Signed by Rabbi Mordekhai ha-Levi, d. 1685).

6. A HUSBAND ARRANGES PAYMENT TO HIS WIFE
Late Seventeenth Century

QUESTION: Reuben is very concerned about his wife Rachel, who does not have a child, is solitary, and is very worried. He has a son from another woman, and that son is a quarrelsome mischief-maker. It is clear as day that after Reuben's death his widow (Rachel) will be launched out of the frying pan into the fire at the hands of his tyrant son. Reuben came to consult with the court, as he wishes to transfer the value of his marriage contract to his wife now, and to ensure her salvation to the greatest extent that he can.

RESPONSE: We have reviewed the marriage contract of this woman and her value is such and such. We told the husband to appraise the belongings and other objects of his wife [so that] the value and weight of each item will be recorded separately. [These items] will be in the hands of the wife when the husband dies. The woman will not have to declare or have them evaluated for the heirs. The woman should be given a one-time payment of three thousand maydis for her living expenses after her husband's death, because that is the amount customarily given to poor women in town. In addition, her husband will ask her to take a solemn oath that she has not taken his belongings and money until now, like the oath that the rabbinical court has widows swear. The husband will also ask the heirs to swear that they will not prevent her from receiving the money he left her for her marriage contract. Then her husband would write a pledge [to the court] that would apply to him and his successors for the whole amount. The husband wants to make his wife happy.

We left a sum of three thousand maydis from her marriage contract in accordance with the sum written in the marriage contracts of poor women living in the city. Therefore, if a quarrel arises between the woman and the heirs, it will be only for a small amount. It is true that her faithfulness (*ne'emanut*) alone [that she only took what she deserved] will protect her against an appeal from the heirs. She will swear a widow's oath, so that the heirs will not claim that she stole a piece of gold. It is better for a woman to have the whole procedure done at once.

(Signed by Rabbi Avraham ha-Levi, d. 1712).

TWENTY-TWO

News from Istanbul at the Turn of the Seventeenth Century

The Chronicle of Selaniki

TRANSLATED BY H. ERDEM ÇIPA

The sections in this chapter are from a late sixteenth-century chronicle. An imperial chronicle was a history that documented events related to the imperial court and the state in a sequential fashion sometimes spanning decades. One can say that it was a "newspaper" of sorts, but with much more limited circulation. The Ottoman term for a historical work was *tarih*; this label was applied to a variety of historical productions. Even though chroniclers are generally assumed to have set aside their own interpretations, it is safe to say that no historical writing is untouched by politics and societal concerns. It was customary for the imperial family and the grandees of the state to support artists and writers with grants, gifts, or scholarships as befit the dignity of the imperial court culture. It is not difficult to imagine that those reflecting on contemporary events were mindful of adopting a favorable approach toward their patrons. As such, modern readers of these narratives must be careful to contextualize the chronicler's connection to his patrons. Histories could be written to justify a political position, glorify a campaign, eulogize statesmen, or investigate controversial current events. Most events worthy of being recorded in such works had to do with the imperial court and the state.

Mustafa Selaniki (d. ca. 1600) was, as his byname suggests, from Selanik (modern-day Thessaloniki). Having held several mid-level positions in the state bureaucracy, he kept a "journal" of sorts in the form of a chronicle, covering the events that transpired mostly in Istanbul from 1563 to 1600 and stretching over the reign of four sultans. It seems Selaniki was not commissioned by a patron to compose this work. Clues in the text indicate that he was hoping to submit the work to a prominent statesman but was unable to do so before his death. The text starts abruptly, without the customary stylistic flourishes and encomia to God and the Prophet Muhammad at the beginning of the work. It is thus safe to assume that the text was still in need of a final revision.

What makes this work valuable is the temporal proximity of its entries to the events the historian describes. Selaniki evidently wrote his entries more or less contemporaneously with events. Most chroniclers wrote accounts of periods before their time, in part because many of the contentious issues described therein would have been resolved by the time of their writing, thus mitigating possible political fallout. Alternative ideas or viewpoints would have been squelched and made to disappear from the historical account, leaving behind only the winning perspective. Selaniki's sources were many—he had access to some state correspondence, he interviewed people and made use of town gossip—but many of his vivid entries reflected his own observations.

As Selaniki failed to secure a patron for the work and thus have it promoted to a wider audience, his chronicle remained little-known until the eighteenth century. The prominent historians of the seventeenth century do not quote him. His misfortune became modern historians' luck: had he found a patron, he might have censored or altered the text. Instead, we have a lucid and bold account from someone who seems to have felt no obligation to any particular patron or faction.

LANGUAGE: Turkish. Fairly precise and uncomplicated language, albeit with the standard amount of Arabic-Persian loan vocabulary, but minimal elements of wordplay or rhymed prose. Curious anecdotes close to colloquial language.

SOURCE: İpşirli, Mehmet, ed. *Tarih-i Selaniki* / Selaniki Mustafa Efendi. Istanbul: İstanbul Üniversitesi Edebiyat Fakültesi, 1989 (225, 227, 232–33, 238, 283–84, 287, 417, 485, 487, 532, 545, 677–78, 849–51). Ottoman print: Mustafa [Selaniki]. *Tarih-i Selaniki.* [Istanbul]: Matbaa-i Amire, 1281/1864. Occasionally the variants listed in İpşirli's edition or the printed version (Istanbul, 1281/1864) were preferred.

THE IMPRISONMENT OF JUDGES IN YEDİKULE (SEVEN TOWERS) PRISON
August 1590

In the orders and decrees regarding public property sent in the direction of Rumeli, judges were strictly warned, "Do not allow sergeants and other assignees [on unrelated business] to collect money from taxpaying subjects." Yet zealous judges who acted with malicious egoism forbade [the appointed tax collectors] who came to gather taxes and refused to show them reverence and kindness. Over time, taxes were not collected, funds did not reach the threshold of felicity in a timely manner, and hardship ensued.

When a judge who impeded the collection of taxes was handed over to sergeants and imprisoned, [other] judges incited theology students and low-level medrese graduates in coffeehouses. They assembled in the courtyard of the Sultan Mehmed Mosque and declared, "What kind of insult to the ulema is this? It affects us all." The leading and prudent ones among them informed His Excellency, the grand vizier, about those who had caused the arousal of sedition. Right away, seven judges were contemptuously captured and imprisoned at Yedikule.

THE EXECUTION OF THE TRAITORS AMONG THE SCRIBES OF THE IMPERIAL COUNCIL

October 1590

When His Excellency, grand vizier Sinan Pasha—*may God Almighty perpetuate his magnificence*—was appointed to the grand vizierate this time, he observed significant disorder and deficiency in various affairs of state. Owing to the negligence and carelessness of those in positions of power and through their intervention on behalf of others, unqualified individuals of the most disgraceful kind were appointed to all businesses. In the imperial council as well as in financial administration, impudent scribes composed falsified warrants and certificates. [Blank] papers furnished with the noble imperial cypher that were [ordinarily] dispatched to commanders participating in the eastern expeditions came into the possession of treacherous scribes, who wrote whatever they wanted, thus causing disorder in affairs of state. Through inquiry and research some valiant and fearless scribes produced a kind of ink, with which all decrees that had been written were erased from paper, and they wrote whatever they wanted. The dealings of those who were addicted to adulterations and misrepresentations became known. The chancery scribes nicknamed "Feeder of the Hungry" and a certain Şems Ahmed called "the Foolish" were captured. On investigation and inquiry, when their villainy, treason, and crimes became manifest, the aforementioned ones were hanged; six other scribes each had one hand chopped off; seven scribes were condemned to the galleys; and several others were dismissed from the imperial council. In the middle ten days of the month of Zilhicce, year 998.

PREPARATIONS MADE BY HIS EXCELLENCY, GRAND VIZIER SİNAN PASHA, FOR CHANNELING [THE WATERS] OF THE AYAN LAKE (LAKE SAPANCA) TO THE GULF OF İZNİKMİD (İZMİT)

March 11, 1591

Formerly, the people of the capital city of Istanbul suffered from excessive expenses for firewood and constantly experienced scarcity in that regard. At the time of the late Sultan Süleyman Khan—*may God's compassion and mercy be upon him*—the late Sinan Agha, the great architect, and a zimmi named Kyrios Nikola accurately estimated an area [at the length] of 21,000 cubits (ca. 12,600 meters) between the Gulf of İznikmid and the so-called Ayan Lake, adjacent to the town of Sabancı (modern-day Sapanca). They planned to dig that area and create a gulf; they determined that the [lake's] waters could be channeled [to the Gulf of İznikmid] but had to quit owing to several impediments. Now, in this blessed year, His Excellency, the prudent, brave, and skillful grand vizier Sinan Pasha—*may God Almighty perpetuate his magnificence*—once again commanded with sound judgment and decisive thought the architects, who were the engineers of the time, to be more careful and exert more effort than previously estimated. He commanded them to apply geometry to facilitate the rerouting of the aforementioned Sabancı Lake to the Gulf of İznikmid as well as to opening a channel six thousand cubits (ca. 3,600 meters long) from the Sakarya River to flow into the [Sabancı] Lake. The altitude was established through land survey computations, every dimension [of the space] was investigated by persons of prudence and maturity, and the matter was aided *by the help and guidance of God Almighty*. When the numerous benefits of all kinds [of this project] for the imperial realm were established with certainty and presented to the throne of the sultanate, the permission and the noble decree of the Padishah of the Place and Time—*may God Almighty perpetuate his sovereignty and caliphate*—was issued.

Accordingly, while cash equivalents were collected in lieu of [the contractual services of] some of the commanders, governors-general, and cavalrymen of the well-protected domains and their foot soldiers; others reported for duty in person. Through thoughtful management and preparation, many men were gathered within one year. Tools and instruments were prepared for the completion of the work; there were approximately thirty thousand skillful masters and workers. His Excellency, Hasan Pasha himself—the governor-general of Anatolia and the son of the late Mehmed Pasha—was appointed supervisor. The organization of military craftsmen and master ironsmiths as well as the compensation for various important expenses and provisions was decreed. On the fifteenth day of the month of Cemaziyelevvel, year 999.

THE CHANNELING [OF THE WATERS] OF SAKARYA RIVER AND SABANCI LAKE TO THE GULF OF İZNİKMİD (İZMİT) AND [SİNAN PASHA'S] VISIT TO INSPECT [THE PROJECT]

April 16–26, 1591

At this time, it was submitted to the throne of the sultanate that grand vizier Sinan Pasha demanded to see with his own eyes the ditch that would be dug for the channeling [of the waters] of Sabancı Lake and Sakarya River to the Gulf of İznikmid. With imperial permission it was decreed that His Excellency, the grand vizier would go together with Ferhad Pasha, commander in chief, and Ali Çelebi Efendi, military judge of Anatolia, as well as other required pillars of state, in admiral Hasan Pasha's galley. On Tuesday, following the imperial council [meeting], they departed for the ship. May God Almighty render their difficult affairs easy. May their auspicious and felicitous arrival be facilitated by God. [. . .]

The location of the aforementioned matter was reached. The site was inspected in detail by the people, architects, and engineers of the realm over three days. [Later,] all measurements and estimates were perfected in the most excellent manner and presented and explained in detail to the ruler of the universe. [Yet,] as peculiar accounts by felicitous notables reached the exalted ear of the Padishah, the Refuge of the Universe, he decreed, "It is foolish to abandon the most important [business] and occupy oneself with the [less] important. [This] is not an affair necessary for religion and state. It is not necessary for the poor of the realm and the weak subjects to suffer hardship and misery, or to operate with various severities of oppression to accomplish something. The most important requisite of the sultanate is to complete the construction of ships for the navy. It is proper to act in accordance with the principles of justice and equity and acquire firewood in the same manner as previously." Indeed, the words of rulers are the rulers of words. Thus, the endeavor His Excellency, the grand vizier, undertook for the permanency of his own glory was put off; his judgment was rendered null and void. On the aforementioned date [in the last ten days of the month of Cemaziyelevvel, year 999].

A CURIOUS ANECDOTE
August 28–September 8, 1592

In this sacred month of God (in which violence is forbidden), a cook of the imperial kitchen drunkenly slapped a fellow cook several times in the face. The latter, who was cleaning a chicken, took a knife and thrust it into the one who slapped him. By God's decree, the fellow [who initially slapped the other] died immediately. Thus, the killer was deemed guilty. His Excellency, the Padishah, the Refuge of the Universe, commanded capital punishment and the killer was executed by hanging the following day. In the location where he was hanged, his fellow cooks said, "The order has been executed." One of the [cooks] cut the rope, and, as soon as the body of the deceased dropped to the ground, covered it with a straw mat, and instantly set out to cross over from Ahurkapusı to Üsküdar to bury the corpse. When he placed the body in the caïque and was about to depart, this fellow displayed signs of being alive. Since the deceased came back to life after being executed, the boatman did not dare to take the body to the other side [of the Bosphorus strait]. Once this anecdote circulated and the news reached the people at the imperial kitchen, they began to say, "O the unfortunate one was not guilty [anyway], God Almighty revived him, what good news!" The following day they brought him again to the imperial council. It turned out that, in truth, the noose of the rope had not been put on properly. When it became evident that the outcome was achieved by a trick, he was put to death by beheading. In the last ten days of the month of Zilkade of the aforementioned year [1000].

PEOPLE CLIMBED MOUNT ALEM TO PRAY FOR THE WARDING OFF OF EVIL AND THE RESTORATION OF HEALTH
September 17–27, 1592

After the passing of the "well-known days" (the first ten days of the month of Zilhicce), in the middle ten days of the month of Zilhicce, announcements originated from His Excellency, the Padishah, the Refuge of Faith—*may God Almighty strengthen his might*—to this effect: "May the entirety of the people of the city, [including] the ulema, the righteous ones, and the dervishes go to Alemdağı and piteously humble themselves in prayer to the throne of God so that the plague epidemic will be repelled from the Muslims." In accordance with a sultanic decree, galleys took the illustrious members of the ulema and the honorable sheikhs over to the Anadolu Hisarı quarter. An immense number of individuals went [to pray]. In the city, shops did not open [for business]. They stayed there for one night. The following day, at dawn, a massive assembly of people lamented and offered to the throne of Oneness supplications and praises for the warding off of calamity, the removal of misfortune, and the restoration of health and wellness. In accordance with [the Qur'anic verse] *Pray to me, and I will answer* (Qur'an 40:60), requests were made in prayer to the court of glory. With humility and vexation, thousands and thousands of proclamations of *"O God, accept our prayers"* ascended to the court of heaven. Sacrifices of sheep were offered as imperial alms. The commander of the imperial guards came. Endless varieties of delicacies were distributed [to the people], plentiful thanks given. The daily count of the number of corpses exiting the gates of Istanbul, which had been 325, decreased to one hundred individuals. The bedridden ones rose to their feet, the health of the ill restored. *By the grace and divine guidance of God Almighty.*

PRISONERS WERE FREED SO THAT PRAYERS WOULD BE ANSWERED
September 17–27, 1592

It was intended that the hearts of prisoners be rehabilitated in order that prayers be accepted [by God]. At first, Çerkes Haydar Pasha, who was incarcerated in Yedikule; Sinan Agha the Younger, the former Master of the Horse, who was imprisoned in Yenihisar; and Mustafa Agha, who had been ordered to relocate from the office of the janissary captain [in Istanbul] to the provincial subdivision of Gazze (Gaza), were pardoned and released—so prayers were answered.

When it was [previously] submitted to the sultan that more than forty aides of the aforementioned Mustafa Agha were deceased, that he had no capacity to travel [to Gaza], and that he preferred to be excused from office, it was decreed, "Let him stay," and he remained [in prison]. In the middle ten days of the month of Zilhicce [1000].

THE CONVERSATION THAT TRANSPIRED WITH A HOLY FOOL AND HOW HIS MYSTERIOUS ALLUSIONS OCCURRED EXACTLY [AS PREDICTED]
November 14–23, 1594

In the first ten days of the month of Rebiülevvel in the year 1003, by divine wisdom, a conversation and introduction took place in the courtyard of the mosque of Sultan Mehmed Khan with a tall, beardless, and ruddy-skinned man named Ahmed [from] among the truth-telling [holy fools], who in appearance resembled a drunkard. He passed as a dervish but was a mentally unstable resident of a dervish convent. As he orated and complained about changes and conflicts of fortune that favor the vile, the felicitous Padishah, the Refuge of Faith—*may God Almighty strengthen his might*—rode by [on horseback] with pomp and majesty. We all made acclamations as we looked on with a large crowd. The aforementioned saint addressed this insignificant humble servant and made many curious statements mingled with mysterious allusions.

First, he said, "Glory be to God, you are experienced and aged persons, who are [still] not able to appreciate others' rights or take lessons from divine warnings, despite having observed so many happenings in these difficult times. How many padishahs have you seen like this one? The frivolous world is not permanent; what kind of indolent indifference is this? The men of knowledge, the righteous ones, the ministers, the viziers altogether rendered abject and despicable the acts of worship that have been entrusted [to all] by God Almighty. Owing to their constant mitigation of the authority of the noble shari'a, [society is] overcome by disobedience. Hearts are darkened. Forbidden things and reprehensible morals unbecoming Muhammad's community and the Islamic faith have become the habit and characteristic of the inhabitants of this city. The fear of God has disappeared and, may God Almighty forbid, they deem disobedience as lawful and legitimate. It is not appropriate for the honor of the manifest religion of the Glory of Existence (i.e., the Prophet Muhammad)—*God's blessings and salutations be upon Him*—to be [in this state] in the middle of polytheist enemies.

There had been numerous divine ordeals, [but no lesson] was taken [from those experiences]. By the knowledge of God Almighty, this will be a harsh winter. Humans and animals, wild beasts and birds will suffer. First, this ruler of yours (Murad III), who rode by, is on his way out! Incapable and deficient in enjoining the good and forbidding the wrong, and obsessed with his carnal ego, there is no remedy or cure left for him. Afterward, Sultan Mehmed Khan [III] will light these candles. He will come and extinguish the flame of our hearth. He himself will burn away; merely a flicker will remain. The enemies of faith will set the honor of the Muslim community on fire. Those who initiated or caused unacceptable acts will meet their punishment in this world and the next. After one or two months, his affairs will [also] be concluded. May God Almighty bestow caution and vigilance on the [ruler] replacing [this one]. He will come alone, his name will be mentioned in Friday sermons, and he will commit shameful acts."

Thus the dervish made clear allusions. He wept and wept, and he caused us great suffering. With such strangely penetrating words he concluded the gathering, bid farewell, and walked away. I paid close attention and observed him carefully; he was wrapping himself into a shroud of mourning and a dirty shawl. This episode was registered here because I was extremely affected by its occurrence. In the first ten days of the month of Rebiülevvel, year 1003.

THE EXPULSION OF CAFER AGHA THE DWARF FROM THE IMPERIAL PALACE

June 26, 1595

Cafer Agha, one of the dwarfs who held the rank of court jester at the imperial palace as a courtier of the late sultan (Murad III), had been in the habit of associating with people outside the palace, and was expert in acquiring bribes. Considered a cause of depravity, he became distant and separate from the benevolent gaze of the sultan and was ordered to move to the house he had acquired outside [the palace complex]. They said that the rejection of the dwarf was at the behest of the sheikhulislam, and the undertaking of Lala Mustafa Pasha. On the eighteenth day of the month of Şevval, year 1003.

THE DECREE ORDERING CASTRATED DWARFS WHO WERE EXPELLED [FROM THE IMPERIAL PALACE] TO LEAVE ISTANBUL

June 30–July 9, 1595

It was ordered that the eunuch dwarfs Zeyrek Agha and Cafer Agha, who were expelled from the imperial palace, leave Istanbul and move to their native provinces, Malatya and Bosnia. It was further decreed that the extravagant houses they had acquired during the reign of the late sultan be sold, compensation be paid out in accordance with shari'a, on confirmation, to those who claimed a share, and that their evil and wickedness be repulsed and removed away from the people. Zeyrek the dwarf remained in the custody of the commander of gatekeepers. In the last ten days of the month of Şevval, year 1003.

THE ARRIVAL TO ISTANBUL OF GIFTS SENT BY THE UNBELIEVERS OF VENICE ON THE OCCASION OF THE IMPERIAL ACCESSION

October 27–November 5, 1595

In the last ten days of the aforementioned month (Safer 1004), one of the doges of the Venetian unbelievers, the accursed Leonardo Donà, arrived at the threshold of felicity for the congratulation of the imperial accession. In accordance with ancient codes of conduct, he brought abundant offerings and gifts and presented them to the sublime council. The [imperial] council assembled with a large crowd, and a feast ensued. In accordance with the ancient custom, splendid robes of honor were bestowed [on the ambassador], who entered [the audience hall] along with his *gentilhuómini*—those are their nobles—and rubbed their faces on the foot of the throne of sultanate. Those faithless and accursed ones presented gifts to the threshold of felicity for the sake of friendship.

Yet, in line with their false rites, they continue to transfer to the kingdom of Hungary ample riches from the treasury of San Marco and infinite armies from accursed Spain, continuously aiding those who draw their swords against Muslims. Our hope and wish is that the miracles of Muhammad manifest themselves soon and that the Powerful and Vengeful God renders the community of true believers victorious and triumphant, the enemies of faith defeated and despicable. *For the sake, and in reverence, of the Lord of the Messengers and the Seal of the Prophets, Amen and Amen.*

THE ESCAPE AND SWIFT CAPTURE OF A PROMINENT UNBELIEVER

November 10, 1595

On the night of the day in question, it became known that an unbeliever from a hostile country and one of the enemies of faith, whose detention was necessary, escaped from prison and disappeared. A sweeping search was initiated; the gates of the city remained shut from dawn onward, and severe restrictions were put in place. As a few janissary guards searched diligently and earnestly, they apprehended and brought forth [the escapee] saying, "We captured him in a wine tavern wearing a white turban, which did not go with his appearance." They rendered a service worth several thousand guruş. Thereafter, the gates of the city were opened. On the seventh of Rebiülahir, year 1004.

THE MISCHIEF CAUSED BY INSOLENT FELLOWS AT THE ÇİZMECİ TEKKESİ DURING THE BLESSED DAYS [OF THE MONTH OF ŞABAN]
April 10–18, 1596

In the middle ten days of the month of Şaban [1004]: At a pleasure ground next to the seashore, in the popular spot known as Çizmeci Tekkesi, some fellows from Galata and Tophane, often also from Istanbul—sergeants, cavalry soldiers, and [members of] other regiments, the most infamous ones among lustful wretches—would gather for socializing. The assembly of [boy]-beloveds, lovers, and rivals proceeded to drink wine. Owing to the reluctance of the ravishing [beloveds] and the wine—the mother of vices—lovers and rivals initiated agitation and quarrels. People present at the assembly rose up and, dagger to dagger, got completely entangled. More than twenty individuals wound up wounded. Three individuals died on the spot. Afterward, two of those wounded died in Istanbul in their hideouts. A youth named Hüseyn, a descendant of the perfect lineage of the Prophet Muhammed, died on site. His father Hamamcızade acquired blood money from those who were at the party.

A cavalry soldier named İbrahim the Younger, an inglorious wretch, who had settled in Diyarbakır and become exceedingly wealthy—in such a manner that the inhabitants of that province shed tears of blood because of his tyranny and oppression—also died at this gathering. The story goes that the corpse of Divane İbrahim Pasha, the former governor-general of Diyarbakır, whose execution had been decreed while he was imprisoned in Yedikule owing to his many injustices, was thrown into the sea. Later, his servants found the dead body and buried him near Çizmeci Tekkesi. Reportedly, before the party on that day, İbrahim the Younger said, "Isn't it a pity that a good commander like you lies alone in the soil?" So they buried [İbrahim the Younger] next to [İbrahim Pasha]. The people of Diyarbakır thanked God abundantly that they were delivered from [İbrahim the Younger's] tyranny. On the aforementioned date.

THE DISMISSAL OF THE OFFICIAL IN CHARGE OF CONSTRUCTION FOR HER EXCELLENCY, THE IMPERIAL MOTHER, THE PATRON OF PIOUS FOUNDATIONS, AND THE APPOINTMENT OF SOMEONE ELSE IN HIS STEAD
March 16–25, 1600

Another event of the age that occurred in the first ten days of the month of Ramazan in the year 1008 is the following: Kara Mehmed Agha, one of the gatekeepers of the imperial palace, who had been selected as superintendent of the construction of the mosque and other charitable buildings of Her Excellency, the mother of [the sultan who is] the Refuge of the World, was [also] appointed as deputy for the handling of all necessary and important affairs pertaining to the management of the pious endowment. Thus, with complete jurisdiction he had become an authority with immense influence to whom everyone would appeal. However, he was in fact not experienced or skilled. Despite being ignorant and vulgar, he would talk pretentiously about correctness and integrity and was careless about acting in accordance with the noble shari'a and sublime prescripts of [sultanic] law. Suffering from the affliction of being opinionated and conceited, he had been doing whatever he wanted. He was Chief Eunuch Osman Agha's steward, so the administration of the pious foundations of illustrious sultans was in his hands. The trusteeships of the sacred mausoleums of the late Sultan Selim Khan II and of Murad Khan III were also committed to his charge.

The area for the building of the mosque of Her Excellency, the mother of the sultan, was vacated. Contrary to the requirements of the sacred shari'a, the total assessed value of the private estates and pious foundations that had been demolished were not paid. Compensation for the demolished pious foundations of Muslims was not provided. For all the pious endowments of viziers and the ulema, as well as other public endowments that had been removed, the payment of compensation totaling twice the value of [those estates] was necessary and legally incumbent. However, owing to negligence and indifference, the wages [for the staff] were not paid out in many pious endowments, thereby leaving the poor foundation servants in distress.

Two old temples of the Jewish and Christian communities were demolished as well. They also came and, contrary to the noble shari'a, demanded the construction [of new temples] as compensation. They persisted for many days. There are various rumors. Apparently, their gifts were accepted and in accordance with their demands, a noble decree carrying the imperial monogram was provided, stating, "May one of their ruined churches [elsewhere] be repaired as compensation." Thereafter, a court confirmation was also issued with the signatures of worthless and ignorant substitute judges, and—God forbid, in compliance with its mandate—a church was built anew in another neighborhood of similar value. [What is more,] the supplies and requisite materials were crafted by the masters, who had been working at [the construction of] the noble mosque, and they were put in their proper place.

When it was the turn of the temple of the Jewish community, [with the idea that such a] mandate cannot be adjudicated without the signature of [one of] the highest-ranking judges, a gatekeeper first brought the court confirmation that had been previously composed and signed by a substitute judge to the Judge of Istanbul, the most learned of all scholars, Mevlana Esad Efendi. As soon as [Esad Efendi] became aware [of the situation], he sent for the substitute judge from the court of Mahmud Pasha who signed [the court confirmation] contrary to the noble shari'a, reprimanded him with harsh words, and dismissed him. He immediately summoned the chiefs of police, the *sübaşı* and the *muhtesib,* to his side and razed the newly built church to the ground. He [later] went straight to His Excellency, Grand Mufti Mevlana Sunullah Efendi, who related that the court confirmation had previously been brought by a gatekeeper to him for signature with a message, "If he does not sign it, the grand mufti to replace him will!"

Right away, detailed letters were written to the glorious attention of the sultan and to Her Excellency, the mother of the sultan, in which it was stated, "Your charitable works and foundations, which will endow the provisions for your hereafter, are contaminated with a breach of individuals' rights. Illegitimate affairs are not stable. It is befitting and appropriate that your legal affairs be made licitly sound by a pious and shari'a-abiding deputy." [Furthermore,] the preacher Hasan Efendi, the sheikh of the Atik Mustafa Pasha Mosque, who was registered as the comptroller (*nazır*) of the pious endowment in the foundation's deed, communicated that one of [the endowment's] caravanserais was demolished without the payment of any compensation, thus weakening the endowment profoundly and bringing the payment of wages to a stop.

After these [two affairs], Kara Mehmed Agha was dismissed. The receipts and expenditures from his time of service as superintendent were examined. Existing building instruments and materials were immediately delivered to Nasuh Agha, who was serving as commander of gatekeepers at the auspicious threshold, and he was appointed the superintendent in charge of construction. On the eighth of Ramazan [1008].

TWENTY-THREE

Propagating the Faith in Constantinople

Catholic Missionary Reports, Seventeenth Century

TRANSLATED BY PAOLO GIRARDELLI

The Latin Catholic communities of the Ottoman Empire were, in most cases, heirs to the colonies established by merchants in the Byzantine and Mamluk states during the Middle Ages. After the Ottoman conquest of Istanbul, the flourishing Latin (Genoese) community of Pera/Galata underwent a dramatic drop in size and influence, even though most privileges enjoyed during the late Byzantine period were ratified by the Ottoman government. In the late fifteenth century, and during the sixteenth century, some religious orders like the Franciscans remained where they had been; others had to move to less imposing establishments as their churches became mosques (like that of the Dominicans) or disappeared altogether.

The three documents presented in this chapter, from the archives of the Congregation "for the Propagation of the Faith" (de Propaganda Fide) in Rome, were produced in the seventeenth century by missionary leaders who controlled and influenced the religious and, in many respects, the social life of Catholics in Istanbul. They reported periodically to Rome—to the prefect or the council of the congregation—about the achievements, problems, and needs of local churches and clergy. The congregation was established in 1622 as a late product of Counter-Reformation efforts to coordinate, reorganize, and enhance missionary activities worldwide. The number of Latin subjects in Istanbul in this period was probably only around six hundred, but they were politically relevant for a range of international and interconfessional reasons: the French protection of the Catholics (including a right of pilgrimage to the Holy Land), their influence over Ottoman Greeks and Armenians (who were far more numerous, and often attended the Catholic schools), and their relationship with non-Latin Catholics (e.g., Greek Catholic Melkites) in the Arab lands of the empire. Missionaries were in fact not only catering to the few local Catholics but also aiming to convert "schismatic" or heretic Orthodox and Armenian subjects of the Ottoman Empire to the Roman confession.

The first document (dated 1622), written by Father Pietro Demarchis, a Dominican, describes the church of San Benedetto, of late-Byzantine origin, better known today as Saint Benoit in Karaköy. This sanctuary was staffed by French Jesuit priests, who were especially active in education. Demarchis takes for granted a very blurred divide between Catholic and Orthodox subjects: these latter are all potential Catholics, only needing to be redirected to the right path.

In the second document, the patriarchal vicar Angelo da Sonnino relates the tragic destruction of the church of San Francesco in the fire of 1639. Staffed by the Franciscan Conventuals, this complex of medieval origin was probably the largest and best-attended Latin church in Istanbul—architecturally and culturally a real fragment of Italy on the shore of the Golden Horn. The church of San Francesco was rebuilt, destroyed by another fire in 1660, and rebuilt again.

The final text, by the vicar Gasparo, describes the funeral procession of the Habsburg ambassador who had the privilege of being buried in 1679 in front of the altar of the rebuilt San Francesco. At the time, the Habsburg embassy was the only embassy still located in the old city, near the Theodosian walls. For this reason, the funeral follows a long processional route, across the Golden Horn and through the streets of Galata, with remarkable pomp and decorum. Gasparo allows us to hear the voices of those Catholics who ranked lowest in the social hierarchy: enslaved women watching the ceremony from the segregation of their masters' homes. San Francesco was again damaged in the 1696 fire, and this time no permission for repair could be obtained. The site was given to a mosque that was itself demolished in the 1950s.

LANGUAGE: Literate Italian, with rare Bible quotations in Latin (marked in italics in the translation), and some regional and archaizing peculiarities especially in the third document. Notes in the margin of the first document were omitted. The original capitalization of the words is preserved in the translation.

SOURCE: Document 1: Archivio Storico di Propaganda Fide, Vatican. Visite, 1, fols. 122a–125a. Doc. 2: Ibid. Scritture riferite. Vol. 162, fols. 195a–197b. Doc. 3: Ibid. Scritture riferite. Vol. 477, fols. 201a–202b. Hofmann, Georg, ed. *Il vicariato apostolico di Costantinopoli, 1453–1830: documenti, con introduzione, 7 illustrazioni ed indici dei luoghi e delle persone.* Vol. 103. Rome: Pontificium Institutum Orientalium Studiorum, 1935 (42–46, 66–68, 75–77).

FIRST IMPRESSIONS AT THE NEW MISSION IN CONSTANTINOPLE, 1622

In the Name of God. Amen.
Visit to the Church of the Jesuit Fathers, named San Benedetto.
[. . .] On the twenty-seventh of the same month of October we personally reached San Benedetto in Pera, a church attached to the Society of Jesus by His Holiness Pope Paul V (d. 1621), of blessed memory, where we were received by the Fathers of the aforementioned Society with all reverence and respect, without challenging in any way the privileges bestowed by the Supreme Pontiffs to their Order.

We then first visited their church, which is small in terms of capacity but beautiful and old, having mosaics that cover and embellish all its walls with sacred representations of the life and passion of Jesus Christ, as well as altars and other embellishments newly accomplished in the period of these Fathers' tenure. In the high altar is kept the Venerable and Most Holy Sacrament, in a gilded, well-executed tabernacle of Roman style, placed between two sculpted angels as high as a youth. The one on the right represents Saint Michael Archangel, and the other one the Guardian Angel, with the Holy Sacrament placed in a silver vase of good craftsmanship. Additionally, there are two more altars of considerable beauty at the sides of the church; one of them dedicated to Saint John Chrysostom (d. 407), and the other to Saints Ignatius (of Loyola, d. 1556) and Xavier (d. 1552). There are confessional booths and separate sections for women, in keeping with the local habit. Outside the church, on the right side, is a corridor in the guise of an atrium, ending in a very beautiful chapel of appropriate size with a small dome, dedicated to the most Holy Madonna, where meetings are held with the participation of His Excellency the Ambassador of France (Philippe de Harlay, d. 1652, term 1620–31) and many other notables of the city. Behind the high altar is located the sacristy with the organ, used for solemn celebrations with music.

We saw afterward their house, entirely renovated and constructed with religious care. Seven clergymen of the mentioned Society are now there, five ordained Priests and two coadjutor Friars: Francesco Canigliac (!) of the French nation, being their superior, Domenico Mauritio from Chios, Lorenzo Aureliac (!) from France, Dionisio, Geronimo Gerosio, the French friar Amabile and the friar Giovanni Claro from Tinos, an island in the Archipelago [in the Aegean Sea]. All of them conduct a holy life with devout behavior.

The revenues of this church are limited; they do not reach two hundred Roman ducats of ordinary coin, and they consist of the rent from houses, a resource administered by certain secular ministers elected every year by the Catholic community of Pera. This revenue is usually spent for the upkeep of the church's houses, for the maintenance of their roofs, for providing the church with oil and wax, and for other expenses that have become frequently necessary [to be paid] to the Turks.

These Fathers also sustain themselves with alms that their most Reverend General obtains for them every year from His Holiness, which do not reach four hundred *zecchini* (gold coins), so that they can hardly support six persons and one secular servant—who is necessary to avoid being forced to go out often to fetch necessary items. Being also absent here, those persons who may give alms for sacerdotal robes and the necessary books, they are often in state of great poverty.

Celebration of Mass and other rituals in this church take place according to the Roman rite, in keeping with the institutions of the Fathers of the aforementioned Society [of Jesus], in all decorum and cleanliness.

These Fathers are committed both to schooling—not only Latins but also Greeks, along with many *calogeri* (orthodox monks) who possess unimaginable potential—and to confessing and preaching, in the times and ways of this Society. This is done to the great satisfaction of both Latin and Greek flocks, which cannot be easily explained in words. We therefore understood that, if they had ways to keep some children in the seminar, it would be highly advantageous, both for the enhancement of the true faith's fervor with Latin subjects and for saving the Greeks from the schism and error in which they find themselves, because in this way it would be easy to instill into young minds the truth of our religion.

The esteem and reputation of these Fathers is not confined to this city, but also penetrates several regions of Greece. They are coveted by the Armenians, and even at the so-called Holy Mountain (Mount Athos, in present-day Greece), with twenty or twenty-two large monasteries of calogeri, where almost all the clergymen of that [Orthodox] confession are trained; all this potential is dwarfed by the reduced number of these Fathers, which prevents their dispersion in other regions.

We have also devised that, because all of Greece uses the vernacular Greek language and books in this language cannot be found in this city, it is necessary to have here in Pera a printing house with Greek characters, so that many spiritual writings authored by these Fathers could be diffused.

We also inquired with these Fathers whether the Christian faithful in this city held and profess all the seven Sacraments professed by the holy mother Roman church, and if these are celebrated with the same ceremonies observed in the Roman ritual regarding their form and content; the answer was positive. The same is true for the celebration of divine offices and the articles of faith, especially regarding the Procession of the Holy Spirit, who proceeds from the Father and the Son.

Even though in this city of Constantinople it is not forbidden by the magistrate and the Ottoman law for the faithful to live in accordance with the holy religion, and to observe all the appropriate ceremonies and rites, owing to the arrogance of many private Ottoman subjects, several prescriptions in the administration of the most holy Sacraments cannot be observed, like bringing to the moribund the Holy Sacrament as viaticum, which cannot be done with the decorum required by the Roman rite. Processions in the streets with the Holy Sacrament and other (sacred objects) are not done, crosses in funerals are not held, and it is not allowed to bury anyone in the city's churches, but only in a common cemetery rather far from town (near modern-day Taksim).

For the rebirth of true Christian piety in this city, it is necessary to endow this church with a good prelate, who would act as the Latin Patriarch. He should be of [this] country, and not suspect to the Turks—of impeccable life, sufficient doctrine, renowned zeal—and he should possess such authority as to be respected and feared by everyone. He should have dignified provisions for his own maintenance, and bear bishopric dignity so as to exert jurisdiction on the entire Levant, especially on the Archipelago, which, owing to its distance from Rome, is out of reach of its authority.

In addition, clergymen attached to this city should only be those of the reformed orders, and of mature age and holy life, to avoid the frequent divergences from correct behavior in many of them.

The most Excellent Lord Ambassador of His most Christian Majesty [the King of France] should have the highest authority to punish and imprison clergymen who perseverate in indecent behavior.

It should also be facilitated that clerics never reside outside their convents and houses, nor go alone to administer the sacraments. This could be avoided if, the Latin flock being of limited size, all parish administrations could be reduced to one, managed by one or more secular priests as it is done in Chios, and not by friars of diverse orders, which causes many disagreements and conflict.

As far as the Greek Church is concerned, in order to regain its loyalty, the first thing to be done is to have the appointed patriarch Cyrillos (Lucaris, d. 1638) removed from office. He is a native of Candia, very hostile to the Roman Church, and is infected with Lutheran and Calvinist heresy. He misleads and alienates as much as he can the Greeks from the Catholics, and he tries to annihilate the name of the Patriarch and the Latin Vicar.

In addition: dispatching missions of *operai* (priests engaged in social activities) in all four patriarchates (Constantinople, Smyrna, Antioch, and Alexandria), to attract prelates and educate common people, especially youth, with a small seminar of eight children for each patriarchate and allotting a salary to each Patriarch would be a very effective means of bringing the Greeks again to their pristine state. This will be all for the present visit.

By Bishop Pietro Demarchis, O. P. (Order of Preachers), (October–November 1622).

FIRE RAZES THE CHURCH OF SAN FRANCESCO, 1639

March 25, 1639.

Thanks to divine favor, I have always brought to the ears of Your Excellency merry news on the positive developments in what, with effort and courageous struggle, has been accomplished to this day in resisting the rapidly growing heresies spread in these countries, and also regarding the quiet and exemplary life that all clergymen live here. But with the present letter, with tears in my eyes, I am going to expose strange and unexpected things that have befallen our church:

On the eighteenth of March, half an hour after dark, a fire broke out in the city of Pera in a house half a mile from us, and it grew so much that it burned all our church and even its bell tower, so that only its main walls are standing. This caused overwhelming affliction to all our Christians because it can be said that, in these regions, *The crown is fallen from our head* (Lamentations 5:16). This was a large, old church where, with the contributions of all these notables and others, the glory of Christian religion could shine with decorum. The brigade responsible for extinguishing the fire, as it usually does in these cases, caused so much harm to the convent, which had been spared by the fire, that not even the roofs, windows, or anything inside was left intact. It was ravaged even beyond what happens to conquered cities during a war. What is even worse, a large part of the city having burned, the houses that belonged to the convent and were rented out have also been destroyed, so that their revenues are lost and we are left only with a ravaged and empty convent.

Regarding divine service, we now celebrate in a chapel of the community of Pera attached to our convent, called Santa Anna, which, thanks be to God, remained free from fire. However, because the only churches spared by the fire are the small chapels and modest sanctuaries of the other religious orders, the old decorum will no longer be observed. The same fire also damaged the site of the Fathers Zoccolanti (the Franciscan observants, based in Santa Maria Draperis, closer to modern-day Tophane, until 1660) and another church of San Sebastiano.

The local notables convinced me to present to Your Eminences the necessity of refunding this church for God's glory, for the reputation of the Apostolic See in this region, and for the honor of the Christian people. They said that any time His Holiness decides to support us with any amount of funds, the other Christian princes will also follow suit. Therefore, as I am obliged to report to Your Eminences that which is relevant to the divine worship and the dignity of the Christian religion, I humbly pray and respectfully encourage you to make this contribution, which should be of about fifteen thousand Roman *scudi* (silver coins). This would aggrandize God's honor in this region, while every nation living in this city would greatly benefit from it. However, I will always comply with what Your Eminences order.

Regarding my condition, Eminent Lords, with due respect I will relate my needs: When the fire brigade entered our convent to have the chance of ravaging it comfortably under the guise of defending it from fire, in the short time that I had I could only save the Scriptures and books that belong to my office. I have therefore lost what little I had. Because the convent cannot offer me the usual support I received before, I beg you to assign me, as to a missionary leader, the salary that is given to other missionaries. I am ashamed to ask similar things and I pray you for God's sake to give me some additional support, because in this country where our Christian flock has suffered so much, we cannot hope for any alms, since the majority is poor, the merchants have left, and a large number of their houses have burned. I remain therefore with all our Christian folk waiting for the resolution of Your Eminences, so that we know what we are expected to do; and in conclusion, with my humblest regard, I kiss in devoted reverence your sacred garb.
Most humble and most devoted servant of Your Highly Revered Eminences,
Brother Angelo da Sonnino, Patriarchal Vicar.

THE FUNERAL OF THE HABSBURG ENVOY IN CONSTANTINOPLE, 1679

Eminent and Revered Lords and most Honorable Masters,
On the twelfth of this month [of September], at two hours after dark, with the benefit of our Church's Sacraments, the Illustrious Lord Pietro Francesco (Peter Franz) Hoffmann, Imperial Internuncio at this Porte, passed to a better life. Although the Ottoman law prohibits anyone to be buried in a church, the Illustrious Lord Giovanni Carlo (Johann Carl) Terlingo de Guzman (d. 1680), ordinary Resident [envoy] of the same Imperial Majesty, would not comply with the customs of this country. Being aware of the negative answers received by others in different times, he nevertheless ventured to request an exception, to which—due

to the esteem that this Grand Vizier pays to the new minister, or out of respect to the Emperor—a gracious rescript was issued against any common expectation. He communicated this to all the Ministers, and after discussing with me the protocol that should be followed to transport him to our Church of San Francesco, this was resolved with utmost pomp, never practiced in similar cases.

On the morning of the fourteenth, at around fifteen hours, the staff and cortege of the most Excellent Ambassadors of France and Venice, with those of the Most Illustrious Residents of Holland, Genoa, and Ragusa, and other Lords, gathered on the shore between Cazzica Bassà (Kasımpaşa) and Galata. We waited for the arrival of the corpse, which was brought from Constantinople with clergymen and courtiers of both imperial ministers, and a crowd of laymen who transported him. As they arrived, three hundred torches were distributed, and we advanced in procession towards Galata, in the following order:

In rows of two, thirty-two Janissaries headed the train, with garb, sticks and the usual distinctive emblems of that militia; they were followed by two heralds in dark garb; twelve grooms in the same order with liveries of turquoise silk; twelve of the Lord Resident in livery of yellow silk; a horse dressed with caparison (the Turks looked with suspicion on these things); six servants of the Lords of Ragusa; four of Genoa; ten from Holland; sixteen heralds of Venice, and six servants of the same; ten for France; then the interpreters—one from Ragusa, two from Genoa, three from Holland, five from Venice, three from France. Then, six Fathers from the family of Terra Sancta, two Reformed, six Conventuals, four Dominicans, the Minister of San Francesco with surplice, stole and cope; then myself with surplice, a short mantle (*mozzetta*), cross and crosier, assisted by five secular priests who wore surplices.

The corpse was carried by eight grooms in turn, in a livery of red cloth from the family of the deceased. All around were ten servants of the same in mourning dress and ten brothers of the company of the Holy Sacrament, with torches in their hands. The coffin could be admired with its ornament of golden brocade. The corpse was dressed in garb of the same fabric with sable lining, other ornaments of velvet and sable, and the aigrette adorned with diamonds from the treasury of His Imperial Majesty. On his breast he held a very large silver cross with reliefs. He was followed by his brother-in-law, an imperial dragoman, one [dragoman] from Poland with the Envoy; the chief Imperial dragoman with the head of the Janissary guard. Finally, the most Illustrious Lord Resident, the two secretaries of France and Venice, the undersecretaries of the same, two secretaries of Holland, four Jesuit Fathers, and 126 notables and merchants. In this service the English did not participate because of some trouble with the French; nor did the Capuchin Fathers appear, out of respect for the rules of their missions which, as they say, prevent them from being at public functions.

The procession went on for two and a half hours along the streets of the city, as far as the courthouse of the Voivode. Many people from every nation and sex convened to watch this, and the streets, windows, doors, and shops were so full that it could be hardly imagined, a crowd impossible to describe. This was so well conducted, and in such beautiful order managed by the Janissaries who were appointed to this function, that it not only ran free from trouble, but was also entirely silent, with the exception of the sighs of some Christian women, who, having seen the cross on the corpse and hearing the priests who, all around the streets, and even in front of the mosques, were chanting psalms, would weep desperately, either for the dead's fate or for their own misery. We almost could not enter the church for the crowd of Turks who took part in the service. The coffin was placed above an eminent scaffold. Ten servants in dark garb attended with torches, and I led the cappella, while the region's Head Father celebrated mass. When the ceremony ended, the corpse was buried in front of the high altar. [. . .]

Constantinople, September 20, 1679.

Most humble, devout, and obedient servant of Your Eminences,

A. Gasparo bishop of Spiga.

TWENTY-FOUR

An Armenian Chronicle of Crimea

Khachatur of Kaffa, d. 1658

TRANSLATED BY NAIRA POGHOSYAN

The Crimean Khanate became independent from the Mongolian Golden Horde and established its own sovereign polity in the early part of the fifteenth century. As the power of the Ottomans grew over the course of the later fifteenth century, the Ottoman state intervened to settle a succession dispute within the khanate, which was located on the northern coast of the Black Sea. This was the beginning of a political alliance whereby the khanate was granted the status of a privileged vassal principality. The Ottomans often relied on the impeccable military craft of the Crimean Tatar outriders and frontline cavalry in their campaigns in eastern and central Europe against the Muscovite Russians, as well as in battles as far away as the Iranian front. In return, the Ottomans protected the khanate's interests; the Ottoman fleet and army kept several outposts on the Crimean coast and at strategic locations across the peninsula, protecting against the khanate's enemies in the north. The khanate existed as a semisovereign polity until the late eighteenth century. Empress Catherine the Great (r. 1762–96) annexed Crimea in 1783, thus marking the beginning of Russian suzerainty over Crimea for more than two centuries.

Ottoman Sunni culture had a considerable influence on Muslim Tatars, particularly among the populations in the southern coastal regions of the Crimea, where the Ottoman legal system was implemented. Located on the Black Sea coast, Kaffa (modern-day Feodosia) was the capital town of the Ottoman administrative region and an important trading port of the peninsula. This lucrative port attracted Cossack and Rus raiders from the region for occasional plunder. Armenians had been the most populous demographic in Kaffa since the Middle Ages. Although it seems that by the seventeenth century the Muslim population had outgrown that of the Armenians, the latter still constituted a sizeable portion of the settlement's estimated twenty thousand inhabitants. The town's population also included Greeks, Jews, and some Rus as well.

FIGURE 19. Kefe (Kaffa, Feodosia), early eighteenth century. Gabriel Bodenehr (artist) (Augsburg).

There are numerous Ottoman state documents and chronicles pertaining to the Crimean Khanate that describe conditions on the peninsula. Khachatur's diary provides us with a different perspective. Born in 1592, the author was an Armenian Apostolic priest in Kaffa. He kept the chronicle as a diary of sorts, which was written more or less at the time of events, as the many highly emotional reflections and missing outcomes in the text attest. Although his style is a bit dry, Khachatur's chronicle is an important source for gleaning the views of a minority group in Ottoman society. The text is only twenty-four folios, but it covers rather a long period of time, from 1615 to 1658, with many long lapses in between. This was not kept as a complete chronicle of events. It was rather a priest's memory book, in which he recorded only what he thought was noteworthy. Among these are accounts of natural catastrophes, famines, plunders, raids, and skirmishes that happened on various parts of the peninsula. More often than not, Khachatur identifies a sin or other cause of as "divine wrath," and is quick to draw lessons from disasters. As a clergyman, he was obviously concerned with hardships that befell his flock. But he was also fairly well-informed and interested in political happenings on the peninsula and in the Ottoman throne city.

Khachatur's chronicle does not have an original title. The autograph manuscript is kept in the Mesrop Mashtots Research Institute of Ancient Manuscripts (Matenadaran) in Yerevan. The author's datings are according to the Julian calendar, which means that in the seventeenth century the dates correspond to a date ten days earlier in the Gregorian calendar.

LANGUAGE: Classical Armenian, interspersed with Turkish terms (transliterated in the translation; plural endings are not included). The orthography of the same words occasionally differs.

SOURCE: Manuscript: Khachatur Kafayeci. No Title. Matenadaran (Mesrop Mashtots Research Institute of Ancient Manuscripts), Yerevan, N 7709 (autograph copy), fols. 220a-244b. Edition: *Manr Jamanakagrutyunner 13-18 dd.* Vol. 1, edited by Vazgen Artasheshi Hakobyan. Yerevan: Haykakan SSr Gitutyunneri Akademiai Hratarakchutyun, 1951 (205-36). Translated into German by Edmund Schütz. "Eine armenische Chronik von Kaffa aus der ersten Hälfte des 17. Jahrhunderts." *Acta Orientalia Academiae Scientiarum Hungaricae* 29/2 (1975): 133-86.

In 1615, zodiac sign of Gemini, Dominical letter 7, golden number 100, epact 21, lunar number 2. On Friday, the twenty-sixth of May of our year, an earthquake took place in the city of Kaffa. The city walls collapsed, the earth trembled, and houses were destroyed. The ground shook. Creatures were frightened; women wept and children cried. The waves of the sea rose and rose, and then ebbed. Praise be to God, who works wonders!

July 20, 1616, on Sunday, at dawn, Yurus (Cossacks) attacked the city of Kaffa and devastated many quarters of the city; however, my city will rise from its devastation yet again. [. . .]

In 1617, Memi Pasha, the pasha of Kaffa, a handsome and good-hearted man, a friend of the country, attacked the Yurus with ten *khadırga* (galleys). The Yurus murdered him, seized three of his galleys, captured many of his people, and slaughtered some of them; others they drove out. In August there was great bereavement in Kaffa and grief was everywhere.

In 1618, Sultan Ahmed died and was received by his God. Sultan Mustafa succeeded him and reigned for three months. However, owing to disagreements that were going on during this time, he was replaced, and Sultan Osman was installed on the throne. A great turmoil took place in the city of Istanbul. Afterward, a fire broke out in the city and many places were burnt down. Disease outbreaks occurred. Heavy rains fell and rivers flooded. Yet again, there was an earthquake in Kaffa on Thursday, July 2.

Then, a woman was blessed with four male offspring; we were all amazed, and admired and praised God the Creator. That Sunday, tempted by Satan, a woman burned herself; she heated up the oven, took off the lid, and jumped in. Her relatives and sons were not at home. When they arrived, she was already burned and the house was on fire. Everyone was crying for her. Her husband was not there; he only came two days later and did not find his wife.

On the thirteenth [of August], another earthquake occurred. In September, in the second quarter of the moon, yet another earthquake took place. After that, a comet was born. In October, a saber (?) was born and in December, again a comet was born. [. . .]

In 1620, Canibek Giray Khan (II., r. 1610–23; 1628–35) minted silver coins. The city was closed for three months; there was no trade until July and August, and then gradually things calmed down. Know, my brothers, that he has been khan for ten years and this is the fourth time he minted coins. [. . .]

On December 18, 1621, zodiac sign of Scorpio, a long and hard winter began. Who could recount [all] the rage that smote us for our sins; even centenarians have never seen such astounding [phenomena] before. The sea by the city of Kaffa froze for three miles out; there was so much ice that the water could not been seen, and people could walk on it. A man went as far as fifteen hundred *daban* (steps) and disappeared for a long time. The springs froze up and we could not find bread or wood. Many poor people died of cold; their feet and hands were frozen and they were crippled.

Dolvetkere (Devlet Giray) Sultan waged *sefer* (campaign) against Korel (western Ukraine). He devastated their *taybur* (camps), ruined many cities, captured many people—men, women, little boys—and also took many books from them, as well as fifty individuals from our [Armenian] people of Lusavorich (Saint Gregory the Illuminator, d. ca. 331). Countless and innumerable captives from their [Eastern Orthodox] people were coming. On the way, it started snowing and it was very cold and frosty; many captives and *asker* (soldiers) died from the freezing cold. Numerous carriages with horses, comrades, servants, lots of provisions, and *mal* and *khazina* (goods and treasures) were left on the road.

In 1622, the Hakaratsink (! Ottomans) were again cursed and punished by God. The rulers and the nobility did not observe the rules, did not obey the sultan's order, and went against divine laws. As they stoned and killed their king Sultan Osman (II, r. 1618–22) and fought against each other; nobles died by the sword, and the city residents plotted and fought against each other. Much evil took place in the country and there was great mourning in the city of Istanbul. On this day, people cried because they had never seen or heard [anything like it]—that servants and nobles, janissaries and palace cavalry gathered and killed the king. Sultan Osman was pitiable and unfortunate, as he was still very young and did not [have time to] enjoy his kingdom; he ruled for just four years and no more. Punishment for the punishers: [eventually] they killed each other with their own swords. Sultan Mustafa (I, second reign 1622–23) was placed on the throne. They (the Ottomans) became the object of scorn and derision for all nations.

At dawn on Monday, June 10 (1622), the Yurus (Cossacks) entered the *liman* (port) of Kaffa with thirty-three *khayıkh* (boats) but could do no harm and went away in shame. They were in the liman (port) of Khughri for five days and caused much damage, taking five ships and ravaging and destroying *bağça* (orchards) of the [Greek] Tats. [. . .]

Thanks to God the Creator, for He did not get too angry with us and had mercy on us. Those damned Hakaratsik (Ottomans) were ashamed and could not gain power over us. Thanks to the King of Kings, our merciful God, who granted power to [the heir apparent, *kalga*] Shahin Giray Sultan and Mehmed Giray Khan. Blessed was the khan; blessed was the sultan who reigned in the region of Sulkhat (modern-day Staryi Krym) and the city of Kaffa. Prosperity and peace, love and reconciliation reigned. A *donanma* (festivity) was organized on September 15 [1624]; there was much rejoicing. [. . .]

At dawn on Sunday, July 5 [1631], our sins called down the wrath of God on the city of Qara-Su (modern-day Bilohirsk). It started raining, and there was thunder and lightning; the whole city was flooded with rain. [The storm] destroyed houses and shops, bridges and *bağça* (orchards), *saray* (mansions) and *çardakh* (pavilions), trees and branches, *dapakh khana* (tanneries) and *boya khana* (dyehouses), *aşci* (cookhouses) and *paçci* (lamb's trotters sellers), *bezaz* (linen cloth traders) and *khazaz* (silk traders), bakeries and *khasab* (butcheries), *bozaci* (fermented millet beverage shops) and *meykhanaci* (wine taverns)—the torrent of floodwaters destroyed everything. A thousand or [one thousand-and?] five hundred or more people drowned—Armenians and Turks, people from Kaffa and Qara-Su, *bazırkan* (merchants) and *musafir* (travelers), *kharib* (strangers), and homeless people. In some families, the wives drowned and the husbands remained alive, whereas in others, husbands drowned and wives remained alive. Some people lost their houses, husbands and wives, sons and daughters, and all their goods. Some lost their husbands and two sons; some lost wives with three or four sons. It was tantamount to Noah's deluge.

[The flood] took out the great bridge of *vardaped* (archimandrites) Minas and the sultan, sweeping away stones and logs, nails and iron—even its tracks disappeared; a third of the city was destroyed. The *çatan* (fences) and the city walls collapsed; two bathhouses were demolished and their *camekan* (dressing rooms) destroyed; two mosques were ruined; the *medrise* (school) collapsed and *sokhtay* (students) were killed. Many other startling things happened: our Armenian church of Saint Auxentius remained intact. However, some of the nearby houses were destroyed, while others remained undamaged. Some of the walls [of houses] collapsed; a number of attics caved in. In some cases the torrent destroyed half of the house, while the other half remained intact. The *arkh* (irrigation canals) and mills were damaged. Many wondrous things happened. In July it rained hard, but the [drinking] water of the city of Kaffa decreased. We will suffer a lot! [. . .]

On February 15 [1633], a fire broke out in Kaffa! Four or five shops burned, and they only just managed to put it out. At dawn on Thursday, two ships of Abaza [Pasha] arrived. They brought the corpse of Ali Pasha's son, who had died in combat. He was taken from the ship with sobs and moaning and brought into the city from the back [route]. It seems God was angry; that night a wind blew, and there was a *hurtuna* (thunderstorm); mills were destroyed, part of the city wall came down and destroyed three houses, and many scary things happened. It was said that Ahmed Sufi, together with his house and all his family—his son and daughter—were wiped out.

On Friday, February 17 [1633], the people assembled [to help]. They gathered and rolled the stones away, and removed six corpses: two men, two women, and two boys had died under the stones and logs. Many other people fell victim to the storm. The man called Ahmed Sufi was a usurer and had a horse-driven mill; his house was destroyed, the mill was ruined, and the pawned items of people remained under the ruins. Some people found and took theirs, while others could not, and remained in distress. [. . .]

Afterward, an income tax of three gold pieces per person, called *hasıl harç*, was levied on inhabitants of the city of Kaffa—may it be cursed! The Christians cried, wept, and said, "We are not able to pay that sum! The imperial *emr* (decree) is for two coins, so take two. If not, we will board ships and go to the king (i.e., the Ottoman sultan). Allow us [to pay two coins]!" There was a judge from Orinberan (modern-day Perekop) who was called Musaoğlu, or maybe Sütçüoğlu; he was the cursed judge who ordered [a levy] of not two but three coins, as he expected to receive *ırışvat* (bribes). The Christians were miserable. When they saw that there was no outcome, they sent a man to the Porte. Our man went, a God-fearing Christian —— and there requested an emr (decree) that just two gold coins be collected. But unfortunately it was not accepted. Many Christians complained, and the pasha of the city was deposed. Later a *tehya* (steward) of the new Pasha came; he was on our side, but the accursed *kadi* (judge) did not accept the decree. Once again, we sent a man to Istanbul and are not sure what will come of it. [. . .]

Three *vardaped*—Sargis, Thoros, Arakel—a delegate, an *abegha* (celibate priest), and an alms-collector *kahana* (married priest) arrived in our city. Our country was in great distress, and there was no trade activity; the khans, the overlords from hell, and the people were shivering, we were abject.

On March 29, 1646, it was our Armenian Easter. There was a considerable food shortage; one *çarek* (quarter) of wheat became two *kuruş*. Who has seen the face of bread? The *fakhir fukhara* (the poor) were in miserable condition. The authorities went from door to door. The *ğadi* (judge) and the *nayib* (deputy judge), wherever they found it, took wheat by force. If there were four quarters [of a bushel] of wheat, one was left with the owner and the rest was distributed to others. There were no ships or *araba* (carriages) [bringing goods]. The city shut down until the middle of the Great Lent (beginning of March 1646). On March 22, many carriages arrived, so that the city was fed—God sent them to the people who had no food and no hope left. Today is Sunday the twenty-third and two araba (carriages) bearing bread have arrived from Qara-Su, so that our region has been supplied with food. The zodiac sign was Capricorn, intercalation 22, lunar number 13, Dominical letter 4, golden number 8. The vizier, who had gone to Malta, was killed in combat.

Let us return again to our country—that is, Kaffa—which we call "the northern country" and "the Land of the Huns," where milk and honey flows. Everything has been very expensive for seven years. Now, the Lord gave everything so that we could acquire *karar* (stability) as it was in cheaper days—praise be to God. But Azak (modern-day Azov) has become a real problem for us; goods from Kaffa were to be brought there. Five ships and five boats sailed off with *zakhira* (provisions) and many other goods to Azak. Then, janissaries came with six ships. Some people said they were five hundred. Seven ships of *ısbahi* (cavalry) antagonized our city. They demanded two thousand *çual* (sacks) and *çatan* (baskets), and a *kharac* (tax) of six *khruş* each from Armenians and Tajiks (! i.e., Turks). Their seizure of goods and beatings went on for three or four days. Four *khadırğa* (galleys) and subsequently thirteen ships left, and five hundred more çual (sacks) were sent later. On August 16, on the Sunday of the Assumption of the Blessed Virgin Mary, the pasha of Trabzon arrived with five or six ships and many asker (soldiers). All the ısbahi (cavalry) came out of the *khula* (*fort*) and set up numerous *çadır* (tents).

The cursed mufti has been devising evil plans for the Monastery of Saint Nshan. He went to Islam Giray Khan (III, r. 1644–54), deceived him, and said, "Your majesty, give me a place to reside in your city of Crimea." [The khan's] heart became confused. He said, "Let it be any place you wish." That godless man said, "There is a monastery where no one lives; people do not enter it." [The khan] said, "I grant it to you! Go and enjoy." *Keş* (shame) on you, godless and sinful creature, brood of evil Satan! You have lied to the ruler that the monastery has no owner, and the Christians did not have any *khaber* (knowledge) about it. The mufti set out from Kaffa saying he would convert the monastery into a mosque and build a *minaray* (minaret). Paronter ("Prince Bishop") Khachatur and Bishop Grigor did not know what to do. The believers gathered, from the Crimeans, from the villages, men and women, and went to the monastery. They entered and barred the gate. When the cursed one arrived, he did not find an entrance and went back ashamed and dishonored. People from Kaffa and Qara-Su went to the khan and requested that the monastery be given back to them. Many treasures were given [as a bribe]. May the Lord execute vengeance on them!

Khaber (news) came from Kezlov (modern-day Yevpatoriya) that the foreigners, following the decree of Islam Giray Khan, had taken over the church. The godless ones came, destroyed, and devastated the church; the Christians did not know what to do. On Friday, March 16, during the week of the Torture of [Saint Gregory] Lusavorich and the start of his imprisonment in the pit.

Easter was on March 25 [1649]. The Christians remained without a pastor, the priests wept, and there was great mourning. Ah, our [poor] Armenian nation and the city of Kezlov! After the event in Kezlev a wondrous thing happened in our city of Kaffa. The Vizier was a pasha. The janissaries of Azak mounted a rebellion and damaged lots of things in the city. Two or three of the pasha's servants were killed; some were beaten; others were stabbed. For this reason, a *divan* (court hearing) was held in the palace. But then a beam broke and the palace collapsed. Many people tumbled down to the lower level and died. Around two hundred people were crippled; some broke their legs and others their hands; some cracked their heads and others their hearts. This miracle took place on [Good] Friday, the day of the betrayal and crucifixion [of Jesus]. However, the godless have not yet calmed down. They did not adhere to the emr (decree) and [collected all the] *ispençe* [poll] tax.

TWENTY-FIVE

On Revenants and Ghosts

Various Documents, Sixteenth Century

TRANSLATED BY MARINOS SARIYANNIS

It is commonly accepted that the folklore of revenants or vampires originated among the Slavic populations of eastern and southeastern Europe. However, some theories identify similar traditions and terminology among Turkic populations, which may imply a central Asian origin for these beliefs. Vampires became widely known in other parts of Europe during the course of the eighteenth century, specifically after Serbia passed into the hands of the Austrians in 1718. Vampire sightings and elaborate vampire tales became more frequent and entered Western European literature at this time. The events quoted below also transpired in Balkan towns; yet, in a manner that is different from what has been assumed so far, the first two texts refer to incidents from the sixteenth century.

A set of fetvas or legal opinions issued by Ebussuud Efendi (d. 1574), the grand mufti of the Ottoman Empire between 1545–74, demonstrates how Ottoman authorities viewed such traditions. The cases probably all refer to the same vampire panic in a Christian village in the Balkans. Ebussuud Efendi's fetvas make a subtle distinction between the revenant phenomenon as it occurs in a Muslim or a Christian corpse. A few decades later, in 1590, the poet Mustafa bin Mehmed Cinani (d. 1595) used Ebussuud's first fetva to illustrate a story of a jinn possession in a work composed mostly of fictional tales. But the author presents a few stories, including the ones translated below, as real accounts. Cinani's accounts combine cases of jinn possession with souls of the dead returning either to implore for prayers or to tyrannize the living. These ghost stories are also set in a Balkan environment. In Anatolian and Arab populations, on the other hand, it seems that jinn interventions, and not vampires or ghosts, were more common.

Although according to the Islamic doctrine the dead cannot be resurrected, the belief in jinn, expounded on by the Qur'an and Islamic angelology, allowed for the presence of "spirits" (not necessarily malevolent) within the context of the dominant theology. The jinn are believed to operate outside the human constraints of the physical world (see chapter 18). Possession of a person by jinns is a known phenomenon in Islamicate cultures. On the other hand, popular as well as scholarly Sufism allowed for the possibility of *insilah*—when a soul departs the body and wanders around the spiritual realm while its host was still alive—as well as the phenomenon of departed sheikhs presenting themselves to the living. Therefore, revenants and ghosts were probably regarded as being within the realm of possibility.

In the final text, a petition concerning a vampire sighting in 1701 or 1702 by the judge of the town of Edirne and submitted to the provincial governor refers to the same fetva, which had been issued by Ebussuud a century and a half earlier, but with some doubt. It notes that the judge was not able to find the grand mufti's instructions about how to deal with corpses coming alive in "Arabic books." The judges were instructed to carefully conduct an investigation of the purported vampire cases. It seems from this account that what mattered to the Ottoman authorities was maintaining order in the villages rather than punishing any unorthodox beliefs.

LANGUAGE: All three documents are in Turkish with genre-specific linguistic characteristics. The fetva is formulated clearly, in a legalistic idiom. The stories are in plain prose, giving the impression of reporting a true story. The chronicler's narrative quotes from official correspondence, replicating the formulaic language and pompous phrasing of the documents.

SOURCE: Grand mufti Ebussuud's *Fetvas*: Manuscript: Süleymaniye Kütüphanesi, Istanbul, İsmihan Sultan 223, fols. 297b-298a. Transcription: Düzdağ, Mehmet Ertuğrul, ed. *Şeyhülislam Ebussuud Efendi Fetvaları Işığında 16. Asır Türk Hayatı*. Istanbul: Enderun Kitabevi, 1983 (197-98) (nos. 980-82). Partially translated by Marinos Sariyannis. "Of Ottoman Ghosts, Vampires and Sorcerers: An Old Discussion Disinterred." *Archivum Ottomanicum* 30 (2013): 195-220. Cinani's stories: Transcription: Ünlü, Osman, ed. *Cinânî Bedâyiü'l-âsâr*. Cambridge, MA: Department of Near Eastern Languages and Civilizations, Harvard University, 2009. Vol. 2, (334-37). Partially translated by Marinos Sariyannis. "The Dead, the Spirits, and the Living: On Ottoman Ghost Stories." *Journal of Turkish Studies* 44 (2015): 373-90. Anonymous chronicler's account: Transcription by Köhbach, Markus. "Ein Fall von Vampirismus bei den Osmanen." *Balkan Studies* 20 (1979): 83-90. Özcan, Abdülkadir. *Anonim Osmanlı Tarihi (1099-1116 / 1688-1704)*. Ankara: Türk Tarih Kurumu Basımevi, 2000 (148-49).

GRAND MUFTI EBUSSUUD'S FETVAS

QUESTION: After some people die and are buried, they strip themselves of their shrouds, blood moves into their limbs, and their bodies become ruddy. Is there any reason for this phenomenon?

RESPONSE: If this is true, it is caused by God's sacred will. There is a saying that "wicked souls attach themselves to the corpses of those who, while still living, were connected to them in their morals and practice, and use [these corpses] as instruments for evil actions." This is not improbable for the divine power.

QUESTION: If a corpse is found in the aforementioned state, what must be done with it?
RESPONSE: It must be covered; no harm comes if the corpse is of a Muslim.

QUESTION: Is it legally permissible to dig someone's body out of its grave and burn it?
RESPONSE: It is not.

QUESTION: In a village near Salonica in Rumeli, an infidel from the Christians died. Some days after he was buried, he appeared in the middle of the night at the door of some of his relatives and others. He said to them, "Hey you, come and visit so-and-so with me." The next day that infidel died in turn. After a few days, he [appeared and] spoke to another person, who died as well. In short, many infidels died this way. If some of the Muslim inhabitants of the village, seeing the undoing of so many infidels, get scared and wish to flee the village, is this legally permissible?
RESPONSE: It is not. Especially, after what they have observed in the town of the infidels, what is required from a Muslim is to leave his affairs to the Possessor of Affairs.

QUESTION: In the aforementioned case, please be so kind as to indicate its reason and cause, along with an efficient way of dealing with it.
RESPONSE: The language falls short and the mind is inadequate to express the reason and cause of such phenomena, and this is not the place to delve into what has been investigated concerning them. The way to stop [this from happening] is as follows: The same day this happens, people should go and nail [the body] to the earth with a single stake through his navel; hopefully, the phenomenon will be repelled thus. If not, and if there is still pinkish color in the corpse, they should cut off its head and throw it near the feet. [The following] is also mentioned in some books: If they find the body looking the same way as it did when they put it in the grave, they should cut its throat and leave it that way. If the body has later altered its position, they should cut off the head and put it at the tips of the feet. In any case, if these measures bring no result, they should disinter the corpse and burn it. In the times of the righteous ancestors (of the early Islamic era), corpses have been burned time and again.

CİNANİ'S STORIES

A VERY STRANGE EVENT: Someone by the name of Ahmed Çavuş narrates the following:
"In the castle of Dıraç (Durrës) in the province of Albania, if someone—be he infidel or Muslim—falls seriously ill and loses his mind, then, without his knowledge and by God's

order, the soul of someone who died previously enters his body and starts relating its own troubles. For instance, the soul says in the voice of the moribund: 'Hey tyrants, why don't you inspect my case? I am so-and-so, son of so-and-so; they torment me greatly in the Hereafter. I had committed this or that sin; my torment is off-limits, and you, you stay in my house and you wear my clothes and you spend my money. Why don't you have any prayers read for my soul? Why don't you make any charity for my sake?' Those who know him understand.

Once, an ill person lost consciousness right next to me, and one of the dead entered the body and said, 'I am the wife of so-and-so Çavuş. When I was alive, I committed adultery with someone. Now they torture me greatly because of this. I am ruined. [My heirs] wasted away so much of my property and money; why don't they think of me?' She was crying. After some time, the ill one came back to his senses. We asked him, and he had no idea of what had happened.

Sometimes the soul of the dead comes onto the roof of his [former] house and cries, 'You are sitting here at ease, possessing my house and property. You do not think of my situation, you do not once repent and give charity for me!' Now, if [the ghost] is a Muslim, they bring a learned man, who reads some verses from the Qur'an and drives it away. If it is a Christian, they bring a priest who reads from the Holy Gospel. Otherwise, the ghost does not cease until the morning." He related thus.

Let this not be conceived as farfetched or marvelous, for it has often happened that the soul of a body or a spirit enters [a corporeal form] and speaks, with God's permission. There are many trustworthy narratives about this phenomenon.

AND IN THE SAME VEIN: Someone named Mevlana Halil, a former assistant of the late [grand mufti] Çivizade Efendi (d. 1587), now a dervish, related to this humble one the following:

"I was once staying at somebody's house in Cairo. One day, when I was sitting in a room, a man came and told me that my host was asking for me. I stood up and went in to him. My host had a concubine who was epileptic. In order to save her, they had brought in an expert exorcist. The exorcist was sitting, and the concubine was lying down. The host said to me: 'This girl lying here is our concubine. Her epilepsy grips her continuously, so looking for a cure we brought this exorcist. He just recited something; he made the concubine unconscious and he summoned the jinn that possesses her and put it into her body.

Once or twice he asked the jinn, "Why are you torturing her?" But the jinn who loves the concubine is Persian; it only speaks Persian! Since the exorcist is an Arab, he does not know Persian. This is why we have summoned you, so that you can translate the Persian words said by the jinn and tell the exorcist in Arabic. By God, you know both languages.' 'Sure,' I said. So I turned to the jinn and asked it in Arabic: '*Ayyuha l-jinn, li-ayy shay tasra hadha* (!) *l-jariyatahu ta'khudhuha,*' which means, 'O jinn, why are you possessing and torturing this concubine?' The jinn spoke from inside the concubine's body with a high-pitched voice and said, '*Az-an sabab ki dost midaram o-ra*'—that is, 'I love her, this is why I am possessing her.' Then, instructed by the exorcist, I said, 'Leave this concubine or else the exorcist will punish you severely.' The jinn said, '*Na-tavanam kardan yira ki basi dost midaram,*'—that is, 'I love her so much; I am unable to leave her.' Then, under the exorcist's orders, they tied the concubine's feet together and started to beat her soles with a thin stick. The jinn, from inside her, cried out, '*Mazan,*' which means 'Don't hit, don't hit!'

Again, as instructed by the exorcist I asked, 'O jinn, are you going to abandon this concubine from now on?' It answered again: '*Na-tavanam kard* (I cannot do it).' Then the exorcist stood up, asked for a pen and wrote [something] on a piece of paper; he rolled up this paper, burned its edge, and had the smoke enter the concubine's nose and ears. She appeared to suffer and cried out very loudly. She could not stand still; [the jinn] did not stop crying, '*Masuz masuz*'—that is, 'Don't burn me, don't burn me! I left her alone and won't possess her again.' The exorcist made him swear a very strong oath on the Prophet Solomon's seal. The jinn took the oath to the effect that it would never again possess the concubine, and then went away. At that moment, the concubine's mind came back to her head and she stood on her feet again. Her master asked her what had happened, but she made awesome and severe oaths saying, 'I have not the slightest idea.' All this happened in my very presence and before my own eyes." He related thus.

There are many stories of this kind, and there is no need to relay them since they are so famous. Many have related, and it cannot be denied, that wicked spirits cling to dead bodies, so that these become enchanted and make strange movements. It is even lawful to nail to the ground by the navel bodies enchanted like this, or to cut their heads, or—if those measures bring no result—to burn them. There are illustrious fetvas on this issue by the grand mufti Ebussuud Efendi.

In this vein, one of the strangest stories that I have heard is as follows.
A VERY STRANGE EVENT: Mevlana Seyyid Muhyiddin from among the equitable judges, who served at the time in the district of Morea (Peloponnese, modern-day Greece), narrated the following:

"It so happened that someone in the district of Morea died. As is the custom there, he had a maidservant, who survived him. One day, three or four months after he died, the aforementioned maid came crying and said, 'My master came, he came to bed and had intercourse with me, just like he used to do when he was alive!' People who heard this laughed and did not believe her. The poor maid continued to protest, 'My master comes to me every night; he destroys my flower and has intercourse with me; you don't believe me!' Finally, she left that house and went to another; she always slept with other people beside her. Still, whenever she was alone, the master came again and had sex with her; there was no solution to be found. Finally, there was a man of knowledge by the name of Piri Dede, who was a medrese graduate. The girl went to him and narrated the story."

The narrator says, "The aforementioned Piri Dede narrated [the following] to me in a face-to-face discussion: 'When the woman first came to me, I did not believe her, but she swore strong oaths; so I decided to go there and stand guard. I told her, "Let me come together with the owner of the house you are staying in and watch over you. When this dead man seeks to take you again, call us and we will come and help you, and we will see him with our own eyes." The woman said, "Well, all right," and left. She also called the owner of the house, and I went there.

We both kept watch outside, on a sofa, and sent the woman inside. It was afternoon and there was still daylight; the woman started to cry, "Help, my master came again!" We rose and ran inside. By the truth of God, who created the world with His power, I saw the man as I knew him in life—he was between the woman's legs and having intercourse with her, like he did while he was alive. As soon as we saw him, we charged him; we thought of hitting him with a sword or a dagger but could not find any. We searched behind the door and found an iron skewer, but when we took it and came back, he had disappeared; we couldn't see anybody anymore. But what had happened to the woman was manifest. Less than ten days later she died as well, and she was buried next to her master. This is a story I saw with my own eyes, God be my witness. God only knows what the truth is.'" He related this story thus.

A STRANGE EVENT: Someone called Mevlana Recayi, who lives near Sandıklı (in western Anatolia) and is one of the assistants of the late Monla Efendi, narrated to this humble one the following:

"With God's permission, in the tribe of the Yörüks who graze on the plateau of Gölcük near Sandıklı a jinn has settled in the body of a ten-year-old girl, and more particularly in her right thigh; it speaks in a strange voice, which resembles the sound of a whistle, but the girl does not open her mouth. This girl has a brother; whenever someone comes to inquire about something, this boy calls the jinn saying, 'Hey beauty, have you come?' and speaks with it [as an intermediary]."

The narrator says, "At this time Monla Efendi had ordained me to construct some watermills on the River Gediz. I went [to the jinn] to ask how many watermills could be built on Gediz. The girl's brother came and as soon as he asked, 'Beauty, have you come?' a voice was heard, saying, 'First we need a cake in front of us.' What could I do? I produced a cake. Then the voice came again, 'Five, the River Gediz five.' At this the boy said, 'What are you saying? I didn't understand a thing.' The jinn answered, 'The inquirer understood my words; it is not necessary that I explain to you.' Indeed, I had understood these words: the meaning was that five watermills could be built on the River Gediz.

People of this area come and make a lot of inquiries and take answers according to their wishes. The girl does not open her mouth at all; she turns into a half-wit of sorts and stays silent and mute." He related thus. And God knows the truth of the matter.

ANONYMOUS CHRONICLER'S ACCOUNT

REPORT BY THE JUDGE OF EDİRNE CONCERNING THE ISSUE OF VAMPIRES (*cadu*): What is requested by this well-wisher of your Excellence is the following: The inhabitants of the

Maraş village, district of Edirne, declared before the religious court that some signs of evil spirits had been observed on the grave of the previously deceased Bıyıklı Ali, in the graveyard of the aforementioned village. The inhabitants were filled with fear. Indeed, in the province of Rumeli, when such signs are observed in some unbeliever's grave, his body has to be nailed with a stake through his navel. If [the signs] persist—that is, if when the grave is opened the corpse is found in a different position and with its color changed to ruddy, it must be beheaded and his head put next to his feet. If the signs are still not halted, the corpse must be disinterred and burned. Such was the fetva of the late Ebussuud Efendi concerning such a case among unbelievers; however, we cannot find such instructions in Arabic books. This is my request.

COPY OF THE GOVERNOR'S DECREE: Virtuous efendi, the judge of Edirne! In order to dissipate this fancy of the villagers, let the court send an experienced and knowledgeable deputy judge to the site of the incident, together with an appointed marshal. On inquiring with the inhabitants, if they agree that the signs of evil spirits are still apparent, the inspector judge should open the grave and ascertain whether the color and position of the dead has changed. You should report accordingly.

A DECREE WRITTEN ON A SIMILAR OCCASION: [To the] head of the police: The inhabitants of the Hacı Sarraf quarter in Edirne declared the following before the court: "In the Muslim cemetery, signs of vampirism appeared on the grave of a woman called Cennet, who died three months ago. Consequently, we are all overwhelmed with groundless fear." The court sent an inspector judge who opened the grave. Four women examined the deceased woman's limbs and reported, "Indeed, it is certain that her corpse has not rotted and her face has turned red; such phenomena are signs of vampirism." You are to open the aforementioned grave and do whatever is accustomed in order to remove the horror and illusions of the inhabitants.

TWENTY-SIX

Miracles of an Anatolian Sufi Saint

The Hagiography of Hacı Bektaş, ca. Late Fifteenth Century

TRANSLATED BY HELGA ANETSHOFER

Hacı Bektaş is arguably the most important and influential mystic of Anatolia ("Hacı" is an honorific). Although his lifetime during the thirteenth century preceded the rise of the Ottomans, his influence continued for centuries and persists in the present day. His teachings found followers especially among nomadic Turkmens in Anatolia, who had rather loose loyalties to the Ottoman central polity. Bektaşi ideas also spread widely in the Balkans. Although there are no contemporary historical sources to determine Hacı Bektaş's actual religious practice, the later hagiographical tradition portrays him as an antinomian charismatic mystic. Bektaşism emphasizes personal spiritual development, and it is generally known to have evolved to be less strict about some of the basic rituals ordained by Sunni Islam, the official religious "ideology" of the Ottoman state—such as praying five times a day or prohibition of alcohol consumption. The twentieth century term "Alevi" comprises a number of socioreligious groups that do not strictly conform to Sunni practices, including the Bektaşis.

The Bektaşi movement is thought to have played a crucial role in the conversion of large numbers of Christian populations in the Balkans to Islam. However, some hybrid religious practices between Christians and Muslims, particularly the sharing of religious sites in the Balkans, did not necessarily result in conversion. Famously, Hacı Bektaş was the patron saint of the janissaries, the elite military corps of the Ottoman palace composed of converted Christian boys, who were originally mostly from these regions.

The sections below are from the *Book of Sainthood* (*Vilayetname*), the very popular book recounting the spiritual deeds and miracles of Hacı Bektaş. Collections like the *Vilayetname* are called hagiographies, which are biographical accounts of influential mystics usually compiled subsequently by the followers of that person. Unlike biographies of notables, the stories in a hagiography commonly move back and forth between the natural and supernatural realms, their main objective being the idealization and glorification of the mystic, as well as the documentation of the miracles attesting to his sainthood. Historians have long ceased treating such accounts as fanciful, as they contain plentiful and concrete information about mentalities, cultural conventions, geographical realities, and more.

The individual biographical accounts about Hacı Bektaş were no doubt first orally transmitted among his followers. Later, probably during the late fifteenth century, as Turkish gradually flourished as a written language in Anatolia, these stories were compiled and committed to paper. However, the earliest known dated manuscripts are from the early seventeenth century. The manuscript from which the excerpt below is taken dates from 1625 or 1626 and represents the "standard" prose version of the *Vilayetname*. The translated sections narrate, among other topics, stories of Hacı Bektaş initiating the contemporary Anatolian mystic Sarı Saltık into the spiritual way of life and converting non-Muslims to Islam. Miracles like walking on water, divining freshwater springs, and surviving the ordeal of being boiled alive are common in Anatolian and central Asian hagiographies. An unusual miracle recorded in the *Vilayetname* and excerpted below is the fate of a man who does not believe in a prophesy of Hacı Bektaş's and is impregnated as a consequence.

Vilayetname remained a semisacred account among Bektaşi communities during Ottoman times and is still revered among Turkish Alevis today. Hacı Bektaş's mausoleum is located in the village of Hacıbektaş (Suluca Karahöyük in the *Vilayetname*) in Cappadocia in central Anatolia and it remains a major pilgrimage site.

LANGUAGE: Turkish. Popular conversational language with short sentences and a fairly archaic sound. Some terminology from early Anatolian Turkish mysticism.

SOURCE: Facsimile and transcription: Duran, Hamiye, ed. *Velâyetnâme*. Ankara: Türkiye Diyanet Vakfı, 2007 (261–66, 350–62, 493–97); including facsimile: *Menakıb-ı Şerif-i Kutbu'l-arifin Hazret-i Hünkar Hacı Bektaş Veli*. Millet Kütüphanesi, Ali Emiri Efendi Kitapları–Şer'iye, 1076, fols. 52b–54a, 75a–78a, 110b–111b.

HACI BEKTAŞ TURNS WHEAT AND LENTILS INTO ROCKS

It is reported that Hacı Bektaş of Khorasan—*God sanctify his secret*—one day went for a walk to the east side of Suluca Karahöyük (Watery Black Mound). At that time, all of the village's grain had been threshed and winnowed and piled up in heaps. A tax collector from Kırşehir would come and weigh the grain, and then the villagers would remove it. According to this custom they had threshed and winnowed the barley, wheat, lentils, rye, and whatnot, piled them up in heaps, and covered them with straw.

His lordship (Hacı Bektaş) stepped forward, lifted his blessed skirts, and said to the owners of the threshed grain: "*Give a little something, for God's sake!*" They said, "Dervish, this is nothing! What should we give you?" The great lord said, "If it's nothing then it shall be nothing!," and quickly turned away. When the men heard the words of the saint, they lifted the covers from the grain and saw that it had all turned into rocks. Those useless men interpreted this miracle as sorcery and said, "Even if this grain has turned into rocks, we still have a lot of gold and silver coins." The great lord again heard what they were saying, and with his blessed words he uttered the following invocation: "That gold and silver that you put your trust in, shall be the same!" Then he walked away. Despairing of their grain heaps, the villagers went home. There they realized that all their gold and silver coins had also turned into rocks. They threw them out into the wild. Ever since, those rocks have been fusing underground and have turned into solid rocks. The grains inside the rocks are distinctly visible, even today. It is a true story.

Following this occasion, Hacı Bektaş-ı Veli's followers gathered, came to him, kissed his hand, and said, "My sultan, you made a curious invocation. All these grains that were supposed to be the people's livelihood turned into rocks and are wasted. No one can benefit from them now." The following words came from the saint's blessed mouth: "My dear ones, these grains will not be wasted. From each one of them a child of ours will come forth. This shall be my legacy to my followers. Whoever eats of the lentils will have a daughter, and whoever eats of the wheat will have a son." This happens under the following conditions: A lawfully married couple shall fast for three days. On Friday night when they copulate, they shall—at the moment of ejaculation—push a rock with the grain inside it into the other's mouth with their tongues, without touching the rock with their teeth. Even when childless women eat the rock, they will become pregnant right at that moment through the miracle of the saint. When they give birth, they shall make a small votive offering to the saint. They should not forget to do it.

AN INCREDULOUS MAN EATS FROM THE GRAINS AND GIVES BIRTH TO TWO SONS

It has been reported that at the time when Hacı Bektaş of Khorasan—*God sanctify his secret*—made the invocation that the grains would not be wasted, and that from each of them a child of his would come forth, a man heard the saint's words and said, "What could possibly happen if you swallow these rocks? How would a child emerge from a rock? Bring them to me; I will swallow two of them!" He took two of the wheat grains in his mouth and swallowed them. Through God's power and by the miracle of the saint, that man instantly became pregnant. His pregnancy progressed day by day, and his belly started to grow. When the time came, he went into labor. He wailed as he was in great pain. He understood what was going to happen and he regretted what he had done. He implored his relatives and friends: "I need help. Ask the saint to forgive my sin and to save me from this suffering." A few close friends and family of the pregnant man came to the noble saint and said, "My sultan, be gracious. Help this unlucky man, so that he can be saved from this suffering." Hacı Bektaş-ı Veli—*God sanctify his secret*—said, "My dear ones! There is no salvation for him; he will die. But split his belly open; two sons of ours are in there, and they will come forth." The man died as the saint had ordained. They immediately split his belly open; the miracle of the saint manifested itself, and two sons were born. They nurtured them and they grew up. Their descendants live today, close to Ankara. They are called the Buğday oğulları, "Sons of the wheat."

HACI BEKTAŞ SENDS SARI SALTIK TO KALIAKRA

It has been reported that the lord Hacı Bektaş of Khorasan—*God sanctify his secret*—one day went to his solitary cave on Mount Arafat (near Suluca Karahöyük). When he approached the Zemzem Spring outside he saw someone herding sheep. The great lord approached the man and asked, "What's your name, my dear?" He answered, "Saltık." His lordship said, "Go now! We are sending you to Rumeli." He stroked Saltık's back, massaged around his eyes, and bestowed on him a gracious glance. The gaze of the saint works like alchemy; if he looks at dirt it turns into gold. At once all the layers that obstructed Saltık's sight from the divine truth were lifted. At that very moment he passed through all the spiritual ranks and stages and reached sainthood.

Saltık became aware of his new spiritual state and said, "King of the holy men, what should we do with these sheep?" The great lord said, "They won't go anywhere until their owner returns. You be a spiritual master and do as we told you!" With his own blessed hand his lordship girded Saltık with a wooden sword and gave him seven arrows, a bow, and a prayer rug. He sent him on his way together with Ulu Abdal (the older Abdal-Dervish) and Kiçi Abdal (the younger Abdal-Dervish). He said, "Go now! Have no doubt about finding the right way—we will guide you." Thereupon Sarı (Blonde) Saltık begged for the saint's gracious glance, kissed his hand, received his blessings and good wishes, and set off. His lordship saw him off and said again, "My dear Saltık, don't be afraid. He who sends you to this mission is with you, don't you worry. Wherever you are, we are with you." He said farewell to Saltık and retreated.

Saltık said farewell to the great lord and went with Ulu Abdal and Kiçi Abdal to the Black Sea coast near Sinop. They sat on a rock called Harman Kaya and conversed for a while. Today grass still grows in a patch as wide as a house on the spot where they sat; it's clearly visible. Then Saltık spread his prayer rug on the surface of the sea, sat on it, and had Ulu Abdal sit on his right side and Kiçi Abdal on his left. Then he said, "Prayer rug of the saint! Go where he sent you!" At once the rug moved like a ship and sailed toward Georgia. Today, when the Black Sea is calm, the route where Saltık's prayer rug sailed can still be seen clearly. The Abdals said, "My Sultan, the rug went left. If it were headed toward Rumeli, it would have gone right." Sarı Saltık said, "It is the saint who is guiding the rug on the sea. Let it go wherever it goes. It is for a reason. Let's see what he will show us." Then the rug moved toward the coast and came close to the land of Georgia.

At that time, a king by the name Güreleş ruled in Georgia. That day he had come to the seacoast to hunt with a hundred men. They saw a silhouette coming from the sea and said, "That does not look like a ship. What could it be?" Some said, "It's a tree trunk that the waves are washing ashore." But when they came closer, they saw three people sitting on a rug floating towards them. When the Georgian king saw this, he said, "These are not ordinary people; not everyone can just sit on a rug and float on the sea like that." The rug came to the coast and stopped. Sarı Saltık Sultan and the Abdals got off the rug and walked out of the sea. Kiçi Abdal shook out the prayer rug and put it on his shoulder. Güreleş and his people dismounted from their horses, stepped forward, kissed Sarı Saltık Sultan's hand, and greeted Ulu Abdal and Kiçi Abdal. Güreleş invited them to his residence. Sarı Saltık Sultan accepted the invitation and they set off. They offered him one of Güreleş's horses, but the sultan did not mount the horse. So Güreleş also proceeded on foot and brought Sarı Saltık Sultan to his own residence. He held a big feast and served them for a few days. Now these were Christians adherent to the religion of Jesus. The sultan invited them to the religion of Islam. Güreleş and his people converted and became Muslims. Sarı Saltık Sultan had them bring felt, and he made a dervish cap similar to the Hüseyni cap, and he put it on their heads with blessing. He then bid farewell and went to the seacoast.

They again rolled out the prayer rug on the surface of the sea and sat on it as before. Sarı Saltık Sultan declared, "Prayer rug of the saint, go where he sent you!" Thereupon the rug turned to the direction of Rumeli and set off. Back at the place where they had been, as long as that Georgian king was alive, he and his people remained Muslims. When Güreleş passed away, his people converted back to their previous religion, but they did not stop wearing the felt cap. That is the reason why the people of this region still wear it. Meanwhile the prayer rug floated on the sea until it reached a fortress called Kaliakra (in modern-day Bulgaria) at the coast of the land of Dobruja. There it stopped and did not continue any further. The sultan and the Abdals got off the prayer rug and Sarı Saltık Sultan said to the Abdals: "There must be a reason why the saint has sent us here. You walk around to the gate, I will climb up to the fortress from here." Ulu Abdal and Kiçi Abdal walked toward the gate. Sarı Saltık climbed up the cliff of the fortress from the seashore.

When he touched the smooth surface of the rock it miraculously moved toward his hands and became handles, and when he pressed his feet against the cliff, they carved out steps in the rock. Thus, he climbed up the fortress. The marks of his hands and feet can still be seen clearly on the rock. Now, this fortress was controlled by an infidel prince of the Laz people. But since a seven-headed dragon appeared, they had abandoned it for another fortress out of fear. As soon as the sultan saw that dragon from the tower of the fortress, he let out a loud cry. When the dragon heard the cry it lifted all of its seven heads, roared dreadfully, and breathed fire. It charged toward the sultan. When Sarı Saltık Sultan saw that the dragon was coming, he climbed down the tower of the fortress and made a move toward the dragon. He prepared the bow and the arrows in his hand, and when the dragon came close, he shot an arrow into each of its heads. But the dragon coiled around the sultan, squeezed him tightly with his tail, and gave him great pain.

The sultan forgot that he had a sword and called Hızır [for help]. That day the prophet Hızır—*peace be upon him*—was sitting in Suluca Karahöyük and conversing with his lordship. The great lord said, "My dear Hızır, a dragon is suffocating Saltık. He has forgotten about his sword and called you. Quick, go to Saltık's rescue and remind him of his sword."

The prophet Hızır—*peace be upon him*—went to Saltık right away and hurled a lance at the dragon so that it pierced the dragon and hit the rock behind him. Then he said to Sarı Saltık Sultan: "O true saint, why don't you draw your sword and cut off the dragon's heads with it?" When Hızır—*peace be upon him*—said that, Saltık remembered the sword and said, "Oh my dear Hızır, for the sake of the saint that I asked for help, I forgot about the sword, otherwise I would not have bothered you by calling you." Then he took out the sword that the lordship had girded him with and cut off all seven heads of the dragon. Blood ran in floods like seven rivers. The prophet Hızır—*peace be upon him*—bid Saltık farewell and set off. Today the footprint of the prophet Hızır and the spot where his lance hit the stone is still clearly visible. After a while Ulu Abdal and Kiçi Abdal came from the gate of the fortress and saw that Sarı Saltık Sultan had killed the dragon. They said, "Blessed be your victorious battle!"

Then they exited the fortress. Saltık said to the Abdals: "I am very thirsty from fighting the dragon. Maybe you could find a sip of water so that I can drink and feel revived." The Abdals searched the surroundings but could not find any trace of water. They returned and said, "We could not find any water." So Sarı Saltık Sultan sat down, dug the earth with his blessed hand, and pure sweet water sprung up. They drank from that water and felt revived.

As they walked around, they chanced on a shepherd and had him inform the lord of the fortress about the slaying of the dragon. When the inhabitants of the fortress heard about it, they rejoiced. The lord of the fortress came and saw that the dragon was slain. He happily and voluntarily became a follower of Sarı Saltık Sultan and gladly accepted the faith. Then Sarı Saltık stayed on and demonstrated various acts of sainthood and miracles. He made the people of this place his followers. A few years later, he came to visit his excellency the lord Hacı Bektaş-ı Veli—*God sanctify his secret.*

HACI BEKTAŞ SAVES CAN BABA'S LIFE FROM A DISTANCE

It has been reported that at that time his lordship Hacı Bektaş-ı Veli—*God sanctify his secret*—was living in Kadıncık Ana's house in Suluca Karahöyük. One day he said to Sarı, the brother of İdris (Kadıncık Ana's husband): "Sarı, our hair has grown long. Come, let's go somewhere where you can shave my head." Sarı grabbed the whetstone and razor and they went to the lower part of Suluca Karahöyük and sat down at a spot across from the mound. Hacı Bektaş bared his head. With his permission Sarı wet his head, took the razor, and started to shave. When he was halfway through Hacı Bektaş gave him a sign to stop with his blessed hand. Sarı stopped shaving. Then the great lord went to a certain spot, dug up the earth with his blessed hand, and said three times: "Flow, my spring, flow!" At the same moment—*through God's power and by the miracle of the saint*—sweet freshwater sprang up and began to flow toward the mound. His lordship said to the water: "Why did you make us tell you to flow three times? Why didn't you come when we told you the first time?" Sarı relates that he heard with his own ears a voice coming from the water, saying, "When you told me the first time, I moved from Khorasan to the city of Nishapur and further to Mount Erciyes (in central Anatolia). The second time I circumambulated Mount Erciyes seven times. The third time I sprang from the indicated spot and flowed to your presence." The lord said, "Sarı, this spring used to be with us in Khorasan and come flowing whenever we needed it. Now we called it again and it came. Our spiritual invocation revived it. Whoever washes themselves in this water will not burn in the fires of hell." With his blessed hand he took some of the water and sprinkled it around. It vaporized immediately and rose up to the sky like smoke.

When Sarı saw this, he could not contain himself and said, "My Sultan, how curious is that! When you sprinkle that cold water on these rocks it vaporizes and rises up to the sky like smoke." The great lord said, "Gülü (i.e., Hülegü) Khan has put Kara Donlu (Black Cloaked) Can Baba in a cauldron. They have lit a fire under him and are boiling him. I am cooling down his water, my dear." When Sarı saw this miracle and heard the voice in the water he called his lordship "abıca." The people of that place used to call his lordship abıca (i.e., "uncle" in modern Anatolian dialects), which in the language of the Oghuz means "saint." They still use this word. So, Hülegü Khan had put Kara Donlu Can Baba in a cauldron and boiled him for three days and three nights. On the fourth day the Tatar (i.e., Mongol) nobles and leaders gathered around Hülegü Khan and said, "My king! Even if that person were made of iron, he would have dissolved within these three days. Let us open the cauldron and see what has become of him!" Hülegü Khan got up and approached that cauldron along with all his subordinates and leaders. They opened the lid and saw Can Baba sitting inside, streaming with sweat. Hülegü Khan ordered him to come out. When they saw this, they were amazed. Hülegü Khan looked at his Christian priest and said, "What do you think?" The priest said, "This is not enough to convince us to leave our own religion and join his religion. Order your soldiers to heap some wood in a plain, ignite a large bonfire, and let this dervish enter it. If he does not burn in the fire, we'll join his religion!" Hülegü Khan said, "Dervish, what do you think of this suggestion? Do you accept it?" Can Baba said, "I accept it. But if I don't burn in this fire and come out safe and sound will you convert to the right faith and become a Muslim?" Hülegü Khan and the nobles and leaders, who were present there, pledged to convert.

TWENTY-SEVEN

A Dispute Concerning Sufi Tombs, 1619

Ömer Fuadi, d. 1636

TRANSLATED BY JOHN CURRY

One of the most widespread and prolific Sufi groups of the Ottoman period was the Halvetiyye order, which took its name from the group's practice of *halvet,* or ascetic, withdrawals from society for lengthy periods of time. While the group originated in the region of Azerbaijan in the fourteenth century, it quickly spread well beyond its original domain, in part owing to a practice of Halvetiyye sheikhs training large numbers of disciples who then traveled to other parts of the Muslim world to extend the reach of the order. Given the vast distances between newly established sheikhs in eras of premodern communication, the rapid spread of groups like the Halvetiyye soon gave rise to various offshoots and subbranches that generated novel variations on the original teachings of the Halvetiyye founders, often bearing a local character. One such group was the Şabaniyye Sufi order, which was founded in the mid-sixteenth century in Kastamonu, a smallish town in the mountains of northern central Anatolia. This subbranch took its name from its founding figure, a man named Şaban Efendi (d. 1569), who trained a number of local and regional sheikhs to carry on the teachings of the group after his death.

The proliferation of Sufi groups, along with their growing visibility in Muslim societies by Şaban Efendi's lifetime, could create intra-Muslim tensions over the acceptability of their practices and doctrines within the Muslim tradition. More legalistic or puritanically minded Muslims sometimes criticized Sufi groups like the Halvetiyye for practices the former deemed incompatible with the religiolegal traditions established by earlier generations of Muslim thinkers. Halvetiyye ceremonies, which often attracted members of the broader public in addition to the devotees, often included musical performances and the formation of circles of participants who then engaged in rhythmic movements. Some Muslims argued that these were dancing circles, and therefore forbidden according to Islamic law. They also argued that the veneration of prominent deceased Sufi leaders, including the building of tomb complexes over their graves, was tantamount to idolatry, as Muslims came to direct their worship to these figures instead of to God.

The author of the text below is a Sufi sheikh named Ömer Fuadi (d. 1636) who left an extensive written record of religious and social affairs that took place in Kastamonu. He is therefore a very different type of historical representative than the vast majority of authors during his period, most of whom hailed from larger cities in the Ottoman Empire like Istanbul. When he was in his twenties, Ömer Fuadi joined the followers of the aforementioned Şaban Efendi, and eventually became a Sufi sheikh himself via the instruction of the last surviving successor to Şaban Efendi's teachings, a pious hermit named Muhyiddin Efendi (d. 1604). After Muhyiddin's death, Ömer Fuadi became a defining leader of this Sufi group in his own right, and he would serve in that role for over three decades. Through his writings and activities, he played a decisive role in consolidating the scattered following of Şaban Efendi into a notable Sufi order that would continue right down to the founding of the Republic of Turkey in the early twentieth century.

The selections below are from a tract called the *Epistle on the Tomb* (*Türbe-name*) written in 1619. Ömer Fuadi wrote it in celebration of the completion of a monumental tomb structure that was erected over the graves of Şaban Efendi and a number of his successors and followers in Kastamonu—a critical moment in the consolidation of what would become the Şabaniyye Sufi order. This tract was subsequently appended to the hagiography of Şaban Efendi that he had written nearly a decade earlier. In it, Ömer Fuadi explains how the tomb came to be built, but he also outlines some of the difficulties that the community had to overcome in order to complete the project.

LANGUAGE: Turkish. Long, convoluted sentences heavily laden with occasionally ambiguous Sufi terminology.

SOURCE: Ottoman print: Derviş Ömer el-Fuadi. *Risale-i Türbename*. Printed in the compilation *Menakıb-ı Şerif-i Pir Halveti Hazret-i Şaban-ı Veli*. Kastamonu, 1294/1877, 130ff. Transcription: Tatcı, Mustafa, ed. *Hazret-i Pîr Şaban-ı Velî Kitabı*. Istanbul: H Yayınları, 2018 (427–67).

INTRODUCTION

Let it be known, not concealed, to the luminous hearts possessing spiritual knowledge of the pure brethren and the faithful spiritual knowers: In order to have firm faith and connection to the sanctified souls of the "poles" (*kutb*) of the age from among the prophets, friends of God, and the holy men who are within the well-known spiritual domes under the vaults of heaven created by God, and [in order to have] confidence and trust in the divine signs [emanating] from their enlightened graves, the scholars, mystics, rulers, viziers, and other notables and wealthy patrons of every age have given respect and preference to two desirable conditions and beloved deeds:

First, the scholars and mystics have gathered together and compiled the biographies of the friends of God, and hagiographies in Arabic, Persian, and Turkish, so that their spiritual states, complete perfection, signs of sainthood, and acts of grace shall be explained to the mystic seekers and sincere friends, and their honorable mention shall be made manifest in the world.

Second, rulers and wealthy patrons have built radiant tombs, which are among the delightfully built and commonly seen domes over the luminous graves [of the friends of God]. They perform this charitable deed because they believe that it will facilitate the arrival of worldly advantage and obtain benefits in the other world for themselves. It is indeed known and proved by experience that through this agreeable deed, many people succeeded in obtaining their desires.

To wit, the reason for the issuing of [these] rightly guided words, and the cause for the manifestation of [the author] Fuadi's intention [to write this epistle] is as follows: The building of a tomb that scholars, mystics, rulers, and wealthy patrons honor and take pride in, was also vouchsafed to his excellency Şaban Efendi (d. 1569). While [the tomb] was being built, by God's will, a situation occurred that seemed contrary to human will: [The Grand Vizier] Nasuh Pasha (d. 1614) had its builder, Ömer Kethüda (the Steward, d. 1611) executed, and the tomb remained unfinished. Subsequently, some ignorant people who knew nothing about the states of the holy men, or the divine wisdom (*hikmetullah*), which reveals itself in the realm of possibility through the divine will, brought forth doubt and suspicion, objections, and false accusations about this matter, owing to envy and rancor. Therefore, this *Epistle of the Tomb* came into being in order to provide a thorough answer to their objections, deflect doubt, suspicion, and evil thoughts, and declare the many evident acts of grace of his excellency, the master [Şaban Efendi].

A STORY

At the time when this poor one [Ömer Fuadi] was finishing up [his Sufi training], our perfected guide, Muhyiddin Efendi (d. 1604), who was among the noble successors of his excellency, master [Şaban Efendi], was giving guidance [while seated] on his prayer rug, and he is thus buried in his illuminated tomb. He spoke the following while in conversation about the spiritual ranks and stations of the knowledge of divine providence, and the secrets of the friends of God:

He said, "I have three wishes in this world. If God Most High were to grant me those wishes, if I were to die at that very moment, death would be a favor to my soul." As soon as this poor one asked for further explanation, he said, "The first of these is that the pulpit of the noble mosque is too long, it creates hardship for the circles of the *zikr* ceremony and hinders the energetic participants in it. The two columns of the mosque also get in the way, and cause trouble in this [same] way. [My first two wishes] are to make the administrator [of the mosque] shorten the pulpit and remove the columns."

At the time, he did not express the third wish, and remained silent. When I requested an explanation of the third wish as well, he disclosed [the following] nonchalantly in private: "If, by the grace of God the Self-Sufficient, our dream manifests in the [visible] world, an exalted tomb shall be built over master Şaban Efendi['s grave]. If it were to occur in my lifetime, and I were to place a woolen cloth on his radiant grave and wrap his black turban [and place it on its top], I would have achieved the greatest of my desires."

After several months, [Muhyiddin Efendi's] sanctified soul passed on to the realm of God's mercy, and his noble body was interred in the area of the grave of the exalted master [Şaban Efendi]. This poor one, by command of God, was bestowed with the service of the order in his lodge and the guidance of spiritual knowledge on his prayer rug. [. . .]

Now, because of an account [about the Prophet] that I had remembered, and by reason of other signs that manifested through silent and spiritual conferrals, permission was given for a tomb structure. Ritual sacrifices were made, and a foundation spot was opened up with the prayers and praises in the noble presences of many scholars and sheikhs, and [thus] the foundation of the exalted building was laid. However, while no one was the target of the attributes of divine wrath or calamity that causes exhaustion, and the builders toiled with joy and pleasure on every side, it occurred to me that it would be better if the builders who worked on one side [of the building], as a result of the architect's decision, didn't work on the tomb of the master, because they were unbelievers.

While waiting to see what would manifest from God's perspective, thinking "what is the truth of the matter, is there acceptance from [Şaban Efendi's] spiritual being or not?" I saw a dream vision by command of God. A notable person from among the exalted sheikhs forbade these unbelievers from the construction, and afterward preached to this poor one (Ömer) with gentle speech and clear words. As soon as he spoke [the words], "Why do you let unbelievers work on the tomb of such a master?" I woke up and warned the architect. He sent them away. Moreover, there was a zimmi laborer among the Muslim builders who worked on one side. As the decision of prohibition [of non-Muslims] was announced to him, and he was instructed about Islam—with the guidance of God Most High—without hesitation, he became a believer through the veneration and love of the exalted master, and was given the name Ali, in place of Arslan.

In short, these types of [spiritual] experiences and signs occurred many times, yet no situation whatsoever appeared that suggested stopping the construction. It was even seen by this poor one previously in a dream-vision that a light descended in the form of the presently constructed tomb onto the enlightened grave of my noble [master].

GOSSIP AND SLANDER

When the wealth of Ömer Kethüda (the Steward) was seized as state revenue, and the tomb remained unfinished, faithless fanatics from among the scholars and other groups, and those who followed and inspected the conditions tied to blaming and slandering the Sufi mystics, found an opportunity at this time to stir up a furor of blame, censure, backbiting, and slander based on evil thoughts, without knowing the states of the friends of God, or having learned the secrets of the spiritual sages.

In addition to imputing to a master like Şaban Efendi the killing of a person (that is, Ömer the Steward), which, according to the shari'a, is one of the most spiteful of grave sins, and by making this kind of massive false accusation, they spread so much inappropriate gossip like this, with ignorance and fanaticism, without knowing the inexorable divine providence and the foreordained state of affairs written on the Preserved Tablet by the will of God. They said, "Şaban Efendi didn't want a tomb. Since the sheikh [Ömer Fuadi] inconsiderately gave license to the building, Şaban Efendi killed Ömer Kethüda (the Steward) through otherworldly intervention." Other rabble and ignorant people lacking knowledge thus gave notoriety to this gossip by following and imitating their substance-free chatter, and people gave credence to this gossip and false argumentation. On account of their persistence, when it became necessary to issue a response using divine knowledge and inspiration, it became possible based on both rational proofs and evidence from figures in authority, which [together] convey certainty.

BUILDING TOMBS IS PROHIBITED: RESPONSE

The existence, and corroborating fact of the Tomb of the Prophet, which was built atop the Lord of the prophets, the Prophet Muhammad, with the wealth of rulers; the visible existence of tombs built atop other prophets and friends of God, and the existence and continuation of this practice by the Muslim community, legal scholars, and Sufis, are a sufficient response to some disbelievers, fanatics, and ignoramuses. These people argue that "it is not permitted to build a tomb over the sheikhs and holy men, to burn lamps and candles at their tombs; it is wasteful expenditure and forbidden. It is never proper to have this done with the wealth of rulers, viziers, and military commanders." [Yet] they know nothing other than the aforementioned perfidiousness and imputing of impossible things [to Şaban Efendi]; they do not have any wisdom; and *guess at something of which they can have no knowledge* (Qur'an 18:22) with undisguised imprudence. [It is also a sufficient response] to those who heed and consider it with a sound mind; hear and remember it with continuous fairness; and who are cognizant of this extensive response. For God Most High has protected [the prophets, friends of God, and so on] from illegitimate acts. If [building tombs] were forbidden and lacked the consent [of these people], then [tombs] would not have existed.

In their existence is a secret wisdom; not everyone must be cognizant of it. It is enough that those who know the secrets and those who have wisdom understand it. [In fact,] there are several types of divine wisdom: Spoken wisdom (*hikmet-i mantuk biha*) and unspoken wisdom (*hikmet-i gayr-i mantuk biha*), known wisdom (*hikmet-i malume*) and unknown wisdom (*hikmet-i mechule*). These types of things (tombs, candles, and so on) belong to the "unknown wisdom." If it were not like that, these situations would not have emerged. On this point, the Lord of the Prophets said, "*My community does not agree on an error.*"

FIGURE 20. The tomb of Sheikh Şaban-ı Veli, Kastamonu, Turkey, 2011. Wikimedia commons.

BUILDING TOMBS IS WASTEFUL: RESPONSE

To those who say that "these types of things (tombs) are wasteful expenditures of money, this is why it is forbidden," the response is as follows: Expenditure [of funds] is not forbidden in every specific case. Expenditure that is forbidden is wealth that is being spent in a useless place without benefit or advantage, and that does not have any use from the point of view of the shari'a, or the purview of the Sufi path. However, the wealth expended on tombs, lamps, and these kinds of places is not useless and without benefit. For according to the meaning of the widely known saying, which is appreciated by the sheikhs who are "people of witnessing" [to God's manifestations of His existence] (*ehl-i şühud*), and the scholars who are "people of intelligence" (*ehl-i şu'ur*) within the Sunni Muslim community: "*If you fall into confusion about a matter, seek help from the occupants of the tombs.*" And according to other well-sourced legal proofs, requesting assistance from the purified souls and sanctified secrets of the holy men is canonically legal. Since seeking help is not useless, this subject [of the tomb], which indicates and facilitates the seeking of help and assistance, is also not vain and without benefit. Hence, it is known to the influential spiritual sages and the penetrating scholars that it is not wasteful expenditure.

BUILDING TOMBS IS AN IMITATION OF UNBELIEVERS: RESPONSE

Some scholars, and ignorant people who blindly imitate them as "scholars," also say that it is never proper to send sacrificial animals and lamps to the sheikhs and their tombs to request help and assistance from the hearts of those [sheikhs] who are alive and the souls of the departed ones. Because it is exclusively God Most High whose assistance should be sought in every matter, and whose help should be requested in every condition. [They say:] "Such acts are akin to the activities of unbelievers: they bow to the graves of their monks and to their idols, and they make them an intermediary between themselves and God. For Muslims, doing this is to imitate them, and it is polytheism."

Given this kind of talk, they think the worst of Muslims and make a serious false accusation. There is no wisdom and soundness in their scientific or spiritual knowledge, which makes false attributions to the most exalted name [of God] in thinking negatively about others in this way, and no luminousness in their hearts or minds. They cannot distinguish and recognize truth from falsehood—that is, the action of Muslims [from that of the unbelievers]—and they do not recognize in reality their intent or beliefs. It is on account of being dependent on their own corrupted personal opinion and dull intellects; on account of their not even knowing the sense of the word "imitation" according to its lexical meaning; or because they negligently do not recall its meaning.

Because by intending worship toward these [monks and idols] and taking a partner in their devotion to God, the unbelievers are in a state of unbelief and polytheism. Yet, the Muslims and believers in divine unity who have needs and desires—in their prayers and supplications to God Most High—do not take the saints and their enlightened graves as a partner in their devotion to God. They certainly do not—with real intention or shallow motives—imitate [the unbelievers] in order to act like them or do the things they do.

VISITING TOMBS IS USELESS: RESPONSE

Some scholars and ignorant people who imitate them deny the connection of the spiritual being of the sheikhs and their holy souls with the world of material things and the manifestation of their signs. Some of them deny [the connection] with the charge of heresy, and [thereby] themselves demonstrate heretical speech. Others do not show heresy and pretend to be believers; [however, they] are not able to tell the difference between the Sunni doctrine and other false schools of thought. They say, "[Those sheikhs] were pious and believing people just like us. They died and arrived at the world of nonexistence. There is no benefit from them for the visitors [of their tombs]. Specifically, in our [Hanafi] school it is not believed that anyone other than the "Ten who were informed [while still alive that they would enter Paradise]" died in faith. If [the holy men] have healing power, it would be [good] just for themselves. There is no benefit from them to others." With such speech expressing conjectures of denial and heresy, they join the schools of the heretics and the Hanbalis. [. . .]

The noble legal opinion by [the grand mufti] Sadeddin (d. 1599) is enough proof and sufficient evidence:

What is the response to this question from the authorities of the Hanafi school, "If Zayd, a member of the ulema, says that there is definitely no benefit to anyone who visits the tombs of the friends of God, scholars and pious ones," what is required for him?

RESPONSE: Repentance and asking for God's pardon. Considering the well-known signs and reports that there is no cutting off of the connection of the holy lights of the souls of the pure bodies of the great friends of God, and since the permissibility of visiting the tombs that are clearly illuminated is the preferred opinion, it is necessary to keep to it. Denying the repeated witnessing of signs and spiritual communion with the righteous ones at the graves of saints by people of perception is a sign of evil acts, a manifestation of ignorance, and leading people astray.

It is notorious that a sheikh of the faulty ones from the zealots of the Hanbali school (likely Ibn Taymiyya, d. 1328) condemned the visitors to the people of the tombs. He was even bold enough to censure the graves of the saints. By writing a book on that topic and deviating from the path of God, he accused the scholars of the age of ignorance and error, and he insulted and humiliated them with prolonged incarceration. When he also openly opposed the sound principles of some [other] religious doctrines, scholarly conferences were held. The scholars then unified and issued legal opinions, saying, "If he transgressed, and does not repent, he shall be executed." It is well-known that he repented and found salvation with a confession of his ignorance and shortcomings. Copies of the legal opinions and tracts of the scholars of that age are not hidden away. Further, [the prophetic saying], *"If you fall into confusion about a matter [seek help from the people of the tombs],"* is a well-known statement and is accepted among the great minds.

[Fetva] Written by the poor one Sadeddin; may he be forgiven.

TWENTY-EIGHT

Preserving Public Health

Court Records and Imperial Council Registers, Late Fifteenth and Sixteenth Centuries

TRANSLATED BY AMIR A. TOFT

Outbreaks of microbial disease have befallen societies across history, bringing with them public health crises and a host of social and economic consequences. Most ravaging and terrible of all diseases in the Old World was the plague. A highly infectious bacterial disease that was usually transmitted from rodents to humans by fleas, the plague broke out episodically in cities and sometimes swept across entire regions. The most destructive plague epidemic, commonly known as the Black Death, is believed to have originated in central or East Asia in the 1340s before spreading through India, the Middle East, Anatolia, and Europe and killing up to half of the population in any given region. The plague continued to hit the Ottoman domains in waves well into the nineteenth century. Another contagious bacterial disease was leprosy, which could damage the nervous system, leading to the loss of extremities, unsightly lumps on the skin, and disfigurement of the face and body. Although it was not always fatal, a profound stigma had been attached to leprosy since antiquity, and its victims often suffered the social penalty of ostracism.

The unseen quality of disease makes it terrifying for people. In an understandable state of despair, some people perceived deadly outbreaks as a reflection of God's wrath for people's sins, and they sought to be spared a terrible fate through prayer and pious devotion. Indeed, in addition to causing mass death, an outbreak could cause famine and dislocation and even break down a society's economic and political institutions. Modern advancements in medical knowledge and technology have helped us overcome most formerly catastrophic diseases. Yet we seem as vulnerable as ever to these resilient and stealthy agents of illness and death. The coronavirus pandemic of 2020 has reached into the lives of virtually everyone on Earth and brought ordinary life to an astonishing halt. With an immediate individual impact ranging from disruption to devastation, its long-term societal effects may continue to be seen for many years.

This chapter is not so much about a particular epidemic as it is about how members of early modern Ottoman society, with the expanding social compact that accompanies ever-growing urban centers and trade networks, addressed threats to public health. Practical measures were adopted to prevent or slow the spread of disease even when effective medicinal treatments were unavailable. It was well known that disease could be spread quickly by mobile groups like soldiers and merchants, especially those traveling around the Mediterranean. A common practice, therefore, was to impose a quarantine (literally, "forty" days of isolation) on merchants arriving from a place beset by plague. Other measures included segregating lepers from town centers. By the eighteenth century, the Ottomans had implemented a successful inoculation against smallpox.

The documents selected for this chapter, comprising court cases and imperial orders, touch on a diverse mix of public health issues. In addition to such dramatic concerns as containing the plague, the sample offers a view of more routine matters, like establishing reliable medical care, access to medicine, and public sanitation, all of which affected the quality of everyday life. An important theme to note is the involvement of legal officials, often but not always at the behest of private persons, in maintaining public health. Increasing state intervention, even in local affairs, is a general trend of early modern empires. As cities grew more complex and densely populated, the ruling apparatus, in an attempt to keep society running more smoothly across its domains, adopted an increasingly hands-on approach to solving public health crises.

LANGUAGE: Turkish. Court records in uncomplicated, formulaic legal language with technical terms interspersed. Imperial Council entries in formulaic administrative language with their particular pompous phrasing.

SOURCE: Document 1: Bursa Court Records 8, fol. 3b. Doc. 2: Bursa Court Records 8, fol. 221a. Doc. 3: Mühimme Registers 5, p. 492, case 1334. Doc. 4: Bursa Court Records 5, fol. 333a. Doc. 5: Bursa Court Records 40, fol. 211a. Doc. 6: Bursa Court Records C 1, fol. 24b. Doc. 7: Antep Court Records 1, p. 23. Doc. 8: Bursa Court Records 45, fol. 165b. Doc. 9: Mühimme Registers 25, p. 108, case 1204. Doc. 10: Mühimme Registers 5, p. 444, case 1189. Doc. 11: Bursa Court Records 152, fol. 45b. Doc. 12: Mühimme Registers 7, p. 67, case 186. Doc. 13: Mühimme Registers 7, p. 607, case 1706. Transcription: Yılmaz, Coşkun, and Necdet Yılmaz, eds. *Osmanlılarda Sağlık*. Istanbul: Biofarma, 2006.

1. ENJOINING A TRIPE SELLER, 1491

The occasion for drafting the following [record] is that the tripe seller Hacı bin Abdullah would bring the intestines, filled with offal, to his shop, which is close to the shop of the late son of Musa, the surgeon, and clean them there. On summer days one could not stay near [the shop] because of the odor. Reliable witnesses have testified, in Hacı's presence, that prior judges had already enjoined him. This being so, it is hereby ordered that he do the

FIGURE 21. Market inspector, ca. 1650s. Artist unknown. Cod.Rål. 8:o no. 10 (*Rålambska dräktboken*), fol. 93. Kungliga Biblioteket, Stockholm.

cleaning elsewhere and not wash [the tripe] in the shop in order that the Muslim residents not be offended.

20 Rebiülevvel 896 (January 31, 1491).

Witnesses to the proceeding: Sadeddin bin Süleyman | Mevlana Muslihuddin bin İbrahim | Muslihuddin bin Musa, the surgeon | Mehmed and Muslihi (?), sons of Oğulbeyi.

2. BOZA SHOPS DURING A PLAGUE OUTBREAK, 1492

The occasion for drafting the following is that the sellers of boza (a fermented millet beverage), who rent the public boza shops, came complaining that, because of an outbreak of plague, their boza shops had gone out of commission and they had suffered losses. A scribe and the [boza shops] superintendent were dispatched to ascertain the difference between a given boza shop's prior and current earnings. When the figures were recorded and it became known that they had indeed suffered losses, the boza shop superintendent, declaring that he would reduce each shop's [daily] rent assessment by a certain amount, then set about doing so as follows (units in akçe):

- Balıkpazarı boza shop; in the care of Ayvagül: sixty-five per day, originally eighty.
- Gallepazarı boza shop; in the care of Hacı Ali: forty per day, originally fifty.
- Odalar boza shop; in the care of Karagöz: twenty-five per day, originally thirty-one.
- Sedbaşı boza shop; in the care of Veli: forty per day, originally fifty.
- Pınarbaşı boza shop; in the care of Babamgeldi: sixteen per day, originally twenty-five.
- The new boza shop; in the care of Bey Yusufi: thirty per day, originally forty.
- Tahtelkala boza shop; in the care of Hacı Yahşi: twenty-five per day, originally forty-two.
- Tatarlar boza shop: seven hundred per month, affirmed at the original [amount].

Approximately 10 Zilkade 897 (September 3, 1492).

3. DETAINING MERCHANTS ON CHIOS, 1566

So ordered to Mehmed Bey:

You had sent a letter [concerning the present matter]. An edict was issued instructing you to find out and present whether it happened that traders arriving at the island of Chios, on account of having come from a place beset by plague, were detained for a period of twenty-five days and made to pay two akçe per day.

When the infidel notables were questioned, they said that it was the ancient law [there] to detain merchants for having come from plague-ridden places, but not to take a fee, and that it was the men standing guard over them who would do so.

You having so reported, I hereby command: "You shall duly admonish and impress on the aforementioned that henceforth they shall not detain Muslims on such grounds. Moreover, they shall not place them indoors [in cells] but rather designate an area [for them to stay]. Thus, from this day forward, they will have no acceptable excuse for detaining Muslims." So written.

Early Ramazan 973 (late March 1566).

4. MEVLANA BEDREDDİN'S BLADDER STONE, 1487

The occasion for drafting the following record is that Mevlana Bedreddin, son of Seyyidi Ahmed, appeared at the court of law. Having summoned the esteemed ophthalmologist and surgeon Seyyid Abdülkadir bin Seyyid İbrahim, rendered the following statement and admission, saying, "I have a bladder stone, and I have given Seyyid Abdülkadir permission and license to split [my bladder] and remove the stone. If I should fail to regain health and die, he shall not be held accountable for my death and none of my family or kin shall bring a claim or controversy."

12 Cumadelula 892 (May 6, 1487).

Witnesses to proceeding: Seyyid Ali bin Seyyid Yusuf | Mevlana Kemal bin İlyas | Mevlana Mehmed bin Nazri (?) | Ayas Agha bin Mahmud Ali.

5. DİMİTRİ'S BLADDER STONE, 1527

The occasion for drafting the following record is that Dimitri bin Nikola, a zimmi residing in the Balıkpazarı neighborhood of the guarded [city of] Bursa, got a bladder stone. Now, seeking to have the stone removed, Dimitri has summoned to the court of law one Seydi Ali bin Berekat eş-Şeybi, a surgeon, accepting the surgeon's fee of three hundred akçe for removal of the stone and making an explicit declaration that, if Dimitri should suffer harm or even die, no claim or controversy shall be brought against Seydi Ali in a court of law. The case was committed to the register in the manner described.

26 Zilkade 933 (August 24, 1527).

Witnesses to the proceeding: Hacı Hasan bin Abdullah | Ali bin Kemal.

FIGURE 22. Circumcision of a male infant, ca. sixteenth century. Artist unknown. Wellcome Collection, London.

6. CIRCUMCISION GONE AWRY, 1555

Ebu Bekir Efendi bin Hasan Efendi, the imam of the noble Hisar Mosque in the guarded city of Bursa, in the presence of the surgeon Halil Çelebi bin Ahmed, rendered, in the capacity of guardian, the following complete statement and deposition in that guarded city's noble and illuminated court of law: "When, at the direction of the named surgeon Halil Çelebi, we circumcised my minor son Mustafa, who is present in the court, [the surgeon] cut off a portion of his glans penis. After his recovery, I had brought, in the capacity of guardian, a claim

Preserving Public Health

against the surgeon Halil Çelebi in accordance with the law expressed by the legal opinion I have in my hand.

Now, [certain persons] have stepped in to mediate between us and negotiated a settlement of my claim against Halil Çelebi for the sum of hundred and fifty guruş. I, in the capacity of guardian, have accepted the stated settlement and have duly taken possession from Halil Çelebi the stated settlement amount. Henceforth, in the present matter I shall have no claim, case, or controversy whatsoever against the aforesaid surgeon Halil Çelebi."

After legal ratification, the matter was written down as it transpired.

Drafted within the first ten days of the noble Zilhicce, in the year 962 (late October 1555).

Witnesses to the proceeding: Haydar bin İzzet | Ahmed bin Hasan | Veli bin Mehmed.

7. SETTLEMENT FOR CAUSING A MISCARRIAGE, 1531

The cause for drafting the [following] record is that Bayram Bey and Abdi, mentioned earlier [in this register], summoned [to the court of law] Mahmud bin Halil, Mehmed bin Halil, Nebikul bin Osman, Mehmed bin Osman, İsmail bin Hasan, Mezid bin Mehmed, and Mehmed bin Kasım, and rendered the following deposition: "The aforementioned came to our home," they claimed, "and quarreled. My [pregnant] wife, Fatıma, miscarried her child, which had been alive [in the womb]. They were the cause of the miscarriage."

The aforementioned individuals, in turn, made the following statement: "Indeed, we altogether entered Bayram's home and quarreled. Fatıma, Bayram Bey's wife, miscarried a stillborn child, and of that [alone] we were the cause."

There then ensued great controversy and fierce contention between the parties, the defendants denying that the fetus had been alive [in the womb]. After this, intermediaries stepped in. In keeping with the hadith, "*Settlement is best*," (in fact Qur'an 4:128) Bayram Bey and Abdi Bey were awarded a settlement sum of eight thousand Osmani akçe to bring an end to the controversy and a resolution to the case, in exchange for which Bayram Bey made the following statement and admission: "In the matter of the aforementioned miscarriage, I no longer have claim or controversy against Mahmud, Nebikul, Mehmed, İsmail, Mehmed, Mezid, and Mehmed. If I should raise a claim or controversy, it shall not be heard by any judges." Abdi also made the following statement and admission: "In the matter of the aforementioned fetus, I no longer have a claim or controversy. If I should raise a claim or controversy, it shall not be heard by any judges." After this statement, the renunciation of a claim between the parties was adjudged and committed to the register.

Written on the twenty-third of the month of Safer, in the year 938 (October 6, 1531).

Witnesses to the proceeding: Ahmed Çelebi bin Boyacızade | Ahmed Kethüda bin Halil | Hacı Ömer bin Zeynüddin | Hacı Hüseyn bin Ali | Hacı Mehmed bin Vahid | Hasan, steward of the fortress | Timurhan bin Mustafa | Ahmed Agha bin Ali | Hilmi bin Cebrail.

8. A DEFICIENT PASTE PREPARATION, 1552

Vefa Çelebi, the current head physician at the hospital in the guarded city of Bursa, prepared a mesir paste using musk. However, great controversy arose with the administrator of the [hospital] endowment over whether saffron had in fact not been added to the musk and whether other ingredients had also not been used properly. Thereafter, Vefa Çelebi undertook to pay back the 1,824 akçe spent for the [preparation of the] pastes. On request, the fact of the matter was recorded in the register.

Witnesses to the proceeding: Those present.

3 Safer 959 (January 30, 1552).

9. APPOINTMENT OF A NEW PALACE PHYSICIAN, 1574

The chief physician has sent a letter, informing that one of the palace physicians, Firuz, who was Jewish and earned a daily salary of thirty akçe, has died; and requesting that, because there are many Jews and few Muslims [serving in the palace], his replacement, with a daily salary of forty akçe, be Mehmed, the head physician at the Sultan Süleyman Hospital.

So ordered.

19 Zilhicce 981 (April 11, 1574).

10. SAFE PASSAGE FOR THE PURCHASE OF MEDICINE, 1566

So ordered to the judges serving along the road to Dubrovnik: "The current king of Transylvania, İştefan (Stephen Báthory, d. 1586), has sent a man to my threshold, the refuge of the universe, in order to seek an order from my grace that, when his personal physician by the name of Blandrata son of Yorgi (Giorgio Blandrata, d. 1588), a zimmi, travels to Dubrovnik in order to obtain some drugs for medical treatment, none shall hinder or molest him on the way there and back. I hereby command: 'Let it be so that, when the aforementioned travels to Dubrovnik and back in order to get some medications, you [my judges] shall not allow anyone to hinder or molest him on the way.'"

So written.

Handed over to janissary captain Mehmed, agent of the head cannoneer.

On 20 Şaban, year 973 (March 7, 1566).

11. ENSLAVED GIRL AFFLICTED WITH SYPHILIS, 1599

The pride of the veiled women, the lady Sultan bint Abdullah rendered the following claim in the presence of one Hüseyn bin Bostan: "Some time ago I bought Peymane bint Abdullah, a slave girl of Hungarian origin, from Hüseyn for eight thousand akçe. I have now been informed and have become aware that this slave girl is afflicted with the Frankish disease (syphilis). I demand, in accordance with the noble law, that she be returned to Hüseyn."

After this statement, when Hüseyn was directly examined, he answered thus: "Indeed, I did sell this slave girl to Sultan for eight thousand akçe, but I did not know that the slave girl had the Frankish disease."

The slave girl was sent to a doctor, one Ali Çelebi—*the pride of the expert doctors,* who, on performing an examination, reported that the slave girl did have the Frankish disease and that it was an old condition. After the request, that which transpired was written down and drafted.

Drafted on the final day of Safer 1008 (September 20, 1599).

Witnesses to the proceeding: Receb bin Hamza | Mustafa bin Mehmed | Mahmud bin Yusuf.

12. A MALODOROUS MOSQUE PRIVY, 1567

So ordered to the judge of [the district of] Havass-ı Kostantıniyye (Eyüp): "You have sent a letter to my court, the refuge of justice, stating that the daughter of Nasuh, the former trustee of Ayasofya [endowment], had built a privy in the precinct of the Ebu Eyyub el-Ensari Mosque; and that many people have complained that, during the summer months, foul odors would emanate from that privy, which, in addition to causing offense to Muslims, would reach the mosque itself, and that they have asked for an imperial order to have it alleviated. Now I hereby command: 'On receipt [of this order], you shall investigate and inquire into the matter accordingly. If the case is indeed as you have presented it, you shall have the harm coming from the privy cured and remedied by lawful means; and you shall let no one raise any unlawful pretext or controversy; and you shall write and refer [to us] anyone who is delinquent or obstinate [in fulfilling this order].'"

So written.

6 Rebiülevvel 975 (September 10, 1567).

13. TROUBLESOME MENDICANTS, 1568

So ordered to the judge of Istanbul: "Some vagrants and certain other persons, though being in all respects healthy and capable of earning a fair living, take to begging in the markets and neighborhoods and, by vehemently insisting and rudely demanding money, vex those of respectable character.

Some beggars buy a blind slave girl or slave boy and force them to beg in the markets and neighborhoods. Some hold up notices (?) and banners and beg around the city. Others put chains on some persons' necks, parading them around the neighborhoods and markets and saying that they are debtors and prisoners.

Medrese students as well go out in groups, demanding money from people in the thoroughfares and streets. Some importunate beggars go out into the markets with a sick person by their side as a pretext for begging in the streets, subjecting people to all sorts of coarse behavior. Some, having been infected by diseases by the will of God, are [seriously] ill: such people, who formerly would have been removed and prevented from [entering] the city, are no longer stopped but instead roam the markets and intermingle with people.

Having been [informed] about these, I hereby command: 'You shall deal with these matters under the supervision of one of the sergeants of my sublime court, the city's chief of police, an exemplar among [his] peers, Hüseyn—*may his esteem be magnified.*

Those mentioned who, being not aged or infirm, are able to earn a fair living—if they should practice begging in the manner described, you shall forbid and prevent them from doing so. You shall not let beggars buy blind slave boys and girls and make them beg in this way, and you shall remove from the city the blind and crippled who cannot be prevented from roaming the neighborhoods and rudely demanding money. You shall by all means prevent and stop from begging all those capable of earning a fair living, and you shall write and apprise us of those who cannot be prevented that they may be sent to the galley. Those really afflicted with diseases you shall, in accordance with ancient custom, remove from the city and not permit to intermingle.

You shall attend to these matters with complete diligence and not let anyone act against my noble decree. Some theology students constantly have some of their relatives and personal connections, though being too young, go about, as though they were medrese students, solely for the purpose of collecting money for religious services. These perform recitations in congregational and neighborhood mosques, making light of the magnificent Qur'an, accosting the Muslims, and disrupting their peace of mind. You shall make them desist as well. However, those medrese students, who are constantly engaged in learning may, as has long been so, seek payment for religious services during their holidays. But you shall admonish them that they, as they have long done, shall not do so anytime other than their holidays.'"

So written.

Delivered to the chief of police [Hüseyn].

On 11 Muharram in the year of 976 (July 6, 1568).

TWENTY-NINE

Traditional Medicine for Everyday Ailments

Anonymous, Late Fifteenth Century

TRANSLATED BY ÖZGEN FELEK

The Ottoman medical system was composed of several interdependent healing traditions. In the sixteenth century, the most conspicuous systems were: (1) folkloristic popular medicine, which was established as a body of knowledge through centuries-old customary practices that differed from region to region; (2) prophetic medicine (*tıbb-i nebevi*)—that is, medical treatment based on the recommendations of the Prophet Muhammad; and (3) mechanistic medicine, which viewed diseases as disruptions in chemical or physical functions, based on the humorism inherited from physicians of Greco-Roman antiquity like Hippocrates (d. ca. 370 BCE) and especially Galen (d. ca. 210). A preeminent name in the history of Islamic medicine is the physician Ibn Sina (Avicenna, d. 1037), who appropriated, updated, and expanded on the humoral approach. His medical encyclopedia *The Canon of Medicine* (*al-Qanun fi't-Tibb*) was used as the standard medical text at various medieval universities in the Islamicate world and across Europe until the eighteenth century.

Humorism was essentially a preventive system founded on maintaining the balances of the humor—that is, the basic fluids of the body: blood, phlegm, black bile, and yellow bile. If one of the body fluids was lacking or present in excess, the balance in the body was thought to be disrupted, and disease symptoms would appear as a result. Each of the four elements had distinct properties, characterized as dry, humid, hot, or cold. Various edible nutrients were assigned these properties and were believed to restore the balance of the body's fluids when ingested. Phlebotomy, or bloodletting, was also a common therapeutic technique used to relieve the patient of surplus humors that upset the balance of the body.

Ottoman medical practices involved both preventive measures and curative therapeutics. There were multiple means to treat all kinds of aches and ailments. Each drug was analyzed according to its humoral characteristics and its effects on the body—whether it cooled, dried, heated, or lubricated. The Ottomans prepared most medication in formulations that would be familiar to the modern patient, such as infusions, decoctions, pomades, pilules, syrups, pastilles, powders, emulsions, suppositories, and clysters (rectal or urethral). Medications were eaten, drunk, or swallowed; ointments were applied topically; therapeutic fluids were bathed in; the fumes of some plants were inhaled; and powders were snuffed.

Most drugs came from plants, but the spectrum of products used by the pharmacists included oils, fats, and dairy products; pulses (like lentils and chickpeas); herbs, seeds, and nuts (cumin, coriander, mustard, cress, pistachio, sesame); sweets like honey, jujubes, peaches, plums, and dates; cooked foods; alcoholic drinks (wine and beer); cosmetics (henna); precious perfumes, pulverized gems; precious metals; and even opium and hashish. Some plants were only regionally available, and there was sometimes a discrepancy about certain plant designations. Authors of pharmacology texts tried to give precise instructions for the correct time to gather certain plants. Furthermore, since chemistry was not sufficiently developed, drug assays of botanicals were difficult, the amount of the active ingredient being uncertain.

The sections below are from a popular medical treatise titled *The Book of Physicians: The Preparation of Medication* (*Kitab-ı Hükema; Tertib-i Mualece*), which is one of the earliest works available about medicine available in Turkish and which was in all likelihood a compilation and partial translation from Arabic sources. A reference to Sultan Mehmed II's (d. 1481) physician Yakub (Jacopo of Gaeta, d. 1484) indicates that at least parts of this text must have been penned after this date. Curiously, these texts were "organic"—that is, they were adjusted and expanded in the hands of subsequent practitioners; it is therefore no wonder that there are sometimes texts with similar titles but different contents.

LANGUAGE: Old Anatolian Turkish with archaic technical terms for illnesses and herbs adopted from Arabic and Persian. Some Arabic loans are of Greek origin in turn. Rather short sentences; some inconsistent usage of grammatical endings creating confusion between actors involved.

SOURCE: Manuscript: *Kitab-ı Hükema; Tertib-i Mualece*. Gümüşhacıköy İlçe Halk Kütüphanesi, Amasya, 05 Mü F 1947. Section 1: fols. 48b–50a. Section 2: fols. 59b–60b. Section 3: fols. 112b–113a. Section 4: fols. 61b–63a. Section 5: fols. 65b–66b. Section 6: fols. 79a–80a. Section 7: 91b–92a. Transcription: Gümüşatam, Gürkan. "Haza Kitab u Hükema-yı Tertib-i Mualece Adlı Eser Üzerine Bir Dil İncelemesi." PhD diss., Ankara University, 2009. The introduction to this chapter is largely based on Shefer-Mossensohn, Miri. *Ottoman Medicine: Healing and Medical Institutions, 1500–1700*. Albany: State University of New York Press, 2009.

---

1. SHORTNESS OF BREATH

Now, if one mixes kite's blood with a little bit of rosewater and has [the patient] drink it, this is efficacious. If one drinks donkey's milk on an empty stomach every morning for a few days, this is efficacious. Dyspnea (*dıyku'n-nefes*) is an illness caused by a shortness of breath, which usually happens as a result of cold [humor] and excessive phlegm.

Now, one type of treatment is as follows: Let them crush a bit of marshmallow plant (*Althaea officinalis*) with raisin and fig and dragon's blood seeds and fennel, and take equal parts lily bulb, violet, and licorice root and then boil [these herbs] with sugar or honey, and filter it, and have the patient drink it.

With the help of a diluent drug, let them remove phlegm; boil honey water or rosewater or peeled marshmallow root and have the patient drink it. If this illness is caused by dryness or black bile, they should have the patient drink pomegranate or common bugloss juice made with sugar syrup or water lily potion. Let them also make the black bile leave [the body]. If swelling occurs, let them medicate the patient repeatedly. The person who is suffering from this illness should abstain from sour and salty [food] and things that cause flatulence, because the shortness of breath is [from] thick phlegm. When the patient walks too much, he cannot properly inhale and exhale.

If the patient is coughing, it is possible to remedy that too. Every time the patient coughs, they must drink hyssop potion and violet potion. Let the patient go to the bathhouse every three days and spread almond oil over his neck. The patient should drink the milk of a red (i.e., reddish-brown) cow as soon as it is milked, without waiting; this is efficacious. If the patient is not weak, they should give [him the milk] immediately. Let them also have the patient drink the urine of a small boy who has not reached puberty; this is efficacious. If they crush two drams of sugar a day and have the patient drink it with warm water for thirty days, this is efficacious. If they pulverize a bit of cumin and mix it with vinegar or water and drink it on an empty stomach in the morning, this is efficacious.

If they boil stinging nettle and add a bit of honey and eat it, this is efficacious. If they boil an arum plant root with honey and knead it into a paste, and then eat an amount not bigger than an almond every morning on an empty stomach, this is effective for shortness of breath and coughing. If they keep two drams of bitter vetch seeds (*Vicia ervilia*) in the mouth until they are completely saturated [with spit], and then chew and swallow them, this is efficacious. Also, whoever crushes the stems of field eryngo (*Eryngium campestre*) until its juice separates, and mixes it with rosewater and drinks it, will be healed with the permission of God; this has been proved.

2. DIFFICULTY IN FALLING ASLEEP OR STAYING AWAKE

Now, if someone spreads violet oil on her head at night, it will make her sleepy. Likewise, rose oil will make one sleepy. Likewise, if one recites the Qur'anic chapters *Tabbat* (Qur'an 111) and the noble *'Amma* (Qur'an 78) and goes to bed, whether he is healthy or sick, he will fall asleep. If they crush opium poppy and mix it with some water and apply it to the heels, they will feel sleepy.

If they wrap chicken stomach in a piece of cloth and hang it on the neck of a very sleepy man, he will not fall asleep. If one wears [the right] eye of a crab [around his neck], he will not fall asleep; if one wears the left eye [of the crab] he *will* fall asleep. If one wears the right eye of a wolf, he will not fall asleep; if one wears the left eye, he will fall asleep. If one spreads fox fat over his forehead, he will not fall asleep. If one wears a nightingale's feather, he will not fall asleep. If one kills an owl and takes out both of its eyes and puts them in water, one will sink in water; the other one will not. Now, he who carries on him the eye that does not sink will never fall asleep. If one wears the one that sinks on his person, he will fall asleep [with ease].

If a patient is uncomfortable and cannot fall asleep, he should buy lettuce for a few akçe and put it under his pillow, and squeeze some of its juice and smear it onto his hands and face; he will be relieved and fall asleep. Also, if he puts an ox's bladder (*Vesica bubula*) on his chest, he will never fall asleep; this has been proved.

3. SLEEP PARALYSIS

Now, the reason for feeling pressure [on the chest during sleep] is excessive eating and sleeping on a full stomach, and feverish heat going to one's head. Its symptoms are as follows: one thinks that something is heavily pressing down on him but when he attempts to scream, he cannot. As soon as the pressure is over, he immediately wakes up. This illness turns into epilepsy or speech and motion paralysis if it happens like this: The illness called epilepsy makes one fall down and foam at the mouth. What is called speech and motion paralysis is almost the same kind.

Now, the remedy is to draw blood. If the patient's eyes appear bloodshot, let him drink a laxative, and abundantly apply warm oils—such as sesame oil or bitter almond oil—on his head, and have him smell pure musk often.

4. HEART PALPITATIONS

Now, whoever consumes lemon balm (*Melissa officinalis*) leaves while they are fresh, and smells [them] and drinks their potion, this is highly efficacious for palpitation. Drinking and applying and smelling rosewater is also efficacious.

What is called palpitation is an illness caused by weakness. Symptoms include frequent thirst, constipation, rapid breathing, and chest tightness. It is also caused by severe anxiety. Cool weather appeals to the patient.

Now, the remedy is to have the patient drink sorrel potion and apple potion and water lily potion and fresh rose-petal potion and pomegranate potion and sandalwood potion, and also Italian bugloss (*Anchusa azurea*) water and rosewater and purslane (*Portulaca oleracea*). Blue violet and willow leaf, and cucumber, myrtle, rosewater, camphor, and pear—smelling any of the aforementioned is marvelous and efficacious.

As for food, the patient should consume soups with pomegranate sauce, unripe grapes, and apples, then apply a bit of psyllium jelly to his breast. The patient should spend time near streams of water, and now and again gladden his heart, and get rid of sorrow and gloom.

FIGURE 23. Physician treating a patient, ca. 1466. Artist unknown. In Sabuncuoğlu Şerefeddin, *Cerrahname*. Supplément Turc 693, fol. 30b, Bibliothèque Nationale, Paris.

However, if this illness is caused by excess of blood (plethora), one should lance [his vein and apply bloodletting?]. If this illness is caused by cold [humor], its symptoms are that warm things appeal to him, and his face is pale. The remedy is to mix musk, apple potion, a bit of aloe and basil, and carnation with common bugloss water and add a bit of saffron, and have the patient drink it. Also let them have the patient eat a dram of butter. Then, let the patient smell aloeswood, basil, musk, bitter orange leaves and celery, and consume calming foods: sautéed chicken, cinnamon, carnation, and saffron. Also let them have the patient eat pistachios with honey.

Then, let them apply sesame oil or jasmine oil to the patient's chest. With God's permission, she shall be relieved.

5. MENTAL ILLNESSES

Now, if one mixes pennyroyal water with a bit of vinegar, and puts drops of it in the patient's nose, this helps the mind. If they drink rose water or rub it [over the face and body] and smell it, this is also efficacious. If they burn the incense of devil's nails (*Unguis odoratus*), this is efficacious. If they smell orange peelings, this is efficacious to the mind. If the patient drinks rosewater for a few mornings, it will remove the forgetfulness and also the palpitations; this has been proved.

Things that give lightness to the heart and serenity to the mind: Now, if one eats orange, it brings lightness to the heart. If they drink common bugloss juice, it will bring lightness to the heart and remove fear. If they eat saffron, it will bring lightness to the heart and serenity to the mind. But if they eat it in excess, it is bad. The patient should consume just one dram of it.

Also, if they every so often eat quail meat, it will bring lightness to the mind and strength to the heart. If they eat it more than that, it will cause muscle spasms; let them refrain from eating too much. If one sprinkles mint over food and eats it, this is efficacious.

There are three kinds of sapphires: one is yellow, one is blue, and one is red. If they make one of them into a seal and wear it, it will bring lightness to the mind and bring serenity to the patient. He will be safe even from the plague; this has been proved and is efficacious.

Now, if one develops the habit of eating cinnamon, his mental health will improve. If one warms up rose oil and applies it to the head, it will improve mental health and comprehension. Also, eating ginger, frankincense, and mustard improves mental health.

Furthermore, if the patient wears the claw, beak, and brain of the hoopoe bird on his head, his mental health and comprehension will improve. If one takes white radish seeds and boils them with a bit of honey and leaves this in frosty weather for one night and drinks it in the morning, it will be seventy-two kinds of remedy, and improve mental health and comprehension. If one consumes Chinese rhubarb (*Rheum officinale*) and some —— together, it is a cure for disorders in the brain. Its benefits to colic, chronic fever, inguinal hernia, swollen liver, and many other illnesses, are countless.

6. TESTICULAR PEARLS AND PENILE CONDITIONS

Now, if there is redness on the testicles, they should draw blood from [the scrotum], close to the body. Whoever crushes mint and mixes it with red grape, and when it becomes like an ointment, applies this ointment to the swelling [on the testicles], will be cured with God's permission. If they crush some basil, and then apply it to the swelling on the testicle, it removes the swelling.

Also, if there is swelling on the penis and it gets inflamed, they should draw blood from his basilic vein, and then beat an egg white [from an egg] that was soaked in vinegar, with rose oil and a bit of starch. When this mixture becomes an ointment, if they put it on a piece of fabric and wrap it over the groin, the patient will be relieved; this has been proved.

If a man's penis is foul-smelling and dirty (balanitis?), it is because of his wife, or because of uncleanliness. Its treatment is thus: if they wash the penis with the patient's own urine as soon as the problem occurs, and apply some vinegar ointment, it will be healed.

If swelling occurs on a man's penis and if they are helpless as to its treatment, they should crush date kernels and —— seeds together, and, when it is softened, mix it with a bit of vinegar to make a dressing, and apply it to the swollen parts. The patient will be healed with the permission of God; this has been proved.

The treatment for swelling of the testicles or another body part is to gather a lot of watercress and then put abundant water in a big cauldron and boil it. If they go in [the cauldron] when the water is hot and sit in it up to the waist or the throat, with God's permission the patient will be relieved and healed from all problems in the major parts of his body, and also from other illnesses. Moreover, if they make a [green?] salad with some olive oil and have the patient eat it, he will be healed. Also, when he [wants to] enter the water again, let the patient pour the water and the herbs into a barrel, then enter the water, and afterward refrain totally from cold and drinking cold water; this has been firmly proved.

7. WARTS

Now, if one crushes leek seeds and applies them to a wart, this will remove the wart. If they crush sparrow droppings with human saliva and apply this after scratching the warts a bit, it will corrode them. If they twist an old piece of cotton into a wick and light it and cauterize the wart, the patient will be rid of the wart.

If they take chickpeas, and at the beginning of the month put one chickpea on each wart, wrap the rest in an old piece of fabric, and toss [the bundle] behind them, it will eradicate all the warts.

If one fumigates all his organs with burned rabbit droppings, it will eradicate all warts. If one squeezes one black nightshade berry (*Solanum nigrum*) on each wart and applies its juice—after letting it soak for one day and one night—the wart will be eradicated. But if the wart is not eradicated, let them apply [black nightshade juice] for up to three days, then it will surely disappear. Also, if they crush one or two eggplants and apply it to the wart, it will eradicate it; this has been proved. But it should be done a few times so that it will relieve the patient. If they crush a few onions with salt and put it on the wart, it will eradicate the wart. If they crush a few grasshopper legs and put it on the wart, it will eradicate the wart; this is highly efficacious.

THIRTY

Snake Medicine and Snake Charming in Cairo

Evliya Çelebi, d. after 1683

TRANSLATED BY ROBERT DANKOFF AND SOOYONG KIM

Born and raised in Istanbul, Evliya Çelebi is famed for his ten-volume *Book of Travels* (*Seyahatname*), which relates his journeys within and outside Ottoman lands over a forty-year period. Evliya not only reports on his personal experiences but also records an encyclopedic wealth of information on people and customs. Thus the *Book of Travels* is at once an autobiographical narrative and a work of human geography.

Evliya was the scion of an established family with ties to the imperial court, his father being chief goldsmith to the sultan, and he received a standard education centered on the religious sciences. However, unlike similarly educated men, he did not pursue a bureaucratic appointment. He instead made travel his profession, having developed a keen curiosity about the world at a young age, as his father's friends regaled him with tales of campaigns and adventures in distant places. Initially, to satisfy that curiosity, he explored Istanbul and its environs, while studying assorted works of geography. Finally, nearing the ripe age of thirty in 1640, Evliya took advantage of his court connections and ventured outside the capital city, eastward to Trabzon on the Black Sea coast.

This marked the beginning of Evliya's travels—to a large extent a grand tour of the vast Ottoman realm. He later ventured south to Ibrim in Lower Nubia, north to Azov in Crimea, to Baghdad on the eastern edge, and to Stolnibelgrad on the western frontier, in today's Hungary. He also visited places beyond Ottoman territorial borders, most notably the Safavid city of Tabriz and the Habsburg capital of Vienna, as a member of Ottoman embassies. In fact, Evliya frequently traveled in the retinue of government officials or as an acting official himself. Many of the travel accounts are filtered through an administrative and imperialist framework. At the same time, a sophisticate from a great imperial capital, Evliya occasionally cast a critical eye on places he found too provincial for his liking.

The *Book of Travels* originated from the detailed notes Evliya took throughout his journeys; despite his prejudices, the information they contain about people and customs are generally presented in a fair-minded manner. Still, Evliya was not immune from embellishments and outright fabrications when reporting on his personal experiences, and the effect is often comic. This, however, is a convention of the genre of travel writing, Ottoman and otherwise.

The following selection is taken from the tenth and last volume, mostly focusing on Cairo, where Evliya eventually settled down and completed the *Book of Travels* as a single, unified work. It is an account of his visit to the Qala'un hospital, a medical complex established centuries before Ottoman rule, to witness the preparation of theriac, a cure-all known since antiquity. The preparation of theriac was notoriously labor-intensive because of the numerous ingredients that had to be collected and processed, particularly the key ingredients of snake flesh and venom, and because the maturation time could last for years. Consequently, although theriac was a widely popular drug in Ottoman lands, Europe, and beyond, it was costly to make and to procure.

LANGUAGE: Turkish. Evliya Çelebi uses many uncommon words, and has a peculiar grammar of his own, employing a lively narrative technique. In fact, there is a separate dictionary for the unusual words that Evliya uses.

SOURCE: Manuscript: Evliya Çelebi. *Seyahatname*. İstanbul Üniversitesi Kütüphanesi, Istanbul, Türkçe Yazmalar 5973, fols. 120b–125b. Transcription: Dankoff, Robert, Seyit Ali Kahraman, and Yücel Dağlı, eds. *Evliya Çelebi Seyahatnâmesi: İstanbul Üniversitesi Kütüphanesi Türkçe Yazmalar 5973, Süleymaniye Kütüphanesi Pertev Paşa 462, Süleymaniye Kütüphanesi Hacı Beşir Ağa 452 Numaralı Yazmaların Mukayeseli Transkripsiyonu, Dizini*. Vol. 10. Istanbul: Yapı Kredi Yayınları, 2007. Translated by Robert Dankoff and Sooyong Kim. *An Ottoman Traveller: Selections from The Book of Travels of Evliya Çelebi*. London: Eland Publishing, 2010.

THE SNAKE HUNT

Let it be known to intelligent travelers that in every country throughout the world there are physicians who make the *faruq* theriac, but they cannot make it like the Egyptian kind. The faruq tablet is peculiar to Egypt. One should understand that the term "tablet" in the first place refers to something that is extracted from the body of a snake.

There are forty persons receiving salaries from the endowments of this hospital of Sultan Qala'un (Mamluk sultan, r. 1279–90) who are charged with providing this service once a year. They are a guild and reside in the villages of the Habiroğlu [tribe] in the district of Giza. Once a year, in the month of July, they hunt the snakes from which the faruq theriac is made.

When it is the proper time to hunt snakes, they gather together and put on clothing of thick felt from head to foot. They even cover their faces; only their eyes are visible. They attach pieces of white felt to long sticks and head for Bahnasa, the Fayyum, and Jabal

Akhdar. They reach the place where the faruq snakes are found in the cool of the morning when the snakes are indolent before being warmed by the heat of the day. Even in that condition it is a great struggle to catch them. Having caught several thousand, they put them in baskets that are smeared with faruq [theriac], and the snakes become intoxicated and bewildered. While the snakes are in this state, they sew up the openings of the baskets. It sometimes happens that while struggling to catch the snakes, one of them will spring at the face of a hunter. If it strikes him in the eye he cannot be saved and falls a martyr to this profession. For they are deadly poisonous snakes. If they bite a camel on the ear or a mule on the hoof, they kill it instantly.

Hunting these snakes is reserved for the abovementioned individuals. No one else is able to carry out the task. By God's command, the members of their guild belong to the Sa'diyye brotherhood; but they are very upright individuals. This group caught a great many snakes, loaded them in baskets on donkeys, and took them to Cairo. On the way, near a garden of Iram called Basatin, one of the snakes escaped and bit the donkey carrying its basket. The poor donkey collapsed headfirst, and in the twinkling of an eye its body swelled up to the size of an elephant. When it died, each leg had turned into a huge pillar. Some of the hunters drove away the people dwelling nearby, saying that the carcass of the donkey would split open and they would be ill affected by the stench. They removed the baskets of snakes that had been loaded on that donkey and placed them on another one. As this was going on, the carcass of the poisoned donkey split open and everything, even the bones, dissolved and flowed away. Thank God no one was harmed. The people who were there immediately piled dirt over the carcass of the donkey and buried it. They brought the cargo of snakes on the other donkeys to the hospital of Qala'un and turned it over to the chief physician and superintendent.

THE PREPARATIONS

This humble one had previously asked the chief physician if I could watch the process; so now they sent me word. I immediately mounted my horse and went to the hospital of Qala'un. They opened the door of the faruq [theriac] chamber and let me in, then barred the door. They do not normally let in outsiders because it is a dangerous place, full of thousands of pitiless snakes, and also because they want to keep their knowledge secret, on the grounds that *the Evil Eye is a reality*.

This faruq chamber is a large medrese. Walls and floor are covered with varicolored raw marble. It is a medrese devoted to the science of medicine. All around the courtyard are terraces that on that day were covered with carpets. We were some thirty people all told, including the chief physician, the superintendent, the secretary of the endowment, the administrator of the endowment, ten assistants of the chief physician, the reciter of prayers, and twelve snake hunters, cooks, and butchers. There was no reason for anyone to knock on the door and want to come in. Still, they barred the door firmly and told me not to fear. I got up on a low stool that they used to light lamps and got ready to watch. All thirty people arose, performed an ablution and two prostrations, then brought out their tools and equipment.

First, there were one hundred blocks of wood, each three spans long. In the middle of each was a *gevele* nail, one span in height. There were one hundred sharp meat cleavers, like so many swords of Dahhak, the backs of which were made of thick Frankish iron. There were one hundred large, glazed, earthenware crocks, large enough for a man to fit inside. Some were full of water, others empty. There were several tinned trays from the time of Qala'un; one *ardeb* (ca. two hundred liters) of finely sifted salt; and some fifty large vessels, like earthenware water jars, glazed inside and out, but with wide bases and mouths big enough for a man to put his head in.

Everyone readied these copper and earthenware vessels. When the reciter of prayers stood up, all those present also rose to their feet. After the *besmele* (i.e., pronouncing the formula, "*In the name of God, the Compassionate, the Merciful*") and praises of God and blessings on the Prophet, he mentioned in order the Ottoman dynasty, the benefactor Sultan Qala'un, the physician Loqman, Pythagoras the monotheist (d. ca. 495 BCE), the sultan of physicians Abu Ali Sina (Avicenna, d. 1037), and the spirits of the other physicians. He then prayed for the safety of those present, mentioning the chief physician, the superintendent, the secretary, the chief cook and all the assistants and servants. After the prayer, he said "*God is great*" and recited a fatiha (i.e., the opening chapter of the Qur'an), and we touched our faces with our hands.

THE SORTING OF THE SNAKES

Now the old chief hunter and three snake butchers cut open the top of one of the twelve baskets that were standing in the middle of the courtyard. Great God! Some thousands of merciless snakes with poisonous fangs slithered out. I was stupefied with fear, although I was watching from a high perch. Some of them jumped as high as a man to the left and right. Hissing and whistling, they threw themselves at the wall.

While the terrified snakes were leaping about, the chief physician's servants joined with the snake hunters and prodded them inside yellow cloaks that were smeared with faruq [theriac], and they all quieted down. The chief hunter and three butchers sat themselves next to the postblocks mentioned above with cleavers in their hands and took the snakes out of the cloaks one by one. One type of snake to emerge was small and white, with an intoxicating musky smell. These the hunters put in their bosoms. I asked the chief physician about them and he said, "That is the musk snake. It is not used for making faruq [theriac], but for other medicaments. You'll see shortly."

As I observed, they collected together all these little white snakes and arranged them on a long red silken cord, hanging by their throats. The cord was tied to a shaded place in a corner of the medrese and stretched from wall to wall. Using cotton, they dripped some Sousse olive oil into the mouths of the snakes, at which they died and began to swell up. The snakes would remain hanging this way for forty days and nights, the snake skins granulating into musk like cardamom seeds, with an odor so sharp that it makes one's nose bleed.

Another type of small snake was short and mottled, with rounded heads like half of a walnut shell. The men set these to one side as well. When I inquired about them, the chief physician said, "They are called snake of Adam the Pure and are descended from the snakes that were banished from paradise along with Adam. These too are not used for making faruq [theriac], but for other medications." He searched through ten baskets of snakes and set aside the musk snakes and the roundheaded snakes of Adam the Pure. The latter, like the faruq snake, does not hatch eggs but gives birth like other animals, by God's wisdom and contrary to the nature of snakes.

Then they counted the faruq snakes that were left. There were 8,300, large and small. They were handed over to the administrator of the endowment, and the secretaries and instructors recorded in ledgers that there were eight hundred guruş worth of snakes.

THE DISMEMBERING OF THE SNAKES

The chief snake hunter and three snake butchers were seated at the postblocks. Uttering a besmele and the intention of healing, he took out a large snake from the cloak, put the middle of the snake on the nail of one of the blocks, and, holding the head and tail together with his left hand, struck once with the cleaver in his right hand. The body of the snake, minus head and tail, began to squirm about the marble floor, while head and tail remained in the chief hunter's hand. He used the back of the cleaver to crush the snake's head and left it on the floor, saying, *"Declare God's unity."* All those present shouted, *"There is no god but God!"*

When he cuts a snake, he does so holding it stretched out and leaving behind [a length of] three fingers (ca. nine centimeters) of the head and tail. Another butcher takes the body of the snake and slices open its abdomen with a golden knife, extracts the intestines and eggs, and throws it to a third butcher who, pulling on the snakeskin with his fingernails, flays it from end to end. Apparently, the skin was makeshift to begin with, so now the white flesh easily slips out. But the snake is still writhing!

With this, the job of the butchers is done and the snake falls into the hands of the physicians. The chief physician's assistants take the peeled snake, wash it thoroughly in the aforementioned crocks, and put it into one of the glazed jars, adding salt. When these jars are full, they place them on the fire. The chief physician holds a watch. They burn acacia wood under the jars, and the fire becomes extremely hot.

Meanwhile everyone is in a state of fear and reciting litanies. Sometimes, when they remove a snake from the cloak, they spit into its mouth, so the snake is intoxicated and bewildered; then they put it on the log and chop it. In this manner the twelve hunters and butchers kill ten baskets of snakes.

As for the heads and tails, they fill large apothecary bottles with them and save them to make other medicaments. I persisted in questioning them about this, but they refused to answer. From what I understand, however—and God knows best—they extract the poison from the heads and send them to the Frankish lands (Europe). Because one time a gift of one thousand snake heads strung on a cord was brought to the king of Dunkerque. He was pleased with the gift, took the snake heads off the cord, and gave them over to the *Graf* (i.e., the count).

If the butchers do not strike accurately while killing these snakes, and one tiny part of the head or tail is still slightly attached to the body, the chief physician immediately leaps from his place and cries out, "*irmi, irmi al-hayya*," which means "Throw it away! Throw away the snake!" [Once] they did not throw the body of the snake with its head in with the intestines and eggs of the other snakes, but they put it in a place apart. That snake immediately swelled up as big as one's arm, although it was originally only as thick as one's thumb. The improperly severed head had affected the body and it swelled up. So [whenever the head was improperly severed] the chief physician immediately cried out and had them throw it away. They also discarded the log and cleaver that were used and brought out different ones. By God's wisdom, on that day seventy-five snakes from ten baskets were not properly killed and the men threw them all away along with the implements. The discarded snakes are not charged on the account of the endowment; rather, they are charged against the account of the snake hunters and butchers and the cost is deducted from their fees. It is an amazing spectacle.

Another noteworthy event occurred that day. When the skins and intestines and eggs of the butchered snakes had piled up like mountains, the snake butchers regrouped and sprinkled some of the aforementioned sifted salt on this snake rubbish. As this was going on, one of the butchers withdrew his hand and gave a heartrending sigh. The chief hunter immediately spat onto the fellow's injured finger, brought three of the snakes that had been washed in the crocks, and wrapped his finger with them. The three snakes immediately swelled to the size of a man's arm. He removed them and wrapped the finger with three more; they did not swell up, but they did change color, and were also removed. Now the chief hunter took the fellow's finger into his mouth, sucked at the wound and spat a yellow substance on the ground. They rubbed a bit of greatest faruq [theriac] on the fellow's finger. The pain subsided; the man was saved from being poisoned.

Apparently, the head and tail of one of the snakes being killed had not been properly severed in a single blow and were accidentally left amid the snakes' eggs and rubbish. Then, while the butchers were sprinkling salt on the snakes' eggs and innards, some poison from that improperly severed snake got on that fellow's finger. They treated him as I described and saved his life. In sum, I never saw such hard-hearted and cold-blooded men as these snake hunters and snake butchers—I wonder if they should even be considered human beings. To be sure, I witnessed a remarkable scene; but at every moment I nearly took leave of my senses, and I began to regret having come to watch.

THE PROCESSING OF THE SNAKE INNARDS

Now I asked the chief physician: "You have salted the skins and innards and eggs of these snakes and pickled them in jars to preserve them. What will you do with them?" "What are you after? Don't ask!" he said. I persisted and questioned him again. Finally, he answered: "There are Frankish *bailos* (i.e., envoys) here. They purchase these jars from us and take them to the physicians of Frankish lands, who use this substance to treat various ailments.

They treat every limb of the body in a different manner, and this substance is very effective."

They put the cleaned and salted snakes into twelve glazed earthenware jars, placed the jars on the kitchen hearths in one corner of the courtyard, and burned acacia wood under them to make the fire extremely hot. The chief physician had his staff in one hand and a watch in the other. The cooks were again his students, having mastered the sciences under his tutorship; the chief physician was only present to watch the time. The snakes boiled for three hours. An amber-like yellow oil appeared at the top of the jars. The chief physician took up a ladle, spooned out yellow snake oil, and filled the large apothecary bottles that were there. Once again, they made the fire very hot under the jars—please note that the vessels used to cook the snakes are not copper saucepans or kettles but, as I mentioned, earthenware jars glazed inside and out.

Next the chief physician weighed the snake oil that he had spooned out with the ladle against olive oil that comes from Sousse in the Maghreb—it is the finest olive oil, like water of life. He filled the bottles with five *okka*s (ca. six kilograms) of snake oil and five of pure olive oil, then put them over a low heat, which they later increased. After three hours the oil took on the consistency of clarified butter and the fragrance of musk and raw ambergris, perfuming the brains of those present. I was impatient to learn what it was for, and again questioned the chief physician.

"To tell you the truth," he said, "there is an enormous number of people in India with leprous conditions, and this oil is very beneficial for that climate. If it is rubbed just once on the bodies of those afflicted with such diseases, by God's command the malady disappears and they become as clear-skinned as pearls or eggs. But it has no benefit here in Egypt, even if it is rubbed on a thousand times. On the other hand, in Egypt, if you make those suffering from mange or palpitations swallow one dram of it for forty days, by God's command they are cured."

They cooked the snakes in the jars for three more hours and boiled off one span of water, then they removed the jars from the fire and put the shredded snake meat on large copper trays to cool. The snake broth left in the jars was for local consumption. For the past month, bowls and ewers and copper buckets had been arriving from the Egyptian notables along with prescriptions, and these were now taken out of the cupboards. The name and illness of each patient were written on a piece of cloth wrapped in paper and attached to each vessel. They filled the bowls and buckets with that snake broth, sometimes adding other medications according to the illness, and returned them to their owners. Thus, the snake soup went to hundreds of places.

THE TASTING OF THE SNAKE BROTH

Their work complete, all the assistants filled dishes with snake soup, crumbled some bread on top, and sat down to eat. I nearly took leave of my senses. The chief physician, the superintendent, the secretary, and the other servants also began to drink the snake broth by the cup. They brought me a cup too. I refused it, but the chief physician and superintendent were insistent: "Truly, my lord, it is very invigorating. It increases the faculty of vision and eliminates the odor of hemorrhoids."

"It is God's to command," I said, mustering my courage. "A trouble shared is a trouble halved. They drank it, so I'll drink it too." I closed my eyes and gritted my teeth, uttered a besmele with the intention of healing, and drank off a cup. It smelled like musk. They brought another cup, in which, with the tip of a knife, they put a small amount of the snake oil mixed with the aforementioned olive oil. I drank that too. God knows, that musky smell did not leave my brain for an entire week.

On the benefits of snake broth: I described before how we were attacked by Arabs on the night we were approaching Badr-i Hunayn after departing from Mecca. During that period I was quite anxious and my body became feverish. Praise be to God, I drank two cups of this snake broth and within a week not a hint or trace of the malady remained; my body turned to pure silver, and I was well again. I experienced other benefits as well. [. . .]

To come to the point—one subject leads to another—after the ejaculation that occurred on that night in Glamoč Castle (in modern-day Bosnia and Herzegovina), this humble one lost sexual potency; I did not even have any nocturnal emission. And I was despondent, thinking that my progeny had been cut off. Now, twenty-seven years later, I came to Egypt and drank two cups of snake broth with oil on the day of faruq in the Qala'un hospital. That night I had two nocturnal emissions in succession. In the morning I went to the hospital and told the whole story to the chief physician. He gave me ten okkas of snake broth and one canister of snake oil and olive oil mixed. I used the snake broth for five or six days and became so healthy that I could break hazelnut shells on my flesh, so hard had my body become. I experienced other benefits as well.

THE READYING OF THE THERIAC TABLETS FOR DISTRIBUTION

In short, the chief physician distributed this snake broth to all the people [who had left their vessels and prescriptions], and the snake stew that they had cooked was cooling on the trays. The chief physician sat down at the trays with his students and attendants. They all washed their hands thoroughly, rolled up their sleeves, and one by one took some snake stew in their hands. From the back of each snake, from both sides of the spine, which they call the backbone, they extracted long cordlike strings as thick as the handle of a pen sharpener. The length differed according to the size of the snake that was cut.

This is what is termed the "tablet" of the faruq theriac, which is the great theriac and is drawn out from the snakemeat like a string. Each snake produces just one tablet weighing one *miskal* (ca. four grams). All this toil and trouble, all this fear and anxiety, is for the sake of tablets weighing one miskal each. None of the other parts of the snake that are cooked are used for faruq [theriac]; they are thrown away, or given to the poor to eat, or else are buried in some out-of-the-way place.

An enjoyable anecdote for sex addicts: Some of it was once given to a man who was no longer able to have sexual intercourse. He ate snake stew and then had sex five or ten times with his wife. She became annoyed because he could not get enough. The next morning she presented a cohabitation suit in court. As plaintiff, her complaint was: "God forbid it, I cannot endure this affliction!" As defendant, he admitted: "I ate snake meat and had sex ten times." The kadı reconciled them to having sex twenty times (a day?). Those who heard of this suit wanted to drink snake soup as well, and prayed: "O God, make it possible!"

In short, they pounded the meat extracted from the back of those snakes with wooden mortars and pestles, pulverized it into a paste, and weighed it on a scale. At this juncture it becomes a white "greatest electuary" and is called "viper's tablet." Now all the medicaments are passed through a fine sieve and weighed out in precise amounts, then mixed with the viper's tablet together with pure Anatolian honey that has been repeatedly boiled.

Every year they cook three cauldrons of faruq theriac. First, they send two jars of it to the felicitous sultan and one jar each to the grand vizier, the grand mufti and chief physician in Istanbul, and the chief kadı of Cairo as gifts. The rest they save for the superintendent of Qala'un's endowment; it is dispensed to the bedridden patients in the hospital according to their illnesses. The faruq theriac is exported from Egypt to Turkey (Rum) and Arabia and Persia and Frankish lands—in short, to the seven climes. It is produced in the manner described. They usually cook it once a year, but while this humble one was in Egypt, the chief physician, being the perfect master, cooked it three times a year.

As for the white snakes of Adam the Pure, mentioned above, their number exceeded one thousand. The medrese where the faruq theriac is made has a small room fitted with glass panes and a cord stretched from one corner to the other. The chief physician hung those white snakes in a row along this cord, attaching them one by one by the tail with red silk thread. Struggling for their lives, the snakes bit one another and, formerly thin and white, they all swelled up as thick as one's arm. Now they closed all the windows of the room and went out, shutting the door behind them. When they opened it forty days later, the snakes of Adam the Pure had shrunk and become like thin strings. Even the bones were now black as cardamom seeds, having turned into a narcotic—the odor deprives a man of his senses, making him intoxicated and dizzy.

As for the snakes with the round head like half a walnut shell that we described above, the snake butchers cut them in two and pickle them with their speckled skins. The halves with heads are strung on strings, the tails are buried in the ground. After forty days they dry out and turn red. Then they are taken [off the strings and out of the ground] and kept in lead canisters. Otherwise they would be eaten by ants, since snake meat and human flesh are very tasty.

THIRTY-ONE

On Smoking Tobacco

Abdulmalik al-Isami, d. 1628; Katib Çelebi, d. 1657

TRANSLATED BY BASIL SALEM AND GEOFFREY LEWIS

Coffee and tobacco, two products that inundated Ottoman markets from the sixteenth century onward, created new anxieties both for the people who consumed them and for the authorities (groups that undoubtedly overlapped). Coffee came from Yemen in the earlier part of the century and quickly became a favored commodity, resulting in the opening of hundreds of coffee houses in Istanbul and beyond within fifty years. Tobacco, on the other hand, was brought from the Americas, and became equally popular in the earlier part of the seventeenth century. It was quickly understood that these were mood-altering and partially addictive substances, a class of substance for which—unlike alcohol—there had previously been no religious legal rulings.

Contemporary narratives report that people started to frequent coffee shops instead of attending places of worship. Such accounts may themselves be the result of the anxieties of pious people, but it is also true that these two products changed the course of daily life for many people. Coffee houses were heretofore nonexistent secular spaces and they were not frowned on by society at large—unlike the popular and more long-standing wine taverns. Because there were no clear religious rulings about coffee, being a regular at a coffee house must not have been viewed as a particularly detestable act. Moreover, drinking coffee or smoking a pipe was inexpensive compared to drinking wine. Additionally, both products were promoted as beneficial for the health of the consumer.

Novel venues for socialization created new concerns for the ruling establishment. It turned out that coffee houses were an ideal venue for airing views critical of the political establishment; in fact, a fair amount of societal unrest was cooked up in coffee houses. They became a new venue for the dissemination of information, a social network where information and gossip quickly spread. As a consequence, Ottoman authorities closed down coffee shops and banned temporarily the consumption of coffee and tobacco several times in the earlier part of the seventeenth century. Around the mid-seventeenth century, coffee began to be consumed in major European cities, where it created similar anxieties.

It is largely accepted that coffee was already being used by Sufis to stay awake during their nightly spiritual rituals, but the new social realities prompted new debates. Scholars tried to evaluate the effects of coffee and tobacco from religiolegal perspectives, considering their social, legal, and health implications. This chapter contains excerpts from two treatises that assess the status of tobacco from several viewpoints. They were written in the midst of heated debates among scholars about these new products, and occasional measures were taken by the authorities against their use.

Abdulmalik al-Isami (d. 1628), the author of the first treatise, was a Meccan scholar and Sufi. The sections below are from his work's introduction, in which he recounts how he set out to write a treatise on the topic and his perturbations about it. Al-Isami's words convey the types of ambiguities and anxieties about tobacco that exemplify his time. Katib Çelebi, the author of the second text, was not a medrese-trained legal scholar, but a self-made polymath from Istanbul. His stance on the developments around tobacco include similar legal reasonings, but it also reflects the societal responses to smoking tobacco. Both authors attempt to gauge the legality of tobacco consumption by looking for indications in the Qur'an and hadith, two major sources of Islamic law, as well as by using the method of analogy.

Demands for these products only rose in the decades following these texts. Historians view the trade and consumption of the new "luxury" items such as coffee, tobacco, tea, cocoa, and sugar from the seventeenth century onward as a part of a larger development known as the consumer revolution. European merchants saw the potential in these commercial goods, which they partially acclimatized and began growing on plantations in the Caribbean colonies. Not only did the new products create new economic models; they reshaped the lives of common people around the world in hitherto unimaginable ways.

LANGUAGE: (1) Arabic. Simple, clear sentences. (2) Turkish. Generally straightforward sentences. The language becomes somewhat convoluted in the sections where the author expounds on legal reasoning.

SOURCE: (1) Abd al-Malik al-Isami. *Risala fi Shurb al-Dukhan.* Süleymaniye Kütüphanesi, Istanbul, Bağdatlı Vehbi 538. Edition and transcription: Acar, Nurettin Muhtar. "Sigara Hakkında İki Yazma Risale: Abdü'l-Melik El-İsâmî'nin 'Risale Celîle Fî Şurbi'd-Duhân' ve Mustafa b. Ali El-Âmâsî'nin 'Risale Fî Tahrîmi'd-Duhân' Adlı Risaleleri." Master's thesis, Uludağ University, Bursa, 2010. (2) Translated by Geoffrey Lewis. *The Balance of Truth.* London: George Allen & Unwin, 1957 (50–59). Lewis's (d. 2008) 1957 translation was partially corrected and edited by Helga Anetshofer and Hakan T. Karateke by comparing it with the manuscript of Katib Çelebi, *Mizanü'l-Hakk fi İhtiyari'l-Ahakk.* TBMM Milli Saraylar Kütüphanesi, Ankara, Halife Abdülmecid Efendi Koleksiyonu 3803 (Y 14), as well as with the printed version in Istanbul: Ali Rıza Efendi Matbaası, 1286/1869–70.

1. ABDULMALIK AL-ISAMI'S *TREATISE ON SMOKING*

The reason that called for the writing of this treatise, and the motive behind addressing such a matter, is that when smoking became popular across the East and the West, people's opinions on the issue were divided: One group saw that [smoking] was permissible; they relied on the fact that there is no explicit proof in the Qur'an or hadith to the contrary. The other group is split into two categories: the first category of people prohibited smoking and forbade being near it, let alone swallowing [smoke]; this category based its assessment on evidence from the Qur'an and hadith and was guided by reason. The second category took a middle ground and declared that while smoking is not forbidden, it is discouraged (*karaha*).

My natural inclination drew me toward forbidding it and my heart leaned toward not permitting it. I searched for proof of its prohibition in the Qur'an and hadith, on the one hand, and used my intellect to prove that it is forbidden, on the other. I also asked the most knowledgeable physicians about the nature of tobacco and about the condition of those who were cursed by inhaling its substance or swallowing its smoke. Furthermore, I availed myself of mystics who have risen to the highest levels of spiritual elevation and of those honorable ones among them who have reached the essence of mysticism and its subtleties. This took a long time, but I persevered in the quest to succeed in this endeavor and I did not tire from searching for what will cure the chest and heart.

While there is no question that the Qur'an does not make an explicit statement regarding the permissibility or prohibition of smoking, [the fact that] God said that there is *nothing moist therein, nor anything withered, but that it is [recorded] in a clear Book [preserved in Heaven]* (Qur'an 6:59) means that the ruling on smoking is in fact contained in the Qur'an and can be extracted through the principles of analogical reasoning; for it can either be generally inferred or can be addressed via analogy. I therefore spent some time reading the Qur'an and analyzing the words of the exegetes. In doing so, I was heeding God's words: *Will they not, then, reflect on the admonitions of the Qur'an; or is it rather, that on some hearts there are their own locks?* (Qur'an 47:24). As such, God guided me with strong proofs, ones that will convince whoever comes across them owing to their attachment to the principles of jurisprudence and its branches.

But I did not have the opportunity to compose a treatise [on the matter] until God guided me to serve the pure Islamic law [as a judge] in the great and exalted city of Medina. After receiving this great honor, I traveled toward Medina by sea [from Istanbul?]. I was fortunate that I arrived in Cairo—*may it be protected from hardships by God's magnificent beneficence*—after a journey that was quick and without difficulties and struggles. But since I arrived there at the beginning of winter, I had to remain there [before continuing on to Medina] until spring arrived, and arrive it did. Some of Cairo's scholars and virtuous individuals used to visit me; sometimes out of custom and sometimes to discuss scholarly issues. One day, the subject of smoking—with which smokers humiliate and betray themselves—came

FIGURE 24. Coffee house; patrons enjoying coffee and tobacco pipes (*çubuk*), early nineteenth century. Antoine Ignace Melling, *Voyage pittoresque de Constantinople et des rives du Bosphore* (Paris: Treuttel et Würtz, 1819), plate 26.

up. They mentioned that some scholars have composed treatises permitting it and others have forbidden it, while others said it was discouraged (*karaha*).

So, I began to transfer to them all the knowledge that God had provided me with in necessitating its prohibition and denying its permissibility. This pleased them greatly. So much so that they insisted that I compose this in written form. I accepted their wish, a wish that would also benefit the people. I began composing [the treatise] and I worked diligently on revising it. I limited my choice of Qur'anic verses to those that contain a clear proof. From the Sufi [knowledge that I had garnered] I chose what was of sound proof, and what showed that smoking causes spiritual harm. I also summarized the medical [knowledge I had acquired] to prove smoking's immediate harm and how it quickens death. Finally, I also relied on what is required by reason and rejected by nature, to show why one must avoid it.

I did not add to this any hadith literature, even though there is plenty of it that is useful for analysis and correct orientation. But I did not want to prolong or add tedium to the treatise for fear that it might distort [its meaning]. This is especially the case since the truth had already become apparent and the aim [of the treatise] had been fulfilled. Furthermore, after having laid the foundation for sound proof, and after the hand had already used the pen to write the final draft, there was no longer time to thoroughly interpret this literature, and, as such, I was unable to transfer it from my rough drafts to the final version of the treatise. But God honored me with the opportunity to reach the garden of the tomb of his beloved and chosen one (i.e., Muhammad's tomb in Medina)—*peace be upon him and on his family who followed his example*—where I was blessed with the occasion to kiss the threshold of his tomb. When I was awarded this honor and arrived in that place that is more noble than any other, I presented [the treatise] to the Prophet—*peace be upon him*—and I placed the papers under the cover of his noble resting place, and I threw it behind the veil of his beneficent shrine. I then departed, awaiting a sign of acceptance or rejection.

May the gratitude be multiplied for the beneficence of the sign [of approval] that I received, which was stronger than what I had hoped. My confidence grew and my commitment to reveal my opinion increased and I continued to revise the treatise and remove what was not necessary and had no justification for inclusion.

I ask God almighty that he accord me and the community the success to work in removing this affliction (i.e., smoking). I ask God that he direct me to the correct path for he is the guide, the merciful, the beneficent. And may he guide me and the community to what is desired and accepted so that he blesses us and is pleased with us. I thus state—and God is the guide, and the reins of guidance to the correct path are in his hands—that smoking is forbidden and not permissible, and that using [the principle of] primordial permissibility (*al-ibaha al-asliyya*, i.e., in the absence of divine commands all actions are permissible) as a rationale for permitting it is not allowed.

2. KATİB ÇELEBİ'S *BALANCE OF TRUTH*

From its first appearance [in the Ottoman domains], which was the Hijri year 1010 (1601–2), to the present day, various preachers have spoken at the pulpits [about smoking], and many of the ulema have written tracts concerning it, some claiming that it is a thing forbidden, some that it is discouraged. Its addicts have replied to the effect that it is permissible. After some time elapsed, the sheikh of the Cerrah Pasha Mosque, İbrahim Efendi (d. 1633), devoted much care and attention to the matter, conducting great debates in the abode of the sultanate—that is, in the city of Istanbul, giving warning talks at a special public meeting in the mosque of Sultan Mehmed, and affixing copies of fetvas to walls. Thus, he attended to the matter diligently, but he troubled himself to no purpose. The more he spoke, the more people persisted in smoking. Seeing that it was fruitless, he abandoned his efforts.

Subsequently, Sultan Murad IV (r. 1623–40), toward the end of his reign, closed down the coffeehouses in order to shut the gate of iniquity, and also banned smoking, in consequence of certain outbreaks of fire. People being undeterred, the imperial anger necessitated the chastisement of those who, by smoking, committed the sin of disobedience to the imperial command. Gradually His Majesty's severity in suppression increased, and so did people's desire to smoke, in accordance with the saying, "*People desire what is forbidden*," and many thousands of men were sent to the abode of nothingness.

When [the sultan] was going on the expedition against Baghdad, at one halting-place fifteen or twenty leading men of the army were arrested on a charge of smoking and were put to death with the severest torture in the imperial presence. Regardless, some of the soldiers carried short pipes in their sleeves; some in their pockets; and [they] smoked whenever they found an opportunity to smoke. In Istanbul, no end of soldiers used to go into the barracks and smoke in the privies. Even during this rigorous prohibition, the number of smokers exceeded that of nonsmokers. After that sultan's death, the practice was sometimes forbidden and sometimes allowed, until the grand mufti Baha'i Efendi (d. 1654) gave a fetva ruling that it was permissible, and the practice won renewed popularity among the people of the world. Although there were occasional reprimands on the part of the exalted sultanate to smokers, [eventually] the issue was completely disregarded. Smoking is at present practiced all over the habitable globe. Such are the vicissitudes undergone by tobacco.

Now there are a number of possible ways of considering the subject, which we shall briefly set forth:

The first possibility is that the people may be effectively prevented from smoking and may give it up. This possibility must be set aside, for custom is second nature. Addicts will not give up in this way. The suggestion should be put to them. If they say, "And what purpose will the prohibition serve?" great thinkers have recommended: "Let the rulers not stint the rod on the backs of the common people." Consequently, it is the rulers' duty publicly to prohibit and chastise; thus they perform their part. As for the people, their duty, if they are addicted to such things, is to refrain from committing a breach of good order by using them in the streets. But in his own house every man may do as he pleases. Then, if the rulers interfere, they will be taking on themselves more than they should. Poetry:

What has the inspector of public places to do within a man's home?

Is this tobacco regarded as good (*müstahsen*) or bad (*kabih*) among the people? If we set aside the fact that addicts think it good, *if it was regarded in and of itself*, common sense judges it to be bad. The criterion of goodness and badness may be either the reason or the law. By either criterion it is bad, for the conditions necessary for rational approval are lacking, while the grounds for disapproval are present. Yet if certain of the lacking conditions are fulfilled, it may then be found good; for example, if it be used medicinally. The fact that the authorities do not use it at public meetings or council meetings, and that it is not used in mosques or other places of worship, is a consequence of its being found bad by the criterion of reason. [. . .]

Is it disapproved (*kerahet*)? There is no word of justification for this, in reason or in law. The following view is accepted by the plurality of people: For a thing to reach the stage of being disapproved, it is an essential condition that it be used to excess. The scent of tobacco smoke and the scent of the tobacco leaf are not intrinsically abominable; in fact, the fumes of burning tobacco are inhaled in moderate amounts for curative uses. But an evil odor arises in the mouth of the heavy smoker, by comparison with which, for the nonsmoker who smells it, halitosis would appear as aloeswood and ambergris. To sum up, just as it is discouraged to eat raw onion, garlic, and leek, which inevitably produce an abominable odor in the mouth, so also heavy smoking is discouraged (*mekruh*) as producing a smell in the mouth, the body, and the clothing. And the reason is that there is incontestable offence in both cases. Just as the prohibition against sexual intercourse during menstruation, on account of offensiveness due to uncleanliness, has given rise to an analogous prohibition against pederasty, so too the use of both [such foods and of tobacco] are commonly discouraged.

In the end it must be unrecommendable (*tenzihiyye*). The fact that addicts do not concede this scent to be abominable is irrelevant and not to be taken into consideration. For they are at liberty not to find abominable the smell of one another's mouths. The purpose of all this is to demonstrate the [reality of the] matter; it is not my intention to interfere with or attack those who have the addiction. To try to put them off is not a practical possibility and is generally agreed to be a waste of time. [. . .]

Is it permissible (*ibaha*)? As the rise of smoking is of recent occurrence, there is no explicit treatment or mention of it in the legal manuals. This being so, some say that in accordance with the principle of primordial permissibility, smoking is permitted and lawful. Formerly, the great scholars of the law have pronounced it discouraged (*kerahet*) for the benefit of the public, while certain provincial muftis have declared it forbidden (*hurmet*). More recently, the late Baha'i Efendi pronounced it lawful (*hill*), not out of regard for his own addiction but because he considered what was best suited to the condition of the people and because he held fast to the principle of primordial permissibility. For the rule about fetvas is to base them on a tradition from one of the founders of legal schools. In the absence of such a tradition, it is necessary to go back to fundamental principles.

Its adverse effects owing to excessive use do not [allow smoking] to be placed in the class of permissibles, yet there is a peril in pronouncing it forbidden or discouraged that overrides any consideration of its undesirable qualities. If one asks what that peril is; it is the serious responsibility (*vebal*) that the people will persist in using the forbidden thing. Further, declaring it permissible is in the general interest, as being an act of compassion toward the addict and protecting the public from this responsibility.

For this reason, preference has been given to declaring it permissible. As most Muslims are addicted to it, they have become inseparably attached to the practice, and will in no circumstance be deterred from it or abandon it, and it has taken hold of the whole world. In matters of this kind, judge and mufti must give their decisions and rulings according to what the Holy Law allows, so that men be not driven into sin. For persistence in a practice that is adjudged to be forbidden and discouraged is not like persistence in a practice for which a fetva has been given to be permissible (*mübah*) and an additional adjudication was issued. In the former there is pure responsibility, but in the latter there is no harm. The judge who decides on the basis of some such legal principle as "choose the lesser of the two evils" is committing no sin and may perhaps acquire merit and reward for delivering a believer from sin.

The late Baha'i Efendi was a man of right nature and sound sense. Had he tried duly and not been addicted to narcotics, he would have become one of the most eminent scholars in the Ottoman domains (Rum). But he did not study any branch of the sciences thoroughly. However, he did possess a talent for deduction, and by his natural ability he used to display his cleverness everywhere. In the matter under discussion he had regard for the condition of mankind and was compassionate. May God be compassionate to him. There has never been a mufti like him since the late Abdurrahim Efendi.

THIRTY-TWO

Divining Past, Present, and Future in the Sand

A Geomantic Miscellany, ca. Sixteenth Century

TRANSLATED BY MATTHEW MELVIN-KOUSHKI

The Arabic practice of geomancy (*ilm al-raml,* or "the science of the sand") was an occult science that ranked in popularity only behind astrology and oneiromancy, or dream divination, throughout the early modern Western (Islamo-Judeo-Christian) world. Indeed, owing to its early incorporation of astrological correspondences, geomancy was often considered a form of "terrestrial astrology," requiring much less astronomical expertise while remaining richly informative. As a divinatory science based on a binary code, it is an Arabic cognate to the *I Ching*, but was significantly more popular over a much larger area than the ancient Chinese oracle. Ottoman elites, like their Safavid and Mughal peers, were also greatly enamored of geomancy specifically for its political, military, and scientific applications. Court geomancers forecast the outcome of campaigns, battles, and sieges, as well as the economic ups and downs of the coming year, among other services rendered to the state. Beyond the court, physicians sometimes used geomancy to help diagnose illnesses, and judges used it to help decide court cases. Geomancy was just as attractive to the common man and woman, many of whom clearly relied on the advice of its professional practitioners for help navigating the hopes and fears of daily life.

The designation "science of the sand" refers to the original practice of drawing sixteen random series of lines in the sand or dirt to generate the first four tetragrams, or mothers, of a geomantic reading. These consisted of four lines of either one dot (odd) or two (even) in descending order, arranged from right to left. It was of the utmost importance that the geomancer be totally focused on the question at hand during this initial stage of the operation. The four mothers then generate four daughters, four nieces, two witnesses, one judge, and a final sentence, whereby 16 possible tetragrams or figures are assigned to these 16 houses according to a simple binary logic to produce a geomantic tableau.

So deployed, this binary code captured the flux patterns of the four elemental energies (fire, air, water, earth) as a means to divine past, present and future events, and indeed the status of everything in the sublunar realm. Each of the sixteen geomantic figures acquired a full suite of specific elemental, astrological, calendrical, numerical, lettrist, humoral, physiognomical, and other correspondences. The first twelve houses of the geomantic chart were likewise mapped onto the twelve planetary houses, and occasionally constructed in the form of a horoscope; astrological aspects (trine, sextile, square, opposition) were adopted as well. Detailed information could thus be derived from the figures and their relationships about virtually any aspect of human experience, whether physical, mental, or spiritual; past, present, or future. They revealed precise categories of data on numbers, letters, days, months, years, astral bodies, and divisions, body parts, physical and facial characteristics, minerals, precious stones, plants and plant products, animals and animal products, birds, fruits, tastes, colors, places, directions, regions, topographies, genders, social classes, nations, weapons, diseases, and so on.

To give a taste of this extremely popular divinatory practice in its Ottoman form, translated below are a few representative passages from a popular geomantic miscellany, presumably compiled in the sixteenth century at the latest, which features a random selection of excerpts and passages mainly in Persian but also in Arabic and Turkish, mostly by different hands. This miscellany offers us a crucial window onto the economic, social, political, familial, sexual, emotional, spiritual, and, yes, scientific life of the average inhabitant of the Ottoman Empire. Most interestingly, it features one of the most extensive—and idiosyncratic—lists of house-specific questions (below) in the entire Western tradition. A majority of the concerns raised and anxieties voiced are deeply familiar to us as present-day readers. In fact, the very personal and pragmatic queries this Persian-Turkish-Arabic geomantic miscellany preserves may be best described as an occult, early modern form of Googling—as well as Facebooking, wiretapping, trade forecasting, job seeking, CT scanning, ultrasounding, metal detecting, home surveilling, and radar.

LANGUAGE: The manuscript consists of an assortment of Persian, Turkish, and Arabic texts; the Persian and Arabic texts contain numerous grammatical and spelling errors. The translations here are all from Persian. Note that the table of house questions has been edited and slightly reduced for clarity.

SOURCE: Manuscript: Anonymous, [*Mecmua-i Reml*], Adnan Ötüken İl Halk Kütüphanesi, Ankara, 06 Hk 5005; translated sections are on fols. 38b–39a, 47b–48a, and 7a–10b, respectively.

If you want to diagnose injuries to the body, see in which house a seven- or five-dotted figure occurs, then to which body part that house corresponds; [the geomantic chart] indicates that is the part that has suffered injury. If the figure in question is auspicious, it will scar well; if it is inauspicious, it will not.

Also, wherever ⁞ appears, the querent is particularly concerned about [matters relating to that house or houses].

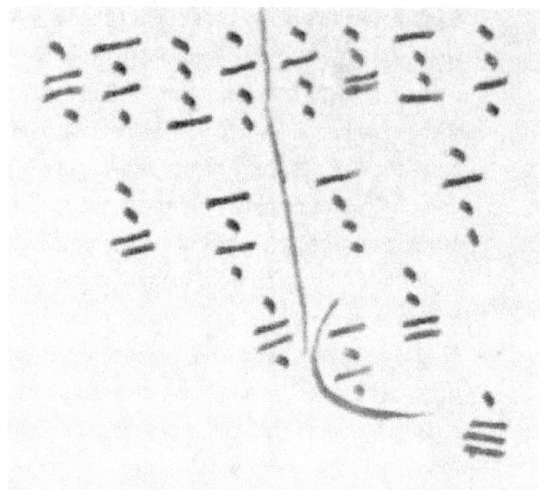

FIGURE 25. Possible configuration of geomantic figures. Anonymous, [*Mecmua-i Reml*], 06 Hk 5005, fol. 39a. Adnan Ötüken İl Halk Kütüphanesi, Ankara.

Fire figures that occur in this house [i.e., the first] are stronger than the other figures; thus [an initial] ∴ is stronger than even ∴, [which is normally the strongest figure].

Also, fixed figures that occur in this house are bad, and indicate that the querent will be frustrated in all his or her undertakings. And if the figure in the first house is repeated in the second, the querent is greatly preoccupied [with their question]. If the figures are weak, their thoughts will be negative; from that figure what he or she is thinking may be known. Thus, if it is ∴, the querent is fearing death or worrying about financial liquidity, and so on.

The ascendant of a person's birth is likewise told from the first house, and that of their conception from the third. If someone wants to find out their ascendant, there are two methods [for determining it]. Either see where ∴ is or see whether the figure in the first house is repeated anywhere. If in the second house, the querent's ascendant is Taurus; if in the third, Gemini; if in the fourth, Cancer; and so on.

If the first figure is not repeated, however, it indicates distress on the part of the querent. For example, say a female client has geomantic charts cast, and this chart is produced:

[The geomancer] will first say, "You're unable to properly focus on your work, and want to know why. But we don't find ∴ [in the main body of the chart], and the ∴ in the first house is not repeated. But we find ∴ [being repeated] instead of ∴, [so the latter] here refers to your husband, who's on a trip—[that's why you're distracted]." The point is that it would be easier [to make an accurate reading in this example] were the initial ∴ to be repeated or if ∴ were present [in the main body of the chart]. The special property of each figure in each house is laid out in the following table. [...]

[An example from this table:] *Horizon Seven, Relating to Marriage, and so on.* First see what associations of this house are present and what are absent. Thus, when a querent seeks judgment [in this respect] see where ∴ occurs, as it governs [questions related to this house], and whether it is strong or weak, as well as the witnesses and any aspects—trine, square, sextile, opposition, conjunction—that it makes, which are among the necessary elements, and derive the judgment from those.

Thus if the question is asked, "How many times will I marry?" seek the answer from the units [cycle], or the sixth house. The geomancer should also ask how many marriages or how many daughters [the querent will have]. But just ⸭ by itself here does not suffice, since it also relates to absent relatives and partners and thieves, as was discussed above. [As that may be], judgment is made on the basis of the strength or weakness [of this figure]. As for an impending marriage [as a legal act], judgment should be sought from the eighth house. Four figures in this house indicate marriage, all of them mutable, and here greatly strengthened: ⸭ ⸭ ⸭ ⸭.

If it is asked whether one's wife will be old or young, tell that from the repetition of [the figure in house] seven. If ⸭ or auspicious figures cardinal or fixed or ⸭, then she will be young. Also, if the querent asks about the quality of the family from which his wife will hail, look to the seventh house: if Tristitia or Carcer occurs there, she will be of bad stock, but if ⸭ or ⸭, her people will be noble. [. . .]

QUESTIONS APPROPRIATE TO THE SIXTEEN GEOMANTIC HOUSES

HOUSE ONE

Will I be happy or not?

How will my request work out?

Will I gain power or fame in the near future?

What's my horoscope, and is it auspicious or not?

The beginning of any business.

How will today be?

When will I die?

HOUSE TWO

Will I have income or not?

Is he or she poor or rich?

Will it be beneficial or not?

What would be a good source of income?

Will my associate come or not?

Will I make more than I spend or vice versa?

When will the money arrive?

Where will my livelihood come from?

Will it be sold or not?

Is he or she generous or stingy?

Will I be able to purchase it soon?

How will my purchase turn out?

How will I make a living?

What's going on with my property?

Will I receive a gift?

Will the lost object be found or not?

Tracking a lost object;

Is the lost object simply lost or was it stolen?

Will my loan be repaid or not?

Will my absent relative return?

How's my friend doing?

Will the trade go through or not?

What's for dinner?

HOUSE THREE

Will a victory be possible on this campaign?

How are my relatives doing?

How did an old concern turn out?

Will it be possible to move an item, and if so when?

Seeing relatives in your dreams.

How are things at home?

Will there be a way?

I sent a messenger—[will he or she arrive?]

How goes it with the messenger en route?

When will the messenger arrive?

Will the person I summoned come?

Will they be found alive or dead?

Whether someone is knowledgeable or ignorant.

What will the end of my life be like?

Going to market or going home.

Will news arrive from abroad or not?

The beginning of a journey.

How will my visit to the bathhouse be?

Traveling through the desert.

How will this business turn out?

Does the dream I had last night mean anything?

Should I go for it?

HOUSE FOUR

How many people are outside the house right now?

How are my children doing?

Will the pregnant woman give birth to a healthy child?

Construction of a building or pool.

Making a sitting area or erecting a column.

Will I have another child?

How will I pass my life?

What's this place like?

How's my father doing?

Will my property be taken from me?

How will my associate's trip go?

How is the city?

What livelihood will I finally settle on?

Should I bury my money or not?

Is there hidden treasure or not?

What's that place like?

Will I be able to leave this place?

Tree planting and the harvest.

Will it be planted?

How's the king's wife?

Is it being stored or transported?

What profit will I have from this purchase?

Will I be able to trade?

Will I be able to sell?

Property of one's brother or associate.

Safe or dangerous?

Coming or going?

How many associates or brothers will I have?

HOUSE FIVE

Taking medicine.

Is this food appropriate [to my condition]?

What's the status of my illness or heart problem?

[Will] this physician's treatment [work]?

Does the physician know what he's doing or not?

Will my child be male or female?

What will my child's horoscope be?

Is the news true?

Revenue from property.

When will news arrive from the countryside?

A brother's traveling.

Will the pregnant woman have an easy birth?

Death of the king.

Wrestling.

Treachery.

Archery.

Boozing.

Gaming.

When will the messenger come?

Will the messenger have valuable information?

Will my lover come or not?

Will my gift reach him or her?

Will a gift reach me?

Someone's being friendly—is he or she sincere?

Will I find relief from this sadness?

How's my lover doing?

What news does the bey have?

What will I eat today?

HOUSE SIX

Will the secret stay a secret or not?

Tracking an escapee.

Will the slave be freed or not?

What was lost?

Who am I thinking of?

Where's the lost person or escapee?

How are my chickens or sheep doing?

Has a spell been cast or not?

What kind of cattle?

How will the chicken trade go?

Has the eye been injured or not?

Will these cattle stay or escape?

Has my turtledove, hawk, or falcon died?

What's the status of the illness?

A slave asking, "Will I be sold?"

Will any harmful creatures come here or not?

Will I be freed or not?

Will my children help me?

How's my servant?

Will the captive be sold or not?

How's the hunt going?

How's the captive?

How's the student?

Should I get surgery, and if so, how will it go?

Is this captive special?

How are the cows and the cowherd?

Disasters and accidents.

Did my captive go off with my animals or were they stolen?

How's the captive or hostage doing?

How are my brothers doing?

Will the lost object be found or not?

HOUSE SEVEN

Was it stolen?

What's the mayor of the city I'm traveling to like?

The state of someone who's away.

Safety of the roads.

Is someone who's away about to die, or has he been revived?

Is the person away still alive or not?

Did this person go there and how is it?

Looking for a wife.

What is the woman like?

Is the woman a virgin or not?

A woman's pedigree and good character—or lack thereof.

Sex talk.

A woman's beauty and grace.

The condition of a caravan.

When will the traveler arrive?

Separation and cutting ties.

If I go looking for someone, will I find her or him?

My future standing.

Enemies and opponents.

Will they oppose me?

Where's my enemy from?

If I make an allegation, will it stick?

Entering into a partnership.

Striking a deal.

Will a deal be struck or not?

HOUSE EIGHT

Will my property return to me?

My lover's father.

How a trip will go.

Will I travel or not?

Taking out a loan.

A father's illness.

Will my inheritance come?

Returning from a journey.

What kind of fear?

The status of a beloved.

A father's lover.

Acquiring an education.

Will I have bad luck or not?

The wife of an associate.

Return on investment.

A father's child.

Giving charity.

Will I get anything from the treasury?

Will I find protection?

Interpreting a dream.

Is the dream I had last night accurate or not?

What did they dream about?

Disappeared property.

Will anyone be suspicious?

Will it be found?

When will I die?

What's the current status of this Islam?

Ritual worship and pilgrimage.

Slaves' departure.

A brother's illness.

Cause of death.

A brother's servant.

Should we expect it or not?

The current state of a wife or partner.

The wife of a collaborator.

Grandchildren.

HOUSE NINE

Is this road safe?

How did the job go?

Will I achieve my goal?

A letter from the king.

Having an audience with the king.

The current state of the king or governor.

A brother's wife.

What's the best thing to do?

My lover's lover.

The end result of a job.

A father's partner.

Will I achieve fame?

Making talismans.

Doing astrology and geomancy.

Will I be divinely graced if I write out this invocation?

How much money will I make?

The return of someone who was away.

How's my mother?

Will I profit from my father's trip?

Is this man a spy?

Is this a prudent thing to do or not?

Is this clean or not?

Between two or three options, which is the best?

HOUSE TEN

Should I go to the judge?

Are [fruits] being eaten from my trees?

What's the thief doing?

A woman's final state.

Will it produce?

A woman's property.

Will my current prestige last or not?

Storms and lightning.

Should I travel to trade or not?

Will it rain or not?

How will the craftwork turn out?

My relationship to the king.

Will my luck change for the better or the worse?

Will God have mercy?

The state of my father's wife.

The property of a wife or partner.

The end result of a partner's condition.

What will my child be like?

Glory and humiliation.

HOUSE ELEVEN

The king's wealth.

Is the court order forthcoming?

Will the official sealed letter arrive?

Will I benefit from the king's wealth?

A mother's property.

The current state of friends.

Meeting up with friends.

Was the promise true?

Will my hope be realized?

A brother's journey.

A father's death.

Reunion with a lover.

How's my lover?

Marrying one's lover.

What is my lover's enemy like?

A son or daughter's marriage.

A daughter's husband.

An old woman.

Is the woman's lover a leech?

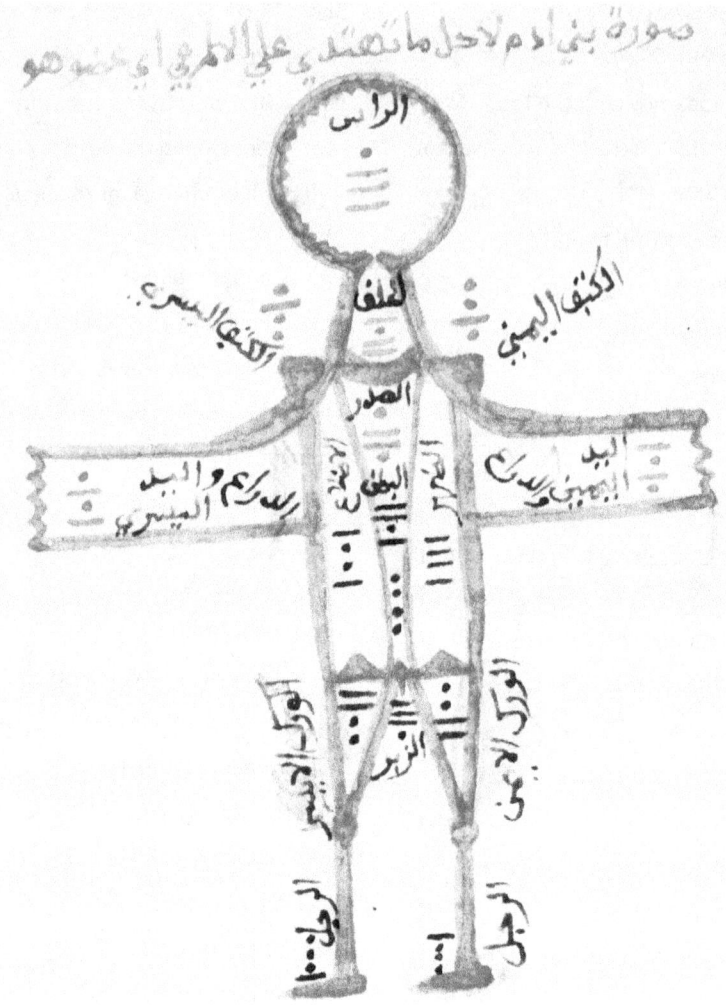

FIGURE 26. Human limbs as they correspond to sixteen geomantic figures. *Kitab fi ilm al-raml*, Département des manuscrits. Arabe 2631, fol. 66b. Bibliothèque nationale de France, Paris.

HOUSE TWELVE

A large animal or slave.

Should I go against him?

How an enemy will end up.

War and peace.

Buying a beast of burden.

The current state of a great enemy.

Freeing the imprisoned.

Fighting an enemy.

Current condition of the prison and its inmates.

What should I do to get the result I want?

Catching doves or pigeons.

Will this worry pass?

Will I face poverty and misery?

Is this jewel authentic?

Will it happen?

Will they repay my loan?

Should I have my blood let?

Is what they're saying about him or her true?

HOUSE THIRTEEN

What's my question?

Weakness and strength.

Will I be safe from these events?

When will this idea stop bothering me?

When will my mind be happy?

Drawing out water.

Distant journeys.

A mother's final state.

A king's final state.

Favor from the king.

The status of a mother.

The partner of a partner.

HOUSE FOURTEEN

Will I achieve my goal?

Will my prayer be answered?

What kind of creature will fulfill my prayer?

Is speaking without listening appropriate?

Has the news been verified?

Expensive or cheap?

Will money come soon on this trip or not?

A friend's status.

Should I go hunting or not?

The brother of an enemy.

An enemy on the move.

A mother's child.

The king's friend.

HOUSE FIFTEEN

Will my representative fight for me?

Will the judge decide in my favor?

The state of the grave.

Will it be gathered or scattered?

Studying philosophy.

Wisdom and corruption.

Economy and waste.

Will it go bad or not?

Will it be a boy or a girl?

Should I confiscate it or not?

Should I educate myself or not?

Will the news remain known only to me?

Should I make an accusation or not?

Should I consult on this problem or not?

Is this person sick or not?

HOUSE SIXTEEN

The result of the result.

Will he achieve his goal?

What will my afterlife be like?

Supervising and checking work.

Will I achieve my goal in the end?

The suffering of friends.

Should I say this?

Will news of my enemy arrive or not?

Will it be in my interest or not?

How will the confluence of all these events turn out?

Will the tax owed be paid?

THIRTY-THREE

Reading Character by Appearance

The Book of Physiognomy, Hamdullah Hamdi, d. 1503

TRANSLATED BY HELGA ANETSHOFER AND HAKAN T. KARATEKE

Physiognomy is a Greek word meaning "judgment of a person's nature (by his or her facial features)." While the idea of extracting reliable information about a person's character by studying their facial characteristics or physical appearance has accompanied some of the worst travesties of modern history, physiognomy has been a popular branch of knowledge since antiquity. A person's complexion and the form and size of his limbs or facial features were believed to hold clues to their character and mind, allowing designated experts to make deductions about the qualities of the person: their intelligence, intentions, defects, or talents. Philosophers and scholars classified typologies and established taxonomies concerning the physical traits of human beings. The external features of a person were believed not only to reveal character, psychology, and moral conditions, but were also thought to hold clues about future potential. As such, physiognomy was a divinational practice and found a wide array of application in daily life. It was popular in premodern Europe as well as in Ottoman society.

The areas of application of physiognomy varied from employing a master physiognomist's testimony in court, to common people bringing it to bear on their decisions regarding daily transactions. One of the areas in which experts in physiognomy were occasionally consulted was in establishing a child's paternity or genealogy. If there was a dispute about a child's parentage, a designated expert would study the physical features of the child and of the possible parents, then make a determination; this had consequences for inheritance. Ottoman officers believed to be expert in physiognomy were instrumental in selecting young men for the different divisions of the army and state service during and after the devşirme process. This was a procedure whereby boys were collected from Christian villages, mostly from the Ottoman Balkans, and conscripted to the sultan's elite army and state service. The officers first gathered only those boys who possessed physical characteristics denoting their "worthiness" for said services. During a second phase, the youngsters were assigned to various tracks—to be trained as foot soldiers or palace guards, or to be educated for bureaucratic positions—again according to physical traits that were believed to convey clues about their future potential.

Similarly, common people made use of the physiognomical knowledge to purchase enslaved people. Not only did slave traders claim to possess some knowledge of the art of discerning character, but the purchasers were also expected either to consult with a person familiar with the art of physiognomy, or to study such manuals themselves in order to be able to make deductions about a person's personality, temperament, and so on.

Being expert in this art partly required training but, physiognomy being also a divinational practice, people with spiritual prowess—for instance, the sheikhs of Sufi orders—were also thought to possess some intrinsic knowledge of character discernment. Judging by the popularity of books written in plain language and evidently with nonexpert audiences in mind, we can conclude that the knowledge penetrated other spheres of daily life, and probably helped to reify stereotypes about physical traits (the manuals were, of course, themselves shaped by preexisting stereotypes and prejudices).

The art of physiognomy was known in Turkish as *firaset* or *kıyafet* (both terms from Arabic meaning "discernment"). Hamdullah Hamdi's (d. 1503) *Kıyafetname* (*Book of Physiognomy*) was one of the earliest and most popular examples of this genre in Turkish and was obviously written for a general readership. Composed as a list in rhymed verse, the poem was conceivably easy to memorize in order to call on whenever needed.

LANGUAGE: Turkish. Simple language in plain verses with several archaic Turkish words and idioms, and many lexical copies from Arabic and Persian.

SOURCE: Manuscript: Hamdullah Hamdi. *Kıyafetname*. Süleymaniye Kütüphanesi, Istanbul, Bağdatlı Vehbi 2162, fols. 20b-27a. Transcription: Çelebioğlu, Âmil. "Kıyafet İlmi ve Akşemseddinzade Hamdullah Hamdi ile Erzurumlu İbrahim Hakkı'nın Kıyafetnameleri." In *Eski Türk Edebiyatı Araştırmaları*, 225-62. Istanbul: Millî Eğitim Bakanlığı, 1998. First published in 1979 by Atatürk Üniversitesi Edebiyat Fakültesi.

APPEARANCE AS THE SIGN OF BEHAVIOR

As God created mankind,
He made individuals diverse.

Though identical in natural constitution (*hılkat*),
They are not identical in appearance (*suret*).

He made His grace manifest to the world,
By making appearance an indicator of behavior.

COMPLEXION

A red complexion is a sign of impulsiveness;
A dark complexion is an indicator of correct judgment.

He whose complexion is yellow,
His heart is changeable and his business is treachery.

Yellow that tends toward black;
The truth is that his character is defective.

A sign and mark of moderation is this:
[The complexion is] either completely fair, or completely red.

But he who is fair with a ruddy tinge,
And has deep blue eyes,

Deceitful, immoral, and a sinner is he;
He prevails in the world for triviality.

CHEEKS

If his cheeks are round,
Wide his forehead, but narrow the chin,

His hair thick, but sparse his beard,
He has no equal in evil.

STATURE

He who is of tall stature,
Artless is he and simplehearted.

If he is short, he is arrogant and malicious,
And a repository of deception and tricks.

When the stature is moderate,
It is a sign of his wisdom and compassion.

FLESH

He whose flesh is soft,
Is of gentle disposition, his intellect sharp.

If the flesh is firm, his body is strong,
Yet he is stupid and imbecilic.

MOVEMENT

He who is fidgety is conceited,
Obscene talk and machinations are his habit.

HAIR

Coarse hair is proof of courage,
And a sign of a healthy brain.

If it is soft, it points to anxiety;
His intellect is blunt, and the brain is dull.

If the hair is ruddy, he is anxious and irate;
If it is black, smart and modest.

If you observe that a person has a lot of hair;
Know that he has not a shred of elegance.

HEAD

If his head is big, he is high-minded;
If it is small, he is short on intellect.

He whose head is flat,
Has no equal in stupidity.

FOREHEAD

If his forehead is wide, bad-tempered is he;
If it is narrow, slow-witted and selfish.

If it is mostly round, lazy is he;
It's best if it is moderately round.

When the forehead is broad with no wrinkles;
An idiot is he, wicked and selfish.

If the wrinkles are long and reach his temples,
Intelligent is he, at least if there are not too many.

If a person has lots of wrinkles on the forehead,
In short, he is all talk.

If there are wrinkles between the two eyebrows,
He who has them is worried with no cause.

EARS

He who has [big] rabbit ears is ignorant,
Though skilled at memorization.

If he has small ears like a cat,
He is a worse thief than a mouse.

Now, there is a sign in [the ears'] big size,
That the owner will have a long life.

EYEBROWS

He whose eyebrows have narrow tips,
Does not lack for mischief and oppression.

If one has thick eyebrows,
Nonsense is his companion; grief his friend.

Good-hearted if the eyebrows are parted;
A thief, if the eyebrows converge.

Thinness [of the brow] is a sign of cheerfulness;
Length a marker of arrogance.

[One with] brows that are black and thin,
Has the appropriate amount of delicacy and coquetry.

EYES

If a person has deep-set eyes,
He has profuse envy and pride.

He who has pig eyes has the heart of a leopard;
His nose will be marked [as a disbeliever] on Judgment Day.

Black eyes are a sign of cleverness;
Bloodshot eyes represent bravery.

He who has blue eyes lacks shame;
He who has grayish blue eyes is rarely a hero.

He who cannot see will live a long life;
A person with eyes like a crane has the boldness of a falcon.

He with big eyes has a lazy mind;
The small-eyed one's [mind] is limited and neglected. [. . .]

FACE

The one with a big face is lazy at any task;
If it is small, he is base and neglectful.

If the face is fleshy, he is rough in manners;
If it is round, it indicates ignorance and gloominess.

If you see one with a pale and lean face,
Run away from his vicious scheming; don't associate with him.

Especially if his neck is also thin;
Only destiny can be as cruel as he.

The person who has an elongated face;
Complains a lot and is impertinent.

One with a sour face speaks many bitter words;
One with a crooked face has no [moral] straightness. [. . .]

NOSE

He who has a narrow and long nose,
Lacks not little in intellect.

If the tip of the nose is close to his mouth,
A lion is he; don't you dare confront him.

He whose nostrils are wide,
Has envy, conceit, and animosity all together.

If a person has a snout-shaped nose,
His anger cannot be contained in his lungs.

He with a flat nose is obsessed with intercourse;
He with a large mouth has courage and diligence.

MOUTH

He who is small-mouthed is cheerful,
But harbors fear in his heart.

You will not find, if you search the whole country,
Faithful words from someone with a crooked mouth.

VOICE

Whoever talks through the nose,
Is a fool; he harbors conceit and animosity.

One with a high-pitched and shrill voice is an ignoramus;
He is shameless and a perfect liar.

Evil is a man with a woman's voice;
And a woman with a man's voice, said the sages.

THIRTY-FOUR

Religious Guidance for Hunters

Ebu Bekr el-Kızılhisari, ca. Late Seventeenth Century

TRANSLATED BY CHRISTOPHER MARKIEWICZ

Like other religions, Islam guides its followers in the proper consumption of meat. Such guidelines have necessarily evolved from the earliest days of Islam in Arabia to this religion's emergence as a global faith. The first of these recommendations and restrictions originated in the Qur'an, while others emerged from the example of the Prophet Muhammad (d. 632). However, alongside the spread of trade networks, the vast expansion of Muslim rule into regions such as central Eurasia, East and West Africa, and South and Southeast Asia brought established Islamic traditions of correct consumption into contact with a plethora of existing dietary habits, procurement practices, and culinary arts as well as an enormous variety of animal species that were not present in the Arabian context. This meant that new guidance regarding the consumption and treatment of different animals was gradually introduced throughout the next centuries of Islam as its traditions gained sway in new human geographies replete with their own distinct cultures and local faunas. It also meant that differing opinions about the permissibility of eating certain animals (e.g., shellfish or rabbits) emerged within different legal traditions and among a variety of Muslim communities or offshoots thereof.

In all cases, these guidelines on animal consumption may have had their origins in particular sociological and anthropological rationales related to knowledge of the nature, hygiene, and associated diseases of certain species. From the perspective of the average believer, however, the act of following such fixed guidelines was likely more important than fully grasping the rationales undergirding them. Be this as it may, a minority of legally minded individuals placed great value in defining the conditions under which any animal was edible or not.

This late seventeenth-century Ottoman hunting treatise by Kızılhisari is itself a compilation of earlier Arabic works with some contemporary additions, all of which reflect the Sunni-Hanafi legal perspective prevalent in the core regions of the Ottoman Empire. Having encountered hunting-related fetvas in Ottoman-era collections, Kızılhisari appears to have seen this topic as an area deserving of further exploration. While the text hints at an awareness of the various scales of hunting, from the large-scale expeditions of sultans and viziers to the more modest projects of the average Muslim, it is nevertheless geared toward instructing all current or aspiring hunters about the most religiously sound ways to pursue this craft, irrespective of class status. For example, the author addresses issues emerging from the use of weaponry, such as rifles or blow guns, which may have constituted a concern when considered against the backdrop of established hunting norms even if they were not completely novel technologies at the time.

Kızılhisari's treatise is a prescriptive text, meaning the degree to which one or the other individual felt bound by its regulations depended on that individual's relative concern for religiolegal rulings. This is an aspect of all prescriptive texts that historians tend to keep in mind as they approach writings on religious law; the perspectives of legally minded scholars do not necessarily reflect the views of wider society. Then again, such texts may nevertheless provide us with hints about the nature of certain contemporary practices or reflect broader concerns and anxieties in the seventeenth-century Ottoman world.

The fact that hunting was a topic covered by theorists of religious ethics may surprise modern readers. However, in keeping with their desire to anticipate and prescribe advice for any situation in which Muslims might find themselves, legal scholars like Kızılhisari sought to extend their discussion of "the good and just life" to hunting animals and all that it entailed. On the one hand, Kızılhisari's work addresses its concerns most directly to individual hunters. On the other, the author's statements sometimes imply that the ethical stakes of hunting extended beyond the individual hunter to the spiritual health and status of the religious community at large.

LANGUAGE: Archaizing Turkish, based on various older sources, presumably mostly in Arabic. Generally short sentences; some sentence structures display signs of translation syntax (based on Arabic and/or Persian). Some words copied from Arabic are not used in their conventional Ottoman Turkish meanings.

SOURCE: Manuscript: Ebu Bekr ibnü'l-Hacı Mustafa el-Kızılhisari (el-Karahisari?) el-İskilibi. *Hidayetü'l-Sayyad.* Milli Kütüphane, Ankara, 06 Mil. Yz. A 1999. Transcription: Aydın, Haluk. "Ebu Bekr İbnü'l-Hacı Mustafa Kızılhisari'nin Avcılıkla İlgili Bir Eseri: *Hidayetü'l-Sayyad.*" In *Av ve Avcılık Kitabı,* edited by Emine Gürsoy-Naskali and Hilal Oytun Altun, 653–96. Istanbul: Kitabevi, 2008. The chapter introduction above was written by Arlen Wiesenthal.

INTRODUCTION

Game is [any] wild animal that avoids humans, whether it is an animal that is eaten, such as a hare or partridge, or an animal that is not eaten, such as a fox or boar—the hunting of which should be for their hides or some other part or to prevent oneself from being harmed, [in which case] hunting is licit. Yet it should not be undertaken as a skill (*san'at*). It is forbidden if it is undertaken as a profession, as is the case among some fishermen. Üskübi (Pir Mehmed, d. 1611) has recorded this view from *Ashbah wa-Naza'ir* (by Zaynuddin ibn Nujaym, d. 1563) in his *Fetava* (collection of legal opinions). However, the author of *Surrat al-fatawa* (Sakızlı Sadık Mehmed bin Ali, d. after 1649) says that even if it is undertaken as a profession it is licit. It is understood also on the basis of *Hidaya* (by Burhanuddin Marghinani, d. 1197) that it should not be done for the sake of amusement, entertainment, or passing time, nor should it conflict with the performance of the five daily ritual prayers or other worship.

[Eating] game is not permissible as long as fifteen conditions are not met, five of which are incumbent on the hunter, five on the hound, and five on the game. The first of the five conditions on the hunter is that he should be someone capable of lawful slaughter of [legally] edible animals. For instance, he should not be an apostate, a Zoroastrian, a Muslim in a state of ritual purity during pilgrimage, or an infidel without scripture (i.e., an infidel other than a Christian or Jew).

The second of these is to dispatch the hound or raptor by hand. If the hound is running free beside the hunter or if it breaks free and rushes to the game and seizes it by itself, the game is not to be eaten. Dispatching is a condition. It is the same for raptors. [. . .]

The fifth of these is that after dispatching the dog or raptor, [the hunter] should not start doing anything else before the game is dead. For instance, if the hunter starts patching his shoes or clothes after dispatching the hound or bird, and the dog or raptor subsequently catches the game, it is inedible.

The first of the conditions incumbent on the dog is that it be trained. We shall describe the trained dog or bird [below], God Almighty willing.

The second is that once the hound or bird is dispatched, it not abandon the game. If it does not run after the game for a while, but [instead] dawdles and frolics to and fro before resuming the chase and catching the game, then the game is inedible. The stipulations of dispatching require that the [hunter] is moving; however, if it is the case that they lie in wait in a certain place and the game passes by and then they catch it, it happens because of their perfect knowledge [about hunting], and then the game that they take is lawful.

The third is that the dogs or birds, with which it is illicit to hunt, should not hunt together with trained dogs or birds. For example, game is not lawful when it is caught through the cooperation of trained dogs and birds with untrained dogs or birds; or with dogs or birds that Zoroastrians or apostates dispatched; or with dogs or birds that have not been dispatched by hand; or with the dogs and birds of someone who deliberately neglects to recite, "*In the name of God the Merciful*" [when dispatching them].

The fourth is that [the hound or bird] wound the game, no matter what part of it. If it [the hound] strangles the game without wounding it or wounds and kills it, then it is inedible. According to a tradition from his eminence, Imam Abu Yusuf (d. 798), wounding is not a necessary condition.

The fifth is that the hound not eat from the game. If it eats from the game that it has taken, then [the game] is inedible. If it does not eat from the flesh, but rather drinks from its

FIGURE 27. Hunting scene, ca. 1580s. Nakkaş Osman (artist) in *Hünername,* Hazine 1523, fol. 182b. Topkapı Sarayı Müzesi Kütüphanesi, Istanbul.

blood, then there is no harm and it is lawful. [By contrast,] a bird is not like a hound, which is to say that if it eats from the game that it has taken, there is no harm and it is lawful. [...]

Game is licit when procured by women, even if they are menstruating or ritually impure, [or by] uncircumcised males, mutes, and those with scripture, like Jews or Christians. If a Jew does not believe that Ezra is the son of God, or if a Christian does not believe that Jesus is the son of God or a god [as they are supposed to according to Qur'an 9:30], then their game and slaughter is not licit.

The game is not licit [when procured by] Muslims in a state of ritual purity [during pilgrimage], apostates, Zoroastrians, and infidels without scripture. Hunting at night is lawful. It is not appropriate to hunt where birds are laying eggs or their young are hatching and when animals are close to giving birth or recently have given birth, because [it would] destroy the offspring ... (?).

When the hunter finds the animal alive on arrival, he has to kill it immediately. He should not make it suffer; for example, he should not break his leg or wing, and then leave it. A hound or a bird should be trained to make [the prey] bleed, [but] not torture it. It is even reprehensible to train the hawk with a live bird, as it would be cruel to the animal.

HUNTING WITH HOUNDS AND THE LIKE

Now, it is permitted to hunt with any animal with fangs, if they are trained—except for pigs because they are inherently unclean and it is not permitted to profit from them. His eminence, Imam Abu Yusuf—*may God Almighty have mercy on him*—records that it is not permissible to hunt with a lion or bear because lions, since they are proud, do not work for others, just as kings do not work for others. Bears, since they are rapacious, also do not work for others, just as no one gains anything from rapacious people.

His eminence, Imam Muhammad (d. 805)—*God Almighty's mercy upon him*—stated that, "I do not know whether or not it is possible to train a wolf. If it is trained, there is no harm in hunting with it." Also, from our companions, it is recorded that it is a custom of both the lion and the wolf that they do not eat the prey immediately. As long as it is like that, it cannot be concluded that they are trained to refrain from eating the game. If their training becomes conceivable, it is permitted to hunt with them. [...]

A bird is trained if it complies when it is called, whether that call is with meat in the hand or not. If, during a training hunt, a dog or other fanged animal catches three or more animals and does not eat them—the first and second animals are inedible because the hunting animal may not be fully trained [yet]. Concerning the third, there are two [competing] traditions. According to the sounder one, it is licit.

If the trained dog eats from the game or the bird, after it has been trained and does not comply when called, it is decided that they are too dimwitted [for hunting], according to his eminence the Great Imam (Abu Hanifa, d. 767)—*mercy of God Almighty upon him*. [...]

If a hunter dispatches a trained dog and if [the dog] catches the game and restrains it until his owner comes, and if the dog, after his owner has taken the game, leaps on the game and snatches a piece of the game with its teeth, and the hunter gives that piece to the dog, which it eats, then the remaining game is still licit. This is because [the dog] perfectly abstained [from eating the game]; it is as if the meat that he ate later came from the hunter's pouch; [therefore,] this case does not indicate that a dog is untrained.

If a trained dog catches up with the prey and breaks off a piece [of flesh] with its front teeth and eats it, and then continues pursuing that game and catches that game or another one, [that game] is not licit. Because by eating that piece, the dog demonstrated it is not trained. However, if it pays no attention to the piece that tore off and continues to pursue the game and, on catching it, abstains from eating until its master arrives, and if the dog, after his master has taken the game, lunges at that piece and eats it, there is no harm done; in other words, the captured game is licit. However, it is not licit [for humans] to consume that [torn-off] piece. Because the most blessed Messenger of God—*may God, the Exalted, bless him and salute him*—said, *"that which [was cut off] from a living [animal] is [considered] dead [meat] (i.e., unclean);"* in other words, the piece that is separated from a living animal is unclean. [. . .]

HUNTING WITH PIERCING WEAPONS

The second chapter describes the conditions of hunting with rifles, arrows, spears, swords, and other weapons. Hunting with a rifle is permitted because it kills by wounding the game with lead bullets or [other piercing] projectiles, and not by [crushing] force or blunt trauma; [therefore,] the condition [of piercing the game] is met.

However, blow guns and pellet bows are not permitted because they shoot pellets (*bunduka*)—what they call *bunduka* is a round thing made from stone or clay. These [pellets] kill the game through blunt trauma or by breaking its limbs without lacerating it. However, wounding lacerations are a condition of the game.

Hunting with a featherless arrow, called *mi'raz* (i.e., a short, blunt arrow with no fletching or head), is not permitted because it strikes sideways and kills the game without lacerating wounds. If the [mi'raz's] head is sharp and the head strikes and pierces [the game], then it is licit. If the hunter launches a mi'raz or [clay or stone] pellets at the game and they hit an arrow that is sitting on top of an enclosure (?) or something else and the arrow in turn kills the game by piercing it, then it is licit.

It is not permitted to hunt with stones or clubs or similar items that do not pierce. If [the hunter] sharpens the ends [of the stones or clubs] so that he kills the prey by piercing it, then it is permitted. However, the hunter must be very careful; if he knows for sure that the game died by means of the [crushing] weight [of the stones or clubs], it is illicit. If he knows for sure that it died of a piercing wound, it is licit. If he is in doubt; in other words, [if] he neither knows for sure that it died through a [crushing] weight nor does he know for sure that it died of a piercing wound, [in this case,] it is illicit as a precaution. [. . .]

If a domestic animal runs wild, it is legally considered game. It is even licit if a camel or a steer flees and is unable to be captured and it dies by any weapon through a blow or a piercing wound—whether in a town or in the country. However, if a sheep flees, it is not to be slayed inside a town; it is to be slayed outside a settlement.

If a chicken flies up in a tree and its master cannot catch it and he fears he might lose it, he may launch a projectile at it (stones or arrows). If he does not fear losing it, he may not launch a projectile at it.

If a pigeon flies from its master's hand and subsequently its master or someone else kills it with a weapon, if it was not tame, then it is licit, whether the weapon used cuts off its head or wounds another part of it. If it was tame, let's have a look: if the weapon struck the throat and cut its throat, then it is licit; if it struck another [body] part, then there are diverse opinions; the correct one is that it is not licit. It is described in this manner in the work of Qadikhan (Fakhruddin Hasan al-Farghani, d. 1196); however, in *Khulasat al-fatawa*, it says that it is absolutely licit.

If a tame deer goes out into the wild and someone shoots a weapon at it while reciting, "*In the name of God the Merciful*," and strikes its throat and cuts it, then it is licit. If that person kills it by striking some other [body part], then it is not licit. However, if it is a wild deer and it will not be caught without hunting it, then it is also licit to [kill it without cutting its throat]. [. . .]

ANIMALS THAT ARE LICIT AND ILLICIT TO EAT

The fourth chapter is a description of the animals that are licit (*helal*) to eat, not licit to eat, discouraged (*mekruh*) to eat and not discouraged to eat. Beasts that have fangs and hunt with their fangs and birds that have talons and hunt with their talons are illicit. The meat of this type of oppressive and raptorial, merciless and rapacious, murderous and predatory animal is illicit as a kindness and beneficence on humankind, because, through eating [their meat], it is possible that something from the seven negative attributes passes on to [the person]. As they are infected, compassion and mercy are removed from their hearts and they torment those servants of God who are weak, as those cruel merciless animals do unto weak animals.

Animals that have fangs are these: lions, tigers, wolves, leopards, foxes, hyenas, cats—whether domestic cats or wild cats—squirrels, sables, martens, monkeys, weasels, elephants, boars, bears, and those animals that resemble these. Birds that have talons are these: vultures, falcons, hawks, eagles, sparrow hawks, black gyrfalcons, gyrfalcons, and those that resemble these. Moreover, it is illicit to eat animals that live in the ground, such as mice, lizards, hedgehogs, snakes, frogs, lesser Egyptian jerboas (desert mice), and similar animals. All animals without blood are illicit except for fish and crickets. If bees, fleas, lice, flies, ticks, and similar animals, that do not have blood, fall into water, milk, or other substances, they do not render these fluids or substances unclean.

Eagles, and crows that feed on carrion are illicit. It is related from Khwaharzada (Abu Bakr bin Muhammad, d. 1090) that crows are of three types: the one that eats carrion and feces, but does not eat seeds, is illicit. The other one that eats seeds but not carrion is licit. The [third] one eats both carrion and seeds; his eminence the Great Imam—*mercy of God*

Almighty upon him—says that this type is licit. Imam Abu Yusuf—*mercy of God Almighty upon him*—says that it is disapproved.

The meat of donkeys and mules is not eaten. [Eating] horse meat, according to the Great Imam—*mercy of God Almighty upon him*—is strongly discouraged and close to unlawful (*tahrimen mekruh*). Its milk is like its meat. According to their eminences the two imams (Abu Yusuf and Muhammad), there is no harm in eating it.

Dead fetuses that come from the bellies of slaughtered animals are illicit. According to his eminence the Great Imam, this is the case even if it is already furry and fully formed. According to the two imams, fully formed fetuses are licit (*helal*) because since its mother was slaughtered it is also considered slaughtered.

THIRTY-FIVE

Cultivating the Land

The Splendor of the Garden, Sixteenth Century

TRANSLATED BY HAKAN T. KARATEKE

The sustenance of premodern societies was a labor-intensive operation. Farming required a massive labor force for all the stages of crop production—plowing, harrowing, sowing, irrigating, and harvesting—as well as for the distribution of crops to larger cities. Disruptions such as population decline were a frequent problem. Generally, in order to keep an optimal area of land cultivated, the relocation of peasantry was discouraged, but if peasants fled their homes for security reasons, which frequently happened in the seventeenth century, labor shortages were inevitable.

Enduring inclement weather conditions also affected the crop yields and placed an additional burden on the peasants, as they had to relinquish a portion of their harvest as in-kind tax. In the seventeenth century, many parts of the world witnessed a sustained period of cold and wet weather now referred to as the "Little Ice Age." This resulted in poor crop growth, and sometimes in failed crops. While certain practices and knowledge about farming passed on from generation to generation, peasants also needed to adapt their farming practices to shortened growing seasons and new varieties of disease.

Apart from the main staples like grains and legumes that were harvested from the fields, other nutrients were obtained from kitchen gardens, orchards, or vineyards; as these mostly needed to be consumed fresh, they were produced locally. The variety of trees, plants, and herbs, but also insect pests, and varying soil and weather conditions necessitated profound knowledge of the cultivation and care of trees and plants. A body of theoretical knowledge had been in circulation in the larger Mediterranean region and Mesopotamia since antiquity, and later authors compiled this information in agronomical treatises. One such work is by a late-sixth, early-seventh century author Cassianus Bassus. The original work in Greek is not extant, but the text has come down to us in Arabic and Persian translations, which found widespread interest in the Islamicate world as the *Book of Qastus*. Another work that became immensely popular was the *Nabataean Agriculture* (*Filahat al-Nabatiyya*) by Ibn Wahshiyya of Kufa (Iraq), written in ca. the tenth century. The book was translated and compiled from earlier Mesopotamian sources. Having been translated into Latin, the information therein also found circulation in medieval Europe.

The Splendor of the Garden (*Revnak-ı Bostan*) is known to be the first treatise on plant and tree farming composed in Turkish. Apparently from Edirne originally, the author remains anonymous. He quotes some of the Arabic sources mentioned above; for example, some of the information about astrological cycles related to farming are excerpted from earlier agronomical works. More importantly, the author relies on the information received from local experts and on his personal and very long experiences. He refers again and again to his own practices, innovations, and seasonal observations, which indicate that he decided to compose the treatise after some years of practice and implementation. Therefore, the detailed information he provides—the types of soil, the methods of growing different varieties of trees and flowers, the pruning and grafting practices, the diseases that befell trees and grapevines and their treatment, the nutritional benefits of different produce—is in part theoretical knowledge gathered from earlier sources, and in part based on practical local knowledge. The treatise ends with instructions for preserving fruits and other produce: this remained a critical practice for continued nutrient intake during winter months. *The Splendor of the Garden* remained a popular manual on garden and orchard farming in the core Ottoman lands through the seventeenth century.

LANGUAGE: Turkish. Simple instructional language scattered with technical terms particular to agriculture, viticulture, and horticulture.

SOURCE: Manuscript: Anonymous. *Revnak-ı Bustan*. Süleymaniye Kütüphanesi, Istanbul, Ayasofya 3736. Ottoman Print: *Revnak-ı Bustan*. Istanbul: Matbaa-i Amire, 1260/1844. Facsimile and transcription: Önler, Zafer, ed. *Revnak-ı Bustan*. Ankara: Türk Dil Kurumu, 2000 (22–23, 25–26, 28–29, 50–51, 58–59). There is no critical edition of this work. Since different copies display many variations, one or the other version had to be preferred to produce this translation.

MY ILLUSTRIOUS GARDEN IN EDİRNE

In accordance with the saying by the most blessed of humankind (the Prophet Muhammad) that *"love for one's hometown is part of the faith,"* the longing for paradise-like gardens has not disappeared from the weak heart of this poor one, who is in want of grace—*may God grant him success in achieving what he wishes*. Undeniably, I was drawn toward vineyards, fruit gardens, and flowering herb and flower gardens, and intended to settle in an abode of good repute and take up residence in a location with impregnable walls. I set out to build an exhilarating garden and a delightful plot, to erect its walls and gates in a favorable location resembling paradise. That is to say, by the grace of God most High, the Helper, I found a distinguished site and an outstanding piece of land comparable to sublime Paradise in the vicinity of the beautiful, exalted, and protected city of Edirne, *the like of which had not been created in the land* (Qur'an 89:8). After weeding and clearing its pure soil of thistles and sticks, I adorned it with roses, fragrant and flowering herbs, hyacinths, wild roses, and select fruit trees, and decided to settle down there.

That uplifting flower garden became renowned as the "heavenly garden," and the reputation of its beauty spread all around. As I worked on cultivating that Paradise-like garden, I followed the words of the sages written in books of farming, and the pearls of wisdom and proven traditions that I heard from experienced gardeners. [Later,] I wished to compile these in a few pages as an exhilarating treatise and a beautiful present for dear friends. Whenever distinguished minds become glad and sad hearts find serenity from the pleasure of adorning kitchen gardens and arranging flower gardens with [the help of] this [treatise], they will remember its miserable author, and kindly grant a prayer so that the gardens of the Compassionate One and the meadows of Heaven may be opened to me.

THE SUPREMACY OF EARTH

Earth, from which the clay of man (i.e., the clay from which humans were created by God) is made, is the most superior of the elements and the most noble of [God's] manifestations. The cursed Satan—*whatever he deserves [shall be] upon him*—was not truthful and, being arrogant, could not perceive the superiority of the noble earth. He became abusively sharp-tongued just like the dreadful flames [of which he was made] and fearlessly said, "*I am better than him (i.e., Adam)*" (Qur'an 7:12) and turned his face from good to evil. He became an unfortunate donkey, a mule carrying the burden of damnation. It is obvious among intelligent and sagacious people that earth is better than, and superior to, fire, because the heart of earth is a mine of prosperity and abundance. It endures torments and calamities; even when it becomes wretched it accepts with resignation and delivers a variety of food. Absorbed in haughtiness, fire is a cold-hearted rebel that sets hearts on fire and melts away souls. It hurts and tortures whoever it comes near and becomes intimate with. Earth has dignity and it is reliable; no matter what things people consign to it [to grow], it protects what it has been entrusted with. Fire is lustful; it destroys and kills everything that it gets ahold of; it is perfidious. Earth, wearing a black-colored veil, rectifies faults and covers defects. Fire exposes secrets and reveals flaws. The products of earth are roses and hyacinths, while fire produces useless smoke, charcoal, and ashes. Since the quality of earth is superior, it was deemed worthy of germinating the eminent tree of honorable Adam.

It is not [necessary] to detail the superiority of earth; [these] hints are enough for intelligent people. The real reason [for this treatise] is not to describe the earth but to explain its types: how many types of soil there are, and which type is able to grow which trees and plants. One has to acquire this knowledge and act accordingly, so that, by the help of God on High, one does not make mistakes and may achieve great benefits with every undertaking.

TIME TO PLANT TREES AND GRAPEVINE

According to astronomers' statements, if a tree is planted a day after, or on the day of, the twenty-fifth day of the second *kanun* (January), the middle of the winter months, which corresponds to the fifth day of the *hamsin* (i.e., the "fifty days" that start ten days before February), that sapling, whatever sort it may be, will take hold and will be free from disease. Water moves into the trees on the third day of February [when the tree comes out of the dormancy stage]; that is the time for pruning and grafting.

It should be known that one should embark on planting, whether grapevine or fruit tree, any day besides the three days at the beginning and end of each month—six days altogether—since the Boötes star (*avva*) rises during these days and is very harmful. The reason that the trees are infested with worms and become deceased after they are planted [on these days] is that the rays of the Boötes star reach them. It is essential for the gardener to avoid the Boötes star. Some say it rises at the beginning of the month; others say it rises at the end of the month. One should not ignore this.

Some say grapevines need to be planted during pruning season; before Hıdr-İlyas (Hıdrellez, usually May 6 in the Gregorian calendar, which marked the beginning of summer). One should prune it with a pruning hook and promptly plant it (?). It is possible to [plant] up to three days after pruning—this is preferable. One can also prune the vine, take a cutting, make a hole [in the ground], deposit some hay into it, spread some dung, place the head of the cutting into the ground with its bottom upward, and then cover it with dung and soil. One should abundantly water it every other day. When it grows roots, one should take it and plant it. This is called sprouting.

Some people knowledgeable about farming say that [grapevines] should be pruned and planted in the fall. In short, wherever water is in short supply, it is better to plant in the fall. It will thoroughly benefit from the winter rains, and its root will be strong, since this is the time when the growth of its fruit will be completed, and the vitality will go to the root and nourish it. In the summer, it will be robust; its cordons and fruits will be sturdy; and it won't be adversely affected by the heat. It is reported by the sage named Qastus that "When I first introduced planting grapevines in the fall, people rejected it. After observing its benefits, they commended and thanked me."

THE METHOD OF PLANTING

It should be known that if someone wants to start a vineyard or an orchard, he first has to plow the field a few times and then harrow it. Then, he should dig the spot where the grapevine or the trees will be planted deep and wide, according to [the size of] the roots, such that there is one wide-open span on every side of the root. The root of the grapevine to be planted should be multibranched [with feeder roots] and healthy. The tips of the roots should be neatly cut with a sharp knife or an axe. After cutting away the [fine] roots that are growing upward, bent like an elbow, or [crowding and] upsetting other [parts of the] root, each branch of the root should be oriented toward the ground while planting. However many layers a root may have, each layer should be covered with soil that was broken up on the surface of the ground as much as the root requires. One should not tramp [the earth] with hand or foot, as it distresses the roots. If the soil is too weak and gravelly, one should mix together the manure of animals other than boar, goose, and duck with the soil, and leave it for a month until they are well-blended. One should then set out to plant.

One should also know that if the soil is too coarse or is up on a plateau, the heat of the sun will not reach the root during autumn or spring. In those conditions [the tree] should be planted shallowly so that the sunlight of the aforementioned seasons can warm the root and have an effect. The root can [also] benefit from the rays of the stars. In a place that is much affected by sunlight, like in thick and soft soil, or on a plain, [the root] should be planted deep in the soil. One observes that the roots of the trees that grow wild on mountains are close to the surface, whereas on the plains it is the opposite. Since the sun does not have too much effect on the ground in the mountains, the root is attracted to the heat of the sun, and hence is necessarily shallow. On the plain, however, since the heat of the sun is profuse, the root moves deep into the ground; there is no necessity; it behaves like it is supposed to. Likewise, the roots of the plants that grow [wild] on the mountains are also close to the surface; the opposite is true for the plains. If it were solely the softness and thinness of the soil that caused the root to go deep, there is no doubt that the soil on the mountains is thinner than that of the plains.

PRUNING AND GRAFTING

According to most people [who are] knowledgeable about farming, the time for pruning is from the middle of the month until four nights before the end of the month. In short, they say that it is appropriate to plant when the moon is waxing and to prune when it is waning. However, the sage called Suriyon (Serapion the Younger, ca. twelfth century) stated that it is possible to plant and prune two nights after the [beginning of] the month and two nights before [its end]. The time for grafting is also the same.

First, know that the time to prune and graft grapevines is March. If the grape is of the "Lady Finger" or (the white, elongated) "Razaki" variety, one should leave eight to twelve nodes on the vine according to its fragility or strength, and prune the rest. With other [varieties of] grapes, one should leave six to eight nodes, and cut the rest. If there is weakness in the old arms, one should leave the strong and cut the weak ones and make the strong ones that remain into a "goblet" [shape], as much as possible.

Know that the later the grapevine is pruned, the better, so that it doesn't suffer cold injury. The pruning of the grapevine depends on the strength of the trunk and the cordons: If it is strong, leave three or four buds; if it is weak, leave two buds. If a stalk close to the ground is weak, leave two buds; if it is supported with a post, leave five or six buds. But one has to observe and learn from the experts.

Know that when pruning a grape arbor or a vine stock one should apply bear's grease to a pruning hook, called *minjal* or *tahra*, secretly, in a spot where no one can see. That hook should then be used to prune. If one crushes garlic, mixes it with olive oil, and applies it to the hook and prunes with it; or if one crushes the insects that are in the ground in the vineyard, mixes them with oil and applies it to the hook; or if one applies beef tallow and frog blood; or if one [burns] a stem from the vine, mixes its ash with olive oil and applies it, and then prunes with that hook, the grapevine is protected from all sorts of diseases and insects.

DISEASES AND TREATMENT

First of all, it should be known that diseases occur in trees because of cold and heat. Thereafter, the tree either dries up, or worms attack it owing to its frailty and gradually kill it. [The tree sometimes] grows roots close to the root collar; they move upward, come close to the surface, and are exposed to the heat from the sun in the summer. Warm water penetrates the tree through these roots, causing dryness and sickness. In the winter the ground freezes, and roots close to the root collar, because they are close to the surface, sustain pressure and become weak. [Otherwise,] in the winter, the strength is in the roots; they become stronger through the warmth of the soil. While other roots grow and thrive, that weak root cannot function: the water inside goes bad, cannot flow, and that section of root becomes sick. Similarly, when humans catch cold, because of the stress on the body, the blood vessels become pressurized and the blood cannot move vigorously. When blood moves slowly, it becomes putrid, fever moves to the limbs, and medication becomes necessary. One either needs to receive blood to help circulation, or to loosen the limbs by sweating so that the blood vessels relax.

Just as humans have a pulse, and illnesses can be detected from it, the pulse of the trees can be read by its leaves in the autumn. You shall observe: if a tree loses leaves before all the others, it has disease. If its leaves have a pistachio color and are not an intense green, it is diseased. Moreover, if you want to know what sort of disease it has, you should examine them in the autumn: If the leaves have a lemon yellow color, the tree is inclined to dry up. If the leaves are speckled and have mottling, it is infested with worms.

If the bases of the branches are weak, and the branches gradually become thinner toward the end; if there are black spots here and there on the trunk or branches of a tree; or the leaves turn sort of dull and matte without their color fading, the tree has suffered heat stress. If the leaves look stunted and are curled, the root has either hit a rock, gotten bent, or was stressed and stunted owing to hard ground. If the tree grows many branches on top, but the trunk is lean, its roots are likewise under stress. If the leaves are brown and look like they are dried up, this is because of a lack of water and the ground being too dense. One has to dig up along the sides of it and water it abundantly. If the disease is not visible on the outside but hidden, the situation of the root is still the same.

If dry, worm-eaten spots are visible, then it is good; an appropriate remedy can be applied. For example, if you cut off the withered parts, and destroy the worms by inserting a brass or metal wire into the withered branch and cutting them open with a knife, they will still appear in another spot. The best [remedy] is that you unearth the roots, see if there are fine roots close to the surface, and cut them off. You should cut the ones that are not growing straight—that is, those that are not directed down deep into the ground. You should also inspect as much as possible to see if the root has hit a rock or if the roots upset each other. Look and make your preparations accordingly.

THE PRESERVATION OF FRUITS FOR WINTER

One harvests the gardens and assembles the winter fruit toward the end of September, the first of the autumn months, provided that it is a place where rain and frost occur late, or at the beginning of October, the middle of the autumn months—in short, during the time of the harvest moon (i.e., the full moon closest to the September equinox), before the rains have started. When winter melons are collected, one should pick them with their stems. They should lie on a rack with a wooden [top] or [be covered with] grass or leaves for about ten days. One should from time to time roll the muskmelons to a different side so that they completely ripen under the sun. Subsequently, if it is possible, in a house into which no other wind blows in apart from the northeast wind, one should drive wooden nails into the walls and construct shelves, on top of which three muskmelons can be placed. Put the muskmelons on the shelf and roll them on to the other side once a week. If it is not possible, one should put them on an elevated spot away from the ground drafts, situated toward the [currents of] air—no wind should touch the fruits but the northeast waft. Place grass or straw underneath. Put watermelons in straw too; one should protect them from the ground drafts as well.

When the grapes are strung on a line, one should hang them inside a hut which must not receive too many drafts. During freezing temperatures, a candle should be lit so that the grapes do not freeze during the day or night, so that their shape will be nice. If you want the grapes to be preserved until the next grape season, you should not separate the bunch from the canes. Place them into a glazed flask or earthen pot, but don't let them press closely together; they should be loose. One should tightly close the lid, bend the branches, bury the pot in the ground, and make sure rain cannot reach it. It will remain fresh until the next year. [. . .]

Pears should be collected after their seeds turn black. If you intend to dry them halved or scored, they should be collected when the seeds are parti-colored. One should halve or score the pears, then leave them to dry in an oven after baking bread or when it is heated to that temperature. One should then take them out of the oven and leave them on a wooden block for drying. If one spreads a loosely woven cloth on top of them while they are drying, the sun will not diminish their taste, and they will dry in tenderness. They will be good.

If one peels the skin of pears and apples, and lets them dry like that, their juice will not disappear; they will preserve their taste. If one scores them, removes the core, and leaves them to dry like that they will be delicious. If one wants to preserve winter pears, one should gather them ten days before or after [the beginning of?] October, during the middle of the autumn months—according to the ripening schedule—after the seeds turn black, [but] before the fruit is completely ripe or while it is semiripe. Then, one lays down saw shavings on a spot and places the pears on them, neither too far apart from each other nor too close, just so much distance that air can circulate between them. Or one spreads the leaves of the Anatolian walnut [tree] and lines up the pears on them to rest for quite a long time, until the spring—[perhaps] even longer.

One squeezes the pears with a press, adds sediment-soil [containing calcium carbonate]—just as they do when making grape juice (*şıra*)—makes it limpid, and then boils it down to produce molasses. One can also place the pears in their juice, and by adding mustard [seeds], make pickles. The pickled pears need to be autumn or winter pears. [. . .] All juicy fruits are preserved by pickling.

THIRTY-SIX

Wonders of Art and Nature

Anonymous, Sixteenth Century

TRANSLATED BY IDO BEN-AMI

Wonders of Art and Nature is an incomplete sixteenth-century manuscript housed in the British Library. The book, which comprises 172 folios and ninety miniatures, is in Turkish, but it was presumably translated from Persian. Several of its stories originally appear in a work titled *Wonders of Creation* (*Ajayeb-e Makhluqat*), written by the Persian compiler Ahmad-e Tusi (twelfth century).

The orientalist Charles Rieu (d. 1902) described the work in his Catalogue of the Turkish Manuscripts in the British Museum in 1888 as containing short, detached sections that relate "to strange stones, plants, and animals, to fabulous monsters of sea and land, to remarkable mountains, rivers, and springs, to wonderful buildings, idols, talismans, etc., and consist for the most part of childish stories and travelers' tales." Arguably, however, the value of this cosmography lay in the sociointellectual function it performed for its intended readers, and not necessarily in the veracity of its contents. A cosmographical work was supposed to prompt its readers to contemplate the wonders of the created world in order to marvel at the creator behind it. Therefore, the significance of Wonders of Art and Nature is rooted in the sensation of wonder that it was meant to evoke. Medieval and early modern readers used the science of cosmography to acquire *ilm* ("knowledge" or "wisdom" in Arabic) that allowed them to practice the arousal of wonder at God's creations.

Cosmographies such as *Wonders of Art and Nature* offered intended readers a detailed list of objects that were meant to generate such wonder. These objects were usually classified into two different categories: marvels (*aja'ib*) and oddities (*ghara'ib*). In his renowned *Wonders of Creation and the Oddities of Existence* (*Aja'ib al-Makhlukat wa-Ghara'ib al-Mawjudat*), the famous cosmographer and geographer Zakariya al-Qazwini (d. 1283) referred to natural things such as the stars, the human body, and the bee as marvels (*aja'ib*). On the other hand, he considered things that rarely occur as oddities (*ghara'ib*): among them are the miracles that several Islamic prophets are renowned for, in addition to phenomena like eclipses, earthquakes, floods, and the birth of animals with strange forms.

Additionally, al-Qazwini offered a theory about wonder that was adopted in later cosmographies. He regarded this emotion as the feeling of bewilderment (*hayrat*), which people experience when they are unable to understand the cause of a thing or how it is supposed to influence them when they see it for the first time. The motif of biting one's finger, which appears occasionally in illustrated cosmographies, indicates this bewilderment and it signifies that the person is confronted with wonder. Therefore, readers of this wisdom literature comprised not only a knowledge community but also an emotional community whose members sought continuous entrance to a "wonderland."

LANGUAGE: Uncomplicated Turkish, with some archaisms and obsolete words.

SOURCE: Manuscript: Anonymous. No Title. British Library, London, Harleian 5500, fols. 17a; 19b–20a; 23b–24a; 51a–51b; 61a; 72a; 75a–75b; 79a–79b; 85b–86a; 112a–112b; 115b–116a; 124b–125a; 143a–143b; 153b–154a, respectively.

---

1. THE AMPHIBIOUS HORSE AND THE ADDERS

It is told that in the Nile in Egypt there is a water horse. When this horse comes out of the water, some of the snakes on the Nile's shore attack it and wrap themselves around the horse in loops in order to bite it. However, the horse snorts on the snakes, and they fall into pieces.

2. FISH THAT ARE AFRAID OF THUNDER

It is mentioned that during Abdulmalik ibn Marwan's time (r. 685–705, the fifth caliph of the Umayyad dynasty) a dead fish was found on the shore of the ocean. There are some fish that never come to the surface of the water but rather swim in groups at the bottom of the sea, on account of their fear of thunder. For as soon as these fish hear the sound of the thunder, they die. They never eat the flesh of a dead animal; however, they eat one another alive. If one of them is dead they do not eat it, because their cadavers are toxic.

3. IMAGES OF HUMANS AND ANIMALS THAT HELP TO CURE ILLNESSES

It is related that in Rum, between the gulf (*halic*) and the boundaries of Constantinople, there is a village. In this place there is a house of stone in which numerous figures of humans and animals exist. It is said that whenever someone suffers from a discomfort, they come to these figures and touch them three times with their hand. If it is a man, [he touches a figure] in the shape of a man, and if it is a woman, [she touches a figure] in the shape of a woman. They put

FIGURE 28. Images of humans and animals that help to cure illnesses. Anonymous. No Title. Harleian 5500, fol. 23b. British Library, London.

their hand on the body part that is giving them pain. Then, God willing, their health will be restored without a delay. No one knows what the cause [for this phenomenon] is.

4. A LONG-LIVED VULTURE REBORN FROM THE ASHES

It is mentioned that the famous bird called *kerkes* (a kind of vulture) lives for a thousand years. When the thousand years are complete, the vulture gathers wood sticks, sets them on fire, and burns itself to ashes. Then, when the wind picks up these ashes, it comes back to life—by God's decree—and lives for another thousand years. It will go on like this until the end of the world.

5. A LION MADE OF STONE

It is mentioned that in Rum there is a certain bathhouse. At its door there is a lion made of stone. If someone puts his hand on this lion's head, it lifts its paw up. It is as if someone was petting the lion, and it then becomes submissive.

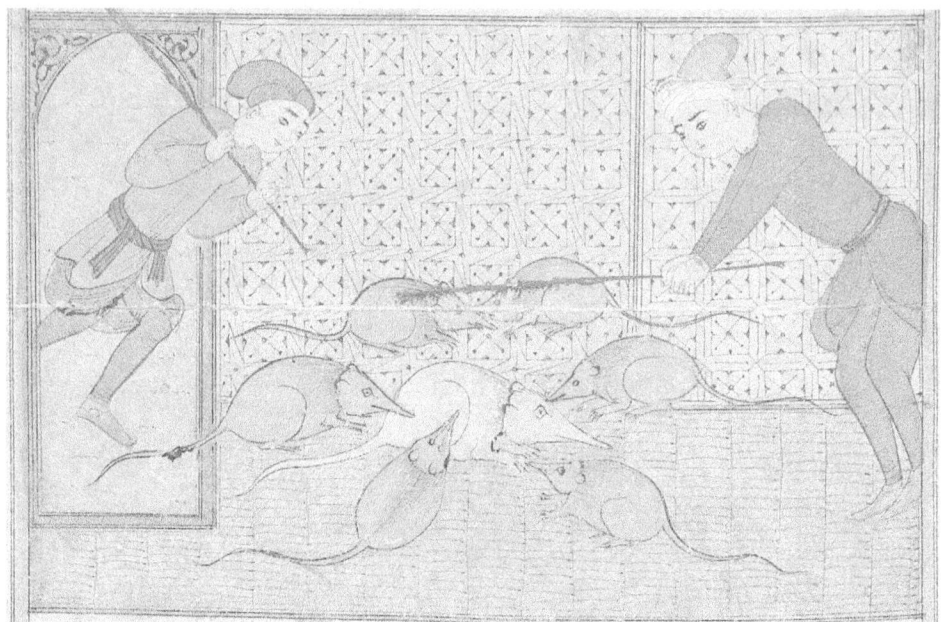

FIGURE 29. A stone that smells like mice. Anonymous. No Title. Harleian 5500, fol. 79a. British Library, London.

6. A MARVELOUS ROSE

In Armenia, there is a rose that never opens while it is on the shrub. Only when someone picks it and holds it in his hand does the rose open, owing to the scent of the hand. It is also said that during the time that the rose is on the shrub, it [only] opens its mouth like a bud, but its color is golden yellow. As long as nobody takes it into their hands, it will not turn red, and its scent will not be pleasant. If someone excessively bleeds, one can give him water from this rose's leaves to drink, and he will be saved and freed from jaundice (lit., yellowness).

7. A TREE THAT CURES TOOTHACHE

It is mentioned that in Turkistan there is a tree whose sticks the local inhabitants use to pick their teeth. Sometimes these people suffer from a toothache, and then they right away burn some of the trees's sticks. The pain only goes away if they hold the tooth into the smoke or smear part of the ashes on it. God—*may He be glorified and exalted*—has given this sort of peculiarity to [this tree].

8. A STONE THAT SMELLS LIKE MICE

It is told that in the Maghreb there is a variety of little stones that are shaped like mice. They smell like rodents. When one of these pieces is in someone's house, all the mice that are in the house will gather around it. It is mentioned that when [the people] are fed up with mice in this land, they bring a piece of this stone and put it [in their house]. Then, all the mice in there run to the stone and gather around it. As the mice gather, the people hit them with various objects and kill them. Thus they will be saved from mice for a while. Basically this stone is the cat for the mice, for there are no other cats in that place.

9. A WONDROUS FOUNTAIN

It is told that in the suburb of Faghfuriyye in Rum, there is a certain fountain. Its water is so delicious and pure that there is no other water like it in all the land. If you put some of this water in a vessel and take it with you, but leave it open [without a lid], the water will become bitter, almost like poison; you cannot drink it. But if you put a lid on it, it will be delicious and pure. It's not like any other water. No one knows why this is so.

10. A WONDROUS MAN

[In the book *Firdaws al-Hikma* (*Paradise of Wisdom*), Ali bin Zayn] relates: In Samaria, I saw a man who had a red face and eyes that sparkled like cats' eyes. People would catch and bring scorpions and centipedes to this fellow. He would eat them fearlessly, and he would not be affected by their poison. Sometimes he would even let the scorpions sting him, and the scorpions that stung [him] would die immediately. But he himself would not be harmed in the slightest. The responsibility [for the reliability of this story] is on the narrator.

11. A DRAGON UNDER A MAGIC SPELL

It is mentioned that in Persia there is a certain mountain, in the center of which there is a dragon. People regularly come from afar to see it. In several places on this mountain there are holes where the back [of this dragon] can be seen. When poked with a javelin or a spit, the dragon even moves; people observe it. The head and tail do not appear. It is said that nothing similar to this marvel and oddity has ever been witnessed. They say, [the prophet-king] Solomon, son of David—*peace be upon him*—has put this dragon under a magic spell. That is why its head and tail cannot be seen.

12. WONDROUS PATTENS

It is told that in the land of the Bulghar (a medieval Turkic people from the Pontic steppe) they have a sort of wooden pattens that is seven ell (ca. 490 cm) high. The local people wear them on their feet during the winter in deep snow. In their hands they each hold a walking staff, carry supplies, and go hunting. The interesting thing is that they can walk fifty parasangs (ca. 165 miles) in the snow with these pattens. They have become used to it; they don't fall over.

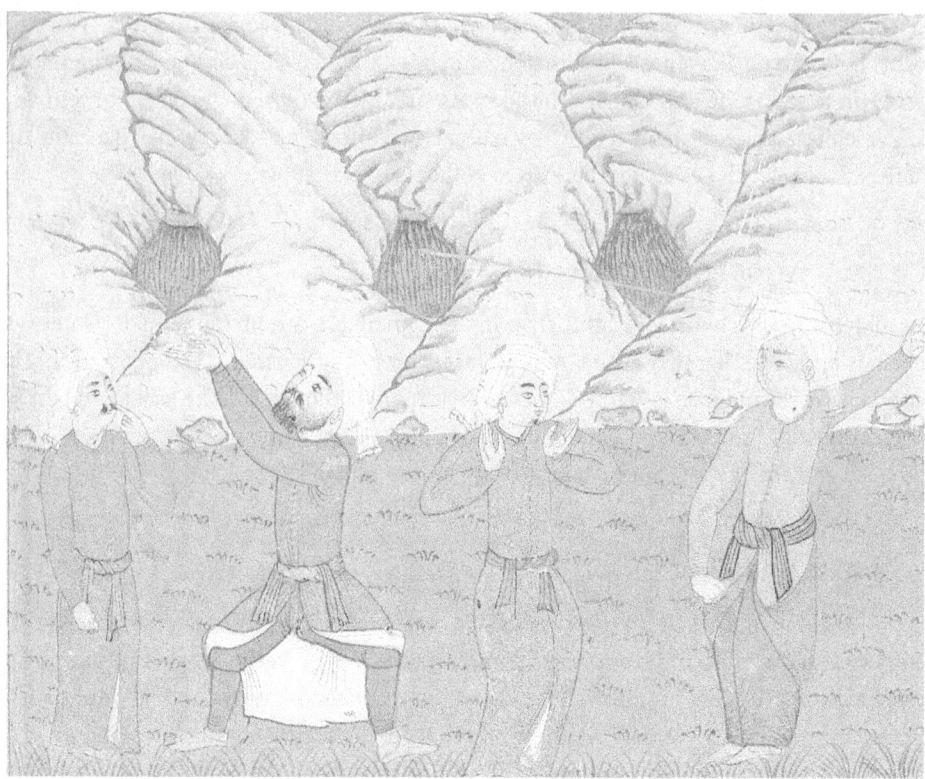

FIGURE 30. A dragon under a magic spell. Anonymous. No Title. Harleian 5500, fol. 115b. British Library, London.

13. A MARVELOUS STRIKING CLOCK

It is mentioned that in the land of Syria there is a certain mosque that has a white marble dome. On top of this dome there are two figures. One is in the shape of a Greek (*Rumi*) man and the other is in the shape of a central Asian Turk (*Türkistan ademi*). When one hour of daytime has passed, a noise emanates from the Greek figure and, with the passing of two hours, two noises emanate from the Turkish figure. In the third hour three noises emanate from the Greek, and so on until the twelfth hour. This is how the locals can tell the hour, night and day. Also, these two figures are constantly moving. The responsibility [for the reliability of this story] is on the narrator.

14. THE SHEEP MADE OF STONE

In Armenia, there is a mountain that is not extremely tall. People have placed a stone sheep on top of [this mountain]. If someone wishes for milk, he approaches the sheep, and says, "Oh sheep! Please, give me some milk because I am parched and thirsty for milk." If this person is genuinely thirsty and filled with a desire to drink, pure and delicious water will flow out from this sheep's mouth. This person can put his mouth on the sheep's mouth and thus drink as much as he desires. But if this person is not genuinely thirsty, however much he asks for it, not a drop of water will flow. This person who wants water can ask in whatever language he wants; it won't make a difference. They say that many people have investigated [this phenomenon] but have not figured out how it is.

THIRTY-SEVEN

On the Natural Advantages of Edirne

Anonymous, Late Fifteenth to Early Sixteenth Century

TRANSLATED BY AMY SINGER

Edirne is an ancient Thracian settlement known in antiquity as Uscudama. Under the Romans the town acquired a walled perimeter and became a fortified urban center known as Hadrianopolis/Adrianople (after the emperor Hadrian, d. 138), which, later, the Ottomans pronounced as Edrene and eventually Edirne. As Byzantine Adrianople, the town continued to have strategic importance in safeguarding the western approach to Constantinople and in serving as a political and commercial hub in the eastern Balkans. Edirne became the capital of the Ottoman state in the early fifteenth century, was adorned with impressive monuments, and remained the most important Ottoman city in Thrace until the end of the empire. Today it is a Turkish city approximately 240 kilometers due west of Istanbul on the Turkish-Greek-Bulgarian border.

The present text, known as *History of Edirne: An Account of* Beşir Çelebi (*Tarih-i Edrene: Hikayet-i Beşir Çelebi*) by an anonymous author, recounts an imagined conversation between the renowned physician Beşir Çelebi and the young Ottoman sultan, Mehmed II (r. 1444–46, 1451–81). The two men talked as they sat by the Tunca River at the pavilion built on the edge of the city by Mehmed's father, Sultan Murad II (r. 1421–44, 1446–51). As related in the *Hikayet*, the sultan was astonished that even on such a warm summer day, Beşir would be wrapped in furs and shivering. This observation elicited the doctor's lengthy explanation of the sources of warm and cool air, the benefits and ills brought by the city's three rivers—the Tunca, the Meriç (Maritsa or Evros), and the Arda—and the climactic advantages of Edirne's location.

These advantages are informed by the basic principle of humorism (see chapter 29), a medical practice maintaining that four humors associated with the four elements—blood/air, phlegm/water, black bile/earth, and yellow bile/fire—controlled health and illness in the human body. This medical philosophy held that each person had a tendency toward a particular kind of imbalance, which the physician was called on to restore when it was too greatly disturbed. By presenting the rivers of Edirne as each associated in a particular season with a specific humor, the author of this text is demonstrating another of Edirne's outstanding qualities—that is, that the town has everything necessary to restore and maintain human well-being. This reinforces his argument that Edirne is "a most excellent place."

The only extant evidence about the physician Beşir Çelebi comes from the works attributed to him. According to his own account, he was originally from Karaman, an independent polity that existed until 1474 in central Anatolia, and he served the ruler İbrahim Karamanoğlu II (r. 1424–64/826–69). The anonymous narrator of the *History of Edirne* relates how, having heard of Beşir Çelebi's talents and already being known for surrounding himself with learned men, the Ottoman sultan Mehmed invited the physician to come to Edirne. The date of this compilation is unknown, but a good guess might be the later fifteenth century, based on the style of the Turkish and the themes of the text.

History of Edirne is unique for this period in its singular focus on the city. It purports to describe the qualities of the town in the mid-fifteenth century, a period for which there is no comparable Ottoman source, and few in any language that offer much detail about the city. The first section focuses on the natural landscape while the second relates the conquest of Edirne by the Ottomans, the construction of Edirne's early Ottoman monuments, and a number of legends connected with these events. It also surveys the older history of the city to discuss the city walls and the churches. In closing, the author emphasizes Edirne's reputation, and adds that the learned men call it *darü'n-nasr* (the abode of victory) and *gaziler ocağı* (the hearth of the ghazis).

LANGUAGE: Turkish. Unembellished narrative prose, with some archaisms and obsolete words. Many insertions of direct speech in question-and-answer form.

SOURCE: Facsimile: Ertaylan, İsmail Hikmet, ed. *Tarih-i Edirne / Hikâyet-i Beşir Çelebi*. Istanbul: Edebiyat Fakültesi Matbaası, 1960 (1–7). Consulted transcriptions: Oy, Aydın. "Risâle-i Beşir Çelebi Menâkıb-ı Medine-i Edrene." In *Edirne: Serhattaki Payıtaht,* edited by Emin Nedret İşli, M. Sabri Koz, and Onur Oral, 71–101. Istanbul: Yapı Kredi Kültür Sanat Yayıncılık, 1998. Erdoğru, M. Akif. "Hikâye-i Tabib Beşir Çelebi ve Tarih-i Edirne İsimli Yazma Eser." In *Tarih Yazıları (Prof. Dr. Tuncer Baykara'ya Armağan),* edited by M. Akif Erdoğru, 174–205. Istanbul: IQ Kültür Sanat Yayıncılık, 2006.

BEŞİR ÇELEBİ'S KNOWLEDGE AND WISDOM

It is told that at the throne city of Greece (*Yunan*)—that is, in the city of Konya—there was a skilled physician whom they called Beşir Çelebi. He had the confidence of all the people; he was very much a master. One day, as he was riding his horse, he chanced on a funeral procession. He called out to those who were carrying the corpse and said, "The person you are carrying is alive." He dismounted, opened the coffin, and drew blood from that person. A little while later the person opened his eyes and sat up. [Those who participated in the funeral procession] said to Beşir Çelebi: "My lord, how did you know that this person was alive?" Beşir Çelebi said, "I knew it from those who carried him, because a corpse is heavy whereas a live person is light. That's how I knew."

At that time, Sultan Ghazi Mehmed Khan had recently acceded to the throne [of the Ottomans] in Edrene. By chance one day the qualities of Beşir Çelebi were mentioned in his royal gathering. As a result of the numerous accounts [he heard], Sultan Ghazi Mehmed Khan developed an intense interest in this physician. Immediately, a letter was drafted to Karamanoğlu İbrahim Bey [the ruler of Konya]; when the messenger reached İbrahim Bey with the letter, he obeyed the royal command and sent the doctor off to the fortune-giving threshold [i.e., the court of Sultan Mehmed II] with every courtesy and dignity. [Beşir Çelebi] completed his journey and arrived at the city of Edrene. He was received by the sultan in the old palace, and they struck up a congenial conversation because Sultan Ghazi Mehmed Khan was also a most educated ruler who was fond of learned men. Whenever he heard of a learned and virtuous man, he would surely ask that he be brought, and be honored with the sultan's company. Indeed, Mehmed was indescribably pleased with the physician. For quite a while [the sultan] did not remove [Beşir Çelebi] from his presence, and he could not do without conversations with him.

Sultan Mehmed Khan had a small pavilion by the banks of the Tunca river. The late sultan Ghazi Murad Khan [Mehmed's father] had had it built. From time to time, as it struck his fancy, the sultan would arrive there to enjoy the fresh air around the river and socialize with some of his companions. One day, the sultan was conversing with Beşir Çelebi at this pavilion. It was in the month of July (Temmuz). The weather was quite hot but the doctor wore two layers of fur, one on top of the other. He had a very frail constitution, so much so that when he would go to the bath, he would spread a felt mat on the marble slab, claiming that the essence (*zat*) of the marble [as a stone] is cold; its body (*beden*) aligns with its essence. Because of his [sensitivity] he used to sit on a stool [and not stand] at the foot of the sultan's throne.

EDİRNE'S CLIMATE

While they were conversing, the doctor shivered and his complexion changed. The sultan wondered at this and said, "How strange it is to catch a chill at this time [of the year], especially since it is now July. In this season the weather is very hot for forty days. There is no breeze from midmorning until the midafternoon prayer. How can you be shivering from so little wind?" Beşir Çelebi said, "My sultan, there are many benefits from the heat, one of which is that it increases the natural body heat and that is the cause of human life, and as for the cold, it increases the coldness [of the body], and thus is evidence of death. And yet this wind did not come from the air, it came from the ground here." The sultan marveled at this and said, "How was this wind born from the ground?" The doctor replied, "My sultan, there are three reasons for the wind being produced from the ground: First, there is a snake's nest in the ground. A snake is a cold animal and the wind emerges from it. Or [secondly], there is marble in the ground or another kind of stone. If it isn't these things either, then [thirdly] there is water [in the ground]. The coldness [of it] is transformed into wind."

The sultan continued: "O doctor, can heat arise from the ground, too?" Beşir Çelebi said, "It can." The sultan asked, "In what way?" The doctor replied, "There are also three reasons for this, my sultan. First, a place can be hollow and if the air and the sun enter it and get hot, then the wind takes the heat and brings it out. Second, [it can come] from a place where treasure is buried, and third, it can come into being in a jinn's dwelling." The sultan congratulated him [for his knowledge]. [Then, the sultan's attendants] dug in that place [where they had been sitting]. A viper appeared, sleeping coiled like a ring. They killed it, dug a bit further, and a mat-shaped piece of marble appeared. They removed that as well. [Beneath it] a pitch-black well was revealed; its water was known as the elixir of life.

So, the sultan gave the noble physician a robe of honor and then said, "O doctor of the age, what would you say about the climate of this place and this city?" The physician said, "It is excellent to be [here] in winter [because it is] neither so high that the wind touches it nor so low that the sun makes it hot. And the air around the river is not harmful because it is sweet water. [But] salty sea air is very harmful. People quickly grow old [from it]. Plato the doctor would go three days' camel journey away from the sea [to settle since] it would harm the life span, weaken the eyesight, and disorient the senses. But this place (Edrene) is protected in winter, and in summer it is filled with pleasant air. It doesn't get too hot because it is open to the north and its south [side] is high, and also in the summer the wind blows from below, reaches up and touches the heights, then returns to spread over the ground. A breeze is never lacking, removing infection and bringing health to the body."

The noble sultan, refuge of the world, said, "Hey doctor, is there any place better around here than this one?" The doctor pointed toward Buçuk Tepe (the hill behind them) and said, "In the lands of Rum (Rumeli, i.e., Thrace and the Balkans) there is no healthier place than this." After that, he pointed toward Deliklü Kaya (a local spot) and praised it, saying, "In winter, one should be careful and you need to wear many clothes. Yet you will live in this place in prosperity; it has a moderate climate, most excellent."

The sultan continued his inquiry, "Doctor, why does the wind blow in the air in winter and on the ground in summer?" The physician replied: "In winter, the sun's strength dwindles, at which point the air gains strength, and the wind blows in the air. In the summer, the sun becomes stronger so that [the wind] blows on the ground and takes its coolness from the earth." "Now, my sultan," he said, "your palace should be here." On hearing the words of the physician, the sultan issued an order that the new palace be built on that spot.

In that time, there was a very skilled architect whose hands and feet were paralyzed. Wherever he went, he was carried on a litter. He [was the one who] built the Üç Şerefeli mosque of the late sultan Murad [II]. Then, that architect built a sublime royal palace that was beyond compare in the inhabited world. He designed a pavilion and enclosed it with iron bands all around. He covered its roof with lead and included a water source inside it. It resembled paradise, and he designed orchards, herb gardens, verdant meads, and rose gardens all around it, all defying description. The noble sultan asked, "What do you have to say

FIGURE 31. Edirne, nineteenth century. M. J. Starling (engraver), in Thomas Allom, *Constantinople and the Scenery of the Seven Churches of Asia Minor* (London: Fisher, Son & Co., 1838), 72–73.

about the climate of Edrene?" The physician said, "My sultan, it is a moderate climate, very pleasant. There is no other such place except maybe for Malkara."

THE RIVERS OF EDİRNE

Next, the sultan asked about Edrene's three rivers. The physician answered, "My sultan, one of these rivers is called the Arda, a sanguine (*demevi*) river. It is pleasant in every way, with water that is good for digestion. If the sick drink it, they become healthy." The sultan asked, "Why is it known as sanguine?" The physician answered, "My lord, if water flows where there is stone, that water is definitely sanguine. But no one should drink it in the summer, it is not healthy then. Now another of the rivers is called Meriç. It is choleric (*safravi*). The sign of this water is that there is sand in the place where it flows. If the sand is fine-grained and yellow, it is choleric. If the sand is clear, it is sanguine. Now the Tunca [the third river] is phlegmatic (*balgami*). Any water that has mud is very good to drink in the summer. But in the winter it should be avoided. If people drink it, they should at least filter it before they drink. This water is rather melancholic (*sevdavi*). Its sign is that in the place where it flows there is a smell of clay and rotting (?). Drinking that water is very harmful." After that, Sultan Ghazi Mehmed Khan became very fond of Edrene. The construction of the new palace was completed and he lived there in prosperity.

THIRTY-EIGHT

The Legend of the Construction of Constantinople

Anonymous, Sixteenth Century

TRANSLATED BY DIMITRIS J. KASTRITSIS

Constantinople was without a doubt the most important city on the Mediterranean Sea in the Middle Ages. Refounded by the Roman emperor Constantine (r. 306–37) as "New Rome" (330) it soon came to be known by his own name. After the original Rome fell out of significance in the fifth century, Constantinople continued to serve as the capital of the Eastern Roman Empire, also known as the Byzantine Empire. When the Sassanian Empire collapsed in the 650s following the Arab-Islamic conquests of Mesopotamia and other regions, the Roman Empire—the other great power in the region at the time—became a natural target for the Arab-Islamic armies. Muslim armies laid siege to Constantinople in 717–18, during the period of the early Islamic conquests. Nevertheless, with the exception of the Latin occupation of the city following the Fourth Crusade (1204–61), the almost impregnable walled city remained greatly coveted, but was considered unconquerable. As the Roman Empire gradually lost territories in its Asian and European provinces, eventually it was left with little more to defend than Constantinople proper. Thanks to the Ottomans' growing zeal and efficiency in using new military technologies—notably massive cannons—they captured the city in 1453. This event is considered a watershed moment for the growth of Ottoman self-perceptions, since it ties in with an imperial vision and affirms claims to inheriting the Roman imperial tradition in the Mediterranean basin.

The Ottomans cherished this age-old imperial city and made it their own. They continued to use the name referring to the Emperor Constantine (Kostantiniyye or Konstantinopol), along with two dozen other names given to the city. As the Ottoman imperial throne city, Constantinople flourished once more and became the center of the world for the Ottoman elite. Within this context, some time after the Ottoman conquest of the city, Turkish narratives based on earlier legendary accounts emerged about the foundation of Constantinople and the construction of its most famous monument, the great cathedral of Hagia Sophia (Ayasofya).

Finished in 537, this imposing church remained the world's largest Christian temple (converted into a mosque after the conquest) until the construction of St. Peter's Basilica in Rome in the seventeenth century. Based on a wide variety of sources from both the Christian and Islamic traditions, including a set of Byzantine legends about the antiquities of the city, the tales about the city became quite popular and had a considerable influence on Ottoman culture.

One way to understand these legends is to view them in the context of the political situation at the time. These stories are often embedded in a number of works known as the *Histories of the House of Osman* (*Tevarih-i Âl-i Osman*), where they play a key role in conveying messages about the nature and abuse of political authority. After 1453, the victorious Ottoman sultan Mehmed II "the Conqueror" (r. 1444-46, 1451-53) took advantage of the prestige he had gained by carrying out the conquest of Constantinople to advance his imperial project, which involved extensive state centralization and reconstruction of the ruined Roman capital. This provoked resistance from groups in the provinces who were threatened with the loss of their advantages by the newly empowered imperial government in Constantinople, now Istanbul. At a time that was also rife with apocalyptic expectations—the conquest of Constantinople by Muslim armies was seen as a harbinger of the end of days—the need to explain the history of Constantinople, an ancient city full of wonders, combined with political messages about the perils of authoritarian government to produce these stories. It is fair to say that they are representative of an age when there was widespread conflict between different religions, universalist visions, and ideas of government. As with the better studied Italian Renaissance taking place at the same time not far from Constantinople, debates about the present were framed in terms of the past in the Ottoman throne city as well. The following passages, translated into English for the first time, are enough to give a basic sense of the style and content of these fascinating Turkish legends.

LANGUAGE: Turkish. Plain prose style typical of Old Anatolian Turkish heroic and historical narratives, including syntactic and lexical archaisms.

SOURCE: Transcription: Öztürk, Necdet, ed. *Anonim Osmanlı Kroniği, 1299-1512*. Istanbul: Türk Dünyası Araştırmaları Vakfı, 2000 (86-93). Also consulted: Yerasimos, Stefanos. *Kostantiniye ve Ayasofya Efsaneleri*. Translated by Şirin Tekeli. Istanbul: İletişim, 1993 (13-19).

PROPHET SOLOMON BUILDS AYDINCIK (KYZIKOS)

After conquering Constantinople, Sultan Mehmed looked on all the strange and marvelous buildings and was left in a state of bewilderment, since they did not look like the work of human hands. So he assembled from the lands of Rum and from the Frankish lands monks, bishops, and people with knowledge of history and asked to be informed as to who had built the buildings of Constantinople, and who had ruled there. These people informed Sultan Mehmed, based on their own knowledge and that found in their books. From the information the entire group provided the following story emerged.

The transmitters of stories about the past recounted that God the Exalted granted the gift of prophecy to the Prophet Solomon, so that he ruled over both men and jinns. All the world's kings were submissive to him, and no place remained on the face of the world over which the Prophet Solomon did not rule. It happened that in the west in the region of the Frankish lands there was an island. That island's ruler was named Ankur. He was a great emperor—greater than any other to be found in all the west and Frankish lands. He commanded over [an army of] several hundred thousand men, and he refused to submit to anyone. He knew that the Prophet Solomon was the master of all humans and jinns, yet out of pride and a tyrannical disposition, he refused to submit to him. One day, the Prophet Solomon gathered all the people, fairies, and jinns and went to that island. The accursed Ankur confronted him and there was a mighty battle. In the end, Ankur was defeated and his army was dispersed. They captured Ankur and brought him to the Prophet Solomon—*peace be upon him*—who offered him conversion to Islam. Out of pride he refused to convert, so the Prophet Solomon ordered his head to be cut off. The island was captured and its people were subjugated. Ankur's wealth and possessions were seized and brought to Solomon—*peace be upon him*—who gifted everything to his soldiers.

When Ankur was killed, he left behind a daughter possessed of great beauty, one renowned and unequalled for her lovely appearance. The girl's name was Şemsiyye Banu. As soon as the Prophet Solomon—*peace be upon him*—saw that girl, he fell in love with her beauty and married her. Whatever that girl desired he happily granted to her. One day, Şemsiyye Hatun said to the Prophet Solomon: "Build for me a palace and lofty pavilion, the likes of which do not exist in all of Creation." So the Prophet Solomon gave orders to the humans, jinns, divs, and fairies. He told them, "Find me a place with a pleasant climate resembling heaven and build for me there a lofty palace." The divs and fairies wandered the earth, visiting the lands of the Arabs and Persians, India and Sind, Cathay and Khotan, China and Machin, the land of Turkistan, and in sum the entire East and West. Unable to find a place with an agreeable climate, they finally ended up in the land of Rum, which is also known as the land of the Greeks. There they found a place on the coast of the White Sea (Mediterranean) with a pleasant climate named Mount Aydıncık (Kyzikos). This is still known in our time; they call it a "Spectacular Place" (*Temaşalık*), and the original building is still there.

In the end, they liked that place and began building the pavilion there. The divs and fairies wandered the earth. From the marble quarries they knew about on Mount Alburz and Mount Kaf, from all the colorful marbles they found there, they cut pieces of multicolored marble, made columns, and carried them away. The eight pieces of porphyry now in Ayasofya were brought over from Mount Kaf. When people say there are no porphyry mines in other places, they mean their location is unknown to all but the divs. When the divs and fairies and humans and jinns were gathered in this way, a pavilion was constructed, the likes of which no one had ever constructed on the face of the earth, with the possible exception of Shaddad ibn Ad. Once it was complete, Şemsiyye Hatun came and settled in that pavilion. She lived there for a while. But in the end, she did not like the place, so she said to the Prophet Solomon: "Take me to Jerusalem." The Prophet Solomon loved Şemsiyye so much that he never refused her desires, so he took her to Jerusalem where she took up residence. But in fact, Şemsiyye had secretly maintained her previous religion. She had not renounced the faith of her father, and worshiped idols—unbeknownst to Solomon. When the Prophet Solomon had taken Şemsiyye to that pavilion, she had left behind a large idol, buried in the palace in Aydıncık. Solomon knew nothing of this, but eventually many bad things befell him for giving his heart to that idolatrous girl, thus abandoning his allegiance to God. [. . .]

YANKO İBN MADYAN SEEKS A LOCATION FOR A NEW CITY

After the Prophet Solomon—*peace be upon him*—departed from this world, a great many emperors came and went. Eventually, a great emperor appeared in the region of Greece, in the land of the Caesar of Rome. He was called Yanko ibn Madyan and he was one of the descendants of Ad, being of that man's lineage. He was descended from the sons of Amlak, who were sons of the son of Ad. His lineage reached Shaddad and he had even seen Shaddad himself. They say that one day, as Yanko ibn Madyan sat on the throne of Aydıncık in the palace constructed by Solomon, the statue Şemsiyye had buried there was suddenly discovered. It was an idol replete with colorful and priceless jewels, and those who saw it were left in a state of amazement. Yanko ibn Madyan said, "O viziers, what do you say? I would also like to acquire a name in this world, so that it may be remembered." So the viziers held council. Among them was a wise and virtuous vizier named Kantur. In Solomon's time, he had fought alongside him in the battle against Ankur, and he had also seen the mosque of al-Aksa constructed in the blessed Jerusalem by the Prophet Solomon. The vizier Kantur said, "O King of the World! You are the Solomon of the present age. So why don't you lay the foundations of a blessed city, so that you may be remembered in the world like Solomon. [. . .]"

Let us now return to our story. What was the reason for the construction of this city? When Yanko ibn Madyan decided to build it, he began to wonder where it should be. As he slept one night with that thought on his mind, he was told in a dream: "Construct that city you are planning to build on the coast of the strait flowing from the Black Sea to the White Sea." Then Yanko said to his viziers: "I have been shown a place that fits this description, but I do not know where it is." The viziers did not know either, so they were left in a state of bewilderment. Then, another night, Yanko was visited again in his sleep, was carried away together with his bedding, and was deposited at the location of present-day Constantinople. He was told, "That city you are planning to construct, build it here." And Yanko woke up and found himself in a strange place. He wondered if he was still dreaming and quietly closed his eyes again. Then he fell asleep again, then opened his eyes once more. He realized this was not a dream and was surprised to find himself alone on the seashore. He wandered all around until he found one of the princes of that region. He explained what had happened to him, and when that prince realized that this was Yanko ibn Madyan, he accepted him as his overlord. He carried out all the requirements of obeisance to the padishah. Horses

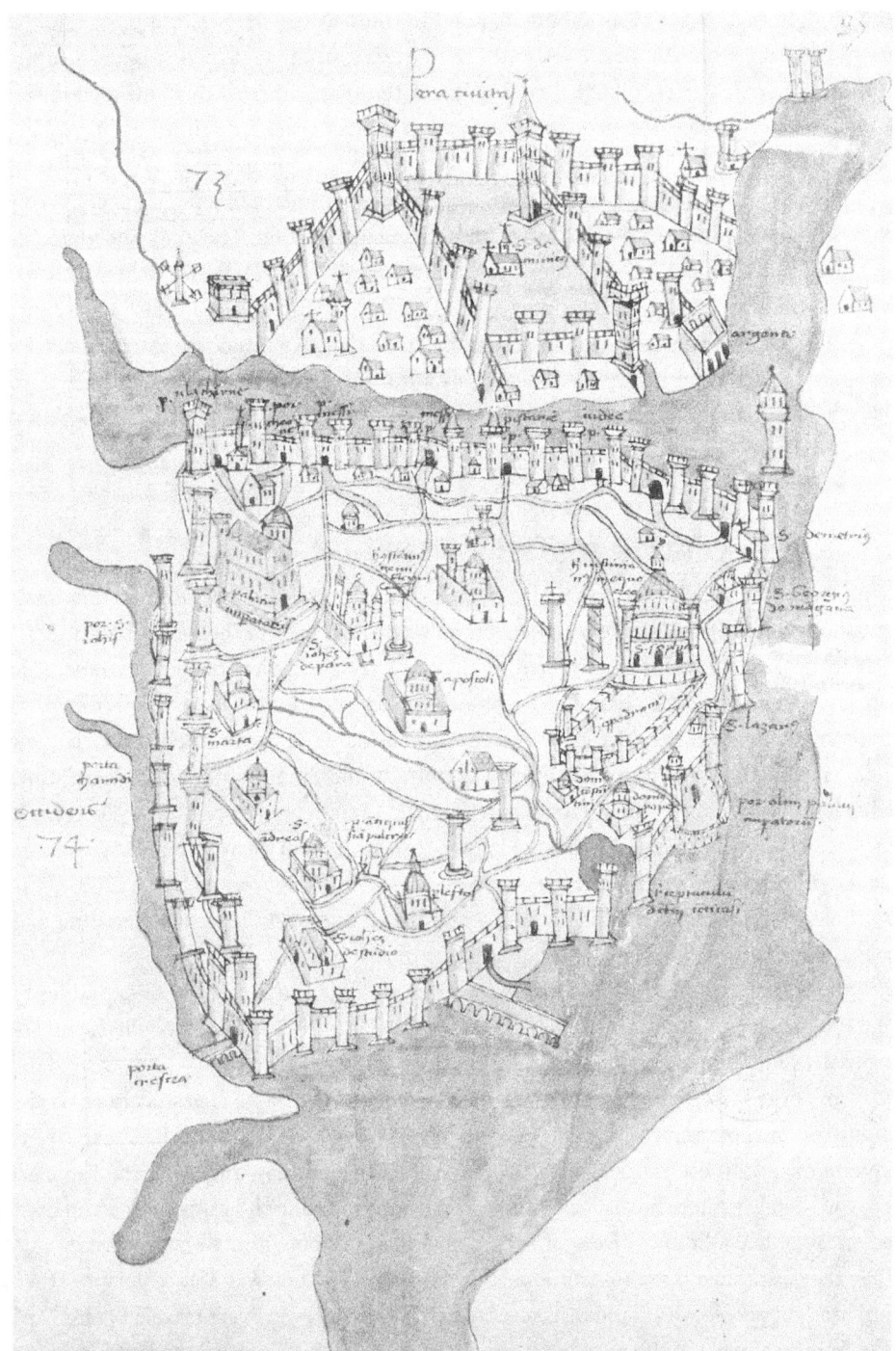

FIGURE 32. Map of pre-Ottoman Constantinople, ca. 1420s. Cristoforo Buondelmonti (cartographer), in *Liber insularum Archipelagi*, Département Cartes et plans, GE FF-9351, fol. 37a. Bibliothèque nationale de France, Paris.

were brought, the two of them mounted, and they toured the surrounding area. They saw that in the strait from the Black Sea to the White Sea a triangle-shaped space had formed whose northern part resembled a peninsula, at the place where Constantinople is now located. When he saw that place, he liked it, for it was the place he had been shown in his dream.

While the padishah was thus engaged, back in the other place the members of his court got up in the morning and did not find him in his usual location. The lords and viziers did not know what had happened to the padishah, for they sought him everywhere and were unable to find him. They sent out men to look for him, but he was nowhere to be found. While they were engaged in this investigation, suddenly news came that the padishah had been found in such and such place. The vizier Kantur set out, went there, and found the padishah, who explained to him the situation. He said, "It has been indicated to us that we should build here a city." And the vizier said, "To hear is to obey."

CONSTRUCTION OF THE CITY BEGINS

So they set out to build a city in that place. Having taken a liking to that location, they busied themselves with the city's construction. Yanko sent emissaries to the lords of all places, to all countries and all padishahs, informing them: "This is what has happened to me. It has been indicated to me that I should build a city. Now, as a token of your friendship, you should also attend to the matter by sending me builders and workmen from your own lands." The matter was discussed all the way in India and Sind, Cathay and Khotan, China and Machin, the lands of the Bulghars and Kipchaks, and in the steppe lands. When the letters reached Hungary, Muscovy, and the lands of the Franks, all the way to the Maghreb, and also the province of Abyssinia, all the way to Mecca, Medina, Egypt, and Syria, the lords and padishahs of those provinces and nations sent builders and workmen, each according to his means. Then they started to construct buildings in that place.

They began by digging a trench, excavating an area equal to forty ells. Suddenly a demonic cupola appeared, whose circumference and height were of forty ells each. They eventually found its door and opened it. There was nothing alive inside, but what should they see? In five places, there were groups of seven [stone] vultures. These vultures had no heads. And in another piece, six magnetic stones in the shape of vultures had been covered in diamonds. All these were standing under the dome, and the vultures in the five places were completely without heads. And of the six vultures in the sixth group, five had no heads, and only one had a head. In front of each was an inscription with its history written on it. When they examined these inscriptions, they found that no one was able to decipher them. They brought people who could read seventy-two languages, who were unable to read them. Wise men, the sages of the age who were among the disciples of Plato and had even seen Plato himself, were unable to decipher them. [. . .]

Every thousand years, that people (i.e., the first people created by God) would come and make a vulture and place it within that dome. When a thousand years would elapse, they would cut off its head and take it away, make another vulture, and place that too within the dome. When yet another thousand years would elapse, they would cut off this vulture's head, too, and would place a [third] one there. In this manner, they placed one vulture there every thousand years. With the completion of seven thousand years, out of the seventh group of vultures the heads were gone from six of them, and only one vulture still had its head in place. From this they knew that the peoples that had existed [before] were six, and they counted the years that had elapsed between then and now, which amounted to 4424 years. But they had no way of knowing about the time before that—namely, how many years had elapsed since the creation of the world. For no one knows that apart from God: *And only God knows that which is hidden.* And that is also why our master Yunus Emre has said:

The world was filled six times
And the seventh time came Adam

Thus they came to understand the significance of what was within that dome: that apart from God the Exalted, everything else that exists will come to an end; and only God will remain, for He does not come to an end and is everlasting.

A PORTENT FOR THE CITY

But let us return to our previous story. After Yanko ibn Madyan spent seven years arranging for the preparation of stone, mortar, and everything else that was needed to construct the city, in the eighth year he gathered armies from all corners of the earth. He prepared the men sent by the padishahs and lords of all lands each according to his means, as well as the army under his own command, which amounted to forty times one hundred thousand men (i.e., four million). Then forty thousand builders and two hundred thousand workmen were standing ready to lay the foundations of the city walls. But according to the assertions of the astrologers, there was a time that came only once in every thirty years. So they were waiting for that hour. Within the city walls, he had pillars like minarets built, on top of which they hung bells so that when that hour arrived, they would ring them, and all at once the builders would lay the foundations that very moment. So the master craftsmen and astrologers were all awaiting that hour, equipped with astrolabes.

The hour had not yet arrived, when one Saturday at the hour of Mars, by celestial judgment and divine ordinance, it came to pass as follows: (No one can stand in the way of God's work, for no matter what plans the wretched sons of Adam make, He prevents them). Out of the blue, in the sky overhead, a stork that was carrying a snake was passing, and out of its pain the snake hit one of those bells and struck it with its tail. Then the bell rang, and when everyone heard it, they thought the time had arrived and started ringing all the other bells. All at once, all the masons and workmen thought the time had arrived, so they rushed forth and laid the foundations. Witnessing this situation, at the risk of their own lives, the astrologers came before the ruler and started lamenting: "The time has not yet arrived!"

But what could the emperor do? It had already come to pass. Predestination had ordained that things happen that way, and like it or not, they didn't find it in their heart to demolish that edifice once they had begun its construction. So they began to build. As for the emperor, he became most dejected, for he understood that it was the fate of the city to go from prosperity to ruin.

THIRTY-NINE

On the Construction of the Pyramids, ca. 1545

Celalzade Salih, d. 1565

TRANSLATED BY GIANCARLO CASALE

Until well into his middle years, Celalzade Salih (d. 1565) lived a comfortable yet circumscribed life as an elite Ottoman scholar. The younger brother of the Ottoman grand chancellor Celalzade Mustafa (d. 1567), Salih was groomed for success from an early age; he apprenticed with the celebrated grand mufti Kemalpaşazade (d. 1534), then began a rapid rise up the Ottoman scholarly hierarchy. By 1536 (still probably in his early forties), he was appointed to the medrese of the Eight Courtyards (Sahn-i Seman), Istanbul's highest-ranking teaching college at the time. A few years later, in 1542, he moved to the equally prestigious imperial medrese of Sultan Bayezid in Edirne.

Salih's career took a dramatic and unexpected turn when he was asked in 1544 to give up his academic position and travel to Egypt. There, he was to investigate the outgoing governor, Davud Pasha, for misuse of government funds—a distasteful task that Salih accepted much against his will. The trip to Egypt turned out to be a life-changing experience, exposing Salih to a distant corner of the empire. The result was a partly autobiographical book he wrote after his return to the capital the following year, the *New History of Egypt* (*Tarih-i Mısr-ı Cedid*), from which the excerpts below are drawn.

In fact, we know of several Ottoman scholars from Istanbul who cycled through Egypt on various administrative assignments in the middle decades of the sixteenth century. Some returned to Istanbul transformed by its learned culture; producing, in the process, hundreds of works based on the texts they encountered during their travels. Nevertheless, at least two elements of Salih's writing are noteworthy. The first is his particular fascination with Egypt's distant pagan past rather than its more recent history as a center of Islamic learning—notably, the vast majority of his text deals with the history of Egypt before the Muslim conquest. Just as remarkable, in writing about this pagan past, Salih openly associates it with magic, star worship, and other forms of occult knowledge, yet with very little indication that, as a Muslim jurist, he saw these subjects as problematic.

In both of these respects, Salih's *New History of Egypt* thus presents striking parallels with the writings of Renaissance humanists of the contemporary Latin West, scholars similarly fascinated by the cultural world of pagan antiquity—including Hermetic magic, astrology, and other occult sciences. But to what extent were such interests, and such a benevolent attitude toward Egypt's pagan heritage, shared by Salih's Ottoman peers? This is a complicated question to answer, in part because his *New History* is not completely original: instead, entire sections are more or less direct translations into Ottoman Turkish from the fourteenth-century Mamluk historian al-Maqrizi's *Book of Exhortations and Considerations in the Description of Territories and Monuments* (*Kitab al-Mawaiz wa'l-I'tibar bi-Dhikri'l-Khitat wa'l-Athar*).

In a sense, this too presents a parallel to the history of the European Renaissance, which at its heart was a great translation movement from Greek and Latin into the vernaculars of early modern Europe. As such, one of the most important lessons of Renaissance history is that translation itself is a creative process, which needs to be understood from the perspective of why, under what circumstances, and to whom, certain kinds of lesser-known texts could be rediscovered and given new meaning. Salih clearly does this in the passages below, by combining a description of his own sense of wonder at seeing the great pyramids with translations from a medieval predecessor who apparently shared a similar attitude toward their meaning. And against this background, it is worth noting that at least a dozen copies of Celalzade Salih's *New History of Egypt* survive today from the sixteenth and early seventeenth centuries—clear evidence that Celalzade Salih was by no means the only Ottoman scholar with a fascination for the magical world of pre-Islamic Egypt.

LANGUAGE: Turkish. Archaic plain prose with short sentences, including some obsolete Turkish vocabulary and grammatical structures.

SOURCE: Manuscripts: Süleymaniye Kütüphanesi, Istanbul, Husrev Paşa 354 and Süleymaniye Kütüphanesi, Istanbul, Halet Efendi 190. Transcription: Bülbül, Tuncay, ed. *Mensur Bir Hikâye: Tarih-i Mısr-ı Cedîd: İnceleme-Metin* / [Sâlih Çelebi]. Ankara: Grafiker Yayınları, 2011 (67–69, 272–93).

SALİH ARRIVES IN CAIRO

Finally, we arrived in the city of Cairo. Here I saw that it is a great city for world-travelers that truly confirms the saying, "Cairo is the world." Yet its doors and its walls, its alleyways and its marketplaces are all falling in ruins, overwhelmed by dust and sand and with owl nests filling every cranny. It is an old city that has aged over the course of time, and its houses, which are its limbs, are falling apart. Each of those doors and walls has become a tongue,

FIGURE 33. Pyramids of Giza, Egypt, seventeenth century. Johann Christoph Wagner, *Delineatio Provinciarum Pannoniae et Imperii Turcici in Oriente* (Augsburg: J. Koppmayer, 1684), 112–13.

speaking in its own language of so many past ages and epochs. Once upon a time it was a well-maintained city on the banks of the Nile, along the flood barriers, a place like heaven, one of its kind in its time. But [now] it looks like a caravanserai in which many travelers have stayed; or a nest from which many birds have emerged; or a house that has passed through many hands; or a cruel beloved who coquettishly laughs in the face of many pleasure seekers. I completely and utterly understood all its past adventures and stories. I saw that both within and beyond its walls the city was full of wondrous buildings and overflowing with marvels of the past. And from those monuments that have since become covered with sand and dust—I heard many stories! And at its abandoned places—I noticed the traces of many vanished peoples!

Best of all, just outside the city, I visited the world-famous great pyramids, which no one gazes on without for a time losing himself in bewilderment and astonishment. I saw that each one is a structure that narrates the events of [a period as long as] a thousand lives of Noah. [The pyramids] appear as old as the eternal time and as having been built at the same time as the heavens. Their sight made a thousand times a thousand impressions on me, and I stood before them completely awestruck for a time. Then my mind turned to the intentions and ambitions of the people [who made them], who with such zeal had gone to such lengths and had exerted themselves so much. I wondered, "Who were they? What rulers could build such monuments?" My mind was spontaneously seized with the desire and my heart with the passion to find the history books and to learn in detail about the following: the history of the king[s] of Egypt and the epoch that passed after them; who settled here before humans; who was the first to build these monuments? And subsequently, who were the pharaohs, the Amalekites, the Caesars, and the Cyruses who ruled in that place? What were the origins of the emperors who reigned this land one after the other? What existed in this area previously and after? Who made [the pyramids]; which rulers ordered them built? [. . .] In addition to what I found in the writings of these scholars, both ancient and more recent, regarding the events and monuments of Egypt, I have added a few more pages containing a different kind of information. Although in many cases people may object to their contents, deeming them improbable or openly dismissing them as lies and fabrications, in truth these are things related to talismans and magic, both of which are true sciences. For magic involves the use of certain charms, processes, and arts in a manner known to practitioners, and whose truth is attested in ancient writings. [. . .]

THE PYRAMIDS

In the land of Egypt, there are a great many pyramids, especially in the district of Abusir. Some of them are large, others small. Some are made of stone and others of masonry, but most are of stone. Some have stepped sides, while others are smooth-edged. All have a flat, square base from which the sides come together into a point as they go up. Originally, there were many small pyramids across from the city of Cairo in the desert of Giza. When Sultan Salahuddin Yusuf bin Ayyub (i.e., Saladin, d. 1193) was ruler of Egypt, he had a lieutenant, a lord who went by the name of Karakuş. On the sultan's orders, he dismantled them, and used the stone to build the fortress of Cairo that still stands today, as well as the ramparts surrounding the city and the stone bridges in Giza.

The largest of the pyramids, which are famous throughout the world and most astonishing to man, are the three pyramids that now still stand immediately across from the old city of Cairo, each of which from afar looks like a great mountain. Two in particular are larger than the third. Exactly when they were made, by whom, and for what purpose, is a subject of disagreement among historians, who have said many contradictory things on the subject. Most often they are attributed to Shaddad ibn Ad, saying he is the one who made them. But the Copts deny this, saying "Because of the strength of our magic, the people of Ad never set foot in the land of Egypt. Rather, the one who constructed them was Surid—son of Shahluq, son of Shiryaq, son of Tumidun, son of Tedresan, son of Husal—who in the times before the Great Flood resided in the city of Memphis (*Emsus*), which is what they call ancient Cairo nowadays.

ON THE REASONS FOR BUILDING THE GREAT PYRAMIDS OF GIZA

The reason King Surid had them built was that three hundred years before the Great Flood, he had a dream in which he saw the earth raised up from below and overturned on top of his people. The people scrambled to escape crawling on the ground, and the stars no longer stayed in the sky, but rather rained down, hitting some of the people as they fell, who made terrifying sounds [as they were crushed]. The king kept his vision secret from the people but, having seen it, he knew for certain that something terrible would happen on earth. Sometime later, he had another dream. The fixed stars again fell from the sky like white birds, as if they were attacking the people. Then they forced the people into a narrow pass between two mountains. The mountains closed in over the people and the stars froze and went dark.

Surid awoke in terror, and in accordance with [his people's] foolish customs, he went to the statue of the sun. Humbling himself before it and pressing his face into the ground, he wept pitifully. Then, when morning broke, he summoned the soothsayers one by one from all corners of Egypt, 130 great soothsayers in all, and held a private consultation with them, revealing everything that he had seen in his dream. They all agreed that it was a highly important matter, and the greatest of them, whom they called Magician Qalimun, spoke as follows: "The visions of rulers are not to be taken lightly. Just as rulers themselves have great power, their dreams are guideposts to matters of the greatest import. So let me now relate to Your Highness my own dream, of which I have until now never spoken, although I had it a year ago. In my dream, o my King, I was in the city of Memphis, sitting together with you at the top of the city tower. Suddenly, we saw the sky separating from its place, falling down on top of us. Once it came down close to us, it took us inside of it, as if it were a great dome. You had lifted up your hands [as if you were holding up the sky]. At this moment, I saw stars falling down on us, moving around us in many different shapes, and saw the people crowding around your palace, crying out, and begging you to help them. You kept lifting your hands up, and holding it at the level of your head, and said to me 'You too, push up like this!' We were both terrified. Then we saw a door opening in the sky, and a light emerging from it—the sun, as it rose around us. We begged the sun for help, and it addressed us, saying 'Fear not! The sky will return to its place.' Then I awoke in fright but fell asleep once again. This time, I saw the city of Memphis with all its people turned upside down, and all of our idols falling from their places and crumbling to pieces. Then I saw many men coming down from the sky, carrying cudgels, and beating the people with them. 'Why do you do this?' I asked. 'Because the people have become unbelievers,' they said. 'They no longer worship their gods, but instead worship others.' I said, 'Will none of them be saved?' They said, 'Of course, those who want to be saved must reach the owner of the Ark.' Then I awoke in fright."

Having heard this, King Surid turned to his soothsayers and said, "Come and consult the stars. Let us see what events they foretell." They did as he asked. After long and careful deliberations, they agreed that a great flood was preordained. Then they said, "There is a fire growing out of the constellation of Leo, it will burn the whole world." "Look again. Will this calamity also afflict our land?" the king asked. "It will," they said, "the water will overwhelm most of our country, and the Land of Egypt will be submerged for many years." "Look again," the King said. "Will the waters then recede, or will Egypt stay submerged forever?" "No," they said, "they will recede, and the land will once more be prosper as before." "Then what will happen?" asked the king. "A king will come against Egypt, kill its people, and take its wealth." "Then what?" the king asked. "A people will come up the Nile, and will rule the greater part of Egypt," they said. "Then what will happen?" asked the king. "The waters of the Nile will run dry, and no people will be left in the land of Egypt," they said. All of this they foretold through the guidance of the stars.

ON THE MANNER OF BUILDING THE GREAT PYRAMIDS

Once King Surid had obtained these answers from the soothsayers, he immediately ordered the construction of the pyramids. First, he commanded that huge blocks be quarried and great marble slabs sculpted from stone. He ordered lead brought from the lands of the Maghreb, and huge black stones from the region of Aswan. The largest blocks of stone were cut, sculpted, shaped, and surfaced where they stood, and were then brought in finished form to the construction site of the pyramids, ready to be placed directly into their structure. Those who undertook this task held a sheet of paper in their hands with some writings on it. They would tap the sheet on the stones they wanted to move, and whichever one they tapped, this stone would immediately jump from its place and fly a distance of one hundred arrow shots in the direction of the pyramid that was to be built with it, before falling to the ground. Tapping the paper on the stone again, it would once more jump into the air as before, and fall down again, and in this way, it was transported as far as they wished. They moved the stones by means of these spells and incantations, for as anyone knows who has seen the huge stones out of which the pyramids are made, without such a cause there is no possibility that these stones could have been moved from one place to another. Whatever artifice you might employ to do so, they are simply not stones that can be moved by animal power.

Then, once all the tools and supplies had been made ready, and all the stones had been brought each to their places as described, King Surid ordered that construction commence on the three great pyramids mentioned previously, one being the Eastern Pyramid, one being the Western Pyramid, and one being the Colored Pyramid. They were constructed as follows: First, a slab was brought into its place and laid down flat. Then, they would grind out round holes in the shape of mill stones in the top of the slab, and into these holes they would screw strong, thick iron clamps. Then, they would bring another slab into place with perfectly parallel holes ground into the bottom, and line it up with the holes below. In this way, the iron clamps in the lower holes would slide into the holes in the upper slab, bringing the two stones together and sealing them tightly. Then they would pour abundant quantities of lead into the holes and all around the stones. By filling the holes with lead, they locked together the stones as tightly as could be.

Once they had made the base of all three pyramids in this way, they then built a door for each one some forty ells beneath the earth. In the Eastern Pyramid, this door was placed below ground one hundred ells below the middle of the wall facing the east. In the Western Pyramid, this door was placed below ground one hundred ells below the middle of the wall facing the west. Similarly, in the Colored Pyramid, this door was placed below ground one hundred ells beneath the middle of the wall facing the south. All of these doors were secret, and anyone hoping to reach them would first have to dig underground to the distance described above, to get to the construction and then get through the door.

The total height of each of these pyramids from ground level to summit was one hundred ells measured in royal cubits, which measures five hundred ells of our modern cubits (ca. twenty meters). The length of each slant height was one hundred royal cubits. Going upward, they brought all sides, opposite to each other, together. For the parts closer to the summit they didn't use clamps. They made the top section narrower, and at the summit, they built a platform with an area approximately large enough for about eight camels to sit down together.

According to King Surid's orders, all the lords of the realm had consulted together and chosen an appropriate time for laying the foundation of each of the pyramids. When all three pyramids were completed according to their wish, they rested from the construction work. [Then, the king] ordered to cover each of the pyramids incomparably from top to bottom in the manner of the Kaaba with colorful and finely woven shrouds and sent word throughout the kingdom that a great festival was to be held. All the people of the realm appeared, strolling around the pyramids, tossing coins and little gifts on them, and feasting, eating, and drinking at the foot of the pyramids for many days.

ON WHAT WAS PLACED IN THE PYRAMIDS

Then, King Surid commanded that the thirty great treasure chambers—which they had built in the Western Pyramid of the hardest, colored stones—be filled to the brim with the wealth of the pharaohs: images and utensils encrusted with rare jewels, sumptuous iron implements, iron weapons with indelible blades, bendable yet unbreakable artistically fashioned crystal objects, all manner of strange talismans, and thousands of exotic drugs from India and beyond of the kind they call "medicinal herbs," and from these drugs every manner of mixed remedies as well as deadly poisons, and many other kinds of products besides all of these.

Then they had domes made in the form of the celestial sphere and decorated with stars. They did this because—according to their foolish beliefs—they thought that by worshipping these [stars], as well as the images their forefathers and ancestors had made, they brought themselves closer to the stars. In addition to these, Surid ordered to record and collect all the wondrous and strange tasks that the experts of the astral sciences had performed up to his own time, in order to know and date what has happened in the world at certain times owing to the condition of the fixed stars and the rotation of the celestial spheres, and what had happened until this time, and who would rule Egypt until the end of the world; as well as all the vessels filled with liquids that could provide a thousand benefits, and many other objects like these. Once they had brought everything, they placed it in the Eastern Pyramid.

Then he ordered that all the bodies of rulers of the past be placed in marble sarcophagi, and that all the corpses of the famous soothsayers of the past be placed in black granite coffins. Each of these soothsayers had a book of his own, in which was recorded the marvelous deeds and occult arts he had performed in his time, as well as his life and appearance, and the great events that had taken place up to his age, and his predictions about what was to come until the end of times. Each of these books was placed together with its owner's body in the appropriate coffin, and then all of them were brought together and placed in order inside the third, the Colored Pyramid, each according to his rank.

Then, on the walls inside the Colored Pyramid, they erected all manner of idols, each in the form of a different kind of [occult] master, and each armed with a talisman. All of them performed in their place their own craft with their hands, so that a person could learn [their craft] by looking at them. Then, in the spaces still left empty along the walls, they also wrote in detail an account of each craft, explaining how it was carried out and what kind of tools and materials were needed. All of this was written down, such that the walls, the doors, and even the ceiling were completely covered. Together, these writings preserved the knowledge of all the most difficult arts pursued by the people of Egypt, including spells, talismans, incantations, engineering, astronomy, alchemy, and natural magic. All these were written down and represented in images, such that none of the sciences or the occult arts of any kind were left out. Alongside these, they placed inside the pyramid all the wealth that they had offered in their worship of the stars, as well as all the wealth of the soothsayers, which is beyond reckoning and whose limits are known only to the most blessed and almighty God, no one else. Then they sealed its entrance with a talisman.

The talisman of the Western Pyramid was made of hard onyx stone, cut from carnelian mines in Yemen. Out of this, they made an idol that stood guard before the door, holding in his hand a weapon like a rod or javelin. Nearby, at a place by his head, they made a snake, lying in a curled-up position. If anyone from outside tried to enter the pyramid to take something, that snake would immediately jump from its place and wrap itself around the person's neck, strangling him to death. Then it would go back to its place, curl up, and lie back down. The talisman of the Eastern Pyramid, meanwhile, was an idol made of a variegated onyx in black and white. It had two luminous open eyes and was sitting on a chair, and it held a rod-shaped weapon. Whenever anyone looked at it, he would hear a terrifying scream from that side that would instantly burst his heart, such that he would fall flat on his face, dead. The third talisman, inside the walls of the Colored Pyramid, was a tiny idol they made of the [magical] eaglestone (*beht*). Anyone who looked at it would suddenly find himself drawn toward it, and then be stuck to its surface, unable to separate himself until he was dead. After making these talismans, they also filled each of these idols with jinns, whom they assigned the task of guarding and protecting them. Then they made countless sacrifices to them and burned incense, so that no one else but the ones who knew the way would ever come across these doors or open their talismans. [. . .]

ON LATER ATTEMPTS TO EXPLORE THE PYRAMIDS

There is still another story, according to which yet another group of people once entered one of the pyramids and descended all the way to its lowest point, exploring throughout its interior. Then they came across a path. This they followed until they entered a place in the shape of a large cistern, with just a bit of water collecting in it, and then flowing out again. They had no idea why that was so. They continued and came to another place in the shape of a house with square walls. They looked closely and saw that the walls were made entirely of tiny square stones, each one of which was beautiful and perfectly made. One of them pulled one of those stones out of the wall and put it in his mouth. Suddenly, he felt a loud buzzing in his ears, which almost made him deaf, but he waited a bit and was able to bear it, resisting the urge to take it out and throw it away.

Then they continued further and came to a place like a great cavern. They looked and saw an endless quantity of gold coins. They estimated that each gold coin weighed about thousand miskals (ca. 4,250 grams). So, they took some gold coins, but once they did, they were no longer able to move from their place. Having no other choice, they put [all the coins] back and were once more able to continue on their way. They walked still further, and came to a place like a huge hall, with the image of an old man made of green stone. Placed in front of him was a whole line of small figures in the form of little boys reading something, as if the old man were teaching them. Here as well there were valuable objects, some of which they took. But as before, they were frozen in place as soon as they did so, unable to move. So they had no choice but to put them back and continue.

Then they came to a house with a sealed door, and frightening sounds of fighting and shrieking coming from inside. They continued on without inspecting it further. Then they entered a square house. Inside, they saw a green column with the figure of a bejeweled rooster perched on top, its two eyes burning like lamp wicks and illuminating the entire inside of the room. When they came close, it let out a terrifying call and beat its wings, so they hurried by in fear. Then they came to an idol made of white stone, in the form of an upside-down woman. She was flanked by a pair of stone lions, one on each side, which looked as if they wanted to swallow her. They were terrified by this, and to protect themselves from its evil they began to recite incantations. Eventually, their faces and eyes grew accustomed to the sight of it. They continued on, and before them a light appeared. They went toward it, and came to the opening of a hole, with a door decorated with two stone figures, each holding a weapon like a lance. They went through that opening, and beyond was the outside world, and a straight path leading away. So they followed the path, walking an entire day, until it eventually brought them back from outside to the base of the pyramid they had first seen. Then they dispersed, each going back to his own home and telling what he had seen to whomever they reached, and word spread throughout the land.

This happened during the time of Yazid bin Abdulmalik, who ruled Egypt. They reported to him about this, and he had those people [who undertook the journey] brought to him and questioned them. They told him everything as recorded above, and he had men sent back with them to the same place. But no matter how much they searched, they could not find the hole they had emerged from. They kept searching all around for many days but could not identify where it might be. Then, the member of the group that had kept the stone in his mouth took it out and saw that it was a beautiful and precious jewel. He sold it for a great sum, and from a pauper he was transformed into rich man. [. . .]

THE SPHINX

As has already been mentioned above, standing between the two great pyramids of Giza is a great stone idol. This was previously known in Egypt by the name of Belhaib, but now the Egyptians call it Abu'l-Haul. This too is one of the wonders of the age. Except for its neck and head, which rise up from the ground, its other members are not visible. They say its trunk is below ground. Some say that it is a talisman built to keep the plains of Giza, where most of the productive fields in Egypt are, from being overwhelmed with the sands of the desert. Its head is extraordinarily large, appearing like a giant dome rising from its resting place on the ground. Judging by its head, the length of its body must be seventy cubits or maybe more.

Its form was in no way impaired, with signs of redness in its face and its mouth that gave it a look of delicate youth and freshness. It had, altogether, a face that was beautifully formed in the extreme and that seemed to smile directly back at the one looking at it. Indeed, when master connoisseurs, who had traveled all over the world, were asked "What are the world's greatest marvels that you have seen?" they answered, "I have seen the sphinx in Egypt, each of whose features is perfectly composed in relation to the other. Its eyes, its mouth, its ears, its nose, and the other elements of its face are all arranged in such a way that they fit together without even the tiniest imperfection."

Today, the idol of the sphinx still stands. But in the year 780 of the Hijra (1378–79), there was a deranged Sufi in Cairo, a man they called Sheikh Muhammad, who was a member of the convent of Salahiyye. He was a man of extremely austere piety, and whenever he found something objectionable, he destroyed it—without exception, and without any regard for the authority of beys or pashas. That Sufi came before the idol of Abu'l-Haul and smashed its face and eyes, damaging its form. When he did so, many places in the region of Giza were overwhelmed with sand and turned into wasteland. The people of that district knew that it was because of the damage done to the sphinx's face because of that Sufi's act of vandalism.

FORTY

An Ode to Istanbul

Eremia Keomurchean Çelebi, d. 1695

TRANSLATED BY HENRY SHAPIRO

Eremia Keomurchean (Kömürciyan) was a prolific Armenian author and intellectual born in 1637 in the Langa neighborhood of Istanbul. He was the grandson of a refugee from the Celali rebellions in eastern Anatolia, the son of a priest born in the midst of migration, and the grandnephew of one of Istanbul's wealthiest Armenian merchants of the seventeenth century. Although Eremia began a clerical education, he ultimately did not follow in his father's and two brothers' footsteps to become a priest. He led a life of scholarly leisure, supported by the patronage of wealthy Armenians. Eremia wrote over fifty works of history, poetry, geography, theology, translation, and epistles in Armenian or Armeno-Turkish (Turkish written in the Armenian alphabet), many of which remain unpublished and unstudied to this day (this is true particularly for those texts written in Armeno-Turkish).

The "Ode to Istanbul," a poem of more than two thousand verses, is a guide to and description of the city. Eremia has a plan and a specific route; he wrote the work at the request of an Armenian *vartabed* (a person occupying a learned rank in the Armenian ecclesiastical hierarchy)—Vartan (d. 1704 or 1705) of the Amrdol Monastery in Bitlis, a city in eastern Anatolia. The work is also dedicated to Vartan. Such an excursion might have never taken place, but the text is constructed as the transcript, as it were, of a guided tour given by Eremia to the vartabed Vartan; several times in the text the author addresses his guest as if he is conversing with him during the tour.

Eremia describes the sites he sees on a trip—mostly on a boat along the shores of the city. The author's gaze is masterfully deployed as a camera that sweeps from one location to the next. He sometimes focuses on a neighborhood as seen from the boat, but he again and again turns the camera away from the shore and depicts what is visible from afar. The tour starts from the Seven Towers on the western walls of the city, then takes the reader from one gate of the

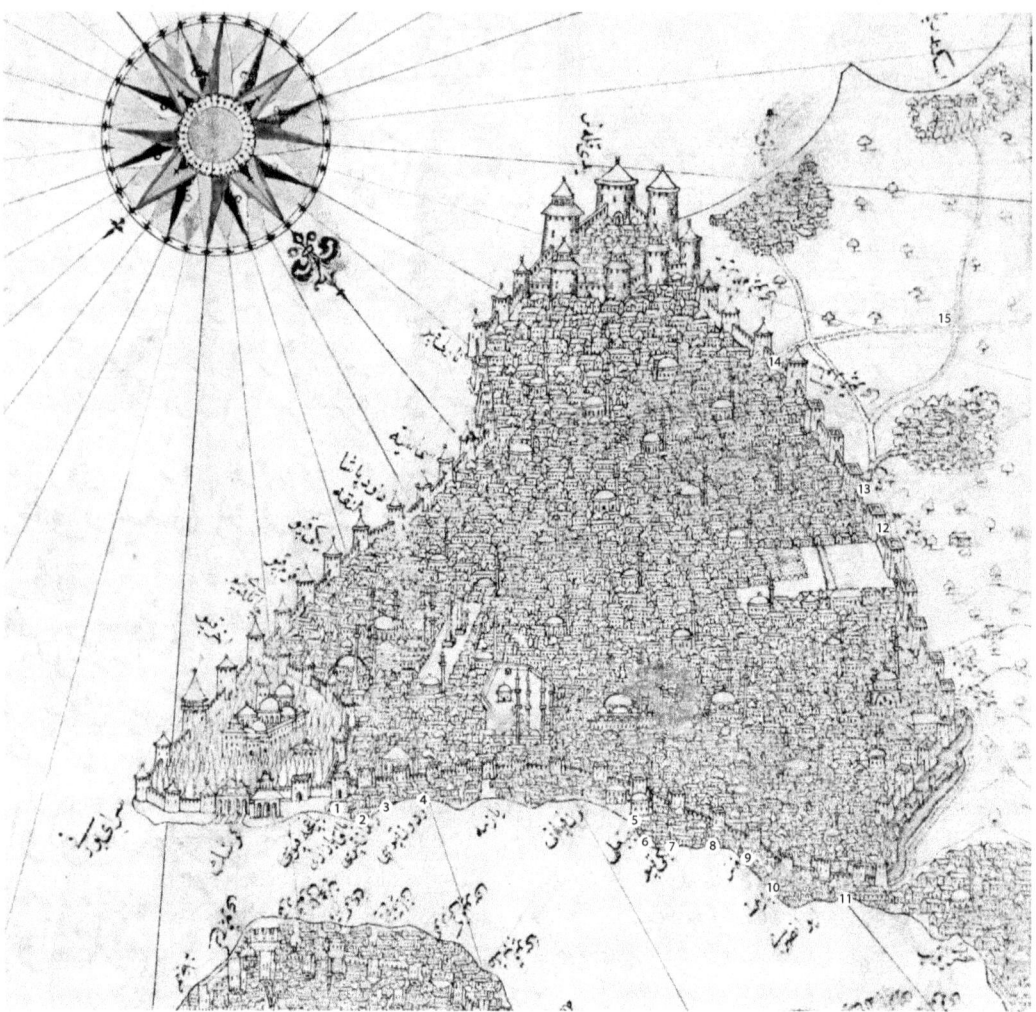

FIGURE 34. Map of Istanbul (view from north), seventeenth century (the numbers on the map correspond to Eremia Keomurchean's excursion). After Piri Reis's (d. 1553) *Kitab-ı Bahriyye*. This copy: Walters Ms. W.658, fol. 370b. The Walters Art Museum, Baltimore.

city walls to the next along the Marmara Sea shoreline. Thereafter, the boat turns the peninsula, on which the Imperial Palace is located, toward the Golden Horn. They move to the inner parts of the inlet, then disembark and mount horses to journey by land and make a full circle of the city walls. Subsequently, the tour continues into the inner sections of the Golden Horn before turning back. After describing Galata and Beyoğlu, they leave the Golden Horn and ride along the western shores of the Bosphorus toward the north. The journey then crosses to the eastern shores, moves south, exits the Bosphorus, and makes its final stop at the Princes' Islands.

As an Istanbulian overwhelmed by the abundance of the city's beauties, Eremia concludes the ode with an apology for what he could not include in this rather short work, and then takes

FIGURE 35. Map of Istanbul (view from east), sixteenth century. Giovanni Andrea di Vavassore (engraver), in *Byzantivm sive Costantineopolis,* woodcut (ca. 1530s).

the opportunity to mention a few more locations. Eremia's work is invaluable for anyone interested in Istanbul's urban, architectural, and cultural history. Thanks to Eremia we are able to imagine sites within the bustle of seventeenth-century Istanbul. The author does not limit his discussion to famed mosques, palaces, and churches, but also describes tombs, Romani people, saints, urban craftsmen, ceremonies, and the religious and linguistic diversity that characterized early modern Istanbul. He also provides information about the famous personalities of various districts.

Eremia's use of language implies that he assumed his audience to be bilingual in Armenian and Turkish. Though it is likely that many Istanbul Armenians of the seventeenth century learned Turkish on the streets of the city, Eremia noted in his diary that he formally began to study literary Ottoman Turkish at the age of nineteen. Eremia was likely exceptional by the standards of Armenians of his time period in his capacity to read Ottoman Turkish historical texts. The autograph copy of the work is preserved in the manuscript library of the Saint James monastery in Jerusalem.

LANGUAGE: Classical Armenian (*Grapar*) mixed with colloquial language, abundantly interspersed with Turkish terms (transliterated in the translation), Persian, Arabic, and Greek words, and technical terminology. At times, a complete hemistich or verse written in Armeno-Turkish.

SOURCE: T'orkomean, Vahram H., ed. *Stampoloy patmut'un* / Eremia Keomurchean. Vol. 1. Vienna: Mkhit'arean tparan, 1913 (30–50). Translated into Turkish by Hrand D. Andreasyan. Edited by Kevork Pamukciyan. *İstanbul Tarihi: XVII. Asırda İstanbul*. Istanbul: Eren Yayıncılık ve Kitapçılık, 1988 (14–23).

---

1. EMİNÖNÜ, THE CUSTOMS DEPARTMENT

Here [the place] is called Eminogi (Eminönü)
   the storeroom of the customs house.
The superintendent of the customs is based here,
   [and] in the *meydan* (square) is a throng of [people], coming and going.
He's called the *gömrük emini* (superintendent of the customs),
   the one who the king appointed as *vekil* (deputy).
[Goods] brought from every country,
   here they are loaded, and from here they are taken away.
Wide-ranging [are] the merchants [who deal in]
   precious stones and *gumaş* (fabrics),
iron, lead, and tin,
   dye and leather, cotton and flax.
Big *fuçi* (barrels) of honey,
   are seen full in the meydan (square),
[And] from the Don, the Pontus,
   and the [land of] the Huns [Crimea] immense [supplies of] oil.
Here is [also] the *pencig emini* (slave-tax collector),
   they sit for the sake of the money from slaves,
some [of whom] are in sorrows of torment,
   while others—the beautiful ones—are in [a state of] opulence. [. . .]

2. BALIK PAZARI, THE FISH MARKET

The ninth gate of the city,
   is called Balıkpazar (fish market).
There are three *isgele* (quays) here,
   Some [boats] go to the other side, while others go to other villages.
Although in Galata
   there are many fish *tükyan* (shops) and sellers,

This place was named [the "fish market" (Balıkpazar)],
   [because] they bring [the fish] for sale to the residents.
With hundreds of species and names,
   in the terminology of the Turks and in the Greek *lisan* (language),
As if you were looking at flowers,
   multicolored in a valley in springtime.
Opposite of the [Balıkpazar] gate is the gate of the [covered] market,
   called Mısri [Egyptian] or Yeni (New) [Gate].
There are many *karagir* shops (made of stone),
   in an edifice with lead-plated domes,
Filled with *bahar* (spices) and *alat* (tools)
   with all the good things of Egypt. [. . .]
The *isgele* (quays) [bound for] Hasköy and Balat
   are [places] of crossing and returning,
[Here are] Jewish *kasab* (butchers) and fruit sellers,
   and [about] a hundred Jewish households.
Ahead on two sides,
   are shops for hide *kundura* (shoes).
Even [farther] ahead jugs and *kyase* (bowls),
   multicolored and gilded.
Here is the *beylik anbar* (state-owned storehouse) for barley,
   And [here] sits the *arpa emini* (superintendent for barley).
[Here] are *kayig* (boats) going to
   Mihaliç, Bandırma, and İzmir.
[Here are] marble stones,
   columns, *ocakh* (hearths), and tombstones.
There are many shops filled with
   vats and platters, black tar and rope.
Fine salt [as big as] hazelnuts
   or walnuts [comes from] Ahyolu and Kefe.
From the Vlachs there comes a piece [of salt],
   [so big] that they carry it on a horse.
It's called Hasır (rush mat) Quay,
   and here are the Egyptian ships,
[Carrying] slender Mısri (Egyptian) *buriya* (mats),
   with *nagşu* (decorations) painted in red.
From Bahçekapı all the way until Unkapan,
   [the shore] is always filled with ships,
From the islands, from the Mediterranean,
   and from Nikomedia (İzmit). [. . .]

3. ZİNDAN KAPI, THE DUNGEON GATE

The tenth gate is Zindankapı,
   on the inner side is the [dungeon of] Cafer Baba,
Where debtors to the residents,
   and murderers here lament.
Here there is a separate place for women,
   and another for Turkish men,
[Apart from] Greeks, Armenians, and Jews,
   but the entrance is in that same large gate.
Here by force the [following people] were tormented:
   Gazaros, Sargis, Istifan,
Topal, Cehennem, Gırbo [Garabet] the *papaz* (priest),
   and Toros and others
These *patrik* (patriarchs) of the city,
   who went astray with the disease of avariciousness,
Here they saw their due:
   may the Lord pardon them in judgment.
Stores for beeswax candles,
   with *kahve* (coffee) and henna outside,
Rice and other produce,
   on the shore of the sea like in a fruit garden,
Are present here dry and fresh,
   [with the result] that the isgele (quay) is called Yemiş (Fruit) [Quay].
Over them sits the *muhtasib agha* (market superintendent)
   on [the upper floor of a] a *çardag* (pavilion).
Here is the *çardag çorvaci* (janissary colonel),
   sitting opposite, he knows everything,
About the multitude of passing men,
   boats and *mavonay* (skiffs).
When the *yeniçer agha* (commander of the janissaries)
   heads for the sea, he sits on a boat,
[And] an *orta çavuş* (middle-[ranking] sergeant) mans the rudder,
   wherever he wills, they go.

4. ODUN KAPISI, THE LUMBER GATE

The [eleventh] gate of the city,
   it's called Lumber [Gate].
Diverse onions, garlic, hens, eggs, and fruit,
   come from Nikomedia.
Nearby is a mosque and *mehkeme* (courthouse),

called Ahi Çelebi.
Here the multitude come and go,
   [and] their legal work is done.
Here [the place] is filled with building materials,
   piled up on the quay from the ships.
On the seashore the shops are filled up [with goods],
   next to the [citadel] wall.
The gate's threshold is unworn stone,
   like *sumaki* (porphyry), made of one piece.
And here on a *çengel* (hook) they would beat
   all the thieves and brigands.
Many are the boats and skiffs,
   in this middle area [between] the gates.
Peasants and common folk,
   they come and go, going in and out from here.
And here three years ago,
   they cut off the city's water a little.
In the meydan (square) of the isgele (quay),
   they saw muddy water outside.
When they dug, [the amount of water] increased,
   as much as instantly it began to gush abundantly,
as much as an arm's measure,
   here a great multitude was cooled.
They built a well and a *musluk* (water tap),
   six fingers in measurement,
[And] they attached a Frankish *tulumbay* (water pump),
   [there, the people] wash with and drink this water. [. . .]
Many are the boats on the shore,
   Opposite is Kasım Pasha,
[Where] the *terskhane* (dockyard), Azapkapı,
   [and] Meyid isgele (quay) are located.
Ahead the houses of the Jews,
   odalar (rental chambers)
Lie on both sides facing the sea,
   with all their shops underneath.
They cook fish for *müsafir* (visitors),
   turşi (pickles), dried *mersin* (sturgeon), and *moronay* (white sturgeon).
The Jewish kasab (butchers) are here,
   [and] the *koltug* (small taverns) [selling] *arag misket* (muscatel arak).
There lies the *gullug* (guardhouse),
   which is the protector of the neighborhood. [. . .]

5. CİBALİ KAPI, THE GATE OF ALİ THE ARMORER

The fourteenth gate is [called] Cibali,
  on both sides are houses,
[and] a quay with all good things,
  whatever is needed for the district comes [here].
There is a Greek church,
  Aya Nikolay.
Here Jews are mixed among the inhabitants,
  [while] Greeks are many on account of the *kilisay* (church).
Many *musafir* (visitors),
  are at the shore here for recreation,
[Where there are] *bakal çakal* (grocers and the like) and *balıkci* (fish vendors),
  kasab (butchers) and *momcu* (candlemakers).

6. AYA KAPI, THE GATE OF SAINT [THEODOSIA]

The fifteenth [gate] is called Ayakapı,
  only this one doesn't have an isgele (quay).
[Here] its fortifications are open,
  but the Greeks are on the side of the sea.
Salakhane (slaughterhouses),
  have been built on the sea.
Here there is [also] a *mumkhane* (candle workshop),
  and a *gullug* (guardhouse) looking out over the sea.

7. YENİ KAPI, THE NEW GATE

The sixteenth is Yenikapı,
  there is an isgele (quay) with boats here.
They come here from the neighborhoods
  of Sultan Muhammed and Selim.
Well-read *efendi* (gentlemen),
  who own homes and orchards,
Alight here to sit on boats,
  touring to gardens by the sea.

8. PETRO KAPISI, THE PETRION [FORT] GATE

This one you count [is] the seventeenth gate,
  it's called the Petrokapı.

The fortifications are open on the outside,
   on the side toward the sea Greek houses are lined up.
Let's enter inside the gate,
   here the fortification is twofold [two parallel walls],
Inside, on both sides live
   Greek nobles who have remained [until] now.

9. FENER KAPI, THE PHANAR GATE

The eighteenth is Fenerkapı,
   inside and out are the Greek people,
And inside is the Patriarchate,
   and the metropolitans with him.
Now they have amassed debt upon debt,
   six or seven hundred purses [of money].
It shocks me how, seizing honors from one another,
   they [do] improper things.
Note that the Patriarchate
   has settled in its third location.
First it was the [church] of the Holy Apostles,
   [built] in the days of Constantine the Great.
There they were honored,
   Blessed Mitrufanes (Metrophanes) (d. 326), and his successors,
Krikor the theologian (d. 390),
   and St. Yovhan the golden-mouthed (d. 407).
Sultan Mehemmed took it,
   [and] he destroyed the holy cathedral from its foundations.
He built [a mosque with its] *mehrab* (prayer niche) toward the *gıble* (Mecca),
   and he named it after himself.
[The Patriarchate] was in another location,
   [that of] a *kilisa* (church) named Pammakaristos,
Which means in translation, "most blessed,"
   the patriarch put his throne there.
Being wicked, they took it,
   in the days of Sultan Süleyman.
Then the [Greeks] brought it to Fenerkapı,
   where [the Patriarchate] sits [now] abjectly.
Near to the Patriarchate
   Is the deputy of Jerusalem.
There is a kilisa (church)
   with a court and garden, [the deputy's] monastery.

Now the patriarch is
   the despot Dositheos (d. 1707).
Until [this patriarch's] arrival, four [others]
   [have been] known to us and our predecessors.
We pass by *yali* (seaside mansions),
   Greek homes on the outer side,
The residences of gentlemen,
   whom they call Wallachians and Moldavians,
They look out onto the land side,
   with open walls and a passage for people.
To the north by sea is Hasköy,
   Okmeydan, and a *bağça* (garden) of the king.
Ahead are Jewish houses,
   for their needs there is a market.
As was said, they live there mixed with Greeks,
   on the shore of the sea.
Long ago a kilisa (church) burned [here],
   [but] when the ambassador of Moscow came again,
He had the church [re]built,
   which remained a place of consolation for the residents.

10. THE BALAT GATE

The nineteenth gate is Balat's,
   let's go until Ayvansaray.
Outside of it Jews live,
   but on the inside is a multitude of diverse [peoples].
Since it has a great isgele (quay),
   ships [with all] needed goods come here.
Going [from here] to Kağıthane
   and to Istanbul, they come with skiffs.
Here [in Balat] there are more Jews
   than in the village of Hasköy or in Galata,
Than in Beşiktaş or Ortaköy,
   Kuzguncuk or Kuruçeşme,
Or, on the edges of Istanbul,
   more than in Üsküdar or Çengelköy.
[The Jews] don't live far away [from the sea],
   they don't budge from the seashore.
Inside is our church,
   named the Hreshdagabed (Archangel).

Up to eight hundred Armenian households,
    scattered around, not in one district.

11. THE AYVANSARAY GATE

The twentieth gate is Ayvansaray,
    from Balat until this place,
All the residents are Jews,
    rich ones dwelling on the seaside.
Inside the gate, nearby,
    there is a ruined and unused kilisay (church),
Inside it there is an *ayazma* (holy spring),
    named the Mother of God of Vılaherna.
Its portico is empty, destroyed and *veran* (ruined),
    and *çingene* (gypsies) have settled by the rampart.
As [is the case] in many other places
    they turned it into a *mescid* and *cami* (mosques).
The great gate is its back,
    now it's closed, fortified with stone.
An image of St. Michael,
    sword in hand, is carved on it.
[It has] an isgele (quay) with boats,
    coming and going to Eyüp Sultan.
For bottles, diverse vessels
    of glass, there is a *kerkhana* (workshop) here.
Ahead is the end and limit,
    of the city [surrounded] by sea on three sides.
We began from the west,
    and with the sun [we've reached] the western limit [again].
Yedikule has been called
    one foot of the city,
and the other foot is this place that we've reached,
    Ayvansaray. [. . .]

12. TOP KAPI, THE CANNON GATE

Ruhım (My dear) vartabed,
    if I may trouble you,
Since it is no longer possible to go on by boat,
    let's mount on horses in our progression.
Putting the north to our back,

Let's go southward.
Let's see the western gates of the city,
    and whatever we run across. [. . .]
The twenty-third [gate] is Topkapı,
    where *top* (cannons) were placed as a sign.
Inside and outside the gate,
    live Armenian gypsies.
Men make sieves at home,
    while women wander around selling them.
[The women are] shameless, with faces uncovered,
    [while] many of their men in this place have Turkified.
Here the *katırci* (muleteer) Armenians live,
    [they are] *kiraci* (porters for hire), they carry loads,
Crying out, saying profanities,
    they come and go to Edirne.
Visible in the distance on our right,
    is the great palace of Davud Pasha,
Its location is seemly and lovely,
    here the king recreates with his family.
Many villages lie on both left and right,
    [that is,] on the southern and northern sides,
[like] Litros, of the Greek *çingene* (gypsies),
    whose women are the singers of the city.
They enter homes,
    and they sing on the streets of the neighborhood.
They enter the *meykhane* (taverns),
    for their admirers they play [music] and dance.
Whenever they learn new verses,
    they sing their fabulous words:
"*Ey derdimend gel gira* (Come on over, oh sorrowful one, enter),
    Koynuma hemen bir zeman (my embrace for a time).
Bose hırid u fürukhd" (Buying and selling kisses),
    the drunken are once again enraptured,
They put money on their foreheads,
    [and] *bir zeman* (for a while) the [gypsies] are glutted [with cash].
When there are words between the Greeks and us,
    this is our answer to them:
Our Armenian gypsies often tour around,
    [and] toil for their livelihoods.
But yours wander around with *dablag*s (drums),
    at taverns making *kef* (merry).

The songs incite and stir,
   "*gela koynuma gir heman*" (come quick, enter my embrace).
Before *garib* (strange) heartthrob youths,
   they dance and go to and fro on foot, [saying,]
"Give a delicious peach [kiss] for scalded hearts,
   negir heman bir zeman" (enter [my embrace] for a while).

13. YENİ KAPI, THE NEW GATE

We've reached the twenty-fourth gate,
   which is called Yenikapı.
Nearby there are *barut* (gunpowder) storerooms,
   and royal guards.
In the gardens are the shelters of
   dervishes and the *mevlakhana* (lodge of the Mevlevis).
The theaters of the residents,
   at a spare moment I'll write about them [later].
There is an ayazma (holy spring),
   called Ayya Treada among the Greeks,
Named after the Holy Trinity,
   [about which some] have written, and [about it] many have lied.

14. THE SİLİVRİ GATE

The twenty-fifth is Silivri,
   inside is a *cami* (mosque), and opposite is a bathhouse.
Nearby the gate, outside of it,
   is a *mezar* (grave) of *Elekci Dede* (Papa Sieve).
He never spoke,
   but he was always eating [the fabric] of sieves.
He would wander behind the Armenian gypsies,
   who would pity him and have him eat sieve.
His whole body was covered in black,
   and he was entirely *arab* (black-skinned) up to the head.
Summer and winter, he was [always] naked,
   he was standing upright, neglected.
With one hand he would eat the sieve,
   and the other hand was on [his] *mefred baba* (big penis)
He didn't have hair or a beard,
   he was brutish and mute like a *hayvan* (animal).
When he died they called him a *veli* (friend of God, saint),

and they hastened to his funeral.
The *agavad* (aghas) and *vuzaray* (viziers),
   they gathered in a crowd at the vile place.
The place of the deceased [man] was filled up,
   a mass of shrouds piled up,
They [all] said, "he came to me in a dream,
   And he said [he wanted] a shroud."
There was a tumult among the multitude,
   [saying] "my [shroud] is worthy [to bury him with]."
They were explaining their dreams to one another,
   and saying, "my shroud is worthy."
Finally, the vizier Ahmed Pasha
   In the year 1102 (1653),
Ordered that it be his [shroud],
   Saying, "let mine be taken."
They wrapped him in it and buried him,
   and made a public procession [with multiple] ranks.
They performed a *meyid namazi* (prayer for the deceased),
   as if he had been a mufti or a sultan.
They said he had been a *veliullah* (friend of God),
   and they considered the *meyid* to be a *sevab* (good deed).
But in my opinion he was a *yaban adami* (savage man),
   a hayvan (animal), [or] *eynehan* (just like) a *torlak* (antinomian dervish).
The priest Markos of Topkapı said:
   "One day I was going
On the Hisardibi Road,
   by the *burc* (tower) on the side of the wall,
Was a *veli* (friend [of God]) adored by the Turks (i.e., Elekci Dede),
   he flung an Armenian gypsy to the ground,
He rode roughshod over her, beat her, and held her,
   and the gypsy cried out in anger."
The Turks were saying about him,
   he's of noble birth, [related] to *Musdafay* (Prophet Muhammad),
A *çelebi* (a man of refinement), a veliullah (friend of God),
   he was deemed worthy of a funeral with great honor.
[In] the dreams of many,
   [he made] requests for *ikram* (gifts) and a *kefin* (shroud).
There was no tasting of water or bread,
   as they got [foodstuff] [by the grace of] God.
They say that his continuing speechlessness was wondrous.
   He was staying silent so much,

Someone answered this, saying,
    "Know you, *kardaş* (oh brother) Muslim:
One day in his life,
    a dear friend of his,
Beseeching and pressing much,
    received an answer from the saint:
'Say my dear,
    why do you torment me so much?
Who is a servant of God?
    Who fulfills the laws of Muslims?
Let me speak with him,
    or let me even give him a *selam* (greeting).
It's not obligatory for a veliullah (friend of God)
    to ever speak with the corrupted.'"
They made a mezar (tomb) and a shelter [for him],
    and they hung a sieve on it as a sign.
Until today guards sit there,
    they preach, saying that it is a place of healing.
Women, *khatun* (ladies), and *khanım* (girls),
    and sultans hastened there in carriages.
Others too read *fatihes* (the first chapter of the Qur'an),
    imploring for *şifa* (healing) from him.
Jugs on the mezar (tomb),
    were placed ready full of water,
As a remedy for those yearning for children,
    to give a boy to women who wanted to get pregnant, or who were barren.
They were rubbing this water
    on their eyes, faces, chests, and *pisdan* (breasts),
Up to the belly and navels they were bringing [the water],
    expunging themselves like this.

15. THE HOLY SPRING OF BALIKLI

On both sides are the *gyor* (graves) of Turks,
    farther ahead is an ayazma (holy spring) of the Greeks,
They call this [spring] Balıklı,
    close by to the Greeks' small cemetery.
Previously there was a monastery,
    named Panayya for the mother of God.
Many men have related to us,
    its miracles of healing.

FIGURE 36. Land walls of Istanbul (view from southwest), nineteenth century. M. J. Starling (engraver), in Thomas Allom, *Constantinople and the Scenery of the Seven Churches of Asia Minor* (London: Fisher, Son & Co., 1838), 80–81.

> It's also called Khrisupiyi,
>   which means "basin of gold" in translation.
> The water is salutary:
>   [once] a half-dead [man was brought back] to life from this [water].
> It's said that in its ceiling
>   was a great *sndug* (chest) two spans in size,
> Which was fastened in an arch,
>   a ring made of iron hung [from it].
> In our times,
>   boys would throw rope at the ring,
> And they would swing on it,
>   those who came on a sacred visit or just on a jaunt.
> A Frankish mechanic named Remil,
>   skilled in geometry,
> He came and waited in the night,
>   and took it without leaving a trace.
> Now there is an opening like a window,

in the place of the sndug (chest) in the arch,
the chest filled with a gold-dyeing *kimya* (elixir),
    if it is true, then may it be *afiet* (good health [to him])!
In our times we saw
    walnut trees nearby to it.
There they excavated deep down under them,
    and they brought up gold and silver.

FORTY-ONE

Passion and Murder on the Bosphorus

Anonymous Tıfli Story, Probably in Circulation During
the Later Seventeenth Century

TRANSLATED BY HELGA ANETSHOFER

Within the varied and understudied genre of Ottoman prose stories and anecdotes, the group of so-called Tıfli stories stand out for their urban realist, or rather protorealist, style. Today we know of a small repertoire of about ten Tıfli stories, which are set in seventeenth-century Istanbul during the reign of the young and harsh Murad IV (b. 1612, r. 1623–40). The stories are named after the protagonist Tıfli Ahmed Çelebi (d. 1660, Tıfli means "child prodigy"), who was a noted poet and a famous professional storyteller (*meddah* or *şehname-han*). He is, however, not the author of the stories. The sultan or Tıfli, who was also the sultan's court entertainer, appears in the stories mostly in supporting roles.

The Tıfli stories offer a unique, realist description of certain aspects of everyday life in Istanbul: they follow the protagonists through their lives in Istanbul, detailing their movements through actual urban locations, their means of transport, their living accommodations and family situations, their clothes and fashion, their professions and workplaces, their consumption of everyday foodstuffs and semiluxury items like coffee and tobacco, and their preferred modes of popular and private entertainment like drinking parties (meclis). The plot of the stories usually revolves around a conflict of semi-illicit desires resulting in sex and violence, adventure and suspense, recrimination and reconciliation. The objects of desire are mostly pubescent boys who have not yet grown coarse facial hair. Their pursuers are sexually mature young men (Sansar Mustafa in our story), as well as adult men (like Sultan Murad) and women. The passion for beautiful boys corresponds to the norm represented in Ottoman love poetry from the late fifteenth century onward. Later, in the Tıfli stories produced from the nineteenth century on, the concept of boy love is abandoned and replaced by heterosexual desire expressed between young men and enslaved girls (and/or women). The descriptions of the protagonists' appearance and character are rather stereotypical (especially for women).

However, the cause-and-effect unfolding of the plot, involving many realistic details, make it possible to imagine the protagonists as real people in a three-dimensional world.

Variants of the Tıfli stories are recorded in manuscript, lithographic, and letter print form. The extract below is from the only story surviving in manuscript form with the generic name Hikayet ("Story"), known in scholarship as the Story of Sansar Mustafa. The extract is around 20 percent of the whole story, which is fifty-five manuscript pages long. In the passage below, Sultan Murad develops an infatuation with the beautiful barber boy Ahmed, who is subsequently abducted by the young rascal Sansar ("the Weasel," in reference to his slyness) Mustafa. The infuriated sultan orders his police officer Hacı Subaşı to apprehend the couple. The police officer hires the prostitute Rukiyye to find them. Later in the story, Sansar Mustafa manages to escape after a suspenseful chase on the rooftops of the Uzun Çarşı ("Long Market," Tahtakale), but Ahmed is captured and sentenced to hanging. In a twist, Sansar rescues Ahmed from the gallows. At the suggestion of Sansar's foster father ("Take your Ahmed and flee this country for a while'") the couple says goodbye to Ahmed's parents and sister and sails to Egypt. This makes for an eventful journey. They earn their livelihood in Cairo with Ahmed selling coffee in the street to a large crowd of admirers. At Ahmed's behest they return to Istanbul five or six years later. Meanwhile Ahmed has become a strong young man with a moustache. Back in Istanbul they seek the mercy of Sultan Murad, who pardons them and makes everyone happy by immediately marrying them off: Sansar to Ahmed's sister, and Ahmed to a beautiful, enslaved virgin girl from the imperial harem.

LANGUAGE: Turkish. Lively, conversational language with many idiomatic and proverbial expressions, including some profanity (which was censored in Şükrü Elçin's transcription). Frequent irregularities in the orthography.

SOURCE: Manuscript: İstanbul Üniversitesi Kütüphanesi, Istanbul, Türkçe Yazmalar 250, fols. 19b-47a. Transcription: Elçin, Şükrü, ed. "Sansar Mustafa Hikâyesi." *Türk Kültürü Araştırmaları* 16, 1-2 (1977-78): 195-224. Sayers, David Selim. "Hikayet." In *Tıflî Hikâyeleri*, 141-63. Istanbul: Bilgi Üniversitesi Yayınları, 2013.

TIFLİ AND SULTAN MURAD TAKE A PLEASURE TRIP TO THE TOPHANE DISTRICT

The story goes that once upon a time Sultan Murad—*may God have mercy on his soul*—had a clever court entertainer by the name of Tıfli Efendi. His majesty Sultan Murad Khan always had a good time with Tıfli, and when the sultan wished to go out incognito, Tıfli would come along. One day Sultan Murad said, "Look here, Tıfli Efendi." "At your service, my Majesty!" Tıfli responded. The sultan continued: "What's a good spot for a pleasure trip today?" Tıfli kissed the ground and said, "Today is the second day of the holy festival, so it is a good day to take a trip to Tophane." "Let us disguise ourselves and go there," Sultan

FIGURE 37. A barber, ca. 1650s. Artist unknown. Cod.Rål. 8:o no. 10 (*Rålambska dräktboken*), fol. 19. Kungliga Biblioteket, Stockholm.

Murad commanded. They immediately dressed up as Mevlevi dervishes and assumed new names. Sultan Murad said, "My name shall be Dervish Hasan, and yours Dervish Hüseyn."

They left through the palace gate and went straight to the Bağçekapı Gate. There they boarded a boat with two tiers [of rowers]. After they had gone out into the sea for a while the boatmen asked, "Where are we going, dervishes?" "Tophane," Tıfli replied. [The boatmen] rowed rapidly and arrived at the Tophane pier. The men paid for the ride, disembarked, and, after closely observing their surroundings, set out for the promenade.

Since it was the second day of the holy festival everyone was out and about: customers and vendors, pickpockets and gropers. Everything was allowed during the days of Sultan Murad— there were people riding on swings, Ferris wheels, and carousels; fancy women were strolling around in large groups followed by flirting casanovas; and, notably, crowds of rosy-cheeked young boys were sauntering arm-in-arm, making their poor admirers suffer with yearning. Everyone was enjoying themselves. His majesty Sultan Murad said to Tıfli: "People are really having a lot of fun here! There are a lot of young boys around; today my heart wishes to ensnare one of them." Fearing he would get into trouble, Tıfli was terrified. [. . .]

THE PRETTY BOY AHMED AT THE BARBERSHOP

In those days there was a barbershop in Tophane called İki kapılı ("Double doored"), which was quite famous. The sultan said, "Dervish Hüseyn, let's eat our savory pastries (*çörek*) and drink our coffee in that barbershop over there." Tıfli said, "Oh no, my padishah, not in such a crowded place!" At that moment, a pretty boy came out of the İki kapılı barbershop—they had never seen such beauty. His sleeves were rolled up and he had a silk cloth wrapped around his waist. His clothes were very clean and he was carrying a silver basin; he was as beautiful as Joseph. He poured the water out of the basin and went back inside.

As soon as Sultan Murad saw the boy, he said, "Tıfli, I am going in there." He walked toward the door, opened it, and went in. Poor Tıfli was petrified, but reluctantly he went in too. The shop was packed, but as he was already inside, Sultan Murad felt embarrassed to turn back. He regretted entering, but it couldn't be helped. When the [customers] in [the shop] looked at their faces he felt ashamed.

The boy had been busy when they entered and did not see them. Eventually he noticed the two dervishes, who were standing because there was no place to sit. The boy promptly greeted them, "Welcome! How good of you to come, esteemed dervishes!" A white-bearded old man (i.e., the boy's father) was sitting at the counter. The boy told him to make space and told them: "Please, sit over here." Sultan Murad and Tıfli sat down next to the old man, and somehow they all fit. But they were embarrassed to take out their savory pastries and eat them. After a while, as it became less crowded the old man greeted them modestly with his hand to his chest: "How good of you to come, esteemed dervishes! Where have you come from?" They returned the greeting. Then Tıfli took out his pastry, broke it in pieces, and offered some to the old man. They began to eat and they drank their coffee.

Afterward they chatted a little and Sultan Murad said to Tıfli: "Dervish Hüseyn, now that we are here, I might as well get my head shaved." "We'll be late, Dervish Hasan," replied Tıfli. Sultan Murad said, "That's no impediment," and told the young man to shave his head. The young man replied, "Of course, my dear sir!" He got up, grabbed his towel, gracefully stepped in front of the sultan, and put the towel around his neck—he was a smart and reasonable boy. He removed the dervish cap from the sultan's head and massaged it with water. When he was done, he took his razor, stropped its blade, and in no time gave him such a shave that Sultan Murad became sleepy from the pleasure of the boy's soft touch on his head. When Ahmed was done shaving, he took a mirror and the dervish cap and said, "May it bring good health to you!" He handed him the mirror and the cap and stood before him. [. . .]

When Sultan Murad and Tıfli left and got back on the boat, Tıfli became uneasy. As he was thinking about how the sultan had set his sights on the boy, Sultan Murad turned to him and said, "Oh Tıfli, I really fancy this boy," and ordered him to find a way to ensnare him. [. . .]

MUSTAFA THE WEASEL, AHMED, AND THE PROSTITUTE RUKİYYE

This is where Sansar ("the Weasel") Mustafa comes into our story: The day after Sansar Mustafa abducted that boy (Ahmed) and brought him to his place, he ordered a tailor-made set of splendid [sailor-style] clothes for him: he bought a grand woolen turban cloth for his head, a —— short, braided waistcoat for his back, peerless baggy trousers for his ass, tight sailor's slip-ons for his feet, and a red coat, and he dressed the boy up with these. The boy looked so beautiful in these clothes that everyone who saw him was smitten. Sansar Mustafa's place was at the Mumhane Gate (in Galata), on the top floor of a wine tavern owned by a man called Panayod. That is where Sansar Mustafa would stay.

Soon the boy became fed up with staying there. One day he pleaded with Sansar Mustafa: "My dear lord, I am getting very bored here. And today is Friday. Let's go and enjoy ourselves in Dolmabahçe today." Sansar Mustafa did not want to disoblige, and he agreed. The two of them set off. As they arrived at Dolmabahçe and strolled around, the passersby who saw the boy at Sansar Mustafa's side were all amazed. But no one dared to say anything—Sansar Mustafa was a valiant, tough, sturdy fellow. The two toured Dolmabahçe and then went back. On the way, the boy observed his surroundings and enjoyed himself. Sansar Mustafa, on the other hand, was on alert for trouble.

[Finally,] the boy said, "My dear lord, I need to ask you for something. Will you hear me?" "What is it? I listen with all my heart," Sansar Mustafa replied. The boy said, "It has been eight or nine days now that you have enjoyed yourself with me and taken your pleasure. How about you entrap a woman for me, so I can enjoy myself with a woman tonight—with gratitude to you?"

At that moment they saw a woman (Rukiyye Hanım) coming toward them with four or five slave girls behind her. She had such a graceful way of walking that there was no limit to the sighs of her helpless admirers. When the boy saw the woman, he said to Sansar Mustafa:

"My lord, you must flirt with this woman and pick her up for me." "Oh boy, that's impossible," Sansar said. The boy said, "If you love me, you'll do it." "What should I say to this woman?" Sansar asked. The boy said, "Say whatever you want." Sansar turned to him and said, "I swear, boy, never in my life have I had a relationship with a woman, or even liked a woman. Surely, if I were to say to her, 'Look, woman! My boy here wants your pussy, come on, give my boy your pussy!', I would be a laughingstock and she would ignore us with disdain." The boy still insisted: "Please pick her up for me!" Sansar saw it was no use. While he was walking and thinking to himself, "What should I say?" Rukiyye Hanım spotted them, took a rose from the slave girl's hand, and walked right toward them. When she was close Sansar barged forward and said, "Hey lady! Where are you going? I have a lot of things to say to you, but [since you're off] take good care." When he said this, the woman laughed loudly.

Then Sansar looked at the boy and said, "Go ahead faggot, there's the whore, and here you are! Tell her whatever you want. I don't know about these things." He took a step back. The boy approached the woman and they started talking. Sansar said to himself, "It's really a different science. Don't imagine womanizing is easy! Among the arts womanizing is more difficult than watchmaking. Not every man can do it." Meanwhile, the boy started imploring the woman to come with them. The woman wrapped up the conversation in a coquettish way.

"Please, follow us," the boy said. The woman turned and followed close behind them. Soon they arrived at Panayod's tavern and took the woman upstairs through the back door. They put her in Sansar's room, and she took off her veil and her cloak and sat on the sofa. Then Sansar Mustafa summoned Panayod. He came upstairs and asked, "What do you wish, my lord Mustafa?" Sansar said, "Housekeeper Panayod, you understand the situation. I want you to prepare the best spread you can." Panayod said, "Of course, as you wish." He went down and prepared an amazing feast for them, then brought it up and set it up before them. They crowded around the dinner table as tight as the pipes of a pan flute. One of the lady's slave girls acted as the cupbearer. She rolled up her sleeves and took the carafe in one hand and a cup in the other. She poured a cup from the carafe and drank it with the words, "First the cupbearer, and then the rest!" Then she poured a cup for the lady, a cup for Sansar Mustafa, a cup for Ahmed, and finally cups for the slave girls. As they drank wine, the slave girls started to sing like nightingales.

Rukiyye Hanım put her arm around Ahmed's neck, Ahmed put his arm around her neck, and they started to exchange juicy kisses. When the dejected Sansar saw how they were kissing, he got up and watched them from a corner. At that moment Ahmed could no longer restrain himself; he quickly untied the drawstring of the lady's drawers, lifted her legs, and finished the job. The lady took great pleasure from Ahmed. They started another round of drinking and got quite tipsy. The woman spoke drunkenly to herself: "Hey disgusting Hacı police officer, I will not sell out such a fine young man just to get your two hundred gold pieces. A mother who gives birth to such a young man should have five children, not just three. A handsome guy like this should live a long time!"

MUSTAFA THE WEASEL BECOMES SUSPICIOUS OF RUKİYYE

Meanwhile, Sansar Mustafa was paying close attention. Because, dear [reader], Sansar Mustafa was a clever, worldly young man who knew every trick. He had already seen a lot of trouble, which is why he remained vigilant.

Sansar didn't let on when he heard these alarming words from the woman. For a while he did nothing. Then he said to himself: "O Sansar! She was going to harm you! I knew such a woman does not get picked up so easily and hang around the corner of a wine tavern. There is something wrong with this picture. Let's see what else she has to say." Without looking in her direction, he listened closely. As she got tipsier, the woman started saying all kinds of things. Sansar said to himself: "Keep talking, you great whore. You did not come here to enjoy yourself. You came to spy on us. This is your moment! Say all you have to say tonight; after this night, you will no longer be able to!"

He pretended to leave the room, stepped behind the woman, and pulled a flame-colored Algerian scimitar from his bosom as if he were pulling out a watch. Making a move as if to pass behind her, he chopped off the woman's head so forcefully that it rolled on the floor. The slave girls sobered up and made to scream. But Sansar shouted at them: "Shut up, you damned creatures, or I'll send you along with her." Terrified, they remained quiet and didn't say another word.

Still, though, there had been some noise when it happened. Panayod heard the sound and said to himself: "Sansar has gotten himself in trouble tonight." Curious, he came upstairs and knocked on the door. Sansar got up and opened it. Panayod entered the room and saw blood everywhere and a dead woman lying on the floor. Freaked out, he turned to Sansar: "Well done, Mustafa! Exactly what a romantic gathering should be!" Sansar said, "Oh housekeeper Panayod, it's not a big deal." Panayod was a rich Christian. He had a few circles (brothels?) operating on the Kapıdağı [Peninsula]. "Look Panayod," Sansar said, "We have to do something about this. Go put the slave girls on a boat at Yalıkapısı; take them to a ship, and tell [the shipmen] to take them to the Kapıdağı Peninsula." Panayod took the slave girls, put them on a ship, and sent them to the Kapıdağı Peninsula.

MUSTAFA THE WEASEL'S PLAN TO GET RID OF THE CORPSE

In the morning Sansar got up and dressed up as a halberdier (*baltacı*, a palace guard). He put a tall felt hat on his head, a cloak on his shoulders, and pulled on trousers with attached boots. He looked like he had been a halberdier for thirty years. He locked Ahmed inside and went to the pier, where he boarded a boat and sailed to Unkapanı. There he disembarked, went straight to the Saraçhane [business center], and came to the area of the chestmakers' shops. He asked, "Which one is the shop of your chief?" They showed it to him. Sansar went to the chief's shop; his name was Hacı Hasan. He was a bon vivant and whiled away most of his hours in the coffee shop.

When the so-called halberdier came to the shop and asked about the chief, his journeyman said, "Halberdier agha; our master has just gone to drink a cup of coffee. If you need him, we can call him." Sansar said, "Call him!" and entered the shop. One of the boys went to his master and said, "A halberdier from the palace is asking for you." The chief hurried back and saw the halberdier sitting in the corner of his shop. The chief said, "Welcome! How good of you to come. Please, come upstairs. Hey boy, quickly bring the gentleman a tobacco pipe and a coffee!"

As Sansar was drinking his coffee, the chief asked, "Sir, what can we do for you?" Sansar replied, "I require a few chests, but they have to be sizable." The chief got up and had five to ten chests taken down. Sansar asked, "Do you have more?" "Certainly, sir," the chief answered. "We have forty to fifty chests." Sansar said, "My dear chief, I will take this one with me now. If they like it, I'll came back and purchase all of them." The chief said, "Fair enough, halberdier agha." Sansar said, "If there is a porter around, fetch him, will you?" The chief told his apprentice, "Go boy, get that Kurdish guy in here." The boy went to fetch the porter. The porter tied his rope around the chest and hoisted it onto his back. The halberdier said goodbye to the chief and led the porter straight to Unkapanı. There he lowered the chest from the porter's back, placed it in a boat, and gave the porter his money. He seated himself in the stern. The boatman asked, "Halberdier agha, where are you headed?" When Sansar said, "Mumhane," he took him there in no time. When they arrived, Sansar got out of the boat, called a porter, loaded the chest on his back, and led him to Panayod's wine tavern. Then he lowered the chest from the porter's back, gave him five to ten coins, and sent him off.

As the evening fell, he held another drinking party, and began feasting with Ahmed. At some point he got up, cut the woman's corpse in two pieces, and put them in the chest. Then he hoisted the chest on his back and left the wine tavern through the waterfront door. He boarded a small rowboat, attached two oars, pulled hard, and came to a spot across from Sarayburnu. "Off you go!" he said, and pushed the chest into the sea with one hand. Then he rowed back as fast as he could. He quickly moored the boat, entered [the tavern] from the waterfront door, and went up to his room, where he continued partying with Ahmed.

That night, through God's intervention, Sultan Murad had a dream. But he could not remember his dream. As he pondered it, he recalled Ahmed and wondered what had become of him. He headed toward the İncili Pavilion (atop the sea walls of the Topkapı Palace facing the Marmara Sea). He lounged there, and then got his telescope and observed the surroundings. He saw that an object was bobbing up and down in the water around the area toward the Red Islands (i.e., Princes' Islands). He said, "I wonder what that is?" and summoned Tıfli, who looked through the telescope too. Though he had a feeling about what it was, he didn't dare answer. Sultan Murad sent for Miço, the commander of the imperial guards. They fetched him and he came, kissed the ground, and said, "At your command, my emperor." The sultan said, "An object keeps sinking and popping up from the water toward the Red Islands. Quickly go there with a boat, find out what it is, and report back!" Miço replied, "The command belongs to my majesty." He left, prepared a boat, and sailed off.

FORTY-TWO

Stories of Guilt and Repentance

Mehmed Nergisi, d. 1635

TRANSLATED BY GISELA PROCHÁZKA-EISL

Mehmed Nergisi was born ca. 1580 in Sarajevo. After finishing his education as a legal scholar, he worked for almost twenty-five years as a judge in various towns in the Balkans. Tired of this itinerant way of life, heavily in debt, and frustrated by the fact that as a judge he could not fully express his literary talents, Nergisi finally sought and succeeded in gaining the attention of Sultan Murad IV (r. 1623–40), who in 1635 appointed him as a chronicler for the campaign at Yerevan. Tragically, only a few miles from Istanbul, Nergisi fell from his horse while passing a swamp and was fatally injured.

During his time Nergisi was regarded as an exceptionally skilled master of elegant and ornate Ottoman prose (*inşa*). He was famous for his exaggerated Persianate style, which was characterized by a richness of new and unusual metaphors and high poetic power—features that contemporary connoisseurs greatly esteemed. However, some two centuries years later, when the simplification of Ottoman Turkish became a subject of discussion, Nergisi was regarded as the archetype of affected, ornate, pretentious, and bombastic diction. Nergisi's language is indeed complicated, but his subtle choice of words, inventive metaphors, and masterly symmetrical arrangement of rhymed prose is also fascinating—though impossible to adequately capture in translation.

One of the benchmark achievements of an author of this period was to compose five major works in verse (*hamse*). Nergisi created a compilation of five works, albeit in prose, as if to submit his flowery style to be recognized by the literati as a poetic form in its own right. Of his five works, the collection entitled *The Sapling Garden* (*Nihalistan*) contains, in its second iteration, twenty-five stories classified into five *nihal*s, or "young plants," each focusing on a particular topic, such as generosity or love. The following two stories are from the final section of the book, which is on the topic of repentance.

The main character in the first story is a thief who hides in a farmhouse with the intention of stealing a horse. From his hideout in a corner, he watches a poisonous serpent slink into a soup kettle. This presents him with a moral dilemma. On the one hand, the family will die should he not warn them about the venom in the soup. On the other hand, alerting them to the danger will lead to his discovery and potentially even his death. In the end, the thief decides to risk his life and warn the farmer's family, who forgive his bad intentions and even present him with the horse that he had planned to steal. He thus realizes the wisdom in the Arabic saying (which is based on a hadith) "salvation lies in honesty" and spends his life in deep remorse.

The protagonist of the second story is an adopted stray dog who is unjustly punished and killed. The dog later appears in the dream of his murderer against the backdrop of Judgment Day and calls him to account for his act. Dreams were a fertile literary landscape for authors to fabricate unlikely instructional conversations or meetings. Such encounters sometimes took place between people who were socially unlikely to meet (a beggar and a sultan) or between sages who lived in different time periods. Nergisi's choice of having the cruel man, the dog he wronged, and God make an evaluation of what transpired—particularly his ability to represent the dog's point of view—is a remarkable literary achievement. In emotional language, the author describes the animal's last moments on earth with empathy and a sense of injustice for the plight of this creature.

LANGUAGE: Turkish. Long, convoluted sentences and flowery imagery. See also the introduction to this chapter for a note on his language.

SOURCE: Ottoman print: Mehmed Nergisi. *Hamse-i Nergisi*. Istanbul, 1285/1868-69 (153-55, 57-160). Transcription: Çaldak, Süleyman. *Nergisi ve Nihalistan'ı*. Istanbul: Kesit Yayınları, 2010 (470-72, 475-77). Translated into German by Gisela Procházka-Eisl. "Gerechtigkeit für einen Hund. Eine Traumgeschichte aus der Hamse des Nergisî." *Osmanlı Araştırmaları* 28 (2006): 165-81.

THE CONSCIENTIOUS THIEF

How a ravening thief, while hidden in a corner of a house, informed the house-owners of a viper that had crept into the food, and how by this action he gained [the horse] he wished for and how this caused him to repent:

An infamous churl from a group of shrewd thieves and cheeky, long-fingered villains had cast an eye of greed and avarice on the strong packhorse of a farmer, who was the finest among his people, but the door where it was kept was locked.

All the servants kept guard during the daytime and had the packhorse stay, out of caution, in their bed chamber during dark nights. Therefore, this long-clawed ravener had no opportunity to succeed. He was completely distraught for a long time out of sheer avarice and ran around restlessly with a desire for the horse. He looked for the moment of opportunity and eyed his possibilities at a place of ambush.

Finally, he saw no other option than to follow this plan: One day, when no member of the unfortunate household was at the farmhouse, he would secretly sneak in. As the bright cell of the world turned dark by the extinguishing of the illuminating torch of the sun—meaning, when night descended and the stokehold of the lime-finished wall of the world, that is, the firmament, changed its color from Nile-blue to black—he would hide in a corner behind the curtain of obscurity. When the residents of the farmhouse came home from the labor of the day, and each being faint and weary, laid their heads on the brickstones of recreation, and when their straying looks were ready for the journey to the campground of sleep to view the shadow figures of the world of dreams, he would carefully untie the rope of the horse and grab the reins with his strong hand.

With this plan in mind, one day the lad secretly set foot in the house, not thinking how to get out again. In a dark, inaccessible corner he noticed a heap of garbage, and he got off to a catnap amid this filth, in the hopes that the busily engaged senses of the residents, returning home tired from the work of the day, would take up the repose of sleep. And while their watchful glances expected the arrival of slumber and were busy trying to fall asleep, he would grasp with his claws the reins of his wish and, like a gazelle, with a small, elegant leap he would fiercely aspire after the grazing grounds of the fulfillment of his desire.

At that point, the house was empty of servants and residents—but they had left a boiling cauldron on the hearth. While the thief was hidden like a disdainful moth amid the garbage, he spotted a wiggling viper of awful appearance, which, attracted by the smell of milk and slithering around the hearth, had fallen into the cauldron.

At dusk, when the owner of the house, free from farming and husbandry, entered the house shuffling and limping, thinking of nothing but food and a quiet sleep, all the members of the household came along one by one and gathered around him in a circle. They were exhausted by their work with cows and donkeys and hungry as oxen. The cauldron, the object of their appetite, was already heated up on the hearth, and the house's caretaker, a smelly old man with shorn hair, noticed that their voracious eyes could not avert their surreptitious, ravenous glances from the cauldron's cover. He set up the tablecloth and a large tray in the middle, brought the cauldron from the hearth, and just when he wanted to pour the food into dishes, it dawned on the upright thief: "These people have no idea that a viper has fallen into the cauldron! With their obvious desire and hunger, they will all be unwittingly destroyed by the viper's poison! But if I warn them about the situation, they will definitely say, 'O evil stranger, what are you doing here?' and will jump and kick me. They will ruin the reins of my life with their destroying hands, and I, who has come here with a wish for a horse, will have to walk on foot to *an evil destination* (i.e., hellfire, Qur'an 22:72)."

After nervously hesitating for some time, he told himself: "According to chivalry and humanity it is better that I get killed by the misguided hand of these people than that such a large community be struck by the ruination of their household."

And like a jinn he suddenly shouted with a gloomy voice from amid the garbage: "O people! Beware and do not stick your spoon into that meal, because it is certain that you will become drowsy and intoxicated from a sip of the sudden death and perish! A short time ago a wiggling viper crept into the bubbling cauldron and was boiled."

When this frightening voice was heard from the dark corner of the house, all were thunderstruck, shocked, and trembled with fear. The eldest and most experienced among them grasped a burning candle and walked slowly toward the place from whence the voice had come. "By God, the Creator of humans and jinn, explain truly what you are! If you are a descendant of Adam (i.e., human), you must make clear what you are doing here and how you know about the viper."

The thief in the garbage recounted the matter in all detail and that he had hidden with the intention of stealing the horse. Some of the family's inexperienced, beardless youngsters began to shout for help: "O relatives, housemates! A thief is hidden in our house! Come over, let us finish him off!" They stood up with a fervor to inflict harm on him.

But the old house owner raised his hand, threatening to slap his housemates, and said, "It is not appropriate for chivalry and humanity to bring about a quarrel as requital for this good deed. Instead, it is appropriate and fair to present him with the horse he desired, and as a reward for the gift [he gave to us], to send him from our community happily with a precious present."

Thereupon they gave him worthy presents besides the horse, and with obeisance and farewell sent him on the way of safety. When the conscientious thief received this divine benefaction, he realized that with [the hadith-based saying] *"Salvation lies in honesty"* as capital, a profitable trade is certain. He knew for certain that the caravan of wishes on the road of divine mercy reaches step by step the store of those who trust in God. He said to himself: "After all, to leave the capital of candor and honesty and to passionately aim at profit through complex deceptions is a source of depravity and disgrace, and sheer deficiency and wrongdoing."

He repented with his whole heart and spent his whole life secluded in the corner of the bazaar of honesty and modesty.

A DOG'S TESTIMONY ON THE DAY OF JUDGMENT

How a pious man of the Islamic community caused an ordinary dog to be killed, and how he became the object of divine reproach in the world of dreams and repented:

With this true and admonitory story, the roar of a persistent, head-splitting dog, who was a ferocious lion in the forest of goodness, came out of the thicket of a nightly conversation.

[The pious man related:] "For a while a weak dog lodged himself in a corner of my dilapidated horse stable. By day he walked along with the sheep in the fields; by night he wandered barking around the house. But one day he clenched his teeth in doggish desire and instinctive ravenousness into the fruits in the garden, otherwise well protected from all directions. When I beheld the evidence of his sharp teeth, my mean doggish soul felt anger toward this situation and I gestured to one of my servants to put an end to his life in some remote corner.

With friendly familiar words the servant called the helpless dog to his side and set off to a lonely place. Although the poor dog followed the order and obeyed, running after the servant, he went in such a sad manner as to suggest he knew that he was on the way to the place of his own demise. Thrice he turned back to me with sorrowful eyes, begging with the language of his body for help, as if he wanted to apologize in the hope of forgiveness for his transgression. The third time he lingered indecisively at the foot of a tree, and his desperate gaze expressed hopelessness. But when he saw in my angry face the resolve to take retribution and the furious furrow of my brow, he abandoned his hope for mercy and postponed the claim for forgiveness to Judgment Day.

Weakly and miserably he followed to heel the executioner, and finally they arrived at the intended place. Just as ordered, and with no hesitation, the bloodthirsty servant hurled a huge stone against the unlucky head of the poor dog. Immediately every sign of his life dissolved into the deadly void, very much like his transient essence.

In the evening I placed my head on a comfortable pillow, free from the fear of the possibility of judgment, of admonition, or of the need to answer for this despicable act before God the Exalted. When my servants, [that is, my] senses, were released to wander about the marketplace of sleep, in [my] dream I found myself in a peculiar and unearthly place. On this field of assembly on the Last Day, the Fulfiller of needs and Teacher for those who pray for salvation—*exalted is His majesty*—had convoked the council of the Last Judgment and arranged the scales of recompense for deeds of good and evil.

All manner of creatures were standing around at this place of punishment and reward, and groups of those who had suffered wrongs and now claimed their due had come in swarms for [compensation of] demands from the past. They stroke their claws into each other's tails. And behold—amid these creatures the poor maltreated dog lamented with his head held high and in an eloquent human voice, "My master, do you recognize this miserable, disappointed one who with heartfelt faithfulness stretching out his forelegs rested for many days in your house? Who showed himself, as far as the likes of us can, a trustworthy servant? I never was short of observing the rules of bread and salt (i.e., hospitality). According to the conditions of truth and benevolence, I did all I could. I kept watch day and night. Day and night in your service I denied my body rest and recreation. And one single time, when I went—avowedly intentionally—in mistaken belief in your generous forgiveness into your garden, you could not tolerate that I had sent a part of God's abundant blessings into the stomach of ravenousness. Owing to the inherent parsimony that is firmly anchored in the human envious nature and the conviction that such a miniscule and futile matter causes harm by diminishing your property, you did not have the grace to ignore my misstep and make [this grace] a golden thread in the robe of honor of humanity. You did not remember the rights due to my service and regarded my murder as appropriate. You saw it suitable to deprive me of roaming the kennel of the world before I was sated with the pleasure of life. Now, in the presence of God the Just, where king and beggar, human and animal are equal, the time has come to face a fair-minded Judge. Let us see what command will be issued according to the order of God, the distributor of justice." Thus he spoke and drew me by force into the court of God's majesty.

In the manner mentioned he made his testimony and claimed his right: "O Lord, when fulfilling on earth my service for this man, he ordered his servant to kill me because of a trifling transgression. I did not behave stubbornly and obstinately but followed him sadly and with tottering gait to the place of execution. Twice or thrice I asked for absolution of my fault—oh yes!—and when we arrived at that tree, I lingered for a while longing for a sign of forgiveness. But he showed no mercy and destroyed the capital of my sweet life." Thus he spoke.

[God] said, "As it has been proved that it was not you yourself who dealt with this matter, but after strict order engaged a servant, the divine order whose refusal is impossible is issued thus: As he has not done this guilty deed himself but through a servant, he will be dispossessed of half of his capital of good actions, his stock of capital of good deeds cut in half."

At that instant I found myself in the shape of a tall tree. And suddenly two fiery guards of hell with frightening gesticulations wielded a saw with sharp teeth, cut my trunk in the middle, and split it into two halves.

When I awoke with an anxiously pounding heart, I found myself trembling like a willow leaf. A stream [of tears] ran from my eyes and I sobbed and wailed. Even now I groan from that heart-rending fear. I seek forgiveness from God. From that day on I must seek shelter with God, the Forgiving and Helping One, not to harm even a defenseless ant. If I trembled like that in the world of dreams in fear of the Almighty's reproach, how could I be so bold as to approach God's true presence in the seen world." Thus he related and assured that this night-adventure was real. *May God overlook his faults through the sanctity of the Qur'an and its verses.*

FORTY-THREE

The Wiles of Women

Anonymous, Sixteenth to Seventeenth Centuries

TRANSLATED BY N. İPEK HÜNER CORA AND HELGA ANETSHOFER

Just as fiction plays a significant role in modern people's lives—in the form of novels, movies, and television shows—it had an important place in the premodern world. Several different genres of fictional stories were in circulation for the Ottoman audience. These stories dealt with people from all walks of life—sultans, townsmen, commoners, or peasants—in numerous realistic and fictional settings, from well-known city centers of the Islamicate world to imagined faraway lands.

Although many Ottoman prose stories had their roots in the rich Mediterranean and Iranian storytelling traditions, they were often rendered as more than just simple translations, and they were appropriated and embellished by Ottoman storytellers to suit their own context and readership. They are thus a rich source of information about the literary preferences of Ottoman writers, narrators, and audiences. While these stories cannot necessarily be considered exact reflections of life, they provide us with invaluable details about a bygone era and, more importantly, they illuminate commonly held beliefs and worldviews. A wealth of information concerning the social norms, expectations, and anxieties of Ottoman citizens are included in these narratives.

The short stories included in this chapter are witty anecdotes that center on the wiles of women. The "wiles of women" (*mekr-i zenan*) constituted a common trope in many stories in the Ottoman, Persian, and Arabic literary traditions. In these stories, the protagonist is a witty woman who tricks a man or men—commonly her husband—in ingenious ways. These women are usually portrayed as more resourceful than malignant in their trickery, and the stories aim at astonishing the audience with the intricacies of the trick. Remarkably, in most of the stories, the clever and wily female protagonist is not punished but wins the day; her actions remain unpunished or even undetected, regardless of their immorality. In the end, men are warned against the devilish nature of women.

The broader genre of trickster stories is not limited to ruses devised by women; rulers, scholars, and even animals could be the protagonists. These stories offered lessons for their readers and listeners, but the fact that the tricksters typically achieved their goals underlines the idea that these stories were not only read for edification. The stories usually do not have complicated plots and were written in a relatively plain language; they created a narrative space in which the societal norms are reversed through humorous and sometimes marvelous plot elements.

It is safe to assume that these stories were read in literary gatherings and circulated both in written and oral forms. An intriguing exercise, then, is to speculate about how the readers might have reacted to these stories. The scholarship traditionally presumes a male audience, because men simply had more opportunities to learn to read. At first glance, the morals presented by the stories support that perspective. However, the oral circulation of the stories and the tradition of reading aloud also make a female audience possible. One might then speculate how women would have perceived these stories of women's wiles. Could these stories be read as subversive? Might they also have conveyed advice to women about tricking men? Would they have given women an occasion to think beyond the social and cultural constraints imposed on them? Or would women be alarmed by the character of the female tricksters? While we cannot arrive at a definitive answer to these questions—not least because there would have been many women with varied interpretations—these and similar inquiries may guide us in pondering how these stories might have been read and perceived by different audiences.

LANGUAGE: Turkish. Lively prose narrative, including conversational elements with many idiomatic expressions and structures specific to spoken language. Some historical Arabic vocabulary, owing to the medieval Arabic source of the respective story.

SOURCE: Story 1-3: Untitled story collection. Türk Dil Kurumu El Yazması ve Nadir Eserler Kütüphanesi, Ankara, A 142, fols. 313b-316a, 323b-325b, 341b-342a. Story 4-5: *Menakıb-ı Hamsin.* Topkapı Sarayı Müzesi Kütüphanesi, Istanbul, Hazine 1279, fols. 128a-129a, 192a-193b.

---

1. THE WOMAN WHO ROBBED THE CHIEF JUDGE'S HOUSE

It is recorded in Süheyli's *Nevadir* (first half of the seventeenth century) that during the time of Baybars-ı Zahiri, the sultan of Egypt (r. 1260–76), there was a crafty and pretty woman in Cairo. She was exceedingly beautiful and attractive; extremely intelligent and sharp. No eye in the world had ever beheld a trickster like her; no mother of any era had given birth to a beauty like her. She was unique and ingenious in craftiness; skillful and fearless in stealing. She could wipe the kohl from someone's eyes [without them noticing], and like a magnet she could pull out money from people's pockets with their eyes open, as easily as if she were pulling a hair out of butter.

One day, the delicate beauty decorated herself abundantly with gold and silver and went to the bathhouse along with seven or eight slave girls. Close to evening she sent the girls home, hid herself in a solitary corner, and stayed there until nightfall. After nightfall, the city's chief of the police saw a woman in the street. He inquired why she was by herself. She said, "I belong to the household of a noble man. Our house is on the outskirts of the city. A friend of mine invited me to the bathhouse. I went with the permission of my husband. After I left the bathhouse, we walked through a crowded bazaar, and I got separated from my slave girls. I am completely exhausted. I cannot just go into anyone's house. I am also afraid of my husband. If there is a safe place known to you where you can have me shelter tonight, it will be easier for me to explain the situation to my husband."

It so happens that the house of the chief judge was nearby. The chief of police guided the woman to the judge's house and knocked on the door. He explained the situation and said, "Let her stay in your house until morning." The judge showed her much attention, and he put her in his private room where all the goods that people had entrusted to him for safekeeping were stored. They treated her with great respect, put a mattress in the room, and left her alone. After resting for a while she got up and opened the chests in that room. She took from the valuable and fine things in the chests as much as she could carry. She took jewels and other things worth twenty thousand gold coins. She had brought with her a bloody robe, a shirt, and a cap decorated with gold and pearls. She dug a hole in the darkness near the judge's outhouse and buried these things. In the gray of dawn, when everyone was sleeping, she opened the door and left.

In the morning everyone got up. They checked on the woman but she had vanished. They entered the room and saw that all the chests had been opened and the entrusted goods of the Muslims were gone. The judge tore out his hair and beard. He immediately sent someone to fetch the chief of police. He said to him: "You cruel man, you schemed to get that damned trickster woman into my house, and you let her plunder goods of the Muslims and my own worth twenty thousand gold coins. Either you have this woman found and brought here, or I will bring you before the sultan to legally contest with you." The chief of police begged the judge on his knees: "Give me a few days to search and find her! If I cannot find her, I will compensate you for the lost goods."

During the next few days, the chief of police scanned every corner of the city looking for the woman. One day he heard a woman cry out from the upper room of a house. He looked to find out who it was. A slave girl answered, "Come in! My lady wants to see you." The chief of police immediately dismounted from his horse and went up to the room. He saw a grand caravanserai, as it were, with abundant goods and chattels. The beautiful woman [from the earlier scam] and the police officer conversed for a while, whereupon she said, "Don't worry! My conscience doesn't allow me to leave you in this sorrow when you have behaved so courteously toward me." She went on: "I have no need for this wealth." She got up, opened the chests, and showed him that they were full to the brim with purses of money. "Now, let's make a deal: If you marry me, after I have resolved this issue, all this wealth will belong to you. You can enjoy it all." The chief of police agreed and swore, "That's what I have always wanted." The beauty said, "Now go to the judge's house at once and say, 'I have searched the

FIGURE 38. Women's bathhouse, eighteenth century. Enderunlu Fazıl, *Zenanname*, T. 5502, fol. 145a. İstanbul Üniversitesi Kütüphanesi, Istanbul.

whole world for this woman; if she were still alive, I would have found her! She was last seen in your house. I suspect you [of killing her]. We need to search your house!'"

The chief of police went to the judge and said what she had told him to. Thereupon the judge answered, "Hey you faithless backstabber! First you play this trick on me, and now you are even slandering me with murder! This is an unbearable attack on my reputation—come and do your search!" The woman had told the chief of police where she hid the clothes. He came in and searched a few spots in the house. In the end he dug up the ground next to the outhouse. The bloody robe, shirt, and gold- and pearl-decorated cap were discovered. The chief of police said, "You tyrant! You are a murderer and on top of it dare to falsely accuse me! Let's bring this case before the sultan and contest each other's claims." The judge was perplexed: *"There is no power and strength but in God!"* said he and fell on his knees before the chief of police. He begged him: "I have lost so much money. The only thing that I have left is my good reputation. Let it not be destroyed!" Finally, they kissed each other and reconciled, and acquitted each other.

The chief of the police felt triumphant and cheerful. He said to himself, "So let bygones be bygones. Not everyone has the luck to get such wealth, property, and such a beautiful woman. Let's go and get married right away and indulge in pleasure for the next few days!" With these words he went to the beauty's neighborhood and knocked at the front door. No one answered. When he knocked louder a nearby neighbor stuck his head out and said, "No one lives in that house. It's empty, don't knock for nothing!" The chief of police said, "Someone was here the other day. I saw them." "You are right," said the neighbor. "The house had been empty for a long time. Four or five days ago a woman came and moved in. But she moved out again. We don't know what kind of person she was. It's the third day now since she has moved out. Here is the key. She left it with us to give it to the owner of the house. Go in and have a look!" He opened the door, went up to the room, and saw there was not even an old reed mat left.

The chief of police returned [to the city] feeling like a battered dog. He was completely perplexed. "Apart from the craftiness of that woman," he said, "How could she fly like the prophet Solomon—*peace be upon him*—and remove so many luxurious goods in one day? Only the prophet Solomon—*peace be upon him*—could do that. What a shame! All the trouble I went through was for nothing." The fact that the crafty woman had showed herself to the chief of police again was actually a trick, a scheme to help him escape a great danger. Afterward she vanished so completely that no one ever found a trace of her.

2. THE WOMAN WHO WANTED TO DECEIVE A MERCHANT BY SWITCHING ROBES

It is narrated that there was a crafty woman in Baghdad. One day she put a gold-brocaded robe in a bundle and handed it to one of her slave girls. Walking in front of the girl she went to a prominent merchant in the draper's market. She took the robe out of the bundle, put it in front of the merchant, and asked, "How much is this robe worth?" The merchant said, "It's worth six hundred thousand akçe." The woman said, "Merchant, let me leave this robe here with you, and you give me one hundred thousand akçe instead, to be paid back in a month. After a month, I will give you back your money and pick up my robe, and I will abundantly return the favor." The merchant didn't want to disappoint the woman, gave her one hundred thousand akçe, and kept the robe with him. The woman walked away with the money but returned soon after and said to the merchant: "I just remembered something. Take your money and give me my robe." The merchant gave her the robe wrapped up in the bundle, took the money, and kept it next to him. The woman took the robe and went off to a solitary place. There she took the robe out of the bundle and put another one in instead. Then she returned to the merchant again and said, "Merchant, I am sorry I am giving you trouble. Please do give me the money!" She put the bundle with the robe in front of him. The merchant took the bundle with the robe and put it next to him. Then he gave her the purse with the money again. She took the money and left.

Three months passed and there was no sight of the woman. The merchant told the story to a friend of his. The friend said to the merchant: "Bring the robe, I want to take a look at it." The merchant brought the bundle and put it in front of his friend. He opened the bundle, saw the robe inside and said, "That robe is worth no more than one hundred akçe." At that moment the merchant knew that the evil woman had played a prank on him, and he had fallen for her scam. Thereupon the merchant went to the chief of police and told him the story in detail. The police officer said, "OK, that woman has played a trick on you, but after all, this is Baghdad, no one knows each other. But if you want this woman to be found I can teach you a trick. That way, I hope, this woman will be found and caught. Go to your shop tonight, break a few of the shutters, take all the goods and money inside your house and hide them. In the morning, lament like this: 'Last night robbers broke into my shop and stole all my goods. But I am not grieving about my own stuff. There was a precious robe wrapped up in a bundle that a woman had deposited with me for safekeeping. They stole this one, too. I don't know what to do or what to say to the owner of that robe!'" The merchant did exactly what the police officer had said. The news spread in Baghdad.

When that crafty woman heard about it, she came to the merchant, put the money in front of him and demanded the bundle with the robe. The merchant said, "The bundle with the robe was stolen." The woman pestered him, saying, "That robe costs nine hundred thousand akçe. The bundle with the robe has to be returned to me. If not, I accept not one akçe less than nine hundred thousand as reimbursement." The merchant said, "Come let's go to the chief of police together. Maybe he can have the robbers found, and I can get all my wares back." The merchant went to the police with the woman. He had the woman wait outside, went inside the police [station] and told the officer that the woman had come on her own account. The chief of police said to the merchant: "Bring the woman here! While I am talking with her, I will give you a sign. Then go and get the bundle with the robe. Say, 'The robe has been found.' Bring the bundle with the robe and put it in front of me!" Thus, the merchant brought the woman to the police officer. The police officer implored the woman: "Have mercy on the merchant!" But the woman completely disregarded him and kept saying "The bundle with the robe has to be returned to me."

FIGURE 39. An Ottoman lady, eighteenth century. Abdülcelil Levni (artist), in Album, Hazine 2169, fol. 11b. Topkapı Sarayı Müzesi Kütüphanesi, Istanbul.

At that moment, the police officer gave the merchant a sign. He went, brought the bundle with the robe to the officer and said, "Woman, I bring good news! Your robe has been found." He thus put the bundle with the robe before the police officer. The officer took the robe out of the bundle, saw it and said, "This robe is worth one hundred akçe at the most." When the woman saw the robe, she was terrified. The police officer said to the woman: "You trickster, you cheat, you crafty woman! Is this all you can do—this kind of trickery in the city of Baghdad?" He immediately got the woman undressed, tied a rock around her neck, threw her in the Tigris, and drowned her.

3. THE MERCHANT WHO TOOK A SECOND WIFE IN BASRA

It has been narrated that there was a merchant in Ahvaz (Iran). He had a wife who was second to none in tricking and deceiving people. When it came to uprightness and chastity, she would pretentiously compare herself to Rabia al-Adawiyya (a mystic from Basra). Her husband traveled to Basra often. As it so happens, he had taken a second wife there, and his first wife in Ahvaz heard about it. So she played a trick. Pretending she was the uncle of his other wife in Basra, she devised a letter addressed to her husband:

> Dear husband of my brother's daughter: Your wife here has passed away. Half of whatever she possessed as well as of her debts is now yours. You shall come now and take your lawful share.

After having penned this letter, she gave it to a sailor, who brought it to her husband, pretending it was sent from Basra. Reading the news of his second wife's passing, her husband became distressed and sad. He told his first wife to prepare provisions, for he had to leave for Basra. The wife started acting up and asked why he was going to Basra so often, wondering whether something lay behind his numerous trips—perhaps another wife? She badgered him so much that her husband became extremely irritated. Assuming that his second wife in Basra was dead anyway, he declared, "If I have another wife, I'll divorce her right now by my threefold *talaq* declaration." Thereupon the wife started grinning and said that it was she who had written the letter. His second wife was alive and well; she only had to be divorced with a threefold *talaq*, and now it was done.

4. THE BUTCHER'S WIFE AND HER LOVERS

In Istanbul, a janissary officer and a tailor were both the lovers of a butcher's wife, though they didn't know of one another. One day, it so happened that the butcher went on a trip. The woman invited the tailor to her house, and he arrived there in the evening. While the woman and the tailor were enjoying themselves with food and drink, someone knocked on the door. The slave girls went to the door and saw that the officer, having heard that the butcher was away on travel, had arrived with his felt janissary headgear and fur coat. He wanted to come inside to be with his lover. The girls hurried the news to the beautiful woman that disaster was imminent. After quickly deliberating on what to do, the butcher's wife decided to pretend to be sick in order to get rid of [the janissary officer]. Thus she hid the tailor behind the cover of the bedding cabinet and called in the officer.

She entertained the officer for a while. Although she flirted with him and gave him coquettish glances, the woman kept him at a distance, pretending she was sick. At that point, a knocking and a perturbed voice were heard outside. The slave girls checked the door and saw that the butcher had arrived. He had ridden his horse until night and had arrived home alone. He also brought a piece of meat wrapped in a cloth on the rump of the horse. Panic-stricken, the janissary officer did not know what to say or where to hide; he was like a moth trapped in a glass lamp or a madman on a chain. His sweetheart, the butcher's wife, came up with a solution for him, too. She wrapped him in an Egyptian rush mat with his headgear and fur, and she set him upright in a discreet corner.

The butcher fastened his horse and, after grooming and feeding it (?), he came in, sat down, and put the meat in front of him. He wanted to roast some of it, have a good dinner, and go to bed. As he sliced the meat and pierced the pieces with metal skewers, a cat snatched an especially good piece. The butcher snapped, grabbed a large knife, and went after the cat. The cat ran away and slipped under the cover of the cabinet. When the butcher lifted the cover, he saw that there was a man there. He pulled the tailor into the middle of the room, started shoving him, and yelled, "Hey, you ill-fated vicious fellow! What are you doing in my house?"

Realizing he would not be able to break away from the butcher, the tailor resorted to a ruse and said, "I didn't come here of my own free will. I am only obeying orders. Do not think me crazy. I came here with my master." The butcher replied, "What? Where is your master? You, come out immediately!" The janissary could not contain himself anymore, knocked down the mat to the ground, and looked for a way to escape. The butcher turned from the tailor to the janissary, seized him, and fought with him. In the meantime the tailor escaped and leaped to safety. He never learned what happened to the janissary officer.

He who cries for others will never stop crying
When the winter comes he will be in trouble again

Even though he helps everyone and is cautious
He won't be appreciated by anyone in the world

They say care of the self comes first
The trick is to save one's own self in this world

5. THE UNFAITHFUL MERCHANT'S CLEVER WIFE

A merchant in Istanbul fell in love with a neighbor's wife. He lost his head from desire and started acting lovestruck. His wife surreptitiously observed him and figured that he was having an affair with the neighbor woman. When she confronted him with the words, "They say you are having an affair with that woman. Everyone is talking about you," he repeatedly swore, "I have no idea what you are talking about. These are my enemies slandering me." Realizing that he would not be honest with her, the wife resorted to a trick.

She went to the house of her husband's lover and said, "I seem to have misplaced the keys to my chests. All my clothes are in them, and I need to go somewhere quickly. Would you lend me your coat, your kaftan, and a few other things I need to wear when I go out? I'll take care of my business and bring them back by tonight." The neighbor woman gave her all the things she asked for. The wife took the clothes, went back home, dressed up looking like the neighbor woman, and headed for her husband's shop.

When the husband saw the woman approach, he thought she was his sweetheart and could hardly contain himself. She greeted him from under her face cover, to which he responded: "Welcome! What an honor! What good winds have brought you here? What can I do for you?" With a thousand flirtatious and coquettish moves, she replied, "I need a plank. That's why I am here." "Of course!" said he, got up and brought out an exquisite red plank. He then placed it in front of her and declared, "Five florins shall be the special price." All the while he was beside himself from pleasure: he melted like sugar in water and ass's dung in clay.

Taking the plank to leave, the woman made a gesture for him to follow along. He quickly closed the shop and cautiously proceeded after her, fantasizing about their time together. The woman hastened to the neighbor's house, made another gesture before entering the courtyard through the gate, and waited for him behind the door. As the man checked his surroundings and saw that there was no one around, he entered through the gate. At that moment, the wife lifted her face cover and hit the man in the face with the plank so hard that he saw stars. She yelled, "You shameless man! You neighbor-disgracing bastard! You sell yourself as righteous to me, and at the same time you charge the 'special' price for the plank! Really?" She grabbed him by the beard and dragged him home.

> Don't say women are deficient in intellect
> Even among them are some smart ones

> They can manipulate and play tricks on you
> Wake up from your idle daydreaming!

> They teach you myriad of stratagems, o dear
> Don't let them fool you, save yourself!

FORTY-FOUR

Social Criticism and Invective in Poetry

Various Poets, Fifteenth to Seventeenth Centuries

TRANSLATED BY SOOYONG KIM

For the Ottomans, poetry was the main medium of literary expression and was considered the pinnacle of rhetorical skill more broadly. Poets were routinely described as nightingales of the garden of eloquence, whereas prose writers received no such high-flown praise. Among the many testaments to the importance of poetry in Ottoman culture are the countless collections, anthologies, and miscellanies compiled over the centuries that privileged this art above all others. And although courtly patronage played a significant part in the cultivation of poetic craft, the audience for poetry crossed the social spectrum.

The forms and genres, as well as an established repertoire of topoi and tropes, were adopted from the Perso-Arabic poetic tradition. The poems were typically composed in couplets and conceived as single yet mostly interrelated grammatical units, and they adhered to specific meters and rhyme schemes. Lyric poetry was the predominant genre, with the speaker assuming the persona of an ever-faithful lover, and the rose of his or her affection being either divine or mundane. Poets, then, put a premium on demonstrating good command of the conventions in a distinct Turkish idiom and style.

Still, even within such limiting bounds, poets had some room for artistic creativity and even for originality, if not for outright invention in the modern sense. Their creativity relied on the manipulation of familiar tropes, often in an allusive manner, to give them a fresh and novel take, and those who could not do this were considered less capable or worse by their peers. The better poets were recognized for their lexical sophistication, as exemplified by their ability to exploit the potential meanings of a term or image. And the intended effect could be euphoric or melancholic, humorous or malicious. However, not every listener and reader comprehended the complexity of the expressions and images. That is, some poems were simply more accessible than others.

Aside from displays of rhetorical prowess, poets broached numerous topics, beyond love and faith, in their compositions. Additionally, despite an expected level of decorum, poets could and did take a critical stance on social issues, from ignorance and corruption to the rivalry for patronage and status. They conveyed their views in the course of an entire poem, in fragments, or through scattered verses. A popular genre for critical opinion was the invective, which could veer from outlandish statements of ridicule to ad hominem personal attacks, frequently in the form of a pithy quatrain. The poets preferred clever expressions based on sharp observations to base insults. The invectives were intended to circulate rapidly among fellow poets, and ideally to elicit a response from the targeted party, if that person had the poetic guts.

The following selection is a representative sample of poems, whole and in part, that can fall under the category of social criticism; a fair number are invectives. The poems are by ten poets, major and minor, spanning the classical period from the fifteenth to the seventeenth century. Included among them is a work by Fuzuli, a provincial poet whose verses in Azeri Turkish had a significant impact on Ottoman literary circles centered mostly around the capital city of Istanbul.

LANGUAGE: The translations try to do justice, as much as possible, to the compressed word play and allusive imagery of the originals in Turkish. Brackets have not been used in this chapter.

SOURCE: The selection is based on poems in: Güfta, Hüseyin. *Divan Şiirinde Cehalet.* Ankara: Akçağ Yayınları, 2011; and Abdulkadiroğlu, Abdulkerim. "Klasik Türk Şiirinde Hiciv." PhD diss., Gazi University, Ankara, 1997. The individual poems have been compared with other published editions and manuscript copies, and a couple have been abbreviated for the sake of space.

---

1. A POET'S APPEAL TO FATE TO CONSIDER HIS IGNORANCE, BY ŞANİ (D. CA. 1534)

O fate, since you favor the ignorant and ill-informed,
That accomplished and well-informed also I'm not.

Thinking of me as wise—why this cruelty to me?
If you assumed I'm learned, God forbid, I'm not!

I'm the most ignorant of the lot, consider me too,
Inferior in folly and stupidity to others I'm not.

Let all the ignorant come, then test my ignorance;
Today, equal to any in slow-wittedness I'm not.

Let me show the ignorant how to get high office;
Especially now, with ignorance, mightier I'm not!

2. A WARNING AGAINST TEACHING MISCHIEF-MAKERS, BY FUZULİ (D. 1556)

O teacher, knowledge for the wicked is tool for fraud;
So beware, don't teach divine matters to deceitful men!

Those who teach knowledge to mischief-makers for trickery,
Hand the executioner a sharp blade for a public massacre.

Whatever fraud the ignorant propagate is just a sprout,
The root of the corruption of the age is the learned's mischief.

3. A RESPONSE TO THE IGNORANT SUFI, BY FUZULİ

O ignorant Sufi, you said, "let's ban the reed-flute's cry,"
Acting against God's law, you devastated Islam's honor.

If you wish to talk about ecstasy with this stature of yours,
My God, like the reed-flute, pierced with holes your body will be.

4. A RETORT TO THE IGNORANT WEALTHY, BY FUZULİ

I've spent the coin of life and acquired knowledge,
As the worldly accumulated wealth, utterly ignorant.

The world's a market where everyone tenders their goods,
The worldly silver and gold, the skilled merit and talent.

I seek not to profit from him who profits not from me;
It's indecent to profit from him who's no profit to me.

I seek not the stash of silver and gold the ignorant offer,
Since it's a sin to enjoy wealth for free from the ignorant.

5. ON SERVICE AND INGRATITUDE, BY NABİ (D. 1712)

Even by choice, being out of office is a strange thing;
It gives the heart, for sure, an out of place sorrow.

A man's house of dignity has been reduced to rubble,
By the troubling and distressing attention of vile men.

Truth be told, on the ruined land of my heart
Having an office or not takes no toll at all.

But those evil-natured with want of opportunity,
Their conduct is the portent of a harsh winter.

Where's he who used to deify me, saying "I'm your servant"?
Now he doesn't even greet back when saluted on the street.

Where's he who used to, out of respect, not sit down?
Now he doesn't even stand up at a gathering where I appear.

Where's he who used to bow his body when he saw me?
Now he shoots sharp arrows when he opens his mouth.

Even if raised by the grace of your bread and salt,
Now your house servants wouldn't respect you.

They make it their lawful doctrine to torment and mistreat you,
They who used to outlaw sleep for themselves to serve readily.

They who used to rush to prepare themselves for swift service,
Now they don't inconvenience themselves with the slightest step.

Where are those who used to race one another to serve first?
Now they, out of disgust, beg one another to go ahead!

Every day someone was once willing to enter your service,
Now every night someone is eager to run away.

6. ON CORRUPTION, BY NABİ

To serve justice in this age is hard, yet
It's invalid where God's law presides not.

It's especially so, most men of law,
They apply not God's commands.

They auction off verdicts in advance,
And whoever bids high wins in favor.

For the poor who can't offer a bribe,
Judges permit them not to litigate.

Most, with no creed or faith, know one thing;
Their eyes only on the crop and the bribe.

In their hands a bushel measure and a scale,
They've turned the courts into shops.

If they want, they make a creditor fall into debt
And convert the bankrupt into a Croesus.

FIGURE 40. Governor general of European provinces (Rumeli). Artist unknown. Cod.Rål. 8:o no. 10 (*Rålambska dräktboken*), fol. 29. Kungliga Biblioteket, Stockholm.

Servants of the Holy Law are the judges, but
Not even vermin perform injustice as they do.

They've branded the bribe a "crop,"
So who now can say no to the crop?

7. ON HAYALİ'S HEADGEAR, RIVAL POET AND OFFICIAL OF THE RUMELİ PROVINCE, BY YAHYA BEY (D. 1582)

Hayali, my favorite, you humor the world;
Your nest of a cap's like a silly Stephen's crown.

O Hayali, you're a venerable bird among birds;
The tassel of yours behind hangs like a pecking bird.

Don't turn yourself into some merchant of sheep,
O opportune fool, by donning the Rumeli cap.

When the sun rises glaring at your cap, under its shield,
Rein free, you lash your horse and ride away.

Heed Yahya's words, don't be people's laughingstock;
Monkey-like, toss your cap away to the wild.

8. ON HAYALİ'S SPARSE BEARD, BY ZATİ (D. 1546)

Spits of hair have dawned on Hayali's face, but bare it remains,
All I want is to describe, to decorate it with a streak of shit.

On both sides of this fool dervish's face hang wisps of hair,
As though two leaves were tied to his cheek-balls and face-ass.

People know there's use in plucking even one bristle from a pig,
So they plucked his beard, hair by hair, and made a barefaced fool.

I said I'd pluck your beard, he replied what guts you have;
He knows not the mischief of my words, see what a fool he is!

We plucked his beard on the sly, then stuck it in his asshole;
But he's a wandering minstrel, thus why his big mouth's pooped.

9. ON YAHYA EFENDI, RIVAL POET AND GRAND MUFTI, BY NEF'İ (D. 1635)

Saying "kismet," from a tyrant and lowlife like Etmekçi*
Thousand gold coins you stole again, o mad Yahya.

But does this greed fall within Islam? Such a sin,
If yet alive, even the hatted Yahya would've rejected.

* Etmekçizade Ahmed Pasha (d. 1618), chief treasurer who amassed much wealth in his lifetime.

10. ON SİYAHİ, MINOR POET, BY YAHYA BEY

None like Siyahi will come to the world,
Ignorant and silly, abject and mad.

Every day because of dying his beard,
He has no time to scratch his head.

O Lord, what black tragedy that,
Dealing with his beard is all he does.

His verses lack color, but odd that
This idler thinks poetry's a picnic!

You can't paint a thing with a fart,
Like this goes the age-old proverb.

O Yahya, if he asks about the meter,
Yakety yak, yakety yak, yak yak yak.

11. ON VEYSİ, RIVAL POET, BY NEF'İ

It suits a bumpkin Turk like that to carry with him
An old sack instead of a purse for a book of deep verse.

If he has skill, let him come to blows with me;
Here's the sword of speech, here's the battle arena!

God's forbidden the fountain of intellect for the country Turk,
Regardless of how much licit magic he uses for his words.

An old-style pen is his, a fresh one—does he have?
He has in hand, indeed, the staff of misguided old men.

The difference between the old and the new style is clear; God forbid,
His prosperous Kaaba should ever be equated to deserted ruins!

The bumpkin Turk's the alley grocer in the city of babble;
His poems are but stones for weighing items in his shop.

12. ON ÉMIGRÉ POETS, BY LE'ALİ (FIFTEENTH CENTURY)

If you wish to be esteemed here,
Do come from Arabia or Persia!

A gem's got no value in the mine,
So can a pearl find worth in the sea?

A witty and quaint saying is this:
Darkness is ever at the candle's foot.

If a man has knowledge and desire,
How does his country show him appreciation?

It's true, a gem comes from stone,
Even so, the cutter's skill is still admired.

Shouldn't Persians pop up in Rum,
Since they're held high with honor?

Whoever comes to Rum from Persia,
He becomes a governor, even a vizier!

13. ON THE FIERY PREACHER, BY NİYAZİ-İ MISRİ (D. 1694)

I went to an assembly today; there sat and spoke the preacher,
Read from his book and made the crowd wail, the preacher.

Divided the folk into two, dispatched one half to Heaven,
The other to Hell, with a hand gesture from the pulpit, the preacher.

Flames that could set damned Satan on fire spewed from his mouth;
You'd think he's the punishment of the seven pits, the preacher.

Crammed people into Hell like that, with no room to stand;
Condemning them there is a laborious job for the preacher.

Advice is truly due to him who utters fiery words all the time;
Niyazi, however, only shares with such a man the title preacher.

14. ON THE SOUP KITCHEN, BY MÜ'MİN (SIXTEENTH CENTURY)

Sir, is it worthy on your just watch
For a soup kitchen to become a mess?

If you wonder about one grain of the rice,
It takes skill to chew, a miracle to swallow!

The bread's unfit to eat, the meat stew raw,
There's no taste or thrill from the meal!

15. ON EGYPT, BY FEHİM (D. 1647)

I've seen much but I've yet to spot a single man, since
My eyes are blurry from the endless donkey dust of Egypt.

The camels are frail and drooly, and the asses tough,
O sir, that's the nature of the old and young of Egypt!

It's worthy as the land of dragons and home of owls,
Treasures turn up, indeed, in ruined corners of Egypt.

If there's a man who's been to Hell, let him give news
Whether sinners can be made to fear the pain of Egypt!

Holy men there wander with bare heads buried in hands,
So hope not for grace or favor from the brazen of Egypt!

FORTY-FIVE

Shrewd Witticisms by a Master Poet

Zati's Anecdotes, Sixteenth Century

TRANSLATED BY HELGA ANETSHOFER

Zati was a poet born sometime during the 1470s in Balıkesir in the northwestern region of Anatolia. He practiced bootmaking at his father's shop, but it seems he also found time to attend literary gatherings in his provincial town and hone his skills as a poet. Composing Ottoman classical poetry generally required a good deal of familiarity with established forms and tropes, and it also required a solid knowledge of grammar and a rich conjoined lexicon of Turkish, Arabic, and Persian. However, occasionally poets like Zati, who lacked an elite education but had inborn talent, took their chances in the literary arena. In fact, aspiring poets viewed poetry as a medium through which they might achieve upward social mobility. Zati's educational and social background is reflected in his poetry in the form of his sincere expressions, and in his proficient use of Turkish idioms rather than copious interplays of loan words from Arabic or Persian, which was common with other poets.

When he was in his thirties, Zati made a bold move: He went to Istanbul. The imperial throne city had perhaps not yet reached the glorious literary glamour that it would by the middle of the sixteenth century, but there was already a thriving scene of literary activity in the early 1500s that drew aspiring artists to the city. But mere competence was not enough to achieve success in this competitive artistic environment. Poets usually presented their work at regularly occurring literary gatherings or at ad hoc venues like the merchandise shop of someone interested in poetry. If the opportunity presented itself, a laudatory ode (*kaside*) submitted to a statesman could mean more than just poetic recognition, and it might come with a handsome stipend or even potentially a long-term income in the grandee's artistic retinue. Keeping an entourage of able poets and artists helped boost the image and prestige of a wealthy person or statesman. It was a symbiotic relationship. Even so, if the patron fell out of imperial favor or died, artists did not have any institutional support.

While Zati received patronage from sultans and high-ranking statesmen in his early years in Istanbul, he later had to make his living from a geomancy shop (see chapter 32) in the courtyard of the Bayezid Mosque, where he wrote amulets, told fortunes, and also acted as a mentor to some of the most celebrated poets of the sixteenth century. He may have had a modest income—sources say he was a contented person—but his artistic reception as a poet had its ups and downs. Zati was a master of lyric poetry. A lyric poem or *gazel* was considered by the Ottomans to be the most noble form of poetry and the main medium by which the poets showed their rhetorical prowess. With thousands of *gazel*s in his collection, Zati proved to be a prolific and inventive poet with a pleasing poetic melody. Although the main artistic realm in which they displayed their talents was lyric poetry, these creative personalities apparently also often had disagreements and rivalries and were fond of engaging in wars of words. Such controversies constituted "media events" among peer poets and the literary aficionados of the court society and were closely followed by many.

The witty anecdotes included in this chapter are selected from Zati's sizeable collection of "pleasantries." His anecdotes are usually set in Istanbul and involve real people. Being the accomplished poet that he was, the anecdotes generally culminate in a clever couplet. To understand the subtleties of Zati's humor requires knowledge of historical euphemisms, as well as the nature and context of the disagreements between the parties. While some of Zati's witty anecdotes were innocent satire, many were obscene taunts that commonly alluded to male-on-male intercourse. The humorous effect was achieved not so much through the use of coarse or vulgar language but by employing highly ambiguous language with multiple layers of wordplay and double entendre. Name-calling or mocking the physical traits of an opponent were commonplace. However, the poets who were exchanging lampoons were often close friends.

LANGUAGE: Old Anatolian Turkish prose with rhymed punchlines. Multiple sexually charged double entendres and ambiguities.

SOURCE: Manuscript: Süleymaniye Kütüphanesi, Istanbul, Lala İsmail, 443, fols. 345b-362a. Transcription: Çavuşoğlu, Mehmed. "Zâtî'nin Letâyifi." *İstanbul Üniversitesi Edebiyat Fakültesi Türk Dili ve Edebiyatı Dergisi* 18 (1970): 1-27. Alternative translations of anecdotes nos. 5 and 12 are found respectively in *Ottoman Lyric Poetry: An Anthology*, edited by Walter G. Andrews, Najaat Black, and Mehmet Kalpaklı, 57. Seattle: University of Washington Press, 2006 and Ambros, Edith Gülçin. "'O Asinine, Vile Cur of a Fool Called Zati!': An Attempt to Show That Unabashed Language Is Part and Parcel of an 'Ottoman Idiom of Satire.'" *Journal of Turkish Studies* 27 (2003): 117.

---

1. Once I had a very bad earache; I was in a lot of pain. Keşfi heard about it and made this joke: "A clyster would do him good." However, Keşfi's head was bald, so I composed the following verse and sent it to him,

FIGURE 41. A social gathering, sixteenth century. Artist unkown, in Sadi's *Gulistan*. Purchase Charles Lang Freer Endowment, F1949.2 Rajab b. Khayr al-Din / Freer Gallery of Art, Smithsonian Institution, Washington, DC.

So Keşfi said of this poor one, a clyster would do him good,
If a bald man knew anything, he would find a solution for himself (lit. for his head).

NOTE: Zati's friend and peer, the poet Keşfi (d. 1538–39). A clyster was a common medical treatment much like an enema and primarily used for stomachache and constipation. It was thought to have many benefits. The insertion of a clyster evokes the image of the anus being penetrated.

2. Once I had a get-together in a wine tavern with a group of sophisticated men. There was an elegant gent among them. His name was Topçızade ("Son of the Cannoneer"). He was continuously teasing this poor and weak one. Finally I said, "Topçızade, be quiet, or I'll let you have it." He said, "That's exactly what I wanted to do, to provoke you to say a verse." Hearing this I said:

Let me satirically shoot a bullet up Topçızade['s ass],
Let me make him fart fire today like a musket.

NOTE: The word *sıkı* is used in the specialized meaning "bullet" here in the phrase "let me shoot a bullet" (*bir sıkı basayın*). Its basic meaning, however, is "thick" and it is often used to allude to the penis. The images of "shooting a bullet" and a "firing musket" are triggered by the name Topçızade, "Son of the Cannoneer."

3. One day three of us went to Trouser seller Şeyhi's store. He had such a tiny store that we could hardly fit inside. So I created this verse:

You live in a place as tight as an asshole (*büzük denlüce yer*),
The three of us could hardly squeeze in.

4. There was a guy called Memi who used to make good ink. I went to his store to buy ink. There was a scribe called Dumbass (*kir-i har*, lit. "donkey dick"), who also came to the store. Memi got up immediately and gave Dumbass thick ink—whereas he gave me a thin one. I couldn't help but say this verse:

Ink-seller Memi, if I only knew what Dumbass is to you,
You got up and gave him a thick one, then turned to me and gave me a thin one.

NOTE: Memi, the illiterate inkmaker and amateur poet Enveri (d. 1547). In satirical poetry, the opposition "thin" (*durı*) and "thick" (*koyu*) is often used in reference to the penis—metaphorically or explicitly. However, "you gave him a thick one (ink or penis)" in Turkish *ana durdun koyu verdün*, can also be read as *ana durdun koyuverdün*, meaning "You got up and penetrated him." "You gave me a thin one (ink or penis)" in Turkish *bana döndün duri verdün,* can also be read as *bana döndün durıverdün,* meaning "You turned around and stayed bent for me."

5. Once I was chatting in Galata with a stunningly beautiful young man from a good family. Many jokes were made during our conversation. This shining light of any gathering of friends got excited by my jokes. He was wearing a smoke-colored Frankish kaftan. He said, "My lord Zati, I want you to have this kaftan. Come tomorrow to pick it up from our place." In the morning I went there, but he said, "It is stored away in the chest for you, no one is home. My mother has the key. You need not come again, I'll send it over to you with a servant boy." "Fine," I said, and left. About a month passed by; I figured he was not sending it. So I made this verse and sent it to him. Seeing it, he sent me the kaftan's value in cash. This is the verse:

> Why are you acting slowly to give us this robe of honor,
> If it was for some dumbass you would have quickly put it on him.

NOTE: *Kir-i har,* literally "donkey dick," was used to describe a large penis, at the same time it was slang for a foolish person, a "dumbass." The second line of the verse, *eger bir kir-i har olsa idi kalkar geydürürdün çüst,* can also mean, "If it was a large dick you would quickly have your anus wear it." Much later, the Ottoman poet Süruri (d. 1816) would use the same image more explicitly in this obscene verse (in his *Hezeliyyat*): "I said (to him), make that unbeliever of a prick of mine wear your anus like a hat. / My catamite exposed his ass and said, as you please."

6. I had a white horse, which had been dear to me for a long time. A smooth-tongued, eloquent, witty guy asked, "My lord Zati, what is the temperament and the coat color of your four-legged animal?" He was hoping I would say, "It is white and soft." I answered with this half verse:

> It is very white, and its head is hard; wherever you squeeze it in, it will go in
>   "clip clop."

NOTE: The color white (often also silver) is a reference to the beloved's shiny and hairless body. The "four-legged animal" is an image for a boy beloved crouching on all fours "doggy style." By answering "white and soft" Zati could be understood as alluding to a beloved boy, since the expression "white and soft" is a stereotypical description for the buttocks of the beloved. Zati, aware of this dangerous ambiguity, in his answer alludes to his penis when seemingly talking about his horse. The horse's treading sound (*darb,* translated as "clip clop") can also be understood as "pounding hard."

7. In Edirne there lived an administrator of a pious foundation called Poll tax-collector Hüsam. He was a poet and his pen name was Feridi. One day I was walking around with him in a garden when it suddenly started to rain. There was a beautiful gazebo with four pillars in this garden. The gardener came and said to Feridi: "Sir, come underneath the gazebo, squeeze in!" When I heard this, I composed the following line spontaneously:

> When the gardeners saw poor Feridi in the rain,
> They said, "O poor man, go under this four-legged gazebo, squeeze in."

NOTE: Poll tax-collector Hüsam, the poet Feridi (died during Selim I's reign, 1512–20). The gazebo resting on four pillars (*çartak*) evokes the image of a boy beloved, crouching on all fours.

8. One day, during a friendly conversation, Feridi flew into a passion and said, "People say, no one has experienced continuous good fortune, but, by my religion, I have!" When I heard these words I said:

> So he says, "By my religion, I have experienced continuous good fortune!"
> Tell him, o Zati, this Feridi should not make meaningless oaths.

9. Once upon a time there was a gentleman by the name of Koçı Bey. Four men with nicknames were friends with him. One was a thin guy; he was called "Peppermint Twig" and he was a bad person. One was a dumb guy; he was called "Ram Balls." One was a bullshitter; he was called "Elephant Shit." One was a polite gent; he would always say, "Hey, man!" So they called him "Man." One day Ram Balls was offended by Elephant Shit and said, "I'm gonna kill him and eat him—however it happens." The friends said, "He's a big fella; you are a weak guy. How will you eat him?" He answered, "Peppermint Twig will help me. The two of us will eat him." Man heard this and got offended. When Koçı Bey heard about this issue he said to Man, "What do you care? Let them do their thing." This humble poet heard about it and created this verse and read it to Koçı Bey. He enjoyed it and gave me a kaftan.

> Is it a wonder that Man would be offended by [Ram Balls's] doings?
> Your Balls have started eating Shit along with Twig.

NOTE: The nicknames take part in creating multiple layers of meaning. "Twig" can be slang for penis, and "Man" is used in the meaning "people, men" in the verse. "Doing, action" (*fi'l*) is a common euphemism for the sexual act. Thus, the verse also reads: "Is it a wonder that people are disgusted by your fucking around (lit. your doing him)? / [By penetrating his anus] your penis and balls have gotten defiled with shit."

10. One day Feridi said, "Whether that Zati tells fortunes by reading the sand or writes poems—whatever food he is being cooked with, he rises up to the top of the pot like a chickpea." I heard about it and spoke this verse:

> Whether Zati is a poet or a fortune-teller, Feridi man,
> Is none of your business. Shut up! You are a pain in his ass.

NOTE: The chickpea rising to the top in boiling water is an allusion to an allegorical story in Rumi's *Masnavi*. There the chickpea symbolizes the believer who has to suffer and go through trials in order to improve his existence. But the chickpea is lacking this insight and keeps complaining about the sufferings it is subjected to.

11. When I used to live in Vefazade district, during Ramazan, close to the festival time, the dervishes would retreat to their cells and pray in seclusion. There was a dervish called Yakini, who was praying in seclusion too. Normally he would always joke with me. When it was time for the festival he came out of his cell. I ran into him and said, "My lord Yakini, what a delightful time you have been having! While you were praying in seclusion this humble one saw Abdurrezzak in my dream. I said to him, 'Our dervishes pray in seclusion, they are doing wonderful things.' Abdurrezzak said, 'They are entrusted to us, we herd and watch over them.' I replied, 'My sultan, our lord Yakini is a very capable person, a peerless dervish.' Abdurrezzak said, 'My lord Zati, are you trying to tell me about the pig that I am herding?'"

12. There was a poetess from Amasya called Mihri Hatun (d. 1506), who used to live in Istanbul. She had grown old without ever marrying; she was a virgin. There was a gentleman called Pasha Çelebi, who was a professor at the Eyüp [Sultan] medrese. One day he asked for Mihri Hatun's hand in marriage. But she did not accept. I heard about it and spoke this quatrain:

> We heard that the Pasha wanted to marry Mihri,
> Should she submit herself to this old man?
> The poor woman has fasted for so many years,
> Should she now celebrate the breaking of the fast with a dumbass (lit. "donkey dick")?

Reportedly, when Mihri Hatun heard this quatrain, she was very amused and said, "I wish I had composed it."

13. There was a guy who was cross-eyed. He was called Cross-eyed (*Şaşı*) Bali. Whoever became the administrator of the İne Bey Subaşı charitable soup kitchen in Balıkesir would make Bali his proxy and go about his business. One day the administrator left, and another

one came. There was an elegant friend called Dervish Hasan, who was good at making witty jokes. When I was talking with him in his shop, all of a sudden Cross-eyed Bali showed up. I said, "I wonder if Bali is also the proxy for the new administrator?" Dervish Hasan said, "He wants a morally straight person, and Bali's eyes don't line up...." When Bali heard this, he was offended. I said to him, "No need to be offended, the guy got confused (*şaşa geldi*) and said something, that's all!" When Bali heard this, he started to laugh.

NOTE: Wordplays based on Bali's strabismus condition. The word *şaşı*, "cross-eyed" is derived from the verbal root *şaş-*, "to deviate, go wrong." Zati uses the same root in *şaşa geldi*, "[his mind] deviated, went astray," to express that Dervish Hasan "got confused." Bali's eyes, which "do not line up" (lit., they have no straightness, Turkish: *doğruluk*), are in opposition to being a morally straight person (Arabic: *müstakim*).

14. I had a vineyard that I inherited from my father. Each one of its grapes was as sweet as a bottle of sugar water. If Alexander the Great had seen them he would not have gone looking for the water of life. There were two guys, one was called Dog (*İt*) İskender, the other one Bird (*Kuş*) Kasım. They happened to pass by the vineyard and ate a lot of grapes. Later they came to me and asked for my forgiveness. I said, "You don't need to ask my forgiveness; when my father planted the vineyard, he said, 'Let dogs and birds eat freely from it.'" On hearing this joke they laughed and took leave.

15. Once a preacher at the Ayasofya Mosque criticized the ceremonial music bandmasters and sang the praises of the school and medrese students. When he finished his sermon, I went to him and said, "My lord, those who have good intentions you criticize, and you praise those who have bad intentions. Why are you doing this?" He replied, "What do you mean?" I said, "Those bandmasters that you criticized—they pray to God that all Muslim women get pregnant and give birth to boys, so that they may go there and play music for them. When a boy is born and they play for his birth, they pray that the boy grows older and his father has him circumcised so they can come back and celebrate again. Then they say, 'May he get married, then we will have another celebration.' Then they pray that he also has sons and daughters. They wish for the growth of the Muslim community. But those medrese students that you praised—they say, 'I wish that an influential man died, and I'd go to see his body to perform the rites, and they'd give me one or two akçe'; they wish for the *decrease* of the Muslim community." When the preacher heard this he agreed.

16. During the reign of the deceased Sultan Bayezid (II., r. 1481–1512) I used to present him with three odes a year: One on the occasion of the spring festival (*nevruz*), and two others for the two religious festivals (i.e., the sacrifice and Ramazan festivals). In the spring he would give me two thousand akçe and at the festivals he would give me kaftans, one side of which was silk brocade and the other side of which was woolen broadcloth. I would never wear

them; I would sell them because they were made of silk brocade. Once I requested a woolen robe (*sof cübbe*) and composed this quatrain:

> O pillars of the state, I am the sea of the pearls of meaning,
> Green and red silk brocade suits quarrelsome soldiers,
> Please give me wavy blue wool instead. May he who sees me in it say,
> "Today this sea was churned up by the wind of the grace of the king."

I brought it to the imperial council. The deceased Ali Pasha (d. 1511) was the grand vizier; I read it to him. He said to the chief treasurer: "Give our Molla Zati a blue woolen robe, lined with scarlet broadcloth." The chief treasurer said, "Poets are not given a woolen robe, scholars (*mollas*) get them." I said, "See, the noble pasha called me 'Molla Zati.' With his confirmation a person can get a whole city, not only a robe." The chief treasurer said, "Him calling you a molla is like calling a blind guy eagle-eyed. He is calling you the opposite of what you are because you are not a molla." I said, "Why am I not a molla? I can well be a substitute judge in Edirne, Bursa, or Istanbul." The chief treasurer said, "Let me ask you a question. If you are able to answer it, then you *are* a molla." "Fine," I said. He asked about a difficult passage on the religious obligations. I realized I didn't know that passage, so I countered, "Go, ask the big kadı!" Ali Pasha said to the chief treasurer: "Now it is proven that he is a molla. Give him the robe." And they gave me a woolen robe.

NOTE: When Zati does not know the answer to the question he resorts to the phrase, "Go, ask the big kadı (i.e., judge)!" (*yürü büyük kadıya*). The grand vizier Ali Pasha confirms tongue-in-cheek that this is a common attitude of ignorant mollas who send people away when they are asked difficult questions. The big kadı could be a military judge or another high-ranking legal scholar.

17. The deceased Ali Pasha reportedly saw one day a few of this poor and humble one's lyric poems, took a liking to them, and asked, "Why doesn't he submit any of these to me?" I heard about it, wrote a few poems, went to his council, and offered them to him. He thought it was a letter of complaint and passed it on to the clerk. İsa Bey (d. 1543), the son of İbrahim Pasha, was sitting next to him and said, "My lord, this is Molla Zati, he has brought you poems." The pasha hadn't seen me before. He looked at my face and said, "I had heard Zati is not pretty, but in fact there is no one uglier." I said, "My lord, 'One man is a mirror to another.'" When the pasha heard this, he burst into loud laughter. He accepted the poems and bestowed on me a generous reward.

NOTE: The phrase "One man is a mirror to another" (*yigit yigidün aynasıdur*) is based on the hadith *al-mu'min mir'atu l-mu'min* ("One believer is a mirror to another").

18. One day, when I was going to the thermal bath in Bursa with a stunning young man, we ran into a few women. The young beauty was a womanizer. When he saw the women he

said, "Do you have a shirt with a split collar to sell? I really want one." One mouthy broad answered, "Since your incised collar came on the market, no one is interested in our split collars anymore."

NOTE: The women's split collar (*yarma yaka*) is an allusion to the vulva; the young man's incised collar (*oyma yaka*) is an allusion to the anus.

FORTY-SIX

Subversive Jokes Featuring a Folk Hero

Nasreddin Hoca Jokes, Sixteenth Century

TRANSLATED BY KATHLEEN BURRILL

Nasreddin Hoca is the protagonist of a number of short, comic stories, or "jokes" that were widely popular in the Ottoman urban and rural domains. He appears as a common peasant in some jokes, and as a judge, scholar, or physician of a small town in others. Versions of some of the stories have been told and loved by Turkic-speaking people from the Balkans to central Asia. From the sixteenth century onward, the witty character and his jokes gradually became more popular, and the compendium constantly expanded, integrating joke plots from other similar characters popular in the wider Middle East.

As his joke collections drew a great deal of scholarly attention, modern researchers sought for evidence for Nasreddin Hoca's historical existence. He is generally believed to have lived in central Anatolia in the thirteenth century, but no near-contemporary source is available. The earliest mention of a character called Nasreddin Hoca is from the late fifteenth century, and the earliest written collections of Hoca jokes are from the sixteenth century.

The Nasreddin Hoca stories are usually set in a village or small town in the countryside, and the protagonists are not real personages but clichéd personality types. Characters are not fully developed; they act according to primal human instincts. The Hoca jokes most certainly appealed to a general public of various backgrounds. The language is plain and the humor is simple and direct. It is important to note, however, that the language and content of the stories changed considerably from its earliest examples in the sixteenth century to nineteenth-century printed editions. The earliest collections contain noticeably more bawdy jokes and coarse language. The jokes in the earliest collections make fun of many established societal conventions. Nasreddin Hoca's character—directly or subtly—pokes fun at religious traditions, institutions, authority figures, sexuality, and social conventions, and frequently uses graphic vocabulary considered vulgar or taboo today, but similar to that found in

FIGURE 42. A rendering of Nasreddin Hoca, seventeenth century. Moin-e Mosavver (Artist). Hazine 2142, fol. 24a. Topkapı Sarayı Müzesi Kütüphanesi, Istanbul.

contemporary Middle Eastern and European jocular literature. That said, the degree of offensiveness of particular words in the sixteenth century is difficult to determine now. The perceived vulgarity of words related to sexuality and bodily functions changes over time, generally in correlation with broader transformations in the social mores of a given community. The figure of Nasreddin Hoca often engages in self-mockery as well. In the early manuscripts, he uses abusive language against his wife and other women, but all the same does not hold a position of authority in the family. His wife is not intimidated, is independent, and is often more sensible than he is.

While Nasreddin Hoca is still remembered in Turkey as a humorous popular hero representing the intellect of humble folk, the subversiveness of the jokes has disappeared and tends to be elided in modern tellings. This is owing to the fact that by adapting the stories for an educated urban milieu after the seventeenth century, the style and language were stripped of their transgressive bawdy humor. Although sometimes still displaying a sense of sarcasm, the Hoca was generally made into a more friendly and conformist character, and the stories were sanitized from obscenities. Their depictions of women and gender roles changed as well; in later collections, male authority within the family appears to be established, whereby the Hoca's attitude toward his wife changes to a patronizing one. These changes were likely the result of transforming norms in Ottoman Turkish society.

Nasreddin Hoca's legacy lives on in modern Turkish culture today. Many of his sharp-witted responses have become idiomatic phrases in Turkish. He is usually depicted with a large turban on his head and as seated backward on a donkey, who also features in many of his stories.

LANGUAGE: Simple everyday Turkish with some archaic vocabulary. Kathleen Burrill's (d. 2008) reading and translations have been minimally corrected and altered by Helga Anetshofer; Burrill's learned euphemisms for vulgar Turkish terms were replaced with equivalent English terms.

SOURCE: Manuscript: *Menakıb-ı Nasreddin Hoca.* Universiteitsbibliotheek, Groningen, HS 488, fols. 79a–62b (reverse pagination). Facsimile, transcription: Translated by Kathleen R. F. Burrill. "The Nasreddin Hoca Stories: An Early Ottoman Manuscript at the University of Groningen." *Archivum Ottomanicum* 2 (1970): 7–114.

RELIGION AND ESTABLISHMENT

1. One day in Sivri Hisar, Nasreddin Hoca was preaching. "Muslims!" he said. "Just you thank God that he didn't put your asses on your foreheads. Why, if He had, you'd shit on your faces each day!"

2. One day Nasreddin Hoca saw the town minaret. "What do they call that?" he asked. "That's the town's dick," he was told. He exclaimed, "Do you have an ass to match it?!"

3. One day Nasreddin Hoca was going to the mosque when he saw a dog at the door. He gave it a "Shoo!" and the dog ran inside and up onto the pulpit where it began to howl. "Well, the silly creature!" said the Hoca. "I guess he used to be the preacher here!"

4. They told the Hoca: "A medrese student is drowning. How shall we get him out?" "Doesn't one of you have a purse?" the Hoca asked. "Show it to him and he'll get out quickly in case there are any akçe in it."

5. One day Nasreddin Hoca arrived in Kara Hisar. As it happened the people were on the lookout for the new moon (as a sign of the beginning or the end of the month of Ramazan), and finally they were just able to see it. "By Allah!" exclaimed the Hoca. "What a strange place this is! In our town when they see a moon as big as a cartwheel, they take no notice. Why do they crowd together here for a moon the size of a sickle?"

6. "So-and-so purposely did not observe the fast (lit., he 'ate' the fast)," they told the Hoca. "My!" he said. "I wish there was another one who 'ate' the ritual prayer!"

7. One day, as Nasreddin Hoca was making his way through the market, a fellow gave him a smart blow on the back of his neck. When the Hoca turned around and looked him in the face the man exclaimed, "Hey Hoca, pardon me! I mistook you for someone else!" "What nonsense this ignorant fellow talks!" said the Hoca. "Come along, we will most certainly take this matter to the judge." To the judge they went, but the judge happened to be a relation of the man's. When the Hoca brought his suit, the judge said, "The penalty for a blow is a half akçe, so you hurry along and fetch the half." The man went off. Left sitting there, the Hoca realized that the fellow was taking a while and not going to come back any time soon. Up he got and gave the judge a smart blow on the back of his neck. "Hey! What do you think you're doing?" cried the judge. "I've got important business," replied the Hoca. "You take that half [akçe] that's coming."

8. One day Nasreddin Hoca went to the mosque. He was wearing a short kaftan and happened to be in the front row. As he bowed down in prayer his balls stuck out from behind, and a fellow took firm hold of them. The Hoca in turn took hold of the imam's balls. "Hey!" cried the imam. "What do you think you're doing?" "What do you mean what am I doing?" said the Hoca. "I thought you were playing 'testicle tag'!"

9. One day Nasreddin Hoca went to the mosque. During the first unit of prayer (*rekat*) the Imam recited [the last chapter of the Qur'an]: "*Say, 'I seek refuge with the Lord of men'*" (Qur'an 114:1) "So!" said the Hoca, "Whatever will you recite in the second *rekat*?" "My balls," he said.

10. One day Nasreddin Hoca was collecting firewood when his donkey got lost. "Have you seen my donkey by any chance?" he asked someone. "Yes, I've seen him," said the man. "He

has become a muezzin at the minaret of such-and-such village." So the Hoca went to the minaret and, looking up, saw a man reciting the call to prayer. Seeing that he had to do something about this, he took a nosebag in his hand and, as the muezzin walked round the minaret, he followed calling, "Whoa! Whoa!"

11. One day, when he was going out, Nasreddin Hoca put a handful of roasted chickpeas into his handkerchief. As he was walking along the road eating them, he came across some children. "Children, shall I give you some chickpeas?" he asked. "Yes, please!" said the children. "Shall I give you as Allah gives or as man gives?" "Give us as Allah gives," said the children. So, to some of them Nasreddin Hoca gave a few, and to some he gave a lot. "Why, Hoca, why don't you give us the same?" they said. "Just look and see!" said the Hoca. "To some Allah gives little and to some he gives much." So now the children said, "Give us as man gives!" At this the Hoca exclaimed, "Allah! Allah! Just listen! Let's admit it, I have never objected to the way you give—but you see, even these children don't like it!"

12. Someone told Nasreddin Hoca: "Your donkey has become a kadı!" Very pleased, he went to his wife. "Wife," he said, "my donkey has become a kadı! I think I'll go and see if he'll make me his deputy." So in the morning he sat off on his journey. When it was evening, he stayed at the dervish lodge and said to the lodge-keeper's wife, "Wake me before daybreak. I've important business and must go on." It happens that in that tekke there were some antinomian dervishes who didn't recognize Nasreddin Hoca, and while he was asleep, they shaved off his beard and moustache. The woman got up and called upstairs, "You up there! Get up! It's morning, if you want to go." Nasreddin Hoca got up, and as he was going on his way he came to the edge of a spring. Sitting down he caught sight of himself in the water. He was amazed to see an antinomian dervish of the Seyitgazi [shrine] and, after pondering a bit, exclaimed, "That fucking woman (*bu amcigin (!) sikdigim*) woke up a Seyitgazi dervish, thinking it was me!"

FAMILY, MORALITY, SEXUALITY

13. Nasreddin Hoca had a field of sprouted barley fodder that was always being trampled. One day he hid and watched the field. It turned out that his daughter had a lover. The lover arrived on the scene and, while fooling around with the Hoca's daughter, said to her: "Come on! Let me be the stallion and you be the mare." She agreed, but while the fellow was playing stallion his eye happened to alight on the Hoca. He skedaddled, and the daughter, taking a bunch of barley in her hand, went after him yelling "Hey! Hey!" "Daughter," said the Hoca, "Is a fellow who goes off leaving such prime pussy likely to come back for a handful of barley?"

14. One day Nasreddin Hoca was fucking someone's donkey when the owner caught him in the act. "Hey! What do you think you are doing?" he asked. "No harm will come to the creature from this," said the Hoca, "but you keep it safe from the wolf!"

15. One day the Hoca had taken a piss, and while he was carrying out his ablutions, a donkey pissed nearby. She was rhythmically contracting her pussy when a fellow came along and said, "Why hello there, gentle Hoca." The Hoca, seeing himself in this state and the donkey in her state, replied, "I didn't do it, I swear! But you go ahead and screw her!"

16. One day Nasreddin Hoca's wife said to him: "Keep that boy quiet until I come back." She went off, but as soon as she had gone the boy cried. The Hoca took him on his knee. The child peed on him, so the Hoca shat all over him. Coming back, his wife demanded, "Why, you idiot! What's this?" "You fucking woman!" retorted the Hoca. "Should a little child like this get the better of me?"

17. One day Nasreddin Hoca's wife said to him: "Keep that boy quiet until I come back." Off she went, but as soon as she had gone, the boy started to cry, and the Hoca, seeing no other solution, put his dick into the child's hand. At that moment, his wife returned. "Why you idiot! What's this?" she demanded. "Why, you fucking woman!" said the Hoca, "Should I hand him a knife and let him cut his hand?"

18. One day when there was no one in the house, Nasreddin Hoca's wife looked at her pussy and exclaimed, "Oh pussy, my luck and happiness! How much good fortune I've met with because of you! And who knows with what good fortune I may yet meet!" As she was talking thus, the Hoca happened to hear and came to look. When he saw what was going on, he quickly went outside, uncovered his dick and started to weep, saying, "It's you that has gotten me into every kind of trouble! And who knows what trouble you may yet get me into!" Now his wife heard from inside the house and, coming out, saw the Hoca standing there ceaselessly weeping, his dick and balls uncovered. "Oh, husband," she asked, "What's the matter with you?" "Why you fucking woman!" exclaimed the Hoca, "I didn't come to your pussy celebration, why do you come to my dick funeral?"

19. One day Nasreddin Hoca's wife said to him: "Go and buy me some light silk fabric." "Is this enough?" the Hoca asked, spreading out his arms. "That's enough," said his wife. The Hoca was on his way to the market with his two arms outspread when he saw a man coming toward him. "Out of the way, brother," said the Hoca, "Or you'll upset the measurement!"

20. One day Nasreddin Hoca was going along carrying his son on his shoulders but, thinking he'd lost the child he began looking for him and searched for a very long while. Finally, not finding him, he turned back toward home. His road passed in front of a halva shop, and from up on his shoulders his son asked, "Oh father, won't you buy a little halva here?" "Ha! There you are! Son of a bitch (*hay anasın sikdigim*)!" exclaimed the Hoca. "Why didn't you say something before? I've looked and looked for you ever since morning!"

21. One day Nasreddin Hoca went on an outing with his assistant. Taking meat with them they went off, but they forgot to bring a cooking pot, so the Hoca said to his assistant: "Go and ask for one at such-and-such village." "All right," he said, and went and knocked on a door in the village. A woman opened it and he said to her: "Ma'am, we have come on an excursion, but we forgot to bring a cooking pot. Will you give us one so that we can cook some meat?" Immediately the woman uncovered her pussy for the assistant. "Wait, wait, my dear lady," he said. "I've got a 'student.' Let me go and fetch him so that he can take it." The woman agreed, so he went and returned to Nasreddin Hoca. "Hoca, this is what has happened," he explained. "Come on, let's go!" The Hoca agreed, and they returned. On their arrival they found the same woman. "Come on now, ma'am, give us the cooking pot," said the assistant. The woman again uncovered her pussy. The Hoca immediately came running up to her, uncovered his dick and said, "Hey now! This will work, my dear lady, and now my hands won't be black!"

22. Nasreddin Hoca had a daughter. Some women came to look her over as a prospective bride. "She's with foal," said the Hoca. After the women had gone, his wife grumbled, "Why you idiot, you! You've completely axed her chances." "You fucking woman!" said the Hoca. "When they sell a horse at the horse market, they say it is with foal. Those who can afford it buy it for more money!"

MORES, SOCIAL PRACTICES

23. One day Nasreddin Hoca bought an ox, and a few days later a man arrived at his home and greeted him. "Why, Hoca!" he said. "Do you know who I am?" The Hoca replied, "No, I don't." "I'm a relation of the man who sold you an ox," exclaimed the fellow, and made himself at home. The following week another person arrived and greeted the Hoca saying, "Why, Hoca! Do you know who I am?" The Hoca replied, "No, I don't." "I'm from the village next to the village of the relation of the man who sold you an ox," said the fellow, and made himself at home. The following week another came, greeted the Hoca, and said, "Why, Hoca! Do you know who I am?" "No, I don't," said the Hoca. "I'm a relation of the fellow from the village next to the village of the relation of the man who sold you an ox," said the man, and made himself at home. When it was nighttime the Hoca put some water into a bowl and set it with some bread before the man. "Why, Hoca!" he exclaimed. "What is this?" "That is soup," said the Hoca, "from the soup of the soup from the meat of the ox that fellow sold me."

24. One day Nasreddin Hoca had been teaching and was returning to his house just ahead of his students. They were walking behind the Hoca. Thereupon he sat himself back to front on the saddle [of his donkey]. "Why, Sir!" they said. "What are you doing that for?" "If you walk in front of me," explained the Hoca, "you turn your backs on my face, and if you walk behind me, I turn my back on your face. I think it's best if we go along chatting like this."

25. One day Nasreddin Hoca cut his nails, and people said to him: "Hey, Hoca! Bury those nail cuttings where people won't tread." So he went off, shat in a particular spot, and buried the nail cuttings with his crap. "Why, Hoca! Whatever did you do that for?" they asked. "Come now," exclaimed the Hoca, "Who would be so blind as to tread on that?"

MISCELLANEOUS

26. One day Nasreddin Hoca entered a garden and found some carrots and turnips. As he was putting some of them into a sack, the gardener heard and came over. "Who brought you here?" he asked. "You know that very strong wind that blew about this time last year?" replied the Hoca. "That brought me!" At this the gardener asked, "And who uprooted these then?" The Hoca replied, "Why, my dear fellow, that was a really strong wind! It just carried me away and whatever I tried to grab hold of came away in my hand!" The rascal of a gardener asked, "And so who put them in the sack?" "By God!" exclaimed the Hoca. "That's what is bothering me too! I don't know!"

27. One day Nasreddin Hoca washed a kaftan and hung it by its sleeves from a tree in front of the house. About to go to bed at night, he went outside and noticed someone in front of the house with widespread arms. Immediately he said, "Here, wife! Bring me my bow and arrow. There is someone here." His wife brought them, and from inside the door the Hoca took aim and shot an arrow exactly in the middle of the figure. Then he firmly closed the door. As soon as it was morning he went outside and saw the state of affairs. "Why, wife! Do you see?" he said, "Thank goodness I wasn't in it—otherwise I'd have done myself in!"

28. One day Nasreddin Hoca had just bought some liver when his son said, "Father, give me the little knucklebone out of that." "You son of a bitch! Can liver have a knucklebone?" said the Hoca and gave his son a beating. The boy went home crying and crying, and the Hoca's wife, coming out to meet them, said, "The devil take you (*bre kanlar kusacak*)! Why did you make that boy cry again?" "He wanted a knucklebone out of a liver—that's why I beat him," the Hoca explained. "How should he know, my poor little one?" said his wife. "He thought it was tripe!"

INDEX

Abdulmalik al-Isami (d. 1628), 236–43
Abdulmalik ibn Marwan (fifth caliph of Umayyads, r. 685–705), 278
Abdurrahman Jami (d. 1492), 73
Abu Ali Sina (d. 1037), 230
Abu Bakr bin Muhammad (d. 1090), 267
Abu Hanifa (d. 767), 265
adulthood. *See* childhood
agriculture, 269–76
Alevis. *See* Hacı Bektaş
Ali Çelebi (military judge of Anatolia), 165
Ali Pasha (d. 1511), 364
animals: eating of, 263, 267–68; hunting of, 261–68; killing of by humans, 335–37; stealing of, 333–34
Armenians: in Crimea, 181–87; in-group social problems, experiencing of, 139; in Istanbul, 307–23; interacting with Greeks, 142
Asiye Hatun ("Lady Asiye," d. second half of seventeenth century), 29–35
Âşık Çelebi (Pir Mehmed, d. 1572), 66–71; *Meşairü'ş-şuara* (The Assemblies of Poets), 66–67
Avicenna. *See* Abu Ali Sina

Báthory, Stephen (d. 1586), 217
Baybars-ı Zahiri (sultan of Egypt, r. 1260–76), 339
Blandrata son of Yorgi. *See* Blandrata, Giorgio
Blandrata, Giorgio (d. 1588), 217

boy love, 66, 242, 324, 327–31, 360–361
bureaucracy: frauds and impostors, 121–25

Canibek Giray Khan (II, r. 1610–23, 1628–35), 183
captivity: conditions of Maltese prisons, 18–22; in a Croatian village, 55–56; of judges, 163; as prisoner-of-war, 53; ransom of prisoners, bargaining of, 21–22; relationship between captive and master, 55; in Rhodes, 45
Catherine the Great (r. 1762–96), 181
Celalzade Mustafa (d. 1567), 60–65, 297; *Tabakatü'l-Memalik ve Derecatü'l-Mesalik* (Echelons of the Dominions and Hierarchies of the Professions), 60
Celalzade Salih (d. 1565), 297–306
childhood, 86–94; adoption, 87–88, 92; child workforce, 87; Christians and Jews, 87–89, 94; violence against children, 87–88, 91, 93
cifr. See lettrism
circumcision in Islam, 36, 215–16, 363
coffee and tobacco, consumption of, 236–43, 324
communication between: Asiye Hatun and Mehmed Dede, 30–32; Zaifi and Rüstem Pasha, 2–7
Constantine (Roman emperor, r. 306–37), 289
conversion: to Catholicism, of Jews (in Spain), 144–45; to Christianity, of Muslims, 59; to Islam, of Christian boys (janissaries), 195; to Islam, of non-Muslims, 61, 94, 136–37,

conversion *(continued)*
196, 199, 201, 291; of Jews, 23, 145–51, 153; to the Roman confession, of Orthodox and Armenians by the Catholics, 173
conversos. See Jews
Crimean Tatars, 50

David ibn Abi Zimra (d. 1573), 150
dervish. *See* Sufism
Divane İbrahim Pasha (governor-general of Diyarbakır), 170
Dolvetkere Sultan (Devlet Giray), 184
Dositheos (d. 1707), 316

Ebu Bekr el-Kızılhisari (ca. late seventeenth century), 261–68
Egyptian soldiers: in naval battles, 12
Eliyahu ha-Levi (fl. early sixteenth century), 146
Emir Hüseyn-i Helvayî ("the helva maker"). *See* Hüseyni
enslaved individuals: Abkhazians, 85; Africans, 84–85; Albanians, 84; Bosnians and Croats, 85; Christian individuals, 78, 84–85; Circassians, 85; conditions of enslaved servants, 80–84; Cossacks, 84; female enslavement, 81–82, 84, 100, 218–19, 324–25, 329, 340; harem (household), 81–82, 84; Kurds, 84; market of enslaved people, 78, 80; slave-tax collector, 310
Enveri (d. 1547), 359
Eremia Keomurchean Çelebi (Kömürciyan, d. 1695), 307–23
espionage, 120–21
Evliya Çelebi (d. after 168), 126, 227–35; *Seyahatname* (Book of Travels), 227–28
exile: to Limnos, 45; to Rhodes, 45
Eyrsperg, Seyfried von, 57–58

Fakhruddin Hasan al-Farghani (d. 1196), 267
faruq (theriac), 228–35
Fehim (d. 1647), 355
Fenarizade Muhyiddin Çelebi (military judge of Rumeli, d. 1548), 62
Ferhad Pasha (commander-in-chief), 165
Feridi (d. sometime between 1512–20), 361–62
fetvas (legal opinions): on conversion from Christianity to Islam, 136–37; on intercommunal spaces and places of worship, 140–41;

marriage between a Christian and a Muslim, 137–38; societal regulations on Christians and Jews, 138–39; taxation of Christians, 143
French Knights Hospitaller. *See* Saint Aubin
Fuzuli (d. 1556), 350

geomancy (*ilm al-raml*, "the science of the sand"), 244–53
grand muftis: Ataullah Mehmed (d. 1715), 142; Baha'i Efendi (d. 1654), 241; Çatalcalı Ali (d. 1620), 140; Çivizade Efendi (d. 1587), 191; Ebussuud (d. 1574), 137, 140–43, 188–89, 194; Erzurumlu Feyzullah (d. 1703), 137, 141, 143; Hocazade Esad (d. 1625), 136, 138, 142–43; Kemalpaşazade (d. 1534), 297; Menteşizade Abdurrahim (d. 1716), 136–38, 140, 143; Sadeddin (d. 1599), 208–09; Yenişehirli Abdullah (d. 1743), 139–40
Greek Orthodox community, effects of a priest's excommunication in, 24–26
Greek language, effects of Turkish language on, 24–28, 311
Greeks: in Crimea, 181, 184; in Istanbul, 312, 314–16, 318–19, 321; in modern-day Greece, 24–28; interacting with Armenians, 142; interacting with Latin Catholics, 175–77
Gülü Khan. *See* Hülegü Khan
gypsies, 102, 109, 317–20

Habsî ("the convicted poet"). *See* Hasbi
Hacı Bektaş (ca. late fifteenth century), 195–201; Alevis, 195–96; *Vilayetname* ("Book of Sainthood,"
Hadrian (Roman emperor, d. 138), 284
Halvetiyye order. *See* Sufism
Hamdullah Hamdi (d. 1503), 254–60; *Kıyafetname* (Book of Physiognomy), 254–55
Hasan Pasha (governor-general of Anatolia), 165
Hasbi, 67–68
Hayim Capusi (d. 1631), 151
Hülegü Khan, 201
Hüseyni ("the confectioner poet"), 70–71

Ibn Taymiyya (d. 1328), 209
İbrahim Efendi (sheikh of Cerrah Pasha Mosque, d. 1633), 240

İbrahim Karamanoğlu (II, r. 1424–64), 285–86
İbrahim Pasha (grand vizier, d. 1536), 63
Imam Muhammad (d. 805), 265
interactions between Muslim and Christian communities, 24–26, 55–57, 61, 134–43
İsa Bey (d. 1543), 364
Islam Giray Khan (III, r. 1644–54), 186
İştefan. *See* Báthory, Stephen

Jacob Berab (d. 1546), 147–48
Jafar al-Sadiq (d. 765), 52
Jawhari (d. 1009), 74; *Sihah* (Arabic dictionary), 74
Jews: circumcision, 149; cloaking as Muslims, 132; crime in Jewish communities, 150–51; in context of Spanish Inquisition, 144–49; *conversos*, 145–51; destruction of Jewish temples, 171; divorce, 153–54, 157–60; *fetvas* concerning lifestyle of Jews. See *fetvas*; *halakha* (Jewish law and jurisprudence), 152–15; inheritance laws, 156; Jewish funeral, 129–30; Jewish life in Istanbul, 313, 316; Karaites, 149; marriage, 146–48, 154–55, 161; portrayed in derogatory manner, 50–51; serving in Ottoman palaces, 217
jinns, 191–93
Job (biblical figure), 26–27
John the Baptist, 51

Kabız, Molla, 60–65
Kadiri Çelebi (military judge of Anatolia, d. 1548), 62
Kaf Mountain, 67, 291
Kara Mustafa Pasha, 129
Katip Çelebi (d. 1657), 236–43
Kemalpaşaoğlu Şemseddin Ahmed, Mevlana (d. 1534), 63–65
Keşfi (d. 1538–39), 358–59
Khachatur of Kaffa (d. 1658), 181
Khwaharzada. *See* Abu Bakr bin Muhammad
Kollonitsch, Cardinal, 59
Krikor (the theologian, d. 390), 315

Lala Mustafa Pasha, 168
land rivalry: between Ottomans and Austria, 53, 57; between Ottomans and Holy League, 53; between Ottomans and Russia, 181
Latin Catholics, 173–80

Le'ali, 354
Lettrism (*cifr*), 45, 47, 49

Macuncuzade Mustafa (d. ca. early seventeenth century), 16–22
Maimonides, 146, 149; *Book of Commandments*, 149
Maulana Jami. *See* Abdurrahman Jami
medicine, 220–26, 278–79; folkloristic popular medicine, 220, 222–26; mechanistic medicine, 220, 222, 224, 284; prophetic medicine, 220–21
medrese, 1–6, 16, 21, 44, 51, 60, 73, 78, 87, 91, 163, 192, 219, 229–30, 235, 237, 297, 362–63, 369; of Davud Pasha, 5; of *Sahn-i Seman* (the Eight Courtyards), 1, 297; of Sinan Bey, 91; of Süleyman Pasha, 4
Mehmed Cinani (d. 1595), 188
Mehmed Giray Khan, 184
Mehmed Mecdi (d. 1591), 72–77; *Hada'ikü'ş-Şaka'ik* (Gardens of Peonies), 72–73
Mehmed Nergisi (d. 1635), 332–37
Melihi, Mevlana (d. early sixteenth century), 73
mental illness: cultural connection to sainthood, 126; mental asylums, 126; treatment of, 224–25; violence, 129–30
Metrophanes (d. 326), 315
Mihri Hatun (d. 1506), 362
Mount Kaf. *See* Kaf Mountain
Muhyiddin Efendi (d. 1604), 203–05
Mü'min (sixteenth century), 355
Mustafa Âli (d. 1600), 78–85; *Meva'idü'n-Nefa'is fi Kava'idi'l-Mecalis* (Tables of Delicacies Concerning the Rules of Social Gatherings), 79
Mustafa Selaniki (d. ca. 1600), 162

Nabi (d. 1712), 350–52
Nasreddin Hoca, 366–73
Nasuh Pasha (d. 1614), 204
naval rivalry: between Ottomans and Malta, 17–18; between Ottomans and Portugal, 10–12; between Ottomans and Russia, 181
Nef'i (d. 1635), 353–54
Nesimi (d. 1417), 51
nightlife: curfews, 113; crime and anti-crime measures, 112–16; fireworks, 111–12, 117; oil lamps, 111, 118; public street lighting, 112,

nightlife *(continued)*
   118; socialization during nighttime, 111, 117–18
Niyazi-i Mısri (d. 1694), 44–52, 354–55

odabaşı (officer in charge of janissary barracks), 42, 53
Ömer Fuadi (d. 1636), 202–09: *Türbe-name* (Epistle on the Tomb), 203–04
Ömer Kethüda ("the Steward," d. 1611), 204–06
Osman Agha of Timişoara (d. first half of eighteenth century), 53–59
Ottoman dynasty: Prince Mustafa, 50, 69; Sultan Ahmed (I, r. 1603–17), 183; Sultan Bayezid (II, r. 1481–1512), 121, 363; Sultan İbrahim (r. 1640–48), 50; Sultan Mehmed (II, r. 1444–46, 1451–81), 284, 286, 290, 315; Sultan Mehmed (III, r. 1595–1603), 75–76, 168; Sultan Mehmed (IV, r. 1648–87), 50; Sultan Murad (II, 1421–44, 1446–51), 284, 287; Sultan Murad (III, r. 1574–95), 168, 171; Sultan Murad (IV, r. 1623–40), 240, 324–25, 327, 332; Sultan Mustafa (I, r. 1617–18, 1622–23), 183–84; Sultan Osman (II, r. 1618–22), 183–84; Sultan Selim (I, r. 1512–20), 361; Sultan Selim (II, r. 1566–74), 171; Sultan Süleyman (I, r. 1520–66), 63, 164; Sultan Süleyman (II, r. 1687–91), 50

physiognomy. *See* Hamdullah Hamdi
Pir Muhammed bin Evrenos. *See* Zaifi
Piri Reis (d. 1553), 8, 308
Pir Mehmed. *See* Üskübi
plague, 210–14, 218
Pythagoras (the monotheist, d. ca. 495 BCE), 230

Qadikhan. *See* Fakhruddin Hasan al-Farghani
Qala'un, Sultan (Mamluk sultan, s. 1279–90), 228–29

rabbis: Avraham ha-Levi (d. 1712), 161; Daniel Estrosa (d. 1654), 156; Mordekhai ha-Levi (d. 1685), 160–61; Yisrael ben Moshe Najara (d. 1625), 154; Yom Tov Tzahalon (d. 1638), 154–55

responsa (by various rabbis), 144–61
Rieu, Charles (d. 1902), 277
Rüstem Pasha (d. 1561), 1–7

Şaban Efendi (d. 1569), 202–06
Sabbatai Zevi (d. 1670), 45
Sadeddin. Mevlana (Sadi, d. 1539), 65
Şani (d. ca. 1534), 349
Saint Aubin (French Knights Hospitaller captain), 18
Saint Eustace (martyred ca. 118), 26–27
St. George, 51
Saint Gregory the Illuminator (d. ca. 331), 184
St. Yovhan (the golden-mouthed, d. 407), 315
Sakızlı Sadık Mehmed bin Ali (d. after 1649), 263
Saladin. *See* Salahuddin Yusuf bin Ayyub
Salahuddin Yusuf bin Ayyub (d. 1193), 300
Sarı Saltık, 198–201
Schallenberg, Christoph Dietmayr Graf von, 59
Seydi Ali Reis (d. 1562), 8–15
Seyyid Hasan Nuri (d. 1688), 36–43
Sinan Pasha (grand vizier), 164–65
Shahin Giray Sultan, 184
Sufi *dede*s: Baki Dede, 41; Fettah Dede, 42; Hacı Ali Dede, 41; Kandilci Dede, 41; Küçük Hüseyn Dede, 42; Mehmed Dede, 29, 30, 32; Nuri Dede, mosque of, 42; Peçeci Kenan Dede, 42; Şaban Dede, 40; Veli Dede, 29
Sufism: abstemious way of life, 36–37, 44; communal feasts, 41, 42, 46; consumption of coffee, 237, 312; daily experiences of a sheikh, 38–43; dervish, 20, 36, 37–40, 51–52, 67, 111, 122, 128, 166–68, 191, 196, 198–99, 201, 319–20, 327–28, 362–63, 370; dreams, interpretation of, 32–34; *esma-i seb'a* (seven names [of God]), 30, 32; funeral, 40; Halvetiyye order, 29, 36–37, 202; Mevlevi dervishes, Sultan Murad and Tiflı disguise as, 327; *Münyetü'l-Musalli* (book on prayers by Sadiduddin al-Kashgari, d. 705/1305), 41; relationship between sheikh and disciples, 29, 30–32; Sünbüliyye branch, 36–37, 39–40; *tekke* (dervish lodge), 36–37, 39–40, 44, 111, 122–23, 170, 205, 319, 370; tombs, 202–09, 319; *zahiri* (exterior) and *batıni* (interior) sciences, 44; *zikr* ceremony, 204

Süruri (d. 1816), 360
Synadinos of Serres (d. after 1662), 23–28

Tam ibn Yahya (d. ca. 1542), 149
Taşköprülüzade Ahmed (d. 1561), 72, 74;
　Shaqa'iq al-numaniya fi ulama al-dawlat al-Uthmaniya (Crimson Peonies Among the Scholars of the Ottoman State), 72
tekke (dervish lodge). *See* Sufism
Tıfli Ahmed Çelebi (d. 1660)

Üskübi (d. 1611), 263

vampirism (*cadu*), 193–94
Vartan (*vartabed,* d. 1704 or 1705), 307
viticulture, 269–76

wine, consumption of: in Sufi context, 74; in taverns, 74–75, 79
women: adultery, 98, 346–47; divorce, 97–98, 100–101; dowry, 100; economic activities, participating in, 97; female enslavement, *see* enslavement individuals; femicide, 330–31; imagery in dreams, 33; miscarriage, 216–17; as object of romance and sexuality through male gaze, 55, 234–35; polygyny, 96–97, 344–45; portrayed as devilish and wile, 338–47; prostitution, 103–10, 328–30; requesting for divorce, 42; as victim of sexual assault, 58, 192–93; widowhood, 98–99

Yahya Bey (d. 1582), 352–53
Yazid (Umayyad caliph, d. 683), 70
Yörüks, 193

Zaifi ("The Frail One," d. after 1557), 1–7
Zakariya al-Qazwini (d. 1283), 277
Zati (d. 1546), 353, 356, 360–62, 364
Zaynuddin ibn Nujaym (d. 1563), 263
Zechariah, 51
zimmi (protected denominational groups, Christians and Jews; i.e., "people of the book"), 89, 115–16, 136–41, 143, 152, 164, 205, 214, 217

Founded in 1893,
UNIVERSITY OF CALIFORNIA PRESS
publishes bold, progressive books and journals
on topics in the arts, humanities, social sciences,
and natural sciences—with a focus on social
justice issues—that inspire thought and action
among readers worldwide.

The UC PRESS FOUNDATION
raises funds to uphold the press's vital role
as an independent, nonprofit publisher, and
receives philanthropic support from a wide
range of individuals and institutions—and from
committed readers like you. To learn more, visit
ucpress.edu/supportus.

www.ingramcontent.com/pod-product-compliance
Lightning Source LLC
Chambersburg PA
CBHW081023240426
43668CB00031B/2355